The Semantics of Colour

Human societies name and classify colours in various ways. Knowing this, is it possible to retrieve colour systems from the past? This book presents the basic principles of modern colour semantics, including the recognition of basic vocabulary, sub-sets, specialized terms, and the significance of non-colour features. Each point is illustrated by case studies drawn from modern and historical languages from around the world. These include discussions of Icelandic horses, Peruvian guinea-pigs, medieval roses, the colour yellow in Stuart England, and Polynesian children's colour terms. Major techniques used in colour research are presented and discussed, such as the evolutionary sequence, Natural Semantic Metalanguage, and vantage theory. The book also addresses whether we can understand the colour systems of the past, including prehistory, by combining various semantic techniques currently used in both modern and historical colour research with archaeological and environmental information.

C. P. BIGGAM is Honorary Senior Research Fellow, English Language in the School of Critical Studies at the University of Glasgow.

The Semantics of Colour

A Historical Approach

C. P. Biggam

University of Glasgow

CAMBRIDGE
UNIVERSITY PRESS

University Printing House, Cambridge CB2 8BS, United Kingdom

Cambridge University Press is part of the University of Cambridge.

It furthers the University's mission by disseminating knowledge in the pursuit of education, learning and research at the highest international levels of excellence.

www.cambridge.org
Information on this title: www.cambridge.org/9781107499881

© C. P. Biggam 2012

First published 2012
First paperback edition 2015

A catalogue record for this publication is available from the British Library

Library of Congress Cataloguing in Publication data
Biggam, C. P. (Carole Patricia), 1946–
The semantics of colour : a historical approach / C. P. Biggam.
   p.   cm.
Includes bibliographical references and index.
ISBN 978-0-521-89992-5 (hardback)
1. Color vision.   2. Color – Terminology.   3. Semantics.   4. Language and culture.   I. Title.
P305.19.C64B54   2012
401'.43 – dc23   2011049120

ISBN 978-0-521-89992-5 Hardback
ISBN 978-1-107-49988-1 Paperback

I have received the greatest help, sound advice and inspiration over many years from Professor Christian J. Kay, of the University of Glasgow, to whom this book is humbly dedicated.

Contents

Contents

List of tables

Preface

In 1970, I was browsing among the linguistics books in Cardiff University (as it is now), when my eye was caught by some bold blue words on a pure white spine: *Basic Color Terms*. Some enterprising academic or librarian had ordered Brent Berlin and Paul Kay's recently published book for the library, and had unknowingly changed my life. That sounds a little too dramatic. I have not been exclusively concerned with colour across the intervening years, nor even with semantics in general, but I have never lost that early fascination, inspired by Berlin and Kay's book, for the classification, labelling and communication of colour. However many times I research other subjects, I find myself drifting back to colour studies with some new angle in mind.

With a background in British archaeology, historical semantics and Anglo-Saxon studies, I nevertheless found myself reading lots of reports by anthropologists on the colour systems of modern-day societies and languages often located in far-flung regions of the world. This was interesting, but I always ended my reading with the same question in mind: how did this particular colour system come to be like that? What was its history? What historical evidence is available? Of course, many of the languages investigated by anthropologists had no historical records, but even where they existed, most of the language-reports were unrelentingly modernist. I watched as more and more publications emerged, reporting on ever more surprising ways (to an English speaker) of dealing with colour concepts; as Berlin and Kay's evolutionary sequence morphed into elaborate and then reduced forms; as criticism of the sequence mounted and faded by turns; or as the origins of a colour term were 'explained' by a quick look in an etymological dictionary, and all the time I was wondering how such statements could be made without thorough historical semantic investigations of individual languages. My own (obviously historically biased) view is that, while a present-day language can be studied exhaustively, providing valuable information, such a study lacks time-depth, the understanding that comes with unearthing centuries of slow development and/or traumatic disturbance, and the changing concepts hinted at by discarded and newly coined vocabulary.

Acquiring this depth of knowledge (where possible) demands a lot of time and work, but the rewards are great because colour, which is involved in so many aspects of our lives, and always has been, can illuminate numerous nooks and crannies of past life. We may find that some people only used colour terms for their animals; or we may find a blaze of brilliant light and shining gold in their religious texts; or a delight in exotic textiles and jewellery; or a long and complex list of colour words used in a particular context; or a dark and devilish store of poetry. All this and more tells us so much about people who can no longer explain in person their delight (or lack of it) in their artefacts and surroundings. With such insights as these, how much better do we understand the colour nuances employed by that society's modern descendants.

This book has been written with more than one target audience in mind, so I hope that, in aiming at multiple targets, I have at least hit one of them. First of all, I have aimed at the general reader with an interest in linguistics. I have tried to explain several basic principles of semantics, and have added a glossary of technical terms, so that such a reader does not 'lose the plot' half-way through (or even earlier). The second target audience is university students studying linguistics, a particular language, literature, anthropology, psychology or perhaps even other subjects in which colour plays a significant role. Finally, I hope my third target, semanticists who are not colour specialists, will find something of use in this book, although they will, with justification, probably skip certain sections.

I would like to thank all those who have helped, advised and generously given information while I was writing this book. With many thanks to: several staff members of AIATSIS, William Biggam, Helen Carron, Adam Głaz, Arnþrúður Heimisdóttir, Carole Hough, Christian Kay, Galina Paramei, Barbara Saunders and Kirsten Wolf. I would also like to acknowledge the valued encouragement and patience of Helen Barton, my editor at Cambridge University Press.

Abbreviations

AD	*anno domini* (any year more recent than 1 BC)
adj.	adjective
AF	Anglo-French
AIATSIS	Australian Institute of Aboriginal and Torres Strait Islander Studies
AND	*Anglo-Norman Dictionary*
B&K (or BK)	Berlin and Kay (1969)
BC	Before Christ (any year earlier than 1 AD)
BCC	Basic Colour Category
BCE	Before the Common Era (any year earlier than 1 AD)
BCT	Basic Colour Term
BML	British Medieval Latin
BNC	*British National Corpus*
BP	Before Present (before 1950)
CSLI	Center for the Study of Language and Information (Stanford University)
DMLBS	*Dictionary of Medieval Latin from British Sources*
DOE	*Dictionary of Old English*
EH	Emergence Hypothesis
EVT	Extended Vantage Theory
f-[colour term]	focal-[colour term]
Ger.	Modern German
HTOED	*Historical Thesaurus of the Oxford English Dictionary*
IE	Indo-European
IPA	International Phonetic Alphabet
ISOR	Interdisciplinair Sociaal Wetenschappelijk Onderzoeksinstituut Rijksuniversiteit (Interdisciplinary Social Sciences Research Institute, State University [Utrecht])
M-[colour term]	macro-[colour term]
[M] (subscript)	a semantic molecule, in NSM
MCS	Mesoamerican Colour Survey
ME	Middle English

MED	*Middle English Dictionary*
ModE	Modern English
n.	noun
n.d.	no date of publication
NF	Norman French
NOWELE	*North-Western European Language Evolution*
NSM	Natural Semantic Metalanguage
OE	Old English
OED	*Oxford English Dictionary*
OLD	*Oxford Latin Dictionary*
OSA	Optical Society of America
P	Partition, in the UE model
PDE	Present-Day English
PIE	Proto-Indo-European
RB	Relative Basicness
SKY	Suomen Kielitieteellinen Yhdistys (Linguistic Association of Finland)
UE	Universals and Evolution model ('Berlin and Kay school' theories)
VT	vantage theory
VT2	vantage theory 2 (a later development)
WCS	World Colour Survey

1   What is colour?

1.1   Introduction

Our world is full of natural colour. Against background swathes of blue sky, yellow sand, green grass and white snow, we prize the startling hues of flowers, fruit, feathers and gemstones. Yet this is not enough for us. Most human societies strive to produce their own colours, namely, dyes and paints of the greatest possible variety. A Palaeolithic cave artist depicting familiar animals, and a modern British home-owner agonizing over the perfect colour-scheme for the living-room, are both exhibiting the same delight in colour, and the same need to adapt it to their own social, cultural and individual requirements.

To say that colour plays multiple roles in human society is a gross understatement. It is everywhere in our lives, sometimes boringly dull and at other times brilliantly eye-catching. It is often taken for granted, yet it also conveys vital messages, as in traffic lights or electrical wiring. It can even signify and engender loyalties and hatreds that influence human history, as in heraldry, uniforms and flags. Since it pervades every aspect of human life, it might be considered essential for our languages to express colour concepts clearly, accurately and in a way that is easily communicable. Yet, when the colour vocabularies of various languages are considered and compared, the researcher finds that there are many different ways in which humans categorize and 'label' colours, resulting in an amazing array of misunderstandings. Monoglot individuals invariably believe that their own colour system is clear and obvious, and they are often mystified when confronted with an alternative system. So the first step which the reader has to take when entering the world of colour semantics is probably the most difficult of all; s/he must restrict his or her own colour system to normal, everyday speech, and learn to set it aside when considering foreign or historical colour descriptions. The aim is to dispose of any preconceptions about how colour 'should' be classified and described, so as to gain insights into the workings of other languages and cultures, and into the nature of colour itself.

The first problem which must be addressed is the word *colour*. If asked to name some colours, the chances are that any English speaker will list words such as *red*, *blue*, *green*, *purple* and so on, but, technically speaking, these denote varieties of only one element of colour, which is called *hue*. In many modern societies, most speakers will interpret the word *colour* or its equivalent, as indicating only hue, but the reader should not assume that all other societies do the same, or did the same in the past, or, indeed, that all societies have a word translatable as 'colour' at all (Wierzbicka 2006: 1–4). A society may be concerned, for example, with the general *appearance* of an entity, involving a mixture of visible features in which hue cannot be separated from one or more other aspects such as shininess, roughness, darkness, wetness and more, in varying combinations. Even more surprising to the English speaker and others is that the so-called 'colour terms' of a language may include *non-visible* elements which cannot be excised from the overall meaning of the word or phrase (Section 1.7).

Certain elements of colour would be much more accurately and fully described by a physicist or vision scientist, but this chapter will aim to present them from the viewpoint of linguistics. A colour impression is composed of many elements, and human societies unconsciously combine them in various ways, and label them with language in order to convey an image to members of the same speech community. While this statement suggests a kaleidoscope of different colour impressions, there also appear to be certain fundamentals in colour-naming which many would argue are universal among human societies, but more of this later. This present chapter aims to introduce the various features which can be observed in colour systems around the world, and it is hoped that this will help readers to understand how their own colour system is simply one possibility among many.

The exact nature of the colours we see is the result of a complicated interaction between the physics of light, the physiology of the human eye, environmental conditions at the time of viewing, the physical properties of the object being viewed and the way in which our brains receive and interpret all this information. In other words, for each viewing, there is a huge number of possible combinations involving phenomena such as illumination, reflectivity, surface texture and many more. In this book, however, the crucial aspect is not the physics and physiology, but the brain's interpretation of the data it receives. With admirable boldness, the human brain adopts a 'no nonsense' approach to the flood of information it receives from the eye, and it simplifies and classifies, so humans can cope with the complexity of their world. This simplification can be glimpsed through language.

Although the various colour vocabularies in the world differ considerably in their details, they most often make use of one or more of four principal phenomena: hue, saturation, tone and brightness. Unfortunately, I have to pause at this point and warn the reader about the terminology of colour semantics. The subject does not yet have a truly standardized terminology and, for certain phenomena, the variety of terms which can be found in published works is amazing. To give one example, saturation is also known as chroma, intensity, concentration, purity and probably more. Worse than this, the same terms are often used by different authors to denote different phenomena (Biggam 2007). In these circumstances, and until there is general agreement, it is essential for writers on the semantics of colour to make clear their own usage at the outset, and to avoid straying from those definitions.[1] My own usage of the four crucial terms, *hue, saturation, tone* and *brightness*, now follows.[2]

1.2   Hue

Of the four principal constituent parts of colour that are significant in linguistic studies, *hue*, or *chromatic colour*, is probably the easiest term for the English speaker to understand. It refers to the spectrum of visible light, parts of which, according to their wavelength or frequency, are perceived by humans to differ from others. The classic natural example of part of the hue spectrum is the rainbow, and its various hues are called *colours* in non-technical English. Examples of English hue vocabulary include *blue, red* and *yellow*. (See Appendix 1.1.)

1.3   Saturation

Turning to *saturation*, this term refers to the purity or otherwise of a hue, in relation to the amount of grey it is perceived to contain. If increasing amounts of grey are successively added to samples of a hue, this creates a range running from a vivid hue (no grey at all) to grey (no hue at all). Thus, to take the example of red, its saturation range will start with a fully saturated red which has no admixture of grey. This can be described in everyday language as *vivid red* or, more commonly, but highly ambiguously, as *bright red* (Section 1.5). The reader should then imagine a range of colours composed of the same red but with increasing amounts of grey added to it. The red becomes duller along the range as the greyness element increases until, finally, the colour is simply grey, as the red element ceases to be perceived. Before this point in the range is reached, the colours could be described as *dull red, grey-red* or even *dirty red*. Using *colour* in its technical sense, it can now be seen that there are colour words which are saturation terms rather than hue terms, and the English words *vivid* and *dull* (as used in the context of colour) are, of course, two examples; they refer to degrees of saturation without specifying hue. (See Appendix 1.2.)

The reader is invited to imagine a hypothetical language in which the roles of saturation and hue, as seen in English semantics, are reversed so that the difference between red and blue is unimportant, but the differences between vivid red and dull red, or between vivid blue and dull blue are highly significant. The vivid hues may be considered prestigious, and be individually named, but the dull hues may be of little interest and may be all designated by only one or two words. This is the sort of colour classification that speakers of many other languages may struggle to understand. To avoid overlooking a classification which is alien to him or her, the researcher into colour semantics needs to keep an open mind, and awareness of the various features of colour can help in this.

1.4   Tone

The next element of colour to be considered is denoted here by the word *tone*. This refers to the admixture of white or black with a hue, creating a range which runs from pale at one end to dark at the other. Taking blue as the example hue this time, the blue tone range runs from very pale blue through shades with successively increasing amounts of blue added to them, so that they range from very pale blues to pale blues to palish blues to fully saturated blue (in which no white is perceived). At this point, the blue tone range begins to add successively increasing amounts of black, resulting in darkish blues, dark blues and very dark blues.

The English words *pale* and *dark* are tonal colour words, and, just like *vivid* and *dull*, they are unspecific as to hue. The English-speaking reader can now attempt to imagine a hypothetical system in which tone plays a stronger role than hue. Such a language would consider the difference between paleness and darkness to be more important than the differences between hues. Its speakers may, for example, have several terms for aspects of paleness and darkness but be unable to distinguish linguistically between pale blue and pale green, or between dark blue and dark green, without launching into a descriptive phrase. They would, however, have no problems in distinguishing linguistically between pale blue/green and dark blue/green.[3]

There is also a special tone range for the achromatic colours. *Achromatic* means literally 'without hue', and it refers to white, black and the greys. The achromatic tone range, therefore, runs from white through very pale greys to pale greys to palish greys to darkish greys to dark greys to very dark greys and, finally, to black. (See Appendix 1.3.)

1.5   Brightness

Brightness is a word which has been used particularly ambiguously in colour studies (Biggam 2007). It is concerned with the amount of light reaching the eye, but the nature and sources of such light are varied. An object may be bright because it is pale and well-lit, or because its surface is made of a reflective material, or because it is itself a light source such as a lamp. The metalanguage used in this book for the various aspects of brightness is described in Section 8.6, and summarized in Appendix 1.4. Where sufficient information exists, a colour description in this book will specify the type of brightness involved, using the suggested terminology. In many cases, however, it is not possible to be precise about the nature of the light, so the words *bright* or *brightness* will be used as unspecific descriptions.

In Present-Day English (PDE), a fully saturated hue is often referred to as *bright*, as in *bright green*, for example, even though the effect is not truly dazzling like a flame. In this sense of *bright*, the eye-catching nature of true brightness is used metaphorically of vivid hues. *Bright* and *brightness* will never be used in this sense in this book, unless in a quotation, but will be replaced by the words *vivid* and *vividness* or the phrases *fully saturated* and *full saturation*.

The last mental exercise for the reader is to imagine a language in which brightness is of far greater significance than hue. This language may have very few basic hue words at all, but may interpret all colour impressions through the crucial contrast of brightness versus darkness, as in daytime versus night-time. The speakers of such a language may depend heavily on daylight, relying on it for hunting, gathering food, avoiding danger, travelling and manufacturing. They are likely to have only limited light-sources at night-time. Small wonder they may have a greater interest in this brightness contrast than in naming the hues.

1.6   Other aspects of appearance

In the sections above, the reader has been asked to imagine colour systems which may seem strange to him or her, namely, systems in which saturation, tone or brightness predominate over hue. There are also languages in which two or more of these colour elements have *equal* importance, forming a network of combinations which may mystify the English-speaking researcher who is looking for a guiding principle in the use of that colour system. In other words, it may be that no single colour element predominates at all (see Hanunóo in Section 4.5).

Even more difficult for our researcher to comprehend is the active inclusion in a colour system of a visible feature which s/he does not normally consider an element of colour at all. A language, for example, may include a phenomenon such as surface texture in its colour system. To most English speakers, the smoothness, roughness, lumpiness or prickliness of an object (to name but a few such features) has nothing to do with colour, but a moment's glance at surrounding items will show that all sorts of surface textures affect a colour impression (see Yucatec in Section 4.5). These aspects of surface texture constitute features of the object's formation, whereas the light-reflectivity mentioned in Section 1.5, although clearly requiring a shiny surface, is concerned with the dazzling effect of what is reflected. This distinction, however, may not be appropriate for some languages, and researchers need to be guided by their findings, and to avoid jumping to conclusions.

This section does not refer to the *unrestricted* use of colour terms with any surface texture. For example, one can say in English 'a shiny grey floor' but this does not imply that whenever *grey* is used, it *must* describe something shiny. English speakers know that *grey* can be used of *non*-shiny things too, in fact, it can be used independently, with or without any surface feature. On the contrary, this section refers to languages in which a colour word *always* includes a particular feature of appearance so that, if Word X indicates 'grey and shiny', speakers of such a language will need a different word, Word Y, to indicate 'grey and non-shiny'.

1.7   Non-appearance aspects

For those who use a hue-based colour vocabulary, the idea of a colour word which cannot be used separately from a feature of surface texture is difficult to comprehend but, even more difficult, are features of colour words which do not refer to appearance at all, and so cannot be indicated on a colour chart even where their presence is crucial to the word's meaning. Such features are extremely varied and include, for example, dryness and edibility, and the researcher needs to understand a society which speaks such a language in order to be aware of these features.

Non-appearance elements of colour terms are closely related to colour symbolism, which is a familiar phenomenon to English speakers. The word *blue* has the connotation of sadness in certain contexts, and *white* can indicate purity but, similar to the discussion in Section 1.6, these connotations are not *always* present when English *blue* and *white* are used. In some languages, however, non-appearance aspects are indissolubly linked with colour aspects in particular terms, and the former may dominate the word's semantics to the extent that considerations of appearance are secondary. This can result in cases where an object seems to have been described with the 'wrong' colour term, because *visible* aspects of appearance have been overriden (see Hanunóo in Section 4.5).

1.8   Explanation

It is important to stress that I am not suggesting that societies base their colour vocabulary on scientifically defined constituents of colour such as tone and saturation, nor that any human, in everyday speech, analyses colour scientifically before speaking about it. The linguistically significant elements of colour are presented here to help readers look objectively at their own colour systems, and to be aware of alternative ways of classifying and labelling colour. Thus, when faced with an unfamiliar system, the researcher has a better chance of unravelling its mysteries.

The investigation of features such as hue, saturation and brightness in colour semantics has been criticized by, for example, Lucy (1992: 155). He argues that this analysis is appropriate to some languages, but has been used as a 'measuring stick' for the investigation of *all* languages. He writes: 'The entire approach guarantees that one will not find interesting and truly novel category differences, for one can only encompass descriptively (or measure quantitatively) what the metalanguage allows.'[4] This is a valid concern where a language's colour vocabulary is studied exclusively from the point of view of hue, saturation and brightness, but I would certainly not recommend such a methodology in isolation. It is perfectly reasonable to ask whether a language shows a particular interest in, for example, dark colours or vivid hues, and to investigate why this should be so, but such concerns need not exclude the various and complex contexts in which the terms are used. The researcher could consider whether darkness terms happen also to be used of large, prickly or wet objects (to name but a few possibilities) or whether they only occur in the context of religious ceremonies or industrial processes (again, to name but a few possibilities). As much detail as possible should be recorded about the context of each occurrence of a colour term, and this requirement may cause the researcher to be concerned with matters such as the age, sex and social position of both speaker and listener, details of the environment, type of event and social mood of each occasion of use and much more valuable data.

1.9   Summary

This first chapter has three main purposes. Firstly, it aims to convey the clear message that colour is more than hue. Secondly, it stresses the need for controlled language in the discussion and description of colour vocabulary in order to avoid misleading ambiguities and, thirdly, it aims to demonstrate to the reader that his or her own colour system is not the only possible way to categorize colours. The first point, regarding colour involving more than hue, has been addressed in introductory form in Sections 1.2 to 1.7. The second point, regarding controlled language, leads me to establish some ground-rules for myself. In this book, the reader will find a (hopefully) systematic use of the terms *hue(s)*, *colour(s)* and *appearance*. *Hue(s)* will be used to denote hues only (Section 1.2), and *achromatics* will be used to denote black, white and grey. *Colour(s)* will be used as an 'umbrella term' wherever hues are not involved in a colour statement, or where both hues and other elements of colour are involved. In practice, this means that *colour* is used frequently, most often indicating hues plus achromatics. *Appearance* will be used for visible features other than hue, saturation, tone or brightness (Section 1.6).[5]

The third point made in this chapter, regarding the fact that the reader's colour system is only one among many, is absolutely crucial. There are many other equally valid classifications apart from our own, and glib assumptions about the meaning of colour words used in languages and societies of which we have little in-depth knowledge are unlikely to be enlightening. It is hoped that examples of 'exotic' colour expressions presented later in this book will make this clear. It is necessary to gain a facility for open-mindedness on colour matters, or many foreign and historical usages will be misinterpreted, certain literary passages will not be appreciated as they were intended and the cultural significance of certain colours will be missed.

2   What is colour semantics?

2.1   Introduction

The academic discipline concerned with the expression and elucidation of meaning in language is semantics. Languages communicate meaning in various ways, making use of a wide range of linguistic features such as sounds, words, phrases and sentences.[1] Certain areas of linguistics, such as the study of sounds (phonology) and of sentence construction (syntax) are well defined, but semantics does not have such clear limits. The semanticist needs not only a broad knowledge of the various sub-fields of linguistic enquiry, but s/he will also benefit from an understanding of other disciplines such as anthropology, psychology and philosophy. Specialists in these, and other fields, have made valuable contributions which the semanticist cannot afford to ignore, but the historical emphasis of this particular book unavoidably results in a concentration on textual studies.

This book is, of course, concerned with *colour* semantics, that is, the means by which languages communicate the types of visual impression described in Chapter 1. Its principal aim is to tackle the question of how such information can be retrieved from past societies but it may seem to the reader that consulting an appropriate dictionary is sufficient to answer such queries. Since the most important semantic area for this present study is *lexical* semantics, that is, the study of meaning as conveyed by words and phrases, understanding both the benefits and limitations of dictionaries is crucial, and will be discussed in the following section. This will be followed in turn by a brief consideration of the development of colour semantics, as illustrated by the work of a few selected important contributors to the subject, showing the steadily improving research behind the dictionary definitions.

2.2   Dictionaries and their uses

A concise or pocket dictionary may offer one or two words as definitions or translations of the word under investigation, and this should suffice to give a general impression of its meaning. If, on the other hand, a large multi-volume dictionary is consulted, the meaning(s) of a word will be presented in the form of a list of senses, beginning with the most commonly encountered one in everyday use, or with the earliest attested meaning in the records. To give one example, if a French speaker were to look up the English equivalent of French *jaune* in a small dictionary, s/he would find the translation 'yellow', and, perhaps, nothing more. Does that mean that our French speaker can now use English *yellow* like a native English speaker? Not at all. If, for example, s/he looked up *yellow* in the *Oxford English Dictionary* (*OED*), s/he would find that certain types of *person* can be described as 'yellow' in English, even though they do not look truly yellow. Such people include the elderly, the sick and members of certain Asian groups. Even further removed from this colour are people who are considered to be jealous, or cowardly, yet an English speaker can describe them too as 'yellow'. Most surprising of all to our imaginary French speaker, and also to many native speakers of English, will be the use of *yellow* to mean 'naval captains retired as rear admirals in H. M. Fleet without being attached to a particular squadron' (*OED*, adjectival sense 1e). English is not unusual in having multiple senses for a single colour term and, if an English speaker were to look up *jaune* in a large French dictionary, s/he would find that it too has various senses, but not necessarily the same as those of *yellow*.[2]

The larger dictionaries, therefore, reveal the multiple roles of certain colour words, pointing out any regional, chronological and contextual restrictions on each function and, in the process, illustrating how they operate within a particular cultural context which may not be obvious to a person from a different culture. The problem for language learners is that the minor senses of a word may affect its more common usage in such a subtle manner that even the native speaker may be unaware of the effect. Poets often make use of these subtle under-senses, by playing on, for example, the English speaker's association of yellowness with sickness and rotting things. To sum up, it is evident that finding a closely equivalent word in a foreign language may prove problematic, as there is unlikely to be a simple one-to-one translation without complications. Semantic studies attempt to investigate the detailed web of meaning, and thereby reduce omissions and misunderstandings.

The reader may be thinking that s/he can manage perfectly well with the smaller dictionaries which usually only present the principal sense of the head-word; for example, '**jaune** yellow' in a French–English pocket dictionary. For some colours, some words, and some languages, this will be fine but, in other cases, this policy will fail. If, for example, an English speaker needs to know the Welsh word for the colour green, s/he will find two candidates in a medium-sized English–Welsh dictionary: *gwyrdd* and *glas*. S/he may wonder which to use, and proceed to investigate each Welsh word in a Welsh–English dictionary. When s/he looks up *glas*, s/he may find, to her surprise, the following English definition: '1. blue; 2. pale; 3. grey; 4. green; 5. young, raw; silver (coins)' (Evans and Thomas 1958). Welsh is an Indo-European language, just like English, and, like British English, it is also spoken in a modern western European society but, in spite of these linguistic and cultural similarities, the definition of *glas* leaves the English speaker confused and puzzled. Languages which are more distant, either in space or in time, can present even worse problems of comprehension, and attempts to understand this phenomenon in Ancient Greek led to the development of modern colour semantics.

2.3   William Gladstone, Hugo Magnus and hue blindness

Throughout the centuries, colour interested various groups in society such as craftsmen and merchants dealing with cloth, dyes and pigments, experts in heraldry, artists, philosophers, early experimenters with light and vision, fashionable gentlefolk, poets and many more. Many of these groups had specialized vocabularies for dealing with their own particular subject concerns, but there appears to have been little interest in the linguistic encoding of colour generally[3] until William Gladstone noticed some 'strange' examples of colour description in Homeric Greek.

William Ewart Gladstone (1809–98) served as Prime Minister of Great Britain four times under Queen Victoria, but it is less well known today that he was also a considerable scholar, having taken a double first at the University of Oxford in Classics and Mathematics. He retained his interest in the Classics throughout his life, publishing, for example, a three-volume work entitled *Studies on Homer and the Homeric Age* in 1858. The third volume contains a large section on Homer's colour vocabulary, and this study can be considered an early precursor of modern colour semantic investigations. Gladstone expresses surprise at several examples of the poet's colour usage. He writes:

Χλωρὸς [*chlōros*] indicates rather the absence than the presence of definite colour . . . If regarded as an epithet of colour, it involves at once an hopeless contradiction between the colour of honey on the one side, and greenness on the other [III.468] . . . In what manner are we to find a common thread upon which to hang the colours of iron, copper, horses, lions, bulls, eagles, wine, swarthy men, and smoke? [III.473] . . . So again with wine-coloured oxen, smutty thunderbolts, violet-coloured sheep, and many more, it is surely conclusive against taking them for descriptions of prismatic colours or their compounds, that they would be bad descriptions in their several kinds [III.487]. (Gladstone 1858)

In his struggles to find some logic behind these and other puzzles, Gladstone makes some important observations, and adopts some valuable techniques. For example, he presents his basic data, that is, the referents (objects or phenomena) described by each colour word, in preliminary lists (1858: III.460–75), and he also realizes that, in certain cases, the *contexts* of referents need to be added, as they can affect the colour impressions described. So, for example, he lists a storm-cloud and a disturbed river, rather than just 'cloud' and 'river' (III.462). He also includes non-adjectives in his research, where they are cognate (derived from the same origin) with colour adjectives (III.457), and he realizes that light (and its movement or absence) played an important role in Homer's works (III.474). Furthermore, he knows that poetic usage of vocabulary must be considered as distinct from that of prose (III.484) and, most perceptive of all for the time at which he wrote, Gladstone rejects the notion that his own culture's classification of colour is the only one possible: 'We must then seek for the basis of Homer's system with respect to colour in something *outside our own*' (my italics) (III.487).

Why is it then that Gladstone's colour studies are often referred to by modern researchers as being almost ridiculous? The reason is that, having carried out a review of the evidence which was thorough and admirable in many ways, Gladstone drew the wrong conclusion. Seeing that Homer's language contained fewer unambiguous hue terms than his own nineteenth-century British English, he deduced that early Greek speakers could not actually *see* those hues for which they had no names.[4] He suggests that the human brain had to be trained to see hues over a long period of time: 'we seem to find, as we go far backward in human history, that the faculty [of discriminating colours] is less and less mature' (1858: III.457); 'perceptions so easy and familiar to us are the results of a slow traditionary growth in knowledge and in the training of the human organ, which commenced long before we took our place in the succession of mankind' (III.496).

Of the early Greeks, Gladstone writes: 'I conclude, then, that the organ of colour and its impressions were but partially developed among the Greeks of the heroic age' (1858: III.488).[5] He believes the Homeric Greeks had no recognition of the hues orange, green and violet, and probably more (III.459), that is to say, they could not see them.

In 1877, Gladstone received a copy of the newly published *Die geschichtliche Entwickelung des Farbensinnes* ('The Historical Development of the Colour Sense') from its author, Hugo Friedrich Magnus (1842–1907). Magnus was a professor of ophthalmology at the University of Breslau, Germany, and, in his book, he had made considerable use of Gladstone's work on Homer. Like Gladstone, Magnus believed that the colour vocabulary of ancient literatures indicated the state of development of human colour vision at the time they were composed. His source texts led him to suggest that the recognition of colours developed sequentially over the centuries, progressing through four stages: firstly, colours of luminous intensity (*lichtstarke Farben*) such as red, orange and yellow; secondly, an ability to distinguish red from yellow; thirdly, recognition of colours of medium luminous intensity (*Farben mittlerer Lichtstärke*) such as greens, as distinct from dark greens and pale greens; and fourthly, colours of little luminous intensity (*Farben geringer Lichtstärke*) like blue and violet (1877: 9–41, taken from Schöntag and Schäfer-Priess 2007: 109–10).[6]

Gladstone was inspired by Magnus' book to do further work on his thesaurus of Homer, and to publish an article entitled 'The colour-sense' in September 1877, a copy of which was sent to Magnus, and later translated into German. In this article, Gladstone accepts Magnus' sequence of colour recognition, and regards this as an evolutionary process which all 'races' experience. He re-evaluates Homer's entire colour vocabulary and usage, and concludes that the poet recognized light, dark, red and, possibly, orange (1877: 388), representing Magnus' earliest category, that is, colours of luminous intensity.

2.4   Grant Allen and colour perception versus naming

The reception of Gladstone's second paper, in which his philological work had been blended with Magnus' typological sequence of colour recognition, was not good. Neither author seemed to have given sufficient consideration to the theory of natural selection, which Charles Darwin had published in his book *On the Origin of Species* in 1859, although Gladstone had certainly read it. Gladstone's work was criticized by a number of scholars, but probably most comprehensively by a follower of Darwin's, Grant Allen, who published *The Colour-Sense* in 1879. He first gives an account of the evolution and adaptation of colour vision in many kinds of animals, and argues that all the higher animals have excellent colour perception, mainly because they are frugivorous (fruit-eating).[7] Allen argues that the principle of natural selection favours animals that can quickly and accurately detect edible fruit, and that the quality of their colour perception is, therefore, crucial to their survival. Humans are also frugivorous, so our colour perception too needs to be of a high quality. Allen concludes that, since animals closely related to humans have the same degree of colour perception as humans themselves, this faculty must have developed in a common ancestor before humans began to evolve independently of the other apes. This, in turn, means that: 'The colour-sense must be a common property of all mankind, in every country, and in every age' (1879: 202). It also implies that the time-scale proposed by Gladstone and Magnus for the development of the 'colour sense' is far too short (page 204).

Allen supports his biological arguments with cultural and linguistic ones. He gathered evidence from many parts of the world by perusing travel books, and sending out questionnaires on colour perception and language to 'missionaries, government officials, and other persons working amongst the most uncivilised races' (1879: 205). He presents his findings in his book, continent by continent, discussing the pigments, artefacts, works of art, and colour terms of many cultures, and concludes that 'all existing races possess a fully developed colour-sense' (page 212).

Allen next proceeds to literary and linguistic arguments, as a preparation for dealing with Gladstone's account of Homeric Greek. He addresses what he and contemporaries refer to as the 'vagueness' of colour terms. He argues that this is the fault of the colour sensations themselves because there are simply too many to label efficiently, so humans have imposed their own various divisions onto the colour space.

Allen then turns to the nature of poetic language, and points out that red is the colour which poets love. He gives several examples of objects described as red in poetry which are not that colour in reality, for example, lions, right hands, kings and wrath. He mimics poetic redness: 'Rosy-fingered dawn spreads crimson glories over the empyrean; the scarlet flush of eventide encarnadines the fiery sky.' Allen then carries out a colour-word count, as Gladstone had done for Homer, of Swinburne's book *Poems and Ballads* (1866). He concludes: 'To adopt the statistical form, we might say (if we chose to reckon the unreckonable) that red is 500 per cent. more poetical than blue!' (1879: 265). Allen carried out further investigations of this type, always finding that red and reddish colours were very much more popular with poets than blues and greens. He did not approve of word-counting as a research technique, but wanted to use Gladstone's own methodology in order to compare results.

Having acquired these results, and made certain linguistic points, Allen turns to Gladstone's and Magnus' accounts of Homeric Greek and Hebrew. As regards the first, he deals effectively with Gladstone's point that the Greeks could not have understood colours because their usage of colour terms was so vague, by giving some examples of imprecise English usage: 'Has Mr. Gladstone never heard of red blood, red skies, red bricks, and red Indians? Do Englishmen never talk of a green old age?' (1879: 267). In other words, it is not only the colour terms of *ancient* languages which are 'vague' in their usage, especially in poetry. The red colours of blood, the sky, bricks and Native Americans differ considerably from one another, but the same English colour word can be used of them all. Allen next argues that everything the Greeks of Homer's time most wanted to describe had variable and mixed colouring, including men, horses and cattle. It was the same in nature: 'the sea, white, or blue, or green, or grey, or purple, in its changeful moods', and a similar number of colour variations could be seen in the sky, mountains, rivers and other natural features. Allen argues that this is why early colour terms are not fixed or regular in their usage, since neither were their referents (pages 271–2), and he stresses in his summary that colour vocabulary, like all vocabulary, evolves only according to the needs of its speakers (page 281). In other words, human colour perception is the result of neuro-physiological development, but colour *terms* are coined only as each culture has need of them. There is no indissoluble link between perception and language.

Magnus began to have serious doubts about the suggested link between perception and colour vocabulary, so embarked on an admirable investigation (for the time) to resolve the matter. He sent out sets of colour samples, along with detailed instructions, to European contacts throughout the world, asking them to test the speakers of local languages, and report their results to him. His informants were mostly colonial administrators and Christian missionaries, and these people needed at least a working knowledge of the languages of their regions of operation. Many such people had much better than a working knowledge, as missionaries, for example, needed to teach in local languages and to translate the Bible. Magnus obtained information from all the inhabited continents, and published his results in 1880 in a report entitled *Untersuchungen über den Farbensinn der Naturvölker* ('Researches on the Colour Sense of Primitive Peoples'). One of the ten conclusions of the report was that colour perception and colour identification are not linked, so a lack of certain colour terms does not, after all, indicate an inability to perceive those colours (1880: 34).

2.5   William Rivers and partial insensitivity to hues

At the end of the nineteenth century, interest in the colour vocabulary of various peoples and particular authors steadily increased, as can be seen in Grossmann's valuable bibliography (1988: 307–66). Between 1880 and 1900, apart from theoretical works on colour language in general, studies in the Classical languages continued to appear, and interest in historical texts, as well as in contemporary languages, is also evident. Examples of languages studied for their colour terms include: Chukchen, Maori, Romanian, Samoan, Berber, Old English (OE), French and 'Eskimo', while examples of historical texts investigated include: the *Rigveda, Chanson de Roland* and the Bible (pages 321–3).

The notion that different peoples perceived colour differently (Section 2.3) was, however, revived in a weaker form when the results of a major anthropological expedition were published.[8] Between 1898 and 1900, an expedition from the University of Cambridge studied the peoples, cultures and environment of the Torres Strait, between Australia and Papua New Guinea, a stretch of shallow sea which contains nearly three hundred islands. The expedition was led by Alfred Cort Haddon, a biologist turned anthropologist, and the team included William Halse Rivers Rivers (1864–1922). Rivers, an anthropologist and psychiatrist, was, at that time, interested in colour vision, and endeavoured to investigate the colour perception and languages of the peoples he encountered in the Torres Strait area.

Rivers used coloured test-wools, as devised by Holmgren, but including additional samples, to test for colour blindness and colour-matching ability, and he also used coloured papers, as sold by Rothe of Leipzig, to help collect colour vocabulary (1901b: 49, 53). The addition of non-linguistic colour standards was a great improvement in the research methodology. In terms of colour matching, Rivers records several unexpected matches, particularly repeated cases of blue being matched with green or violet (pages 49–53). The blue hue also posed problems for Rivers in terms of vocabulary. He found that the languages he encountered either had no word at all that could be translated with Modern English (ModE) *blue* or they had what he calls an 'indefinite' term (for example, 1901b: 94). Like most of his European and North American contemporaries, he used *indefinite* and other pejorative terms, such as *confused* and *defective*, to refer to colour categories that differed from his own. These 'exotic' categories usually included a broader range of colours than their nearest English equivalents (Section 5.5), and so were interpreted as indicating an imprecise, vague or muddled designation of hues.

On Murray Island, Rivers found that the most frequently used word for blue was *bŭlubŭlu*, a reduplicated and adapted form of English *blue*. However, the old men told Rivers that the proper word for blue was *golegole*, the principal word for black. As Rivers amazedly records, 'they regarded it as quite natural to apply this [black] name to the brilliant blue of the sky and sea' (1901b: 55). Amongst what Rivers calls 'the Western Tribe' on the islands of Mabuiag and Badu, he found that the colour word *maludgamulnga* could indicate blue or green (pages 57–8). These are just some examples of the many colour terms that clearly surprised Rivers.

Rivers was aware of numerous studies of colour vocabularies around the world, and he knew that many of them had revealed colour terms whose meanings were quite alien to English speakers. His colour-matching exercises had convinced him that, even where his subjects had no word for a hue such as blue, they could still see it (which Gladstone had denied). He writes 'the matches . . . [showed] that they could certainly see blue and distinguish it from other colours' (1901b: 95). Nonetheless, it was evident that, although the various hues could be distinguished, the 'wrong' ones were often chosen as matches, for example, green to match blue, blue to match black, and others. His findings seem to have left Rivers in somewhat of a quandary. His work had disproved Gladstone's extreme position that, without a name, a colour was not perceived, and yet he had found a number of 'defective' colour words that did not name single hues. He took a middle path, and decided that some peoples suffered from *partial* colour insensitivity: 'the colour vision of the Papuan is characterized by a certain degree of insensitiveness to blue (and probably green) as compared with that of Europeans' (page 94). Yet he was loath to say that the cause of this insensitivity was purely physiological: 'There can be very little doubt, however, that any physiological insensitiveness which may exist, can only be one of the factors determining the characteristic features of primitive colour nomenclature' (page 95). His conclusion was that 'One of the chief interests of the work described in this report is that it shows that defect in nomenclature for a colour may be associated with defective sensibility for that colour and so far lends some support to the views of Gladstone and Geiger' (page 49).[9]

2.6   Edward Sapir, Benjamin Whorf and linguistic relativity

In the early twentieth century, there emerged an increasing number of publications on colour. In the first twenty years of the century, they included, apart from general books on colour, works on 'primitive' colour vision (of peoples in the then 'third world'), comparative studies of two or more languages, individual word-studies, and a number of items on 'the colour sense' (German *Farbenempfindung*) which is best modernized as 'colour perception'. Interest in the colour terms of individual languages remained strong, with studies appearing of Old English, Modern English, Latin, what is now called Proto-Indo-European, Ancient Greek, Romanian, Middle High German and Spanish, although there was a very literary tendency to concentrate exclusively on, or at least to emphasize, poetic usage in these languages. There was also an interest in the colour imagery of individual writers, such as Victor Hugo, Pindar, Goethe and Tirso de Molina (Grossmann 1988: 323–5).

The increased number of reports on how the world's peoples categorized and named colour provided fertile ground for an idea which had its roots in the theories of certain philosophers and linguists of the late eighteenth century, and, as MacLaury has shown, was already fully formed by 1920 in the mind of Franz Boas, the Professor of Anthropology at Columbia University (1997a: 18–19). In its developed form, this theory is now often referred to as the 'Sapir–Whorf hypothesis', named after Edward Sapir (1884–1939), a Prussian-born American anthropologist and linguist who was a student of Boas, and Benjamin Lee Whorf (1897–1941), a fire-assessment specialist in an insurance company who also established a substantial reputation as a linguist. The Sapir–Whorf hypothesis, which evolved out of their, and other, writings involves two main principles which relate closely to one other: linguistic relativity and linguistic determinism.

The theory of linguistic relativity suggests that the various languages differ arbitrarily from one another in the way they classify, structure and communicate aspects of the real world. This reflects the fact that different speech communities can have very different world-views. Sapir wrote: 'No two languages are ever sufficiently similar to be considered as representing the same social reality. The worlds in which different societies live are distinct worlds, not merely the same world with different labels attached' (1929: 209).

It was but a short step from suggesting that every language reflected a different world-view, to suggesting that a society's world-view was dictated by its language. This is the theory of linguistic determinism.[10] Sapir had touched upon this idea, writing: 'what if language is not so much a garment as a prepared road or groove?' (1921: 14) but, eight years later, he expressed himself in more positive fashion: 'We see and hear and otherwise experience very largely as we do because the language habits of our community predispose certain choices of interpretation' (1929: 210). Two years after the publication of his 1929 article, Sapir moved from the University of Chicago to Yale, and Benjamin Whorf was among his first students there. Whorf was to develop investigative techniques for researching and testing these views in various, mostly North American, languages.[11]

It is recognized today that there are both mild and extreme versions of the Sapir–Whorf hypothesis, and it is possible to find precursors of both versions in their writings.[12] Briefly put, the mild form of determinism suggests that language *influences* thought, but the extreme form suggests that language *determines* thought. Whorf writes of the latter: 'This organization [the 'geometry' or 'pattern-system' of each language] is imposed from outside the narrow circle of the personal consciousness, making of that consciousness a mere puppet whose linguistic maneuverings are held in unsensed and unbreakable bonds of pattern' (1956: 257).[13]

Research on colour vocabulary and semantics between the 1920s and 1960s was carried out against the background of, or under the influence of, the Sapir–Whorf hypothesis.[14] Taking an imaginary case, field researchers studying the colour vocabulary of Language X may have found, for example, that it had no principal term for blue. At this period, researchers would not have assumed that speakers of Language X had no *perception* of blue, as Gladstone had assumed, but, if they accepted the strong version of the Sapir–Whorf hypothesis, they would have believed that such people had no concept of blueness in their minds; that is, they had no *cognition* of blue because there was no principal blue term available to 'create' such a concept.

The Sapir–Whorf hypothesis affected both within-language studies, as in the hypothetical case above, and cross-language comparative studies. Colour became the principal area for research into whether a correlation could be established between linguistic and non-linguistic factors.[15] A linguistic factor could be, for example, codability, that is, the ease (or otherwise) of *naming* colours.[16] A non-linguistic factor might be memorability (recognition); that is, the ability to *remember* colours. Where a correlation was established, showing that it was easier for subjects to remember those colours for which they had principal colour terms, and more difficult for them to remember a colour for which they had no principal colour term, then it was believed that the Sapir–Whorf hypothesis was supported by that language. In other words, the belief was that it was easy to remember a colour for which one had a name, because the name had created the concept of that colour in the mind.

In 1956, an article was published which presented a cross-language comparison of colour within the linguistic relativity approach (Lenneberg and Roberts 1956).[17] Speakers of American English and of Zuni, the language of the Zuni people of New Mexico, were tested on their ability to recognize sections of the hue range denoted in Modern English by *yellow* and *orange*. The Zuni have a single principal word for this range, whereas English has two. The researchers found that English speakers were always able to distinguish between the colours yellow and orange, but monolingual Zuni speakers frequently failed to do so. Bilingual Zunis, who also spoke English, exhibited results that fell between those of the English speakers and the monolingual Zunis. Experimental results appeared to show, therefore, a link between codability (having two principal terms that divided the yellow/orange range between them) and memorability (easily distinguishing between yellow and orange). Brown and Lenneberg point out, however, that these experiments do not establish the *direction* of causality; that is, whether language prompts the concept, or the concept prompts the language (1954: 461). Other writers were somewhat less open-minded, and MacLaury comments: 'The relativity of language had become a crusade with color as its banner' (1997a: 20).

2.7   Brent Berlin, Paul Kay and linguistic universality

The event which challenged relativism in dramatic fashion was the publication, in 1969, of a book entitled *Basic Color Terms: their Universality and Evolution*, written by Brent Berlin and Paul Kay, both, at that time, at the University of California at Berkeley. This book, described as 'a pivotal challenge to an unfettered linguistic relativity' (Smith *et al.* 1995: 203), is usually taken to herald the modern era of colour semantics, even though certain of its proposals have since been challenged, revised or rejected.

As with many new theories, earlier and contemporary scholars had introduced ideas which fed into and nourished the work of Berlin and Kay. The principal influence doubtless came from the work of Noam Chomsky who had suggested that a 'deep structure' exists in the human mind from which languages generate meaningful sentences (Taylor 2003: 15–16).

Berlin and Kay started from the observation that 'color words translate too easily among various pairs of unrelated languages for the extreme linguistic relativity thesis to be valid' (1969: 2). They began a process of testing this hypothesis in a graduate seminar in 1967 in which data were gathered from several languages. Data from further languages were added, both from native-speaking informants and written sources, until the total reached ninety-eight languages from several language families. Berlin and Kay used these data to test the prevalent relativity hypothesis: 'We suspect that this allegation of total arbitrariness in the way languages segment the color space is a gross overstatement' (page 2), and their hypotheses have been revised and up-dated ever since as research results have accumulated.

Berlin and Kay suggested that two major aspects of colour cognition and naming were universal. Firstly, they suggested that there is a total universal inventory of eleven Basic Colour Categories (BCCs) (Chapter 5) which are successively named, usually over a considerable period of time, with Basic Colour Terms (BCTs) in each language (Chapter 3). Secondly, they also suggested that although languages differ, often considerably, as to the number of BCCs they have distinguished and named at any one time, the *order* in which they do this constitutes another language universal (Chapter 6). These universalist views are not without their challengers, from relativists and others, and such criticisms and alternative approaches will also be considered here (Chapter 7).[18]

As the previous paragraph indicates, there is a crucial difference between BCCs and BCTs, that is, between categories and terms. Categories are concepts in the mind, belonging to the cognitive domain, whereas terms are words and expressions, as represented in speech and/or texts, which belong to the linguistic domain. In very rough terms, colour terms are labels which enable concepts to be communicated to others who understand the same language. These two things, the concept and the name, may have a one-to-one relationship in which a single word denotes a single concept, but this is not always the case, so it is essential not to confuse them. It is a convention (although not an invariable one) in linguistics to separate them visually in print, when required, by means of SMALL CAPITALS (concepts) and *Italics* (words). For example, I may say 'In English, RED is denoted by *red*, but in Spanish, RED is denoted by *rojo*' (see Appendix, Section 2).

3   Basic colour terms

3.1   Introduction

The last chapter presented a selective account of the steadily increasing quantity of colour semantic evidence up to the late twentieth century, and the gradual improvement in the quality of its interpretation. It is time to turn to the features of colour vocabulary which have been studied, disputed and/or become established in more recent times. The main concern of this book is, of course, to tackle the difficult matter of how we interpret the colour terms of text-restricted languages (which have no surviving native speakers), but this work is often guided by what is known of the nature and behaviour of colour vocabulary in *living* languages. For this reason, it is now necessary to consider various features of colour semantics as illustrated by the extensive available data from currently spoken languages. Although, of course, the semanticist must not assume that historical languages operated in exactly the same way, modern languages can often suggest explanations for apparent anomalies and mysteries in historical data when no other information may be forthcoming.

3.2   Basicness

Colour semantic studies of individual languages are often greatly concerned, some would say obsessed, with the matter of basicness. Which colour words are Basic Colour Terms (BCTs) and which are not? As with other basic vocabulary, BCTs are frequently used, in both speech and writing, and they are well known to all adult speakers of the language. English speakers all know words such as *mother, arm, red* and *green* but they are less likely to encounter and/or understand *sibling, pancreas, burgundy* and *taupe*, which suggests that the second word-set contains *non*-basic terms. Although the phrase *basic colour term* became famous with the publication of Berlin and Kay's 1969 book (Section 2.7), it did not represent a new idea, as phrases like 'Level I terms' had already been used by, for example, Conklin (1955: 341).[1] This distinction reflects the common feeling that some colour terms are more important than others. For example, on Bellona Island, in the Solomon Islands, the people refer to their BCTs as 'the big names for colours', 'the mothers of colours' or 'the base of the colours' (Kuschel and Monberg 1974: 218).

Even *within* BCTs a further distinction can be made by dividing them into primary and secondary terms.[2] In many languages, there is a sense that some BCTs are more basic than others. In English, for example, *red* (a primary BCT) 'feels' more basic than *orange* (a secondary BCT). To express matters more objectively, the primary BCTs appear to denote colours which correspond with the six Hering primaries. Ewald Hering (1834–1918), a German physiologist, proposed the theory that the human visual system works on the principle of colour opponency, by which the brain interprets colour through the three opponent processes of black versus white, red versus green, and blue versus yellow (Wooten and Miller 1997: 66–70). These six colours (Hering's *Urfarben*) are called 'unique' or 'elemental' colours in English, and they are named by the primary BCTs.

It will become evident later in this book (in Chapter 5) that the recognition of BCTs in a language can reveal aspects of the native speakers' cognition of colour, so effective and appropriate means of recognizing them are highly desirable. Berlin and Kay set out four primary criteria to help in the recognition of BCTs in any language, and these were expected to be sufficient for this task in most cases. However, they also provided another four secondary criteria for cases where the application of the first four had left an element of doubt as to a word's basic status (1969: 6–7). One point which is easy to miss is that their criteria were not presented as 'laws' but as guidelines (I missed this myself, and am grateful to Robert MacLaury for pointing it out to me).[3] This fact became increasingly relevant after 1969 when it was found that some of the guidelines were inappropriate for some languages, as can be seen from the example of Samoan discussed in Section 3.3.

Major contributions to the debate on BCT recognition have been made by Berlin and Kay (1969), Hays *et al.* (1972), Crawford (1982), Boynton and Olson (1990) and Corbett and Davies (1997).[4] This chapter will introduce various aspects of colour vocabulary which have been suggested as means by which basic terms can be separated from non-basic ones.[5] Thus, the purpose of this chapter is fourfold: to present criteria for use in recognizing BCTs; to emphasize those criteria which can be applied in historical studies; to persuade readers that the evaluation of basicness is not a matter for guessing, even where they know a language well; and to simultaneously introduce certain techniques of colour semantic research.

In the BCT criteria which follow, the first eleven (Sections 3.3 to 3.13) represent Berlin and Kay's list of four primary and four secondary criteria (1969: 6–7) with their fourth criterion, psychological salience, split into the four suggested ways of how this may be assessed. It has been considered useful to describe even those criteria which are inappropriate for historical studies since historical semanticists may have to make use of comparative data from modern languages, so need to know something of how the results were obtained.

3.3   Non-predictable ('monolexemic') character

Berlin and Kay's criterion i, the first of their four primary criteria, states that a BCT should be monolexemic. Unfortunately, while their explanation of this criterion is clear, the name they give it, and one of their examples, have proved somewhat confusing. They explain *monolexemic* as 'its [the colour term's] meaning is not predictable from the meaning of its parts' (1969: 6).[6] Thus, while *green* and *purple* are monolexemic, compound words such as *lemon-coloured*, phrases such as *the colour of the rust on my aunt's old Chevrolet*, and lexemes exhibiting morphological variation, such as *bluish*, are listed as non-monolexemic.[7] It could be argued, however, that *bluish* consists of one lexeme (*blue*) which is also a morpheme, plus another morpheme (*-ish*). In other words, for *bluish* to be non-monolexemic as Berlin and Kay suggest, we would have to consider *-ish* a second lexeme, which it is not.[8]

Objections were raised against this criterion by those who were familiar with reduplicative languages. These are languages which, as part of their normal structure, duplicate words to create a new, but usually related, meaning. In Samoan, for example, *mū* means 'red hot; to burn', and *mūmū* means 'red' (Snow 1971: 386). Many have argued that, in cases like Samoan, a monolexemic structure should not be required for BCT status. This is not a case of simply rejecting an inconvenient criterion, but a matter of accommodating a particular and intrinsic feature of a language. As a result, the Samoan colour terms which are acceptable as potentially basic are *pa'epa'e* 'white' (from *pa'e* 'to bleach white'), *uliuli* 'black' (from *uli* 'dog, guide, helmsman'),[9] *mūmū* 'red' and *samasama* 'yellow' (from *sama* 'turmeric powder mixed with coconut oil'). From what Snow says, however, the two Samoan words for green are *not* monolexemic, and he readily accepts this. The meanings of *lanumeamata* (literally, 'colour of something that is raw') and *lanulau'ava* (literally, 'colour of the leaf of the kava plant') are clearly predictable from their parts, for example, 'kava leaf' and 'colour' clearly predict some form of green, provided one knows what a kava leaf looks like (1971: 386–7).[10]

When he comes to the blue hue, however, Snow is in a quandary. He reports that the Samoan term is *lanumoana* (literally, 'colour of the deepest part of the sea') and, in spite of the fact that this word has a comparable structure to that of the definitely non-monolexemic Samoan words for green, he enters into a somewhat unconvincing argument as to how *lanumoana* could be considered monolexemic (pages 187–8). This article on Samoan is an early example of the difficulties some researchers experienced in applying certain of Berlin and Kay's criteria.

The present writer knows nothing about the Samoan language, but suspects that Snow (and many others) were interpreting *monolexemic* in a particular way. They consider a word such as Samoan *mūmū* to consist of two lexemes (*mū* and *mū*) which makes it non-monolexemic but Snow is convinced *mūmū* is a basic term. It is very likely in fact that, in the case of reduplicative languages, a construction such as *mūmū* should be considered an independent single lexeme.

It would appear then that the 'monolexemic' criterion has perhaps been misleadingly named, and I have used Berlin and Kay's description of 'non-predictable' in its place.[11] Most of the Samoan colour expressions listed above would pass this test since there seems no logic in an argument that states 'burn, burn' must predict 'red' (why not 'destroyed' or 'cooked'?), and certainly not that 'dog, dog' predicts 'black'.[12] On the other hand, the meanings of the colour terms starting *lanu-* certainly *are* predictable, consisting of 'colour' and '[entity name]', and so fail this test.

It is not only reduplicative languages however which can fall foul of this criterion. MacLaury researched the colour terms of Karuk, a people and language of north-west California, and found that almost all their terms, several of which must be basic, consist of compounds of '[entity name]' and 'like'. Thus 'red' is *ʔa•x-kúniš*, literally 'blood-like'; 'white' is *čánča•f-kúniš*, literally 'foam-like'; and 'black' is *ikxáram-kúniš* 'night-like'. This creates a new dilemma. These colour terms are predictable from their parts, but *only* if the hearer knows that colour is the subject of conversation. If not, the phrases could refer to other qualities of the entities, such as the flowing or oozing of blood, the bubbly nature of foam, or the coldness of night. MacLaury came to a sensible conclusion, suggesting that these data 'underscore that a basic color term is best identified by the way it is used rather than by how it is formed or where it comes from' (1992b: 8).[13] This view is very much supported for cross-cultural studies by Alvarado and Jameson (2002) who show that the English speaker's greater use of monolexemic terms is not paralleled in Vietnamese and other languages in which the use of modifiers, such as the equivalents of *light*, *dark*, *vivid* and so on, and compound terms, is much more common and constitutes an essential element of their colour-naming strategy.

In historical studies, the researcher can apply this criterion to a certain extent, provided s/he fully understands the structure of the language. Even so, without native-speaker insight, it is best considered as a supporting criterion only, always requiring corroborating evidence.

3.4   Hyponymy

Berlin and Kay's criterion ii states that a BCT cannot be a hyponym of another colour word, and this has been generally accepted as a useful indicator of basicness. A hyponym is a word whose meaning is totally contained within the meaning of another word. Thus, the meanings of PDE *crimson* and *scarlet* are contained within the meaning of PDE *red*, so they are hyponyms of *red*. *Red*, on the other hand, is a hyperonym (*hyper-* not *hypo-*) or a higher-level, superordinate term, so it can be considered a potential BCT.

Hyponymy can often be recognized from conversations, expressions or descriptive texts. A question such as 'What sort of red is it?' is likely to be answered with a hyponym, while a sentence such as 'It was an amazing emerald green' suggests by its structure (in English, at least) that *emerald* is a hyponym of the superordinate *green*. Where expressions like these, or semantically equivalent constructions in other languages, are found in historical texts, hyponyms and hyperonyms can be recognized.

3.5   Contextual restriction

Berlin and Kay's criterion iii, namely that a BCT must not be contextually restricted, has also proved generally acceptable.[14] It states that a BCT's usage should not be restricted to a narrow class of objects, in the way that PDE *blonde* is restricted to human hair,[15] or *roan* to animals. Consider the incorrectness of phrases such as **blonde paper* or **roan sofas*.[16]

John Lyons argues that 'context-restrictedness' should not debar a colour word from basic status, but he understands *basic* in extremely broad terms (1995a: 207). He refers to 'Level-1' words like English *black*, *white* and *red* as basic, and 'Level-2' words like English *scarlet*, *mauve* and *turquoise* as 'less basic' (page 202) but Berlin and Kay would regard his Level-2 words as *non*-basic.

The difference of opinion over context-restrictedness also relates to the *direction* of restriction. Some languages have two salient colour terms for the same colour, and the two terms may operate in a complementary fashion, as regards the referents they can describe. In French, for example, there are two colour terms roughly equivalent to English *brown*; they are *brun* and *marron*. Lyons points out that some referents can only be described by one of these terms so, for example, brown shoes must be *marron*, not *brun*. Similarly, in describing human hair or skin, a French speaker would use *brun*, not *marron*. Lyons refers to both these cases as context-restricted (1995a: 206) but this indicates a subtly different definition to that of Berlin and Kay. Lyons is describing a limitation on the colour terms applicable to a particular referent, whereas Berlin and Kay are describing a limitation on the referents describable by a particular colour term.

Berlin and Kay's (1969: 6) interpretation of contextual restriction specifies restriction to a *narrow* class of objects, indicating colour terms such as *blonde* (see above). As regards the French words for brown, Forbes, after questioning 139 French speakers living in France, was able to show that *marron* can be used of eyes, clothes and material, trees, leather, wooden furniture and food. In addition, some of her informants used *marron* of hair, animals, paint and earth (1979: 301–2). This by no means exhibits a *narrow* restriction so, in Berlin and Kay's interpretation of contextual restriction, *marron* is not restricted.

An interesting angle on contextual freedom is described by Rakhilina and Paramei (2011), and called *combinability*. This refers to the ability (or inability) of a colour term to describe both natural phenomena and human artefacts. Through their research into the Russian language, but with supporting evidence from several other languages, they notice that some terms which are coined in order to indicate a shade of colour which is typical of a newly produced or newly imported artefact, can later expand to become applicable to the natural world. Rakhilina and Paramei therefore suggest that combinability with both artefacts and natural entities is a likely precondition for basic status.

In historical studies, contextual restriction can be suspected or demonstrated, depending on how much evidence is available. It is particularly prevalent in the contexts of human colouring (especially hair, skin and eyes), animal colours (especially of horses and cattle), textiles and dyes, but can also occur in other contexts which have economic or social importance in a particular society. When a colour term is found in one of these contexts only, and there is sufficient data to confirm the researcher's suspicions, that term should be considered contextually restricted.

3.6   Elicited lists

Berlin and Kay's criterion iv.1 is their first of four suggested methods of assessing psychological salience. Their four methods comprise my Sections 3.6 to 3.9. Psychological salience refers to whether a concept comes to the forefront of a person's mind when a particular subject is mentioned. When a person is faced with the subject of colour, for example, which colour words are among the first to leap into his or her mind? Elicited lists can be used to investigate this. Native speakers are asked to list their colour terms, and occurrence at or near the beginning of such a list suggests that a term is likely to be a BCT, although further corroboration is required.

In the late 1980s and the 1990s, researchers, mostly psychologists, expended considerable effort on establishing criteria for BCT recognition which could be measured and were susceptible to statistical assessment (for example, Davies and Corbett 1994).[17] The elicitation of lists as a test of basicness was evaluated with Russian speakers by Morgan and Corbett (1989).[18] The informants were asked to write down all the colour terms that came to their minds in five minutes, and to draw a line across their lists at the end of each minute.[19] It was hoped that this experiment would cast some light on the well-known problem of the Russian blues.

Russian has two principal terms for the blue region, *sinij* (синий) and *goluboj* (голубой), and doubts had been expressed over the years as to whether they could both be BCTs. In the elicitation test, *sinij* was named by 24 of the 31 informants within the first minute, and *goluboj* was named by 27 of them within that same period. These results are better than those for some accepted Russian BCTs such as *černyj* 'black' (21); *želtyj* 'yellow' (21); and *belyj* 'white' (18). Furthermore, the results for both blue terms were considerably better than those for non-basic terms, of which the highest score was 13 informants (Corbett and Davies 1995: 320, Table 6). The test results appear to support the basic status of both the Russian blues, but other experimenters have warned that reliance on salience tests alone can be misleading (Taylor, Mondry and MacLaury 1997: 420).[20]

Similar tests on speakers of American English, British English and French (Corbett and Davies 1995: 320–5) found that English *white* and *black* scored relatively low (listed by 272 and 314 subjects respectively out of 442), but Corbett and Davies suggest this is because English speakers are uncertain as to whether white and black are proper colours.[21] In conclusion, list elicitation tests involving time limits are not applicable to historical studies since they require native speakers. However, in some cases, the historical data may include classified word-lists, colour terms noted down by early anthropologists, and similar information which may be of limited value in indicating lexical salience.

3.7   Consensus

This is part of Berlin and Kay's criterion iv.2, which is their second suggested method for assessing psychological salience (the second part of criterion iv.2 is described in Section 3.8). They referred to this criterion as 'stability of reference across informants'. Boynton and Olson, calling it *consensus*, devised a testing procedure in which seven English-speaking subjects were asked to name 424 randomly shown Optical Society of America (OSA) colour samples on two occasions each, making 14 namings for each sample. The subjects were asked to name the samples with 'monolexemic' colour terms only. Consensus was interpreted as a given sample being named with the same colour term 14 times, and this was achieved for 128 samples (1987: 95–9). Although this seems a reasonable way in which to test consensus, when Boynton and Olson carried out a similar test a few years later, the number of samples on which there was consensus dropped to only nine (Boynton and Olson 1990: 1313). They point out that the later group of subjects chose to use non-basic terms for 33 per cent of the time compared with only 10 per cent of the time in the earlier study and, since this provided the later group with a much larger selection from which to choose, consensus was inevitably reduced.[22]

Something which both the Boynton and Olson studies showed was that there is no consensus on the use of any *non*-BCTs. A similar result was achieved for Japanese colour terms in which full consensus (100 per cent) was recorded for the BCTs *shiro* 'white'; *midori* 'green'; *cha* 'brown'; and *murasaki* 'purple'. A high consensus (90 to 99 per cent) was recorded for *kuro* 'black' and *aka* 'red'.[23] This should be compared with results for *non*-basic terms where, leaving aside two exceptions,[24] the highest percentage achieved was for *oudo* 'yellow soil' (60 per cent) and the next highest score (45 per cent) was recorded for *kusa* 'grass green'; *yamabuki* 'globeflower'; *ai* 'indigo'; and *cream* 'cream' (Uchikawa and Boynton 1987: 1828, Table 4). These studies indicate that percentage of consensus successfully separates most of the BCTs of a language from most of the non-BCTs.

In historical projects, there may be sufficient data from known authors to enable consensus among individuals to be assessed. However, where it is not possible to recognize the work of individuals in sufficient numbers, it has been suggested that types of colour vocabulary may be used instead to indicate consensus among different social groups. Types of vocabulary may be retrieved from, for example, learned, specialized, poetic and popular texts (Biggam 1997: 89), and it is assumed that such types roughly represent, respectively, those who have been educated, those involved in colourful crafts and industries, those with a particular interest in linguistic style, and those who belong to none of these groups. It is suggested, for example, that colour terms which occur in all such groups are more likely to be basic.

3.8   Consistency

This is the second part of Berlin and Kay's criterion iv.2 (the first part is described in Section 3.7), and is their second suggested method of assessing psychological salience. They called it 'stability of reference across occasions of use'. Boynton and colleagues, calling it *consistency*, calculated their results from the same data as those used for consensus testing, as described in Section 3.7. Subjects were each asked to name 424 randomly shown OSA colour samples on two occasions, using 'monolexemic' colour terms. On the second occasion, the samples were shown to each subject in the reverse order to that used on the first occasion (Uchikawa and Boynton 1987: 1825–6).

Consistency was defined as the assigning of the same colour term to the same sample on both naming occasions. In a study with nine English speakers, it was found that subjects named samples consistently 75 per cent of the time (range 57 to 86 per cent) when using a BCT, but only 45 per cent of the time (range 24 to 59 per cent) when using non-basic terms (Boynton and Olson 1990: 1313). Consistency results have been published for Russian, Japanese and two separate studies of American English (Corbett and Davies 1995: 318,

Table 5), and they show that the majority of BCTs are used more consistently than even the highest-scoring non-basic terms.

Without modification, this criterion is inappropriate for historical studies since it requires the testing of native speakers. However, in historical projects which can draw on numbers of works by individual authors, the researcher can investigate the meanings and uses of colour terms across an author's texts, and thus evaluate his or her consistency. Where there is much less data available, or where authors are unknown, a possible modification has been suggested (Biggam 1997: 88). Where the range and quantity of surviving texts are appropriate, historical researchers may consider replacing the consistency of individuals with consistency across categories of text. This involves classifying texts into categories such as religious works, chronicles, encyclopaedias and others, and evaluating consistency across these categories.

3.9   Idiolectal evidence

Berlin and Kay's criterion iv.3, the last of their suggested tests for psychological salience, specifies that a potential BCT should occur in the individual speech habits (idiolect) of every native speaker.

Under certain conditions, this criterion can be applied in historical studies. Where the amount of surviving evidence is limited, anonymous or unrepresentative of the various genres of recorded speech and writings, it is impossible to be confident that a particular colour term would have been known to almost everyone. However, where there is ample material available to survey, for example, from the nineteenth century, the researcher may be able to show that a particular colour term is found in the work of a large number of individuals. This would be a satisfactory outcome since, even with living languages, the researcher is not expected to question *every* native speaker.

Berlin and Kay's criterion of psychological salience (Sections 3.6 to 3.9) came under particularly heavy criticism. It was considered inappropriate to mix this psychological approach with the linguistic nature of the three other primary criteria.[25] The salience criteria were also originally criticized for being somewhat unclear and not conducive to measurement. Kay suggests that most of the problems with this criterion occur with colour terms or in colour regions that are undergoing change (2001: 2250–1) (see Chapter 6).

Berlin and Kay were aware that, after their first four criteria had been applied, there could still be doubts as to the basic status of some words, so they provided four secondary criteria aimed at settling such problems (Sections 3.10 to 3.13).

3.10   Derivational morphology

Berlin and Kay's criterion v, the first of their secondary criteria, concerned *derivational morphology*, which they called 'distributional potential' This means that, where a known BCT can, for example, attach suffixes or pre-fixes in the way that ModE *green* can attach *-ish* to make *greenish*, the potential BCT under scrutiny is more likely to be basic if it can do the same.

Wescott has a similar suggestion which he calls 'polytypy' (1970: 354–5). This involves counting the number of 'grammatical categories' or parts of speech which a colour expression can exhibit. He gives English *black* as an example, which occurs as adjective (*blackish*), noun (*blackness*), verb (*blacken*) and adverb (*blackly*). This differs from Berlin and Kay's suggestion in that the idea is not explicitly to compare morphemes with those of a known BCT, but rather simply to count them. It is not clear whether a comparison with other colour terms in the same language is involved or not.

Crawford rejects Berlin and Kay's criterion because he cannot see why dis-tributional potential should be relevant to basicness (1982: 341). He illustrates his objection with the case of ModE *orange* which, unlike all other English BCTs, most often adds *-ey* in place of the usual *-ish*. Crawford maintains that this reluctance of English speakers to generate *orangish* from *orange* suggests it may not have the same distributional potential as accepted English BCTs, and this casts doubt on its basic status. Nonetheless, *orange* is an accepted English BCT, so Crawford concludes that there must be something wrong with the criterion. Crawford's choice of example is unfortunate for his argument, since any tendency on the part of English speakers to prefer *orangey* to *orangish* is almost certainly because the juxtaposition of the two sounds represented by *g* and *sh* in *orangish* is simply considered awkward to pronounce.[26] Although useful as a clue, this criterion is only partially successful in some languages, as in English, where the suffix *-en* appears in *whiten*, *blacken* and *redden* but is not added to the other English BCTs (for example, **greenen* and **bluen*).[27]

Corbett and Davies retrieve derivational morphology data from their investi-gations of Russian and French, and conclude that this feature has only a limited ability to separate basic from non-basic terms in these two languages (1995: 325–7). Steinvall, however, is unhappy with their data-collection method which relied on particular word-forms appearing in appropriate dictionaries. Steinvall maintains that the failure of a dictionary to list a particular morphological vari-ant does not mean that that form is unacceptable. Furthermore, he considers the frequency of occurrence of such forms as retrieved from a corpus (a database of the language) to be more significant (2002: 83) (see Sections 3.15 and 3.16).

In historical studies, the researcher should certainly gather data on the mor-phological variations of his or her language of study but it seems likely that this criterion would only provide supporting evidence for basicness, since irregu-larities resulting from, for example, ease of pronunciation, may not be easily assessed in historical languages. There are similar difficulties with Wescott's version of this test. Whether or not to apply this criterion would very much depend on the structure of the language under study and the amount of surviving evidence.

3.11   Homonymy

Berlin and Kay's criterion vi, the second of their secondary criteria, suggests that the researcher should harbour doubts about a potential BCT which also names a similarly coloured object. Thus, *turquoise* is a colour word but it is also the name of a gemstone which is often a green-blue colour. Berlin and Kay point out that the English BCT *orange* would also be doubtful if it had not already passed the four primary criteria (1969: 6).

Colour terms often evolve out of words for concrete objects, just as *orange* (the colour) has evolved from *orange* (the fruit), and the main concern of this criterion is that, for the colour word to be a BCT, its meaning must be divorced from that of the concrete object. The *form* of the two words can remain the same, but their meanings must have diverged to the extent of having become independent of each other at the date relevant to the research, although this is often difficult to evaluate. This means that BCTs can be homonyms (words with the same form but different meanings) such as *orange* (the colour) and *orange* (the fruit), but they cannot be polysemous (one word having more than one meaning) such as *chartreuse* (a colour and a liqueur).[28] Another way of expressing this requirement is to say that the colour sense must have become abstract, that is, no longer inseparable from a concrete object in the mind of a native speaker.

This is a difficult criterion to apply in historical studies but, with sufficient material available, it is possible to make a reasonable assessment of the situation. It is recommended that the researcher peruse his or her texts carefully to ascertain whether there are a number of contexts in which the concrete meaning of his or her colour term would be inappropriate; for example, *orange shoes* in English could have no connection with fruit. Some would argue that the concrete object, namely, the orange fruit in this case, is never totally absent from the mind of a native speaker, regardless of the referent, but such links are of variable strength, and likely to weaken with the passage of time. Such subtleties are impossible to test for when studying a dead language, but the extant range of referents has the potential to be of supportive value.

3.12   Recent loan words

Berlin and Kay's criterion vii, the third of their secondary criteria, suggests that a word's basicness may be doubted if it is a recent foreign loan word into the language being researched. This criterion has often been criticized for the vagueness of the word *recent* (for example, Crawford 1982: 341). A moment's thought, however, will reveal how impossible it would be to specify a particular time-span, since this criterion involves the widely differing social and economic circumstances in which individual languages are spoken.

In historical studies, this criterion would require considerable knowledge of the language's development over time. It would be necessary to know when the foreign word was adopted into the target language, and how widespread it was in the available records. Clues such as changing spellings of the word, indicating increasing naturalization in its new language would be helpful, as would indications that the adopted word was functioning as a semi-technical term restricted to literate individuals. This criterion could, in most cases, only provide supporting evidence.

3.13   Morphological complexity

Berlin and Kay's criterion viii, the fourth and last of their secondary criteria, is linked by them to their criterion i ('monolexemic' structure, Section 3.3). It is suggested that, where it has been difficult to judge whether the potential BCT is monolexemic, a consideration of morphological complexity may help. Berlin and Kay are very doubtful about this criterion, saying 'The English term *blue-green* might be eliminated by this criterion' (1969: 7). Since they use *might* in this sentence, it is clear that they are not necessarily recommending that a BCT should consist of a single morpheme, but they are probably thinking in terms of a low number of morphemes within the limits appropriate to a particular language. This criterion has always been tricky to understand, since *blue-green* is the only example provided, and it would seem that its lexemic status is not at all difficult to assess: it consists of two lexemes, so is non-monolexemic. As a result, there is no need to assess it further in terms of morphological complexity.

In historical studies, it would certainly be possible to assess the morphological complexity of colour terms from the surviving records, but any judgements as to the norm for BCTs would need to be made in the context of the language's overall lexical structure. Two examples of why this is necessary are discussed in Section 3.3.

The publication of *Basic Color Terms* in 1969, including the BCT criteria listed above, was followed by a flurry of articles.[29] Anyone with knowledge of a (preferably) exotic language wanted to test it against the new theories, eager to disprove or support Berlin and Kay's suggestions. Such articles raised worthwhile queries and expanded colour semantic information, but there are two problems that frequently occur in them and which need to be understood by the researcher who makes use of their data. Firstly, many of these language-specific articles of the 1970s and 1980s (and later) attempt to fit the language into the procrustean bed of BCT criteria, when it would have been better if the researcher had, after having collected his or her data, rejected any criteria that were inappropriate to 'their' language. It is often clear from a researcher's protests that a criterion is unsuitable for a particular language and that, where it is retained in the survey, it may distort the overall results. As explained in Section 3.2, the considered rejection of certain criteria does not contravene Berlin and Kay's suggested procedures.

The second problem which the reader of these language studies may encounter is usually impossible to evaluate. While it was sensible, and even necessary, to avoid establishing a fixed list of criteria for assessing basicness in every language, this imposes a heavy burden on each researcher. S/he has to know the language whose colour terms are under scrutiny extremely well, and be able to make judgements as to which BCT criteria are appropriate in the context of that language's structure and usage but, unfortunately, it is common for the earlier colour semantic studies to omit any account of the extent of the researcher's knowledge of the language and its culture. Some researchers suggested additional or alternative criteria for BCT recognition, and these will now be added to the list.

3.14   Expression length

Durbin suggested that a BCT should have a comparatively short expression length (this includes single word length) (1972: 270–2) and this was included in a list of new types of evidence published by Hays and colleagues (Hays *et al.* 1972: 1110–11). Expression length was considered especially useful in diachronic studies as a test of Berlin and Kay's evolutionary sequence (Chapter 6), but it is included here as a possible criterion for synchronic studies in certain languages.[30]

Durbin assessed expression length according to the number of phonemes they contained (1972: 270–2).[31] The idea was based on Zipf's Law of Abbreviation, named after the American linguist George Zipf, which concerns the relationship between frequency of occurrence and word length. Zipf (1949) maintained that the more frequently a word is used, the shorter it becomes, and examples of this phenomenon can easily be found in English where, for example, *omnibus* has become *bus*, and *television* has become *telly*. This is often referred to as 'the principle of least effort', and it implies that BCTs are likely to be shorter in pronunciation than non-BCTs, as the former are used more often.[32]

Corbett and Davies investigated word length, using both phonemes and syllables, in English, French, Russian and Spanish (1995: 333–5). For the first three of these languages, they had data for some non-basic vocabulary and, when this was compared with that for basic terms, the conclusion was that word length fails to distinguish accurately between the two types of vocabulary. In French and Russian, there is at least one non-basic term which is shorter than the shortest BCT, and in English, the three shortest non-basics are shorter than six of the BCTs. French and Russian show statistically significant differences in the syllable counts between primary and secondary BCTs, but the test appears to be of dubious value for distinguishing between basic and non-basic terms.

In historical studies, this test could be applied to some languages, but it is recommended that the results should only be considered as supporting evidence for the indication of primary, but not secondary, BCTs.

3.15   Frequency of occurrence in texts

Hays and colleagues also drew attention to the frequency of occurrence of colour terms in texts, pointing out that the more salient a colour term is, the more often it is used (Hays *et al.* 1972: 1111–13). They had in mind that this criterion would suit diachronic studies by helping to assess the age of BCTs (which they call 'focal colour terms') but this test can also be a useful criterion for the assessment of basicness.[33]

Hays and colleagues looked at published word-frequency tables for six languages, and extracted figures for the known BCTs. The highest-scoring BCTs in each language were almost always ModE *white*, *black* and *red* and their equivalents. The first and second highest scores for each language were as follows: English (3 sources): *white* is first in all three lists, while second place is held by different words, namely, *brown*, *red* and *black*; Castilian Spanish (2 sources): *blanco* 'white' and *negro* 'black' are first and second in both lists; French (1 source): *blanc* 'white' is first, and *noir* 'black' is second; German (1 source): *weiss* 'white' is first, and *rot* 'red' is second; Russian (1 source): *belyj* 'white' is first, and *krasnyj* 'red' is second; Romanian (1 source): *alb* 'white' is first, and *negru* 'black' is second; Japanese (1 source): *shiro* 'white' is first, and *kuro* 'black' is second.

The published frequency lists available in 1972 were of greatly varying quality, scope and date but they nonetheless appear to have produced useful results.[34] Where possible, researchers used frequency lists compiled from various genres of text, such as newspapers and magazines, poetry, prose literature, non-fiction, children's literature and so on. Results by genre can be compared, and a combined total retrieved. Corbett and Davies published frequency tables in 1995 for colour terms in twentieth-century Russian texts (1995: 328–33).[35] They found that the primary BCTs had scores ranging from 471 for *belyj* 'white' to 109 for *želtyj* 'yellow', while the highest scoring non-BCT was *belosnežnyj* 'snow-white' with 67. While the division between primary BCTs and non-BCTs is clear, the secondary BCTs had more erratic scores, ranging from *seryj* 'grey' with 116 to *oranževyj* 'orange' with only 15.[36] The results for modern British English are comparable (Corbett and Davies 1995: 330), so it would seem that this test is useful for separating *primary* (but not always secondary) BCTs from *non*-BCTs. Frequency studies have increasingly come to depend on lexical corpora held in computer databases (see Section 8.5) but such resources are by no means available for all languages.

The researcher cannot take the results of frequency studies as they stand, without considering potential problems for his or her particular research. A list of such problems is provided in Leech, Rayson and Wilson (2001: 19) and, although it relates to lists retrieved from corpora, it also holds warnings for manually compiled lists. Firstly, attention must be paid to *dispersion values*, that is, the representative nature (or otherwise) of the texts included. It is essential to avoid the misrepresentation of a particular term or terms as a result of including a specialized tract; for example, a manual on indigo dyeing, while excluding manuals on other dyes. This would result in an over-representation of blue words. Secondly, there is a need to beware, especially in computer-generated lists, of spelling variations such as that between French *brun* and *brune* (the masculine and feminine forms respectively) as they will be separately listed, and the researcher may prefer to combine their totals. Thirdly, frequency figures are not influenced by context so the totals may include unwanted cases such as personal names. Fourthly, it should be remembered that frequency results refer to words, not *meanings*, so, for example, the total for Modern English *turquoise* will include the gemstone as well as the colour.

Frequency of occurrence is clearly an appropriate test to use in historical studies although, in many projects, it will be difficult to judge how representative the surviving texts are likely to be. This test would clearly be most valuable where there is ample surviving documentation.

3.16   Frequency of occurrence in speech

The criterion above (Section 3.15) is concerned with the frequency of occurrence of colour terms in texts, but the same test can be applied to speech.[37] Basic evidence can be obtained from corpora of the spoken word, where available, from data-gathering exercises based on verbal communications of various types, or from verbally elicited lists of colour terms (see Section 3.6). Section 3.6 is concerned with the position or rank of a colour term in a list of such terms, or (more likely, and to be preferred) the mean ranking of a colour term across *several* elicited lists. For this present criterion, however, it is necessary to calculate how many times a colour term is included in several elicited lists regardless of its position.

Bolton acquired lists of Spanish colour terms from 113 students (ranging in age from 13 to 26) in two locations in Peru (1978a: 290). He recorded both the mean ranking (page 292, Table 2) and the frequency of occurrence of each term (page 291, Table 1). Considering the latter dataset, it is interesting that even the most salient terms such as *rojo* 'red' (mentioned 104 times), *amarillo* 'yellow' (102 times) and *verde* 'green' (101 times) were not listed by *all* of the 113 students. Nonetheless, with certain exceptions, there is a clear distinction between BCTs and non-basic terms. The lowest scoring BCT is *morado* 'purple', mentioned 22 times, while the highest scoring non-basic term is *plomo* 'grey', mentioned only eight times. This ignores two exceptions. *Celeste* 'pale blue' is listed as non-basic but occurs 39 times in the lists. As Bolton mentions, this word should possibly be considered basic (1978a: 294). The second exception is *gris* 'grey', listed as a BCT but with only four occurrences in the lists. Bolton explains that, of his 113 informants, only one listed *both* the grey terms, *gris* and *plomo* (page 293), suggesting that the availability of a second widely used grey term had reduced the score of the grey BCT. The results for *celeste* and *gris* usefully indicate terms which require further investigation.

Corbett and Davies used similar measurements obtained from verbal naming experiments (1995: 315–16). They compared results from four sets of data, one each for Russian and Japanese, and two for American English. For each dataset, the total basic-term frequency of occurrence figures, expressed as percentages, were higher than for the *non*-basic figures (page 316, Table 4).

Urmas Sutrop has devised a cognitive salience calculation based on the naming frequency of colour terms in experiments with native speakers, and on each term's mean position in elicited lists (Section 3.6). The formula is $S = F / (N \times mP)$, where S is salience ranking, F is frequency, N is the number of subjects, and mP is the mean position. In cases where all subjects name a particular term ($F = N$) and the mean position is 1, the salience ranking is also 1. Basic terms have the lowest results, indicating high salience.[38]

In historical studies, this criterion can only be considered for recent periods which may benefit from corpora of the spoken language or the survival of extensive sound-recordings of speech.

3.17   Response time

Response (or reaction) time had been suggested by Hays and colleagues as a good way to test colour terms for psychological salience (Hays *et al.* 1972: 1120), and Boynton and Olson (1990: 1314–15) took up the idea. The theory was that a BCT would require a shorter response time than a non-basic term. The procedure involved showing nine subjects 424 randomly ordered OSA colour samples under controlled conditions, and asking them to name each one monolexemically in English. The samples were then shown a second time in reverse order. The time taken by the subjects to name each sample was measured, and a mean calculated for the time taken to use each colour term across the total nine informants. The results showed that all BCTs were elicited in shorter response times than was recorded for any of the non-basic terms (1990: 1315, Figure 3).

Corbett and Davies also presented and compared response times obtained from testing speakers of Russian and Japanese, and from two sets of American English speakers (1995: 313–15). In each language, the mean response time for BCTs was faster than that for non-BCTs (page 313, Table 3). However, this test is inappropriate for historical studies since it requires the presence of native speakers.

3.18   Type modification

Bolton recognized the importance of cultural context in the use of colour terms, specifically in what he called the domain of economic importance, and he suggested that a BCT is more likely than a non-BCT to feature in the naming and discussion of such items. He provides studies of two such contexts in Peru (1978a). He first considered names for potatoes in the Quechua language in the highlands of southern Peru where this crop has been grown, and varieties have been developed, over many centuries. Colour terms regularly feature in both the names of potato varieties and in discussion about their cultivation. Interviews with eighteen informants produced an astonishing 350 names for varieties of potato, of which approximately 38 per cent included a colour term. This Task I [one] produced results which consisted almost entirely of BCTs: the three most frequently occurring were *puka* 'red' (113 times), *yurah* 'white' (106 times) and *yana* 'black' (84 times).

In Task II, the informants were asked to describe the characteristics of fifteen varieties of potato and, in Task III, they were asked to name fifteen potato varieties and answer questions about them. The results for each task included *puka, yurah* and *yana* in the top three places, although not always in the same order (Bolton 1978a: 297–8). The other BCTs feature less frequently, and the only non-basic terms mentioned are *garnet* and *maroon* (no Quechua terms provided) in the context of potato skin (page 298).

Bolton's second cultural investigation was into the keeping and consumption of guinea pigs in the same area of Peru (1978a: 300). Interviews with local informants produced 192 occurrences of colour terms connected with guinea pigs, of which 97.4 per cent were BCTs. The only non-basic terms used (five occurrences) were all in Spanish, not Quechua: *castaño* 'chestnut'; *medio manteca* 'half lard'; and *color de vicuña* 'colour of the vicuña' (an animal related to the llama) (page 300). It seems that, in distinguishing between multiple items of the same type on the basis of colour, there is a preference for basic vocabulary.

What Bolton had found is not, however, restricted to domains of economic importance, and his examples belong to the feature known here as *type modification*. It has long been observed that colour adjectives can be used in ways which are not purely descriptive, but classificatory.[39] This means that, while a phrase such as *the blue hat* simply describes the colour of the hat, a phrase such as *the white wines of France* does not accurately describe the colour of the wines, since they are not the colour of snow or milk. In this second phrase, the colour adjective is *classifying* the wines rather than describing them, and it successfully excludes red and rosé wines (the only other possibilities) from consideration. While it is true, as Bolton suggested, that many of these classificatory uses of colour occur with items of economic importance, such as guinea pigs and wines, they are also used in areas like hair colour and skin colour. A 'red-haired' person does not have hair which is naturally the colour of a tomato, but s/he clearly does *not* have blonde, brown or black hair.

Most recently, type modification in Modern English colour adjectives has been researched by Steinvall (2002; 2006) who used two language corpora to look for patterns in the occurrence of this phenomenon. He first studied examples from the *Oxford English Dictionary* and applied a rank correlation test which showed a significant correlation between BCTs and adjectives used in type modification (pages 111–16). There was, however, no clear dividing line between the less commonly used BCTs and non-basic colour terms (page 112). Steinvall also studied the colour adjective collocations with nouns in cases retrieved from the *Bank of English*, and his results again showed that BCTs occurred much more commonly in this type of collocation than non-BCTs (pages 116–21).[40] Steinvall writes: 'It became apparent in both the dictionary and the corpus studies...that there are, in fact, very few terms which are frequently used for type modification: there are the six Primary BCTs and to a certain degree also *brown, grey, golden* and *silver*' (page 122).

It seems clear that this criterion is likely to be valuable for distinguishing the primary BCTs in certain languages, and for offering indications of basicness for the secondary BCTs which would, without doubt, require corroborating evidence. In historical studies, provided the researcher has sufficient material to offer a significant amount of this type of evidence, the results should be useful in connection with the primary BCTs, but would provide only somewhat unreliable supporting evidence for the secondaries.

3.19   Domains of expressive culture

A further suggestion of Bolton's which emerged from his Peruvian studies was that a BCT was more likely than a non-BCT to feature in the naming and discussion of items in domains of expressive culture (1978a: 300–3). He researched the colour terms occurring in four areas of Peruvian culture: rituals, folktales, folksongs and truck-names. The colour-term data for the ritual domain were retrieved from interviews with local specialists in the subject.[41] Data from folktales were collected from seventy-four tales in two publications, one in English and the other in Spanish. Folksong data came from Bolton's own collection of 723 songs (*huayños*) from southern Peru, mostly in Spanish, and the truck-names came from the collections of Bolton, and of Farfán (1957), collected from various places in the Andes. In all four domains, Bolton found that BCTs predominated, and non-basic terms were rare.

Although I suspect that this criterion may be useful, there are problems with using Bolton's data. At the time when he was writing, it was widely believed that there was a direct and straightforward (universal) equivalence between BCTs in all languages, because they were believed to name the same underlying colour categories. It is probably this prevailing belief that persuades Bolton to amalgamate evidence from different languages so that his results from the four domains are presented in a single table, even though they appear to be taken from three languages: Quechua, Spanish and English. We now know that this is a risky thing to do, especially where one language (English) is not native to the culture being studied.[42] Nonetheless, Bolton shows that this criterion may be valuable in both anthropological (cultural) and linguistic colour studies.

In historical studies, the researcher could only apply this criterion if s/he had sufficient evidence of the required type. The nature of the material would depend on the cultural interests of the individual society, but could involve distinctive styles of poetry, songs, tales, riddles and others such as the insult-competitions of, for example, sixteenth-century Scotland (*flytings*) or the improvised verse singing of the Basques (*bertsolaritza*). This criterion is most likely to provide only supporting evidence.

3.20   Embedded expressions

It has been remarked that colloquial and sometimes 'fossilized' expressions involving colour usually employ basic terms although this phenomenon has not often been suggested as a criterion of basicness. Waszakowa uses only three basicness criteria but, without including it in her list, she also refers to the need for a BCT to be 'well entrenched' as shown in its appearance in set phrases (2000: 19).[43] Hill points out that although Polish has at least five terms for blue, only two are used metaphorically (*niebieski* and *błękitny*) (2008: 76–7). Wescott suggests that the 'metaphoricity' of colour terms in a language can be measured to see if they have additional non-colour senses (1970: 355). Examples of embedded expressions include similes, metaphors (Section 4.3), proverbs, idioms and names.[44] Similes provide good examples of this type of evidence.

Similes stress, and usually exaggerate, one feature of the subject by comparing it with a different type of entity. Thus, in the simile *James is as strong as an ox*, the feature of James which is being stressed is his strength, and this is dramatically emphasized by comparing him with a notoriously strong animal. The listener is not expected to believe that James really does equal an ox in strength but s/he will understand that James is strong for a human being. In addition to describing James, this simile tells us that, in the culture that uses it, the ox is iconic of great strength. In the same way, *colour* similes inform us of what a culture considers iconic or typical of a particular colour. A sentence such as *The sheets were as white as snow* or *The miner was as black as soot* indicate that (British) English speakers consider snow and soot to be good examples of the whitest white and the blackest black. Similes of this form simultaneously express both a colour category and its focus,[45] and, since BCTs name whole categories, not parts of categories, a colour term in such a figure of speech is likely to be basic.

Wescott suggested that the extent of what he called 'onymicity' could also indicate a basic term (1970: 354). This refers to the tendency for basic colour terms to occur much more frequently than non-basics in the specialized embedded forms of traditional place-names and personal names. He shows how English *white* commonly occurs in personal names such as Whyte, Whiting, Whitman and more (page 355). In place-names, it can be found, to use some British examples, in Whitchurch, Whitley, Whitfield and others (Hough 2006: 194). The use of a non-basic term in, for example, a place-name such as 'Turquoise Bay' would immediately suggest a non-embedded, recently invented commercial name for a holiday development or the like. Examples of embedded expressions should be collected as part of the research on historical texts, and are likely to be of value in identifying BCTs.

3.21   Cultural–historical significance

This criterion is probably best considered as a last resort, when basic status for a particular term is still in doubt after more objective criteria have been applied. It has proved particularly important in the infamous case of the Russian blues.[46] There are two principal colour terms for blue in Russian: *sinij*, which is usually translated as 'dark blue', and *goluboj*, usually translated as 'light blue', and the problem is that they appear to have a relationship whereby *sinij*, as an abstract colour term, covers almost the entire field of Russian blue, but it cannot be used of *all* blue referents in a descriptive function (Paramei 2005: 14–15). If basic status were denied to *goluboj*, that would mean that the colour of certain blue entities could not be described at all by a basic term.

The Russian linguist Revekka Frumkina suggested that cultural and historical factors should be taken into consideration in problematic cases such as this. Paramei summarizes her argument as follows:

The idea is that differentiation [between the meanings of terms such as *sinij* and *goluboj*] is encouraged and reinforced by the culture to which native speakers belong, such that speakers encounter special conditions that make certain color differences, which may otherwise be nonsignificant, crucial and behaviorally important. (2005: 29)

Frumkina argues that, because *sinij* cannot be applied to all blue referents, *goluboj* has a basic role in those contexts.[47] Russian shows an interesting scenario here in which the basicness judgement for *goluboj* is so much on a knife-edge that it is essential to involve the insight of native speakers and the cultural history of the word.

In historical studies, the insight of native speakers is denied to us, but cultural history may be of use as supporting evidence. This would very much depend on the nature and amount of the evidence available about a particular society.

3.22   Discussion

The nineteen potentially useful criteria discussed above have all been suggested by researchers as offering some indication of whether a colour term may be basic or not.[48] A few, especially non-hyponymy and contextual freedom, have been almost universally accepted as indicators of basicness. The importance of psychological salience has also featured in nearly all colour semantic studies, although the means of assessing it has varied. It should also be understood that none of the criteria are foolproof by themselves and, also, that there is no guarantee that what appears to work for one language will work for another. Researchers into particular languages need to select the criteria which are appropriate for that language. This is not to suggest that they should freely select the criteria which are attractive or convenient for them, but rather the criteria which are appropriate to the structure and usage of the language they are researching. Once the appropriate criteria have been selected, they need to be used consistently within a particular language.

Some researchers, such as Crawford (1982) and MacLaury (1982), have taken a minimalist approach, reducing the criteria they use to non-hyponymy and contextual freedom only, although Crawford also considered psychological salience.[49] In 1982, Crawford suggested a pared-down minimal format for BCT recognition, based on Berlin and Kay's criteria. He weeded out the monolexemic criterion and elicited lists, and then excised all four of Berlin and Kay's secondary criteria with judgements such as 'irrelevant', 'vague' and 'impossible'. In conclusion, he recommends that the following criteria should suffice to define a BCT: it should occur in the idiolects of all informants (Section 3.9); it should have stability of reference across informants and occasions of use (Sections 3.7 and 3.8); it should not be a hyponym (Section 3.4); and it should not be contextually restricted (Section 3.5) (page 342). If I understand correctly, these criteria are not guidelines which an individual researcher may select or reject but, taken collectively, it is suggested they constitute a universal BCT definition.

Others have gone to the opposite extreme and, instead of selecting a minimum number of criteria, have employed as many tests as were known to them and

Table 3.1 *Basicness criteria of particular value in historical studies*

Criterion	Section
Hyponymy	3.4
Contextual restriction	3.5
Morphological complexity	3.13
Frequency of occurrence in texts	3.15
Frequency of occurrence in speech	3.16
Type modification (for primary BCTs)	3.18
Embedded expressions	3.20

were applicable to their languages. The American linguist Roger Wescott, for example, applied all of Berlin and Kay's 1969 criteria, both primary and secondary, but with unsettling results. Wescott (1970) had long-term interests in Bini, a language of Nigeria, and he proceeded to investigate Bini colour vocabulary. His main problem with Berlin and Kay's criteria was that he found he could assess the total number of Bini BCTs as anything between zero and eight, depending on the degree of strictness he used in applying the criteria. In other words, he found the criteria too imprecise, and he had particular problems with monolexemic structure (Section 3.3), derivational morphology (Section 3.10) and morphological complexity (Section 3.13) which he calls 'Berlin and Kay's "difficult" criteria' (pages 351–2).

Unfortunately, Wescott appears to misunderstand that Berlin and Kay's secondary criteria, to which two of these 'difficult' ones belong, should only be applied if the primary criteria leave room for doubt. Without knowledge of Bini, I cannot say whether this correction would make a great difference but it is clear, for example, that Wescott dismisses the potential BCTs *ùfúa* 'white yam' and *iyélò* 'yellow' because the first is a homonym (Section 3.11) and the second is a loan word, borrowed from ModE *yellow* (Section 3.12).[50] Although ModE *orange* is also a homonym, it is, nonetheless, a BCT because it passes Berlin and Kay's first four criteria but Wescott does not clarify whether these Bini words pass or fail the four primary criteria. He also interprets Berlin and Kay's criteria as 'exclusionary rules', rather than suggestions to be adapted to individual languages or even rejected where appropriate (1970: 351) (Section 3.2). Because of these misinterpretations, his criticisms cannot stand.

For the historical semanticist, there are certain criteria which are likely to be useful in judging basicness, as can be seen in Table 3.1. Several of the remaining criteria have a value as corroborating evidence, as described in the sections above, but the value of most of the criteria will vary according to the structure and surviving texts of each language.

Having arrived at the close of this chapter, two final points need to be stressed. Firstly, when studying the colour vocabulary of a language, the researcher should never assume that the BCTs are obvious. This is often a temptation where s/he knows the language or where a dictionary is available but, unless a previous colour semantic study has already been carried out, it is best to apply the appropriate tests and thus come to an objective (as far as possible) conclusion. Secondly, although it is useful to know which are the BCTs of a language, this division between basic and non-basic terms should not be allowed to impose itself on every aspect of the research. In some cases, it may be preferable to consider the colour terms in a project as a spectrum of vocabulary ranging from high frequency to rarity, rather than dividing them between the 'privileged' BCTs and the rest. The study of basicness is just a tool in the semanticist's toolbox which has its uses on certain occasions.

4 Non-basic and non-standard colour expressions

4.1 Introduction

In the previous chapter, we grappled with the concept of the basic colour term (BCT), and it is now time to turn to *non*-basic terms and non-standard uses of BCTs. At first sight, it is easy to define a non-BCT: it is quite simply any colour term which is not basic. Can they be recognized from their forms? The brief answer to this is 'No'. Non-basic terms can take many forms in various languages. In English, for example, non-basics can be simplex terms like *scarlet* or *aqua*, compound terms such as *sky-blue* or *rose-red*, or phrases such as *dead leaf colour* or *the colour of a tropical sea*.[1] As has been seen in the previous chapter, other languages have different rules of morphology, syntax and lexical coining, so will construct different types of colour description. Whether dealing with a modern or historical language, the researcher needs to acquaint him- or herself with the structure of that language in order to recognize valuable clues such as an unusual morphemic variation or a 'foreign' lexical form.

Turning from form to meaning, the reader can ascertain those features which a non-basic term may exhibit simply by reversing the BCT criteria given in the previous chapter. Thus, non-basics may have meanings which are predictable from their parts, as in the case of *reddish brown* (Section 3.3); or they may be hyponyms of a BCT, as *crimson* is a hyponym of *red* (Section 3.4); or they may be contextually restricted, as *swarthy* is restricted to descriptions of the human complexion (Section 3.5) and so on.

This chapter will also consider some uses of BCTs which deviate from their 'standard' sense, sometimes in terms of the colour area they denote or its focus, or in terms of their non-colour associations. These will be referred to as 'non-standard' BCT uses, indicating a non-standard *meaning* with a standard form (spelling and/or pronunciation). It should be stressed that the word *standard* is used in relation to the norms of individual languages, and not in relation to some supposed universal norm.

4.2 Sub-sets and models

Non-basic terms and non-standard BCT uses are often found in sub-sets. These are collections of two or more words, some of which are used exclusively, or very nearly so, of one particular subject. The reader has already encountered contextual restriction (Section 3.5) as a feature which is incompatible with basic status, and the example was given of ModE *blonde* in the domain of human hair-colour. *Blonde* belongs to a sub-set of hair-colour terms such as *brunette* and *auburn* and, although such words may not be *strictly* limited to their primary subjects, these associations are understood by native speakers as the most salient. It was shown, for example, that *blonde* can now be found in some rather eccentric collocations used in marketing and advertising, but these are not the contexts that first spring to mind when the word is mentioned.[2] Sub-sets may also contain BCTs, just as *red* and *black* are used in the context of human hair but it should be noted that, although these words have the *forms* of BCTs, they do not always have the same sense, and can be described as 'sense-modified' or 'non-standard'. Red hair, for example, is never the colour that an English native speaker would describe as 'typical red' in an unrestricted context. The 'red' which occurs in the context of hair is much closer to orange (see Section 3.18).

Most sub-sets are concerned with items of importance to particular societies or they may survive from items of *historical* importance. As mentioned in the previous chapter, Bolton noted the significance of colour in domains of economic importance (Section 3.18) but the same applies to the spheres of social and cultural importance. Although Bolton found mostly sense-modified BCTs in these domains, other members of a sub-set may be contextually restricted and, therefore, non-basic.

The vocabulary of sub-sets can be remarkably complex, and cause substantial translation problems. An example will be given here of horse-colour terms in Icelandic and British English.[3] Colour sub-sets may contain BCTs which are used in a very nearly standard and normal fashion. An example is Icelandic *svartur* 'black' (an Icelandic BCT)[4] which is used of black horses, and is translated by the English horse-colour term *black*. What could be simpler? A person with no knowledge of horses would have no difficulties with this translation but there is a complication. In both countries, a 'black' horse must have a black coat, skin, mane and tail, although white markings on the face and limbs are acceptable.[5] The presence of other non-black areas, such as the mane or tail, renders the description *svartur* or *black* inappropriate, even though the largest visible area, the body-colour, is black. Many Icelandic horses which are otherwise completely black, have dark, reddish-brown manes so, even though the manes were originally black (they have been lightened by the sun) such a horse is not *svartur*: it is *brúnn* '(literally) brown'.[6]

Some BCTs used in the English and Icelandic horse-colour sub-sets are apparently sense-modified to a surprising degree. In British English, *grey* (horse-colour) can be used, not only of horses which are indubitably grey, but also of animals which are black or white (Packer and Ali 1985: 22–3).

Similarly, in Icelandic, *grár* 'grey' can be used of horses which are black or white, as well as grey. What is going on here?

The fact is that these horse-colour terms are being used as a means of classification, and are not, therefore, truly descriptive. In English, the 'grey' horse can be defined as having 'an uneven mixture of white and dark-coloured hairs with the skin darkly pigmented. As the animal ages the coat becomes lighter as the percentage of white hairs increases. The change in seasons can also result in changes in the shade of the coat' (Packer and Ali 1985: 22). If we now turn to the Icelandic 'greys', we find a similar description: 'In Iceland we usually don't call a horse white, all shades of grey and white are called grár ... The [*grár*] horse is usually born coal black, red or in any other colour, becomes grey-dappled when around 2 years old, and is often snow-white at the age of 10' (Heimisdóttir).[7] An Icelandic 'grey', therefore, can have different coloured coats throughout its life but it will always be called a 'grey'. In Britain, a horse with white body-colour may be called 'white' by some authorities, provided the animal has a pale skin, while a white horse with *dark* skin is called a 'grey' (pages 28–9).

The reader can already see that the body-colour of some horses will coincide with the standard meaning of the colour term applied to them but, in other cases, the relationship between horse-colour and colour term will be eccentric or non-standard. This is a valuable lesson for colour semanticists, namely, that there may be principles of colour-naming in operation which owe very little to the salient or even visible colour. Sub-sets are dangerous places for the unwary explorer.

Non-basic terms often mix happily with BCTs in sub-sets. In English horse-colours, the words *bay*, *chestnut*, *dun* and *roan* are non-basic colour terms which are only rather vaguely understood by the majority of native speakers who would probably be content to describe horse-colours with BCTs used in the standard way. Those involved in the world of horses, however, have found even such specialized terms to be inadequate for their purposes. Thus *bay* is often popularly sub-divided into *light bay*, *golden bay*, *red bay* and *dark bay* (Packer and Ali 1985: 12–13).[8]

While the types of *bay* are simple enough to understand for the outsider, the subdivisions of other principal terms are more obscure; for example, *liver chestnut*, *palomino* and *strawberry roan*.[9] More precise terms like these are often culturally distinct, that is, unlikely to translate literally into horse-colour terms recognized in another culture. A liver-chestnut horse is dark reddish-brown,[10] similar to the colour of liver. In Icelandic, this horse-colour is *sótrauður*, literally 'soot-red'. Both languages understandably stress the dark tone of the hue but with reference to different objects, and these suggest that English speakers see the liver chestnut as dark brown whereas Icelandic speakers see it as dark red. This should not, however, be taken as evidence that the red and brown categories in the two societies *always* differ. The semantics of colour sub-sets can be distinctly odd.

The palomino horse, which originated in the United States, is pale golden-brown with white mane and tail. Presumably because of its origins, there appears to be no British English name for this type of horse, and the Spanish name was, therefore, adopted. In Iceland, there has been a long-standing preference for coining terms in Icelandic rather than adopting foreign words, so the Spanish name was apparently rejected in favour of a native construction. *Palomino* is *leirljós* in Icelandic, which means literally 'clay-pale' or 'mud-pale'. The two languages are on completely different wavelengths here, representing a big difference in the transparency of the terms for native speakers. While *palomino* has no transparent meaning for the English speaker at all, an Icelander would be able to envisage the colour of the horse in question as a pale earthy colour.[11]

The term *roan*, as used of horses, indicates an animal with a coat consisting of an equal quantity of white hair mixed with hair of another colour. Common subdivisions of this type in English are *bay roan*, *strawberry roan* and *blue roan*. The strawberry roan has white hairs mixed with chestnut, and this is said to look pinkish. The Icelandic roan too has mixed hair-colour on the body but it undergoes dramatic colour changes from one season of the year to another. The white under-coat is the predominant colour in spring and autumn while, in winter, this is covered by longer hair which grows in the darker colour. In summer, the horse often shows a mixture of the two. The change of colour is so startling that such animals can be hard to recognize after a period of separation. Not surprisingly, a strawberry roan in Icelandic is called *rauðlitförótt*, literally 'red-colour-changer'. An Icelandic strawberry roan will have a chestnut colour in the winter but will still be referred to as 'red' when in its summer white coat. As with *palomino*, *roan* is not transparent in meaning to the non-horsey English speaker, and *strawberry* is downright misleading. Thus, the exact colours of the strawberry roan represent information which has to be learnt, while the Icelandic term is more helpful to Icelandic speakers. The colour semanticist may be wondering whether the BCT criterion of not being a recent foreign loan word (Section 3.12) could have any relevance at all to Icelandic in which such borrowing and adoption is rare.

Closely related to sub-sets are colour *models*, in which the entire colour vocabulary of a language is interpreted through the colour set of an entity or phenomenon which is well-known in that society. For example, Turton describes the eleven most commonly elicited colour terms of the Mursi of Ethiopia as being sometimes the equivalents of English terms, and sometimes the names of cattle-colours. Thus *golonyi* can be translated as 'red' or, in the context of cattle, as 'reddish-brown', and *chagi* 'green-blue', when used of cattle, means 'slate grey; bluish-grey; ash-coloured' (1980: 326). Turton states 'there are no colour terms in Mursi other than cattle-colour terms' (page 320) but he also makes it quite clear that the Mursi colour categories are focused in the same general areas as they are for English speakers. In other words, cattle are not the prototypes for their colour categories in spite of these vitally important animals dominating the Mursi colour system. Turton found that the Mursi were quite capable of naming colour samples of all kinds, including many shades which 'they had almost certainly never seen before' (pages 321–2). He concludes that the Mursi have equated the differences between cattle colours with the differences between universally recognized colour foci, thus employing a 'cattle model' for their colour system (page 334).

Several other languages, such as Maa (Kenya and Tanzania), have a large colour vocabulary for the areas of grey and brown because of the importance of cattle in their economies (Payne 2003: 182) but this differs from Turton's argument for an all-encompassing cattle model in Mursi. *Historical* semanticists need to be cautious about recognizing models, especially in cases where the data are limited, since it is first necessary to understand *all* a language's principal colour terms.

This section is intended to show that sub-sets and models consist of collections of colour words which are constrained by the 'real' colours of the subject involved. A word like *red* can be used of a horse because everyone knows it cannot be vivid red. However little we may know about horses, we all know that much. Within the context of horses, therefore, we mentally explore our red category until we reach the reddest colour that a horse can be, that is, reddish-brown. In most other contexts, we would probably include this colour in our concept of brownness. This contextual distortion of the standard semantic range requires vigilance when working in a language not one's own, such as a historical language.

4.3   Metaphor and metonymy

In Section 3.20 we discussed BCTs in embedded expressions such as similes and metaphors. A metaphor is a word or phrase which is used figuratively (metaphorically) in a certain subject area in which it is, literally speaking, inappropriate.[12] Thus, it is appropriate to say 'She swallowed her soup' because *swallow* can operate in the conceptual domain of food, but it is literally *inappropriate* (but figuratively acceptable) to say 'She swallowed the argument'. In other words, the target domain of 'ideas' (for example, 'argument') has been expressed in terms appropriate to the source domain of 'food' (for example, 'soup'). Let us consider a colour example. An inexperienced young person struggling with his or her first day in a new job may be described by colleagues as 'green'. In this case, the target domain of 'experience' has been expressed in terms appropriate to the source domain of 'plants', as the young person is metaphorically described as if s/he were a young, fresh seedling.[13]

While metaphors involve an *imagined* link between two concepts, metonyms involve a *real* link. A classic example is the use of *London* as a replacement for 'the British government' in the sentence 'London was furious at today's news'. There is a real link between London and the British government because London is the location of the government.[14] As can be seen from this example, metonyms require a certain amount of shared knowledge in order to convey the desired message. While a British person will understand the London metonym perfectly, the sentence 'Majuro was furious at today's news' may not be recognized in Britain as a metonym at all, and taken to refer to a person.[15] Niemeier stresses this point, showing that, even with two languages whose basic colour terms translate easily, as between English and German, the metonymic uses of such terms often cause problems for 'intercultural translatability' (1998: 134).

There are numerous examples of colour expressions which originated as metonyms, and one has already been encountered in the horse-colours above (Section 4.2), in which *strawberry*, a fruit-name, was used to indicate a horse-colour.[16] This colour term originated when the entity 'strawberry', belonging to the domain of fruit, was made to stand for 'strawberry', belonging to the domain of colour. This is a colour example of an *ontological metonym* which can be expressed as 'Entity stands for entity's colour' (Casson 1994: 17).

It was shown in Section 3.11 that a BCT has a colour meaning which is divorced from that of the entity which was responsible for its name. In other words, it should have acquired an abstract colour sense, the origin of which is often not obvious to native speakers. More recent colour metonyms, however, retain close semantic links with their parental entities, with the entity sense remaining dominant, so they are likely to be *non*-basic. If the colour sense remains in use for a long period of time, of course, such a word may take on BCT attributes and, eventually, like ModE *orange*, a few may even cross the line and become truly basic.

In the midst of the publication blizzard on BCTs which followed the appearance of Berlin and Kay's 1969 book, Ronald Casson (1994) published a paper about English *non*-basic colour metonyms.[17] He divides them into 'novel' or 'creative' terms on the one hand, and 'conventional' terms on the other.[18] His novel terms are invented for particular needs and circumstances, and these new coinings, or newly invented colour senses of established non-colour words, are rarely found in standard dictionaries of the languages concerned. He gives some examples of hosiery colours which illustrate colour term coinings: *desert dusk, Arabian night, gold coin* and *burnt sand* (pages 5–6). Although these are familiar phrases in other contexts, they are new inventions as colour expressions.

Also described as 'novel' are certain established words which have acquired a colour sense in addition to their standard definitions, for example: *cranberry*, *pewter*, *chalk* and *brandy* (page 8).

Casson's 'conventional' non-basic colour terms, unlike the creative ones, can be found in dictionaries with their colour senses recorded, and examples include: *rose*, *lilac*, *gold*, *cream* and *navy*. These metonymic colour terms are widely used in marketing, advertising and poetry but many of Casson's novel terms constitute an endangered species which may be popular for a season and then pass out of fashion completely.

As mentioned above, Casson lists some very creative hosiery colours, and many other examples can be found in ranges of products such as cosmetics, house-paints, clothes and cars, to name but a few. I suggest there are three types of metonymic colour expression used in marketing, ranging from the logical to the imaginative. The examples given here have all been found on the colour charts of paint manufacturers but many of them are also used of other products. The first category is called 'logical' because the colour of the entity in the metonym tallies with the colour of the paint. Examples in English are *lavender* and *terracotta*.

My second category is called 'evocative' because, although the colour connection is still obvious in most cases, there is an added non-colour element which the manufacturer hopes will evoke pleasant feelings in the potential buyer. Colours such as *Mediterranean sea* and *lemon zest* refer unmistakably to blue and yellow respectively but are, simultaneously, likely to remind the shopper of summer holidays and zingy tastes, motivating them to buy the product.

My third category is called 'obscure' and it refers to colour names which, in literal terms, are either non-specific or downright meaningless as regards colour. One of the best cases I know is a range of paint-colours called 'New England Paint Company' which was once sold by the British household-goods chain B&Q. The range drew its inspiration from the work of Cary Hazlegrove, a photographer who lives on Nantucket Island, Massachusetts.[19] The paint chart, dated 2000, consists of very pale colours which include some logical names such as *canvas* and *vellum*, as well as evocative names such as *apple pie* (pale green) and *cheesecake* (pale yellow). The chart includes, however, several obscure names which denote entities that are either not usually considered to have a typical colour or have no colour at all. For example, the names *jetties* (pale brownish-cream) and *driftwood* (pale pinkish-cream) are taken from entities which can be found in a wide range of colours while the names *homecoming* (pale bluish-purple) and *windswept* (pale blue) are taken from abstractions which are without colour. Presumably, these names have been chosen because they are considered to be evocative of New England but they are not evocative of particular colours.

A wide variety of entities have provided metonyms for colours in English. Casson broadly classifies the origins of his dataset of hue metonyms into five: plants, animals (including humans), minerals, food and drink, and artefacts (1994: 10–12).[20] He also makes the important point that metonymically extended entity hues are *idealizations* of the entity's colour. In other words, the British English concept of *lemon* (colour) will be the hue of a perfect lemon of the variety most often seen in the UK (page 20, Note 7). Casson's classification of hue metonyms shows the large number of items which are available in the United States, either naturally or by importation, but in societies with fewer resources and trade links, colour metonyms can be quite revealing. They must, after all, use the names of entities which are widely known in their societies in order to successfully convey meaning, and such information may be of particular value to the historical researcher with limited social and cultural data to hand.

4.4   Specialized colour terms

'Specialized terms' refers to colour terminology which forms part of the technical language belonging to particular crafts, trades and industries. Colour is a major component in an astonishingly large number of occupations; for example, dyeing, painting, embroidery, cartography, printing, software and website development, glass-working, photography, mosaic work, teaching, weaving, cosmetic art and many more. It is likely that the specialized colour terminology of such workers includes words which are unknown to other native speakers, and this is one of the disqualifications for basic status (Section 3.9). Other terms may be familiar to laymen and -women, but may have a non-standard meaning in a particular trade. Some names for artists' paints will now be considered.

Although pigments have been used in artwork for tens of thousands of years, artists were restricted to naturally occurring substances, such as minerals and biological materials, until the first years of the eighteenth century. At this time, the first synthetic pigment, later called 'Prussian Blue', was discovered by accident by Heinrich Diesbach, a paintmaker ('colourman') working in Berlin (Eastaugh *et al.* 2004: 309).[21] The first aniline ('coal tar') dye, called mauveine, was developed by the chemist Sir William Henry Perkin in London in 1856 (page 256) and, after that date, there followed a steadily increasing number of synthetic products.

Pigment names fall into two major categories. Those in the first category include a BCT or a widely known non-basic term making their colour at least partially obvious to everyone. Other elements of the name, however, are specialized terms which make little sense to those not involved with pigments. Examples from artists' paints include *quinophthalone yellow*, *cadmium orange*, *disazo scarlet* and *manganese violet* (Wilcox 1991: 38, 68, 93, 130).

The second category of pigment names consists of those which do not include any standard colour terms, thus making the meanings of the names opaque to the majority of native speakers. Many of these names would not even be recognized as having a connection with colour at all. Examples, again from artists' paints, include: *gamboge* (usually a slightly reddish yellow), *raw umber* (various browns), *burnt sienna* (orange to reddish-brown), *chrome antimony titanium buff rutile* (pale yellowish-brown) and *lithopone* (white) (Wilcox 1991: 32, 211, 212, 213, 270).

Specialized terms are clearly similar in type to sub-sets (Section 4.2) but they often contain a far larger number of names, as with artists' pigments. In some subject areas, the researcher may find both a sub-set and a list of specialized terms, and this can be illustrated by wine-colour words. Most people know the wine-colour sub-set which, in English, consists of *red* and *white*, or *red, rosé* and *white*. However, those who work with wines sub-divide these colours into more precise designations. Thus, for example, 'white' wines can be described as: *yellow green, straw, gold, yellow brown, amber brown* and *brown*.[22]

The semantic researcher may encounter specialized terms in product catalogues and in the speech or manuals of artists and craftsmen. S/he needs to bear in mind that such terms may be unique to a particular occupation or may have popular meanings in addition to their technical meanings. Probably most surprising of all is that someone who uses, for example, *brown* in a highly restricted and specialized sense in his or her working day, will use the same word with its *standard* sense once s/he has left the work environment.

4.5   Significant non-colour features

Many colour expressions, both basic and non-basic, also have a non-colour sense, often arising from symbolism, metonymy or some other association accepted by the society which speaks the language. This section is concerned more narrowly with colour terms in which a non-colour feature is highly important or even dominant compared with the colour feature. When this subject is considered, colour semanticists return time and time again to an article published in 1955 by the American anthropologist Harold C. Conklin.

Conklin wrote about the colour categories and terms of Hanunóo, a language spoken by people of the same name living on the island of Mindoro in the Philippines. The Hanunóo are a group belonging to the Mangyan people, and are sometimes referred to as the Hanunóo-Mangyan. Conklin's main concern was the study of Hanunóo folk-botany, involving their plant-names, crops and system of agriculture. Discussion of plants and crops often involves the use of colour terms, and Conklin became aware that Hanunóo colour vocabulary posed considerable comprehension and translation problems for the English speaker. He listed what he called the 'Level I terms' (BCTs) of Hanunóo with their meanings:

(*ma*)*bīru*: relative darkness (of shade of color); blackness[23]

(*ma*)*lagti?*: relative lightness (or tint of color); whiteness[24]

(*ma*)*rara?*: relative presence of red; redness

(*ma*)*latuy*: relative presence of light greenness; greenness

Conklin found that the focal points of these categories (the areas considered most typical of their colours) 'could be limited more or less' to what English speakers might call *black*, *white*, *orange-red* and *leaf-green* respectively (1955: 341). He describes the extent of the categories as follows:

> *mabīru* includes colours which can be denoted in English by *black*, *violet*, *indigo*, *blue*, *dark green* and *dark grey*, and also includes 'deep shades of other colors and mixtures'.
>
> *malagti?* includes white 'and very light tints of other colors and mixtures'.
>
> *marara?* includes colours denoted in English by *maroon*, *red*, *orange* and *yellow*, and also includes 'mixtures in which these qualities are seen to predominate'.
>
> *malatuy* includes light green and mixtures of green, yellow and light brown. (Conklin 1955: 342)

The reader has now encountered a set of colour categories which may be very different from his or her own, but the *colour* composition of the Hanunóo categories is only one of the comprehension problems faced by the English speaker. As Conklin cautiously explains: 'The basis of this Level I classification appears to have certain correlates beyond what is usually considered the range of chromatic differentiation, and which are associated with nonlinguistic phenomena in the external environment' (1955: 342). These 'extra' means of differentiation involve three sets of contrasts: light versus dark; fastness (lack of fading) versus fading; and dryness versus wetness.

The light versus dark contrast which forms an integral part of the Hanunóo colour system is evidenced, for example, in the ranges of *mabīru* and *malagti?*, which could be roughly glossed as 'darkness / blackness' and 'lightness / whiteness' respectively. As was seen in Section 1.4, colour, technically speaking, consists of more than hue, and it would seem that a tonal contrast is involved in the Hanunóo system in addition to hue distinctions. I have retained Conklin's term *light* (rather than using *pale*) because this light versus dark distinction may involve brightness as well as paleness, but that is not clear from his article.[25]

Conklin describes the fastness versus fading contrast as consisting, on the one hand, of 'deep, unfading, indelible' and, on the other, of 'pale, weak, faded, bleached or 'colorless' (1955: 342). This contrasts *mabīru* and *marara?* with *malagti?* and *malatuy*, that is (in very generalized terms), darkness and redness versus lightness and greenness. The first two are more highly prized than the second two so, for example, fabric which has been dipped several times in indigo dye (making it darker than fabric dyed once only) is admired, and red trade beads are more valued than white ones. This second contrast appears to be related to the dark versus light (tone) contrast and also to saturation, but with an additional element of colour stability. Some items are strongly coloured (dark or vivid) and many remain so, while other items look 'washed out' either because they are intrinsically pale or because they have lost their original colour.

It is, however, the third contrast occurring in the colour vocabulary of Hanunóo which has been quoted many times and which English speakers find particularly surprising. Conklin describes the dryness versus wetness distinction as 'dryness or desiccation' versus 'wetness or freshness (succulence)' (1955: 342). This distinction is reflected in the meanings of *mararaʔ* 'redness, dryness' and *malatuy* 'greenness, moistness'. Any kind of succulent, uncooked food but especially fruits and vegetables, is described as *malatuy*, and many of them are green (*malatuy*) in colour but what happens if an item is succulent but not green? Conklin shows that it is moistness that triumphs over hue. He gives the example of newly cut bamboo, which is shiny and wet but brown in colour. The word used in this case is still *malatuy* ('green') not *mararaʔ* ('red') so the wetness of the bamboo is more salient than its hue (page 342).[26]

Conklin's paper is invaluable as a dire warning to colour semanticists, and it has encouraged generations of researchers to look out for the unexpected. It may be, however, that the 'strangeness' of the Hanunóo colour system has been exaggerated. Kay points out that there are many languages which connect the colour green with notions of immaturity and/or succulence (2006: 122), and Borg gives examples from various modern Arabic vernaculars, as well as German and English (2007: 283–4).[27] Given the metonymic importance of plants in many languages, this is to be expected, so why all the fuss about Hanunóo?

On the basis of Conklin's article, the Hanunóo language has often been said to have *inseparable* colour and non-colour semantic elements in certain colour terms. To give just one example, Lyons writes: 'the color vocabulary of Hanunóo, as analyzed by Conklin, might appear to us to be exotic in the extreme, especially in its failure to separate hue, or chromaticity, from texture and succulence' (1999: 54). Although Lyons' interpretation of Conklin's article is the same as that of the majority of commentators, Kay has pointed out that there is a degree of ambiguity in Conklin's phraseology. Conklin's only statement on the relation of Hanunóo BCT colour senses with their non-colour senses is the sentence quoted earlier in this section, and which, to paraphrase, surmises that the BCTs appear to have non-hue senses which are associated with environmental phenomena. Kay rightly says this statement does not establish that the Hanunóo BCTs denote *inseparable* colour and non-colour elements (2006: 122) although Lyons takes this to be the case (1999: 60). Kay reminds us of the important distinction between *conjunctive* and *disjunctive* interpretations. In disjunctive usage, the colour and non-colour senses can operate separately (as in ModE *orange* (COLOUR; FRUIT)) while in conjunctive usage, they are inseparable (COLOUR+FRUIT). It would appear that *malatuy*, at least, has disjunctive semantics (2006: 124).

The Hanunóo debate will, no doubt, continue but I have introduced it here to show that, whatever the situation with this particular language, semantic researchers need to be aware of the possibility of colour terms having non-colour senses which may be so significant that they affect the colour sense in some way. Examples can be found which are even more semantically complex than in Hanunóo, involving several non-colour elements which affect the choice of colour terms. Brief mention can be made of Bricker's study of the colour terms of the Yucatec language of Mexico.[28] She found semantic elements indicating a three-way contrast in colour terms between objects that are small and discrete, small and clustered, and large and undifferentiated. She comments: 'colors cannot be described as glossy, gleaming, or brilliant if they are associated with small, rounded objects'. In addition, there are elements in Yucatec for wetness and dryness, and five features involving texture: softness; hardness; puffiness and lumpiness; prickliness and rashes; and abrasions and rawness (1999: 286–8).

Bricker's conclusion includes the following salutary sentence: 'The Maya [Yucatec] and Tzotzil data I have presented here suggest that, in the future, it may be fruitful to move beyond the variables that are cognitively salient in English (hue, brightness and saturation) and consider those that are more salient in other languages' (1999: 297). The fact of the matter is that the researcher needs to open his or her mind to *any* possible variables in a colour system, and be aware that they may have been overlooked in earlier investigations. This is likely to involve a rethinking of data-gathering procedures. A final, related point needs to be made. If the reader is exclusively interested in Indo-European languages, s/he may think that s/he can ignore Bricker's warning, but this is not the case, as we already know enough to say that the historical and dialectal colour systems of Indo-European languages may involve elements which the reader has hitherto regarded as exotic.[29]

4.6   Contact languages

The colour terms of a language (the target language) can be affected in several ways through contact with a second language (the source language). The target language may adopt basic and/or non-basic terms from the source language, either to supply a name for a colour or shade which had not thus far been separately labelled, or to replace native terms.[30] The motivation for either process may involve more than the desire for increased precision, as the target-language speakers may be more concerned with sounding 'modern' or fashionable in cases where the source language is prestigious. The motivation may, however, be entirely practical, and involve the necessity of communicating with speakers of another language for reasons of trade in coloured goods such as textiles or furs. Borrowings may be short-lived, since social and economic circumstances change, or, as long-term adoptions, they may become naturalized in the target language.[31]

The amount of borrowing and adoption which takes place from one language to another depends on the intensity of the contact. Thomason and Kaufman (1988: 72) list the factors which affect contact intensity as follows: the length of time the contact is in operation; the number of source-language speakers as compared with target-language speakers; whether or not speakers of the source language have socio-political dominance over those who speak the target language; and whether or not the two languages have close contact in mixed households or other social milieux (see also Section 9.4).

The researcher cannot safely assume that a colour word adopted into another language retains the full and unaltered meaning it had in the source language (Biggam 2006c: 168–9). Speakers of the target language may be unaware of the minor semantic elements of a foreign word, or they may even have an erroneous understanding of its principal sense. Part of the researcher's investigation into borrowings and adoptions needs to include a consideration of the extent to which speakers of the target language speak and understand the source language. The likelihood is that the researcher will uncover a varied situation, ranging from those who are completely bilingual to those who have only a slight acquaintance with the source language. This situation often reflects the social standing or occupation of the adopting speakers. People of high rank are likely to know a prestigious neighbouring language well, and those who have, for example, commercial dealings with speakers of the source language may develop a good working knowledge of it. Obviously, those who have only rare contact are at a greater disadvantage, and this last group may even be unaware that a new colour term had foreign origins.

Heidi Lazar-Meyn studies the colour systems of the Celtic languages, and has noted the effects on them of close contact with English which has more BCTs. In 1991 she published a survey of Celtic colour terms, principally those in Irish and Welsh. Of her three Irish-speaking informants, two gave no term for pink but the third informant gave *pinc*, a clear borrowing from English (1991: 231). That two of the informants appear to be unacquainted with *pinc* is a clear indication that it was unlikely to be (in 1991) an Irish BCT (see Section 3.9). Lazar-Meyn's list of Welsh BCTs, based on the answers of seventeen informants, shows no terms at all for pink but near unanimity for purple. Fourteen of the informants gave *piws* for purple, a loan-word from English (*puce*). Of the remaining informants, one gave no purple term at all, another gave English *purple*, and the third gave both *piws* and *purple* (pages 233–4). Within this sample of native speakers, it would seem that *piws* is in an unassailable position and is likely to become established, but a small number of the informants are unsure and have a tendency to borrow a different word although it is still a foreign loan-word.

Finally, Lazar-Meyn makes an interesting comparison of her findings with the colour vocabulary found in Celtic language translations of a picture dictionary for small children (Amery 1979). The full range of English BCTs has been translated, and this results in *bándearg* in Irish for 'pink' (meaning literally 'white-red'). Lazar-Meyn's sample of informants for Irish was very small but none of them suggested this word. It is possible that the translator into Irish was aiming to avoid loan-words, which is a common and understandable reaction in a language under pressure from another. The Welsh translation has *porffor* for 'purple' and *pinc* for 'pink', neither of which tallies with the answers of any of Lazar-Meyn's seventeen Welsh informants (1991: 238). It seems likely, at least from the informants used in these surveys, that Irish and Welsh words which could be translated into English as *pink* and *purple* are in a state of flux (or were in 1991) but that speakers are most likely to adopt English terms.

It is hoped that the reader is now familiar with the difference between BCTs and non-BCTs, and with the many, perhaps unexpected, ways in which colour terms are used around the world. We have seen colour terms working 'cooperatively' in groups (sub-sets) and singly, with both standard and modified meanings, in various contexts and associations. Chapters 3 and 4 have concentrated primarily on colour vocabulary with little attention paid to the concepts that they denote, so the next chapter will aim to correct the balance.

5 Basic colour categories

5.1 Introduction

The previous two chapters were mainly concerned with colour *terms* (words and expressions) while the present chapter is concerned with colour *concepts* or categories. Before proceeding, it is wise to remind ourselves of this crucial difference. While it may seem obvious that a concept is not a word, the two things are, nevertheless, often confused. For example, a person may read a Middle English (ME) text which includes the word *rēd*. The reader may assume this word is identical with ModE *red* but this could lead to a misunderstanding of the text because the same *form* of a word (in this case, the spelling) does not necessarily indicate the same *meaning*. Meaning is a slippery thing, constantly evolving into different shapes, often imperfectly shared even by co-speakers of a language, only clumsily transmitted through translation, and frequently evolving new and unexpected nuances. All this can happen while the word labelling the concept retains the same form. Thus our reader of Middle English may be surprised to find that the object described as *rēd* was actually purple or pink because Middle English did not have basic categories for these hues, so they were included in the Middle English red category.

In synchronic studies (concerned with a particular period in time; Chapter 9), the sometimes elusive, sometimes volatile, nature of meaning can be a problem in research that involves different regions, social classes, occupations and other groups who may employ subtle differences in their semantics. In diachronic studies too (concerned with research *across* periods of time; Chapter 10), the history of a word may involve drastic or subtle semantic shift, or no change at all. The researcher may find that some words have retained the same form *and* meaning over long periods of time but, initially, s/he can never be sure. When first dealing with the semantics of a language, or a phase of a language, therefore, it is safest to consider the concept and the term as separate entities until they are better understood.

5.2 The significance of basic colour categories

In the previous two chapters, basic and non-basic colour terms were discussed, and the reader may have wondered why it is considered helpful to distinguish between the two. One reason is that the *basic* terms of a language usually give some indication of the principal abstract colour categories in the minds of native speakers. The vast majority of non-basic terms can be described as denoting 'a type of red', 'a type of blue', 'a type of green' and so on, and if the non-basic terms of a language were all described in this way, the researcher would end up with groups or 'families' of colour terms, classified as the red group, the blue group and others. The *basic* terms of a language, however, are not susceptible to this treatment. We cannot describe, for example, English *blue* as denoting 'a type of [particular hue]' it is just blue. This situation indicates that Modern English speakers have a concept of 'blueness' in their minds which they have labelled with the word *blue*, and which they are free to apply to any appropriately coloured entity or to use in any figurative construction. They have, in other words, a blue cognitive category, and, in the case of a living language, this conclusion can be further tested by psychological investigation techniques.

The assumption that BCTs reveal underlying conceptual structures is broadly true but requires constant vigilance on the part of the researcher since s/he may encounter exceptions, distortions, unexpected complexities and situations which represent transitional phases from one conceptual structure to another. The best way to guard against error is, where possible, to deal with large numbers of small investigations. In the case of a living language, this means questioning a large number of native-speaker informants representing various socio-economic groups. The individual results can then be studied in order to gain an overall impression of their society's colour system. Results from only a small number of informants should not be extrapolated to the whole speech community, since it has been shown that individual speakers may differ in the number and nature of their colour categories: men may differ from women; young people may differ from older generations; bilinguals may differ from monolinguals; cloth dyers may differ from farmers; and so on (Sections 4.6 and 5.7). Readers are asked to bear in mind, therefore, that when I speak of a language's colour system, this may not be true for *all* that language's native speakers.

5.3   The basic level of categorization

Categorization theory in linguistics involves hierarchical structures of categories in various domains. A commonly cited example is FURNITURE. The hierarchy of categories from less to more specific can be expressed as follows: ARTEFACT − FURNITURE − CHAIR − KITCHEN CHAIR, in which single examples have been selected at each level. These levels, however, are not of equal cognitive importance. Various tests show that, in British society for example, CHAIR is basic in the above list and is equal in basicness to, for example, TABLE or BED (Taylor 2003: 48–51). Categories below this basic level often have to be described with a basic-level term plus a modifier, as in *kitchen chair*, while categories above the basic-level term can be missing altogether or irregular in some way. For example, FURNITURE is uncountable in English, that is, we cannot say **a furniture* or **furnitures*. Basic-level terms exhibit a high frequency of occurrence, and they are likely to be short and/or structurally simple (2003: 51).

Turning to colour, the basic level of categorization is represented by BCTs such as English *blue* and *red*. Non-basic terms and phrases below the basic level often use a BCT plus modifier, such as *dark blue* or *pale red*, but this is not an invariable rule since words such as *peach* and *burgundy* occur on the same level. As Taylor (2003: 51) points out, English has no level above the basic one in colour categorization. He excludes the word *coloured* from this role since, in everyday usage, it does not include the achromatics.[1]

5.4   The structure of a basic colour category

Where a particular society has a basic colour category for GREEN, for example, it can be thought of as a concept which has a focus, a boundary and an intermediate area. The focal or prototypical area of the category represents the shade which a speech community considers to be the best example of the category, and which they might describe as 'the greenest green' or 'typical green' although not everyone's typical green is located at exactly the same point on a colour chart (Section 11.3). Close to this focal area of the category are shades of green which are not quite the greenest possible, perhaps because they are slightly paler, darker or duller than 'typical green', or because they contain too much blue or yellow or any other detracting element. As we move further out from the focus, the shades of green become less and less like typical green. In language, the degree of distance from the focus, as judged by the speaker, can be conveyed by means of *hedges*, that is, terms or phrases such as *almost*, *virtually*, *slightly* and so on. Still moving away from the focus, we finally come to shades which are barely green at all. This marks the approach to the category boundary where membership of the category is tenuous. It is at the boundary that disagreement among members of the same speech community is most often found; for example, some may consider a particular shade of turquoise as green but others may classify it as blue. The category boundary is crossed when a colour is considered to be more like one of green's neighbours on the hue spectrum than like green itself, but the position of the boundary will not be exactly the same for every native speaker.

A speech community may, therefore, have a number of basic colour categories which are shared by members of the community, and are named by colour terms in their language. Aspects of this categorization vary from society to society, and nothing should be taken for granted or assumed from the researcher's own colour categories until evidence has been retrieved and evaluated. The category foci of various societies are most often in roughly similar positions in the colour space, probably because fully saturated hues are widely preferred (van Brakel 1993: 117) but the number of intermediate shades, and the general extent of the categories vary considerably between cultures. Edwin Ardener published an expanded version of Hjelmslev's comparison table of colour categories in certain languages. Ardener illustrates how five English categories compare with their equivalents in Standard Welsh, Modern Colloquial Welsh and Ibo (or Igbo, spoken in Nigeria and Cameroon). The categories differ radically in extent, with the exception of those for English and Modern Colloquial Welsh, which are the same. To take one example, the English and Modern Colloquial Welsh green categories are equivalent to all the Standard Welsh green category plus one third of its green+blue+grey category, and the English category is also equivalent to one half of the Ibo green+blue+grey category (1971a: xxi).[2]

5.5   Macro-categories

While readers will, no doubt, find it easy to understand a category such as RED or GREEN, they may have greater difficulty with a category which does not consist of a single hue. Although speakers of English, French and Hungarian, for example, may draw the boundary between GREEN and BLUE at different places, they all, nonetheless, have a distinct boundary between the two. What about societies which have no boundary in this area at all? These societies have a single green+blue category, which is an example of a *macro-category*, also known as a 'composite category' or 'extended category'.

The macro-category of GREEN+BLUE is often called *grue*, a modern construct from English *green* and *blue* to indicate the oneness of this category in some colour systems. Grue, and other macro-categories, have similar structures to the single-hue categories, consisting of a boundary and a non-focal area. They may, however, have two or even three foci (MacLaury 1997a: 265–78). In a grue category, for example, there may be one focus in the green area and another in the blue area, and one of the foci may be of lesser salience than the other (Section 7.4). Societies differ as to the nature of their macro-category focus or foci, and, moreover, so do individuals within societies. In a macro-category, the intermediate shades are the non-focal shades of both hues, and the category boundary surrounds them all. Such a macro-category is, typically, denoted by only one BCT (see also Section 6.3).

It should not be imagined that a community using macro-colour categories cannot visually distinguish between the two hues; they just regard them as two varieties of the same colour, since the one merges into the other and the community has no compelling reason to regard them as fundamentally different. They are very likely, of course, to have *non*-basic terms appropriate to each separate hue so that those who need to, such as painters, can adequately communicate a specific colour area. For example, Zulu speakers can specify with phrases: 'grue like the sky' and 'grue like the grass' (Taylor 2003: 12).

5.6   Micro-categories

Macro-categories are clearly larger in coverage than an English speaker would expect to find, but there are also basic colour categories which are smaller. While English has one basic term for BLUE, Russian appears to have two, denoted by *sinij* and *goluboj* (Sections 3.6 and 3.21), usually translated as 'dark blue' and 'light blue' respectively.[3] This suggests that Russian speakers have two separate micro-categories which are each smaller than the more usually encountered single blue category, but the situation is not quite as straightforward as it sounds.

At this point, an important semantic distinction must be introduced. It was recognized by John Lyons, and referred to by him as the difference between 'referential' and 'descriptive' (or 'attributive') usage. *Referential usage* occurs when there is reference to, or discussion of a colour as an abstract concept, for example, in the statement 'I don't like brown'. This communicates a dislike of *anything* brown, and the topic of the sentence is brownness. *Descriptive usage*, on the other hand, occurs when there is reference to an object which has a particular colour as, for example, in the statement 'I don't like brown coats'. Unlike referential usage, this does not imply that the speaker dislikes objects such as brown horses or brown books, since the topic of the sentence is not brownness but coats (Lyons 1995a: 206).

Returning to the Russian blues, their referential usage (indicating abstract colours), as shown by a colour-naming test, reveals that *sinij* is the nearest equivalent to English *blue*.[4] With no further research, this finding might have suggested that *goluboj* is not basic, but mapping exercises, in which individual colour samples were named by native speakers, have shown that, although *sinij* covers a much larger area of BLUE than *goluboj*, it cannot be used for the entire blue area since *goluboj* is required to name the paler and greener areas (Paramei 2007: 87–9). This situation suggests that *goluboj* is not a hyponym of *sinij* since these two words, and the categories they label, are in a complementary relationship.[5]

Turning from the referential use of the Russian blues to their descriptive use, it is found that the two words are again complementary. *Sinij* specializes in darker and more saturated blues, with connotations of strength and intensity, while *goluboj* is used for paler and less saturated blues, with connotations of dilution, dimness, airiness and a tarnished appearance (Alimpieva, reported in Paramei 2007: 78). Paramei provides an interesting example of this complementary use: the mundane description of greyish-blue or pale blue eyes in, for example, identity documents in Russian, uses *goluboj*, but where a person is described as having *sinie glaza*, this implies eyes of a startling cornflower-blue, considered to be beautiful (Paramei, personal communication, 11 August 2009).

The considerable psychological and linguistic research which has been carried out into the Russian blues has mostly concluded that Russians have two basic categories in the area of the colour space occupied by a single category in many other languages. I refer to categories like the Russian blues as 'micro-categories', in contrast with macro-categories. Although micro-categories are, to my knowledge, relatively rare, researchers should be aware of their existence, and consider this alternative when they investigate what may, at first, appear to be a highly salient hyponym.[6]

5.7   Intra-language variation

In the 1960s there was a prevalent assumption that any speech community within a relatively restricted geographical area was linguistically homogeneous, in other words, that everyone who was a native speaker of a language or dialect, shared with their contemporary fellow-speakers the same lexicon and the same rules and conventions of grammar, phonology and semantics. In terms of colour categorization, the assumption of homogeneity meant that contemporary native speakers were all expected to have the same number of BCCs (and BCTs). Evidence was building, however, to suggest that linguistic *variation* (heterogeneity) was the norm, and that this variation was the source of language vitality and change.[7]

Linguistic differences of various kinds were found between age-groups, men and women, monolinguals and bilinguals, urban and rural dwellers and so on. In investigating variations in the designation of colours in the Luganda language of Uganda, Pollnac took account of these and several other factors which had the potential to affect the colour lexicons of individuals. These factors included: duration of formal education; occupation; frequency of visits to Kampala (the capital); and even whether, and for how long, subjects had owned a radio (1975: 103). Pollnac's Sub-Group 7, with the most elaborate colour system, was the youngest sub-group, speaking the greatest number of languages, including the highest percentage of those who knew English, had possessed radios longer than any other sub-group, came second in terms of frequency of visits to Kampala, had received the longest formal education, and had the lowest number of members living in rural areas. Most of these valuable statistics can be boiled down to the statement that the more contact an individual has with those from different communities, and the greater selection of goods and products s/he sees on a regular basis, the more elaborate his or her colour system is likely to be. This means, of course, that, with living languages, interviewing only a small number of native speakers risks missing one or more of these variations. For historical semanticists, it emphasizes the need, which cannot always be fulfilled, to gather representative data.

5.7.1   Monolingualism versus bi- or multilingualism

The remainder of this chapter will consider three of the contexts in which intra-language variation occurs in colour systems: monolingualism versus knowledge of other languages; male versus female language; and the usage of younger versus older generations. Turning first to monolingualism versus bi- or multi-lingualism, in Section 4.6 the reader saw the effects on languages (in this case, Irish and Welsh) of having constant and significant contact with another language with a greater number of basic colour categories (in this case, English). Most adult speakers of Irish and Welsh also speak fluent English, and these bilingual people not only correctly manage the purple and pink categories when they speak English but, perhaps inevitably, the more they use them, the more likely they are to develop the same categories in their Celtic languages. The practice of code-switching between languages (Section 9.4), of adopting vocabulary from one language into another, and the need to translate in various circumstances often means that bi- and multilinguals are likely to have addi-tional developed or evolving colour categories compared with those of their monolingual compatriots.

Even where both monolinguals and bi- or multilinguals have the same num-ber of basic categories, the foci and extent of some categories may be different for the two groups. It is often the case that the categories of bilinguals, for example, have shifted under the influence of their second language. Caskey-Sirmons and Hickerson found that the category boundaries of Korean/English bilinguals had more variation than those of Korean monolinguals. Similarly, the monolinguals were much more consistent than the bilinguals in their place-ment of category foci on a colour chart. The Korean bilinguals also showed a tendency to extend their categories further to the right on the chart so that, for example, their yellow category extended towards the green–yellow area, and their green category extended into the blue–green area. A particularly pro-nounced shift was evident in the blue category: monolinguals placed their focus in blue-green, while bilingual informants chose five separate focal locations, all of which were located between blue and bluish-purple. This destabilization of the Korean foci among bilinguals shows the influence of English whose blue focus is *not* in blue-green (1977: 360). Caskey-Sirmons and Hickerson also studied monolinguals and bilinguals in English and the following languages: Japanese, Hindi, Cantonese and Mandarin, and they concluded that 'All of these observations are indicative of a tendency to generalization, which appears to be typical of bilingualism and multilingualism... that is, terminological categories of bilinguals become broader and the available choices more varied' (page 365).

5.7.2   Male versus female language

Now let us consider male versus female colour concepts. Many women have the impression that men are less interested in colour than they are, less confident about creating colour-schemes, and less able to describe subtle shades of hues. Is there any evidence to support this impression? There are several studies to show that men and women use basic colour *terms* to differing extents, but evidence of the sexes having differing numbers of basic *concepts*, that is, categories, is more difficult to find. Elaine Rich published a study of a colour description exercise designed to reveal, among other things, any differences in male and female colour vocabulary.[8] Her informants were each shown twenty-five cards and asked to describe the colours on them with a word or phrase. To evaluate the results, Rich (1977: 405) classified colour terms into four types which she called: 'Basic' (BCTs); 'Qualified' (BCTs qualified by modifiers such as *light* or *dark*, or by forms based on other BCTs as in *yellowish green*); 'Qualified Fancy' (BCTs qualified by 'special' terms, as in *sky blue* or *hunter green*); and 'Fancy' (non-basic colour terms such as *lavender* or *magenta*).[9] Rich's four categories were assigned values of from one to four points, so that the use of a basic term received one point, and the use of a fancy term received four. The most pertinent of Rich's results for our present concerns was that her female informants used 'fancier' words than the male informants, the latter preferring basic and qualified terms. Her two male groups taken together had a result of 3.7 for qualified fancy terms, and 5.4 for fancy ones, whereas the two female groups (excluding a group of nuns) had corresponding results of 5.6 and 7.5 (pages 405–7, Table 3).

Nowaczyk (1982: 259) also found that his male informants relied on BCTs more than the females when they were all asked to perform a matching task which involved assigning *provided* colour terms to colour samples. Since the terms (both basic and fancy) were provided by the researchers, it is clear that the male informants actively avoided the fancier terms. When fancy terms were used, women were significantly more accurate than men in matching them to the correct colours (page 261).

There has been considerable speculation as to why differences in the experimental results consistently occur. It is often postulated that women's larger and more elaborate colour vocabulary results from their traditional interests and hobbies which are often strongly colour-related, for example, cosmetics, embroidery, clothes, flower-arranging, interior decor and so on. As part of a larger experiment on unrestrained-choice colour-naming by males and females, Swaringen, Layman and Wilson recorded their subjects' hobbies, and graded them according to the degree of their involvement with colour. This grading resulted in a mean score for males of 1.5 and for females of 2.79. Since the female subjects provided a significantly higher number of colour-names for the twenty-one chips used in the experiment, the authors suggest there may be a correlation between the extent of colour-related hobbies and of colour vocabulary (1978: 441–2). Simpson and Tarrant (1991: 61) also investigated the influence of hobbies, and found that their male subjects had significantly fewer colour-related hobbies than the females.

Another experimental result supports the view that everyday contact with, and consideration of, colour has an effect on colour vocabulary. Rich found that a group of nuns used more basic and qualified colour terms than other women, and fewer qualified fancy and fancy terms. For example, they scored 6.2 for fancy usage while lay women scored 7.5 (men scored 5.4) (1977: 407). The fact that nuns who wear habits (as did these particular nuns) do not have to decide daily which colours to wear and whether various parts of their ensemble are chromatically compatible appears to have affected their vocabulary, although they still have a higher score than the men.

Researchers should be warned not to extrapolate results from one society to another. All four studies so far described in this section (those by Rich, Nowaczyk, Swaringen and colleagues, and Simpson and Tarrant) were conducted among English speakers in Western societies (in the United States and the United Kingdom). Researchers should be prepared for the possibility that, in other societies, it may be *men* who work on colour-related tasks and so have an extensive vocabulary of fancy terms.[10]

Even when individual women do not have colour-related interests or occupations, the general expectations of society may encourage them to favour fancy non-basic terms. Greene and Gynther (1995: 31) suggest that gender differences in colour identification and naming may result from the differential socialization of men and women. They note that the colour of women's clothing is more often described with fancy terms whereas the colour of men's clothing is more often described with BCTs, as if fussing with details was not manly. The gender differences in colour naming may be a feature of adulthood since Machen's (2002) experiment, concentrating exclusively on 14- to 16-year-olds, found no significant difference in colour naming between males and females.

Since this is a chapter on *categories*, the crucial question is whether the difference in adult vocabulary, as described above, indicates a cognitive difference. There is an increasing amount of evidence for colour-related psychophysiological differences between males and females. Furbee and colleagues conducted experiments which showed strong male/female differences in both the perception and cognition of colour, with women performing better (1997:

224–5, 233). Most humans are trichromatic, that is, they possess three types of photo-sensitive pigments in the cone cells of the retina which absorb light of differing wavelengths (see also Section 7.2). The three types of cell feed into three neural channels to the brain where the signals are interpreted as a colour sensation. Recently, however, evidence has been accruing to show that a certain percentage of women, perhaps a substantial percentage, are *tetra*chromats, that is, they have *four* types of photo-pigment, which enables them to perceive more chromatic variations than trichromats (Jameson, Highnote and Wasserman 2001: 244–5).

While it is tempting to see a connection between female tetrachromacy and the larger and fancier colour vocabulary of women in certain societies, does this mean that women have more basic categories than their menfolk? It seems unlikely that this is the case among those of similar age. Nowaczyk (1982: 264) speculates that women may have more 'internal representations' of the colour space than men but he does not envisage these representations as being the same as basic categories. A promising case was published by Thomas, Curtis and Bolton, concerning experiments with Nepalese subjects. They found that the mean number of BCTs listed by their male subjects was 6.36 whereas females listed 7.47. Their subjects consisted of both urban- and rural-dwellers, however, and they point out that more of their female subjects lived in an urban environment (Kathmandu) than their male subjects, which may indicate that the apparent difference between the sexes in this case actually relates to a city versus rural environment (1978: 77).

There appear to be many factors involved in the gender differences apparent in colour perception, cognition and naming. We have seen that physiology, socialization, extent of vocabulary, environment and occupation may all have separate or interacting roles in various experimental results but the cultural context of experimental work should itself be considered, as Smith and colleagues rightly suggest. They carried out a survey among students at the University of South Florida, and found there was 'little or no difference' between the elicited colour term lists of males and females, with BCTs being ranked in 'almost identical fashion'. They suggest that such results are not surprising where the socio-cultural context is minimal, that is, in a linguistic exercise rather than in 'real' contexts such as buying clothes or repainting a car (Smith *et al.* 1995: 215).

5.7.3 Older versus younger people's language

The next topic is the question of whether age affects the number of basic colour categories an individual possesses. In 1969, Berlin and Kay had assigned languages to one of the seven stages of the evolutionary sequence (Section 6.2) according to the number of their basic categories but, with the acceptance of

Table 5.1 *West Futunese colour category types with average ages of the informants using them*

Group no.	No. of categories	Average age of informant
1	4	45.0
2	5	48.3
3	6	35.1
4	7	11.0
5	9	10.0

intra-language variation, it became clear that some languages belonged to one stage amongst older people but to a later stage amongst younger people. In other words, younger speakers, in some cases, used one (or even more) additional basic categories to those of their elders. The case of the West Futunese language is of relevance here.

West Futuna, also known as Futuna Island, is in Tafea province of Vanuatu in the South Pacific, and the language is a Polynesian outlier. Janet Dougherty reported on the colour categories of forty-five adults and twenty-four children from this speech community. She found that all her subjects had the basic categories which were listed at the time as WHITE, BLACK, RED and GRUE. Five (11 per cent) of the adults had no further categories (Group 1), but eighteen (40 per cent) of them had an additional yellow category (Group 2), while twenty-one (47 per cent) of them had separate green and blue categories (Group 3).[11] As for the children, many of them had a brown category in addition (Group 4), and one child had orange and purple categories as well ('Group' 5) (1977: 103; 105). This represents an astonishing range of colour systems, all operating contemporaneously in a single society. Dougherty provides average ages for the five groups (1977: 116, Table IV), and this information appears here in Table 5.1.

Table 5.1 indicates that age may be a significant factor in the number of basic categories used by any one West Futunese speaker. There is, of course, a 'blip' in the steadily decreasing age shown in the third column, since the average age of Group 2 is higher than that of Group 1, but it should be remembered that Group 1 consists of only five informants.[12] Although this pattern is initially convincing, it would be wise to check for other possibilities. It may be significant, for example, that male informants predominate in Groups 1 and 2 but, in all the groups thereafter, females predominate. On the other hand, it is *certainly* significant that the members of Group 3 were among the first West Futunese to attend school, and the children's groups were learning English. This has had an evident influence on their colour systems, as shown by their BCTs. The BCTs known to Group 1 and others are all denoted by West Futunese words:

hkeŋo 'light, white'; *uri* 'dark, black'; *hmea* 'red'; and *uiui* 'grue'. The naming of some later categories, however, appears to indicate that the language is in a state of tension between native terms and borrowings from pidgin English. The yellow category, for example, can be named *hleu* (West Futunese, meaning literally 'ripe') or *fero fero* (a yellow term from the neighbouring island of Aniwa) or *iela* (pidgin English, from English *yellow*). Other BCTs are clearly from English, whether from pidgin or school-English, for example: *plu* 'blue'; *krin* 'green'; and *praon* 'brown' (Dougherty 1977: 106, Table II).[13]

In this chapter, the reader will, no doubt, have noticed that both individuals and their societies in general categorize colour, but not necessarily in the same way. Although this poses obvious problems, especially in historical studies, the complications are well worth tackling since, as Lakoff writes: 'An understanding of how we categorize is central to any understanding of how we think and how we function' (1987: 6).

6   The evolutionary sequence

6.1   Introduction

At this point, we know quite a lot about basic colour categories, such as their structure, their abstract nature, their variability within societies and how they can be recognized. This chapter is concerned with the *evolutionary sequence*, a widely known interpretation of how these categories develop over time (diachronically). It is here that the reader unavoidably encounters the old battle between relativism and universalism (Sections 2.6, 2.7 and 7.6) because the sequence represents a universalist hypothesis on colour category acquisition.

From the beginning, the evolutionary sequence has been bedevilled by two words: *universal* and *evolution*. Part of the criticism of the sequence has, I believe, involved unnecessarily narrow interpretations of these words, so the latter will be considered in Section 7.3 while the former is tackled here. What exactly is meant by *universal*? In its literal sense, *universal* indicates applicability to everyone and everything but it also has a more modest sense of applicability to every member of a stated group. Even here, however, it is often used rather loosely, indicating something like 'extremely common', as can be seen in the sentence 'tea-drinking is universal amongst the English'. While colour categories and their foci have frequently been claimed to have a perceptual basis which is determined by (universal) human biology, the evolutionary sequence was, from the beginning, described as having 'a *partially* fixed order' (Berlin and Kay 1969: 5; my italics), thus denying the literal sense of *universality*.[1]

It is impossible to write about colour category acquisition and not devote many pages to what may be called the 'Berlin and Kay school' or the 'UE model' (the latter name taken from the words 'Universals' and 'Evolution') (Kay 2006: 117). From 1969 to the present, Berlin, Kay and their colleagues have revolutionized, popularized and constantly developed linguistic and anthropological colour studies. At the centre of their diachronic hypothesis lies the evolutionary sequence, itself regularly evolving to take account of new discoveries, and proving deeply satisfying to those who want to believe that there is order in human affairs.

Table 6.1 *Inventories of basic categories, as represented by the numbers of basic terms (1969)*

No. of BCTs	Basic categories present
2	WHITE, BLACK
3	WHITE, BLACK, RED
4	WHITE, BLACK, RED, GREEN *or* WHITE, BLACK, RED, YELLOW
5	WHITE, BLACK, RED, GREEN, YELLOW
6	WHITE, BLACK, RED, GREEN, YELLOW, BLUE
7	WHITE, BLACK, RED, GREEN, YELLOW, BLUE, BROWN
8 or more	WHITE, BLACK, RED, GREEN, YELLOW, BLUE, BROWN *and one or more of*: PURPLE, PINK, ORANGE, GREY

6.2   The 1969 evolutionary sequence

How many basic colour categories does a society have at any one time? The standard reply to such a question is between two and eleven, and this brings us back to Berlin and Kay's book (1969). We have already seen their work on basicness criteria for BCTs (Sections 3.3 to 3.13) but the proposal for which they are probably best known is the evolutionary sequence.

Berlin and Kay collected information on BCTs from native speakers of twenty languages, and they also added further data from textual evidence for another seventy-eight languages. On considering their results, they could find none of their ninety-eight languages which provided evidence for more than eleven basic categories, although at least two, Hungarian and Russian, appeared to have more than eleven BCTs (1969: 35–6).[2] However, *below* the maximum of eleven or twelve, they found widely differing numbers of basic categories.

Although the numbers of categories represented by BCTs differed from language to language, Berlin and Kay found that a certain pattern of acquisition emerged from their data. Firstly, they found that every one of their languages had BCTs denoting categories with foci in white and black. Then the researchers noticed that any language with more than two BCTs always had one which denoted a category focused in red, and that, if a language had even more BCTs, they always had one focused in either green or yellow. So the pattern continued, and it can be tabulated as in Table 6.1, in which BCTs are taken to represent the foci of cognitive categories.

Berlin and Kay's ninety-eight languages from around the world had differing numbers of BCTs but all apparently fitted into the general pattern shown in Table 6.1. In other words, the number of BCTs a language possessed could be located in the first column, and, from there, it appeared that the basic categories

Table 6.2 *The evolutionary sequence of colour category acquisition, as represented by category foci (1969)*

Stage I	Stage II	Stage III	Stage IV	Stage V	Stage VI	Stage VII
white *and* black	+ red	+ green *or* + yellow	+ yellow *or* + green	+ blue	+ brown	+ purple *and/or* + pink *and/or* + orange *and/or* + grey

existing in that particular speech community could be accurately predicted by looking in the second column. This means that Table 6.1 lists a set of *implicational universals*. Berlin and Kay then drew up the first version of the diachronic evolutionary sequence (Table 6.2).

This sequence has appeared (not usually in tabulated form) in hundreds, perhaps thousands of publications, and has been discussed, criticized and praised. Few linguistic hypotheses have aroused such enthusiasm or vituperation, or motivated more research around the world. However, if s/he is to enter into the fray, the reader should ask precisely what these English-language colour terms represent. Berlin and Kay recorded basic colour *terms* in various languages, and these were taken to indicate underlying cognitive *categories*. However, the sequence shows only a part of each category, namely, their *foci*, or most 'typical' areas. This is because Berlin and Kay's research had showed that, although category foci in the various languages they had investigated could be plotted in similar and distinct areas of the colour chart, category *boundaries* refused to be so accommodating. Berlin and Kay write:

> In fact, in marked contrast to the foci, category boundaries proved to be so unreliable, even for an individual informant, that they have been accorded a relatively minor place in the analysis. Consequently, whenever we speak of color categories, *we refer to the foci of categories, rather than to their boundaries or total area*, except when specifically stating otherwise. (1969: 13; their italics)

Berlin and Kay had carried out mapping exercises with their native-speaker informants, and the results can be seen in their book (1969: 114–33). Their informants were asked to map the position of the foci and boundaries of their categories on the 'stimulus board' which showed a Munsell array of 329 standard colour chips (pages 5, 7).[3] It was covered with clear acetate so that informants could draw on it.[4] As we have seen, the results for category boundaries varied considerably but the results for foci, although not perfectly spot-on every time, were all placed in similar areas of the Munsell array (pages 8–9, Figs. 2–3). It was this similarity, across several unrelated languages, which led Berlin and Kay to claim there were universal features underlying colour terminology: '*color categorization is not random and the foci of basic color terms are similar in all languages*' (page 10; their italics).

The fact that the 1969 sequence involves category foci *only* has caused problems of representation in print. When writing in English, there is a need to distinguish, for example, between English *green* (a BCT that denotes an entire category used by English speakers) from Berlin and Kay's 'green' (claimed to be a universally recognized focal area). Sometimes, small capitals have been used, as in GREEN, but, because of the linguistic convention of using small capitals to indicate concepts, this practice obscures the fact that the 1969 sequence is restricted to foci. The reader will find other conventions, for example, that of Lyons (1995a: 209–10), who refers to the foci as BK-red, BK-green and so on, in which 'BK' stands for 'Berlin and Kay'. In this book I shall use f-red, f-green and so on, to indicate focal areas.

There is, however, more that the reader needs to know about the 1969 sequence. Because the English names on the sequence represent category foci, it is easy to understand that, for example, the label 'green' indicates 'typical green', the salient area of the assumed GREEN category, but 'black' and 'white' are more problematic. After all, 'typical black' is simply black, and the category does not extend to a counter-intuitive 'pale black' or 'dark black'. It is clear, however, that Berlin and Kay envisaged f-black and f-white as the 'typical' areas of the DARK and LIGHT categories: '*black* plus most dark hues, and *white* plus most light hues' (1969: 17). The confusion arises from the fact that the labels 'black' and 'white', while by definition indicating foci, are simultaneously being used to denote macro-categories (Section 6.3). If the reader is wondering why a dark blue, for example, would not be in the blue category, it is because a Stage I language has no other categories than DARK and LIGHT (see Table 6.2): there simply is *no* blue category. This sequence represents a gradual (and optional) development over time, and a Stage I language has only just begun to develop basic categories.

There is a further difficulty with the 1969 sequence which reflects the linguistic thinking of the time, and that is the assumption of native-speaker linguistic homogeneity. This means that, in terms of colour categorization, speakers of the same language or dialect, living at the same period in time, were all expected to have the same number of basic categories but, as we have seen (Section 5.7), this is now known to be incorrect, since *variation* (heterogeneity) within a speech community has been shown to be the norm. It is worth bearing this in mind when considering Berlin and Kay's classification of languages according to their stage on the sequence.

It only remains to issue a crucially important warning. Readers are likely to find the 1969 sequence presented by numerous authors in publications dating from the 1970s to the present, but many writers are apparently unaware that there were later revisions of the sequence, starting in 1975, which resulted from further research and assessment. It is necessary to discuss the original form of the sequence here, not only because earlier language studies are still useful, but also because it is still appearing in print as if it had never been revised. The major amendments to the sequence will be presented below.

6.3   The role of macro-categories

In 1975, Paul Kay published a paper to revise certain aspects of the 1969 evolutionary sequence. One of the most persuasive reasons for doing so was the work of Eleanor Rosch Heider (1972a, 1972b) among the Dugum Dani of Indonesian New Guinea, which provided an unexpected picture of what seemed to be a Stage I system. This type of colour system consists of only two basic categories which classify all colour experiences on the basis of brightness and tone. The two BCTs are usually glossed as 'dark' and 'light', the latter term covering both paleness and brightness.

Rosch Heider found that the Dani system was not that simple, since, in addition to brightness and tone, it also appeared to have some basis in hue. Kay summarized Rosch Heider's results as follows: Dani *mili*, the dark term, includes cool hues, while Dani *mola*, the light term, includes warm hues. In other words, the distinction between the two terms can be expressed as DARK+COOL (*mili*) versus LIGHT+WARM (*mola*) (1975: 258). This summary of Rosch Heider's research on Dani, which was crucial in the recognition of macro-categories, has been so frequently quoted that the Dani language ranks with Hanunóo (Section 4.5) as an icon of colour semantic research.[5]

The Dani language provided a second surprise. Berlin and Kay had labelled the foci of their Stage I categories as 'black' and 'white' but Rosch Heider found the Dani foci were not in these positions. Various Dani-speaking informants placed the best examples of *mili* among the darkest greens and blues, and not at black. They were divided over the focus of *mola*, usually locating it, not at white, but in the dark red area or, less commonly, in pale pink. Rosch Heider asked each informant whether the black and white samples were not better examples of *mili* and *mola* but no one agreed with this (1972a: 451, 453).

Rosch Heider also found that roughly half her informants used further colour terms: *pimut* or *boksu* 'red' was used by 50 per cent of her forty informants, and *bodli* 'yellow' was used by 45 per cent. In addition, 28 per cent of her informants used *juaiegen* 'blue' (1972a: 451, 454–6), although none of these terms could be regarded as a BCT.

Table 6.3 *The evolutionary sequence of colour category acquisition, as represented by categories and foci (1975)*

Stage I	Stage II	Stages IIIa and IIIb	Stage IV	Stage V	Stage VI	Stage VII
WHITE and BLACK	+ RED	+ GRUE (IIIa) or + yellow (IIIb)	+ yellow or + GRUE	+ green and + blue	+ brown	+ purple and/or + pink and/or + orange and/or + grey

By the early 1970s, therefore, it was clear that Stage I of the sequence needed to be rethought but other stages too were beginning to cause concern. Although Berlin and Kay had known that the Stage I categories were macro-colours,[6] it became clear that other such categories existed, and, moreover, they appeared to be the norm in the early stages of the sequence. Berlin and Kay had noted in 1969 that Japanese *ao* 'blue' had once covered green in addition to blue (1969: 42), and, by 1975, it was evident that other languages too had these grue categories, for example: Aguaruna (Berlin and Berlin 1975: 71–2, 81–3); 'Eskimo' (his term) (Heinrich 1973); and West Futunese (Dougherty 1974).[7] The realization of the extent of macro-categories in the early phases of the sequence prompted Kay to make revisions, as seen in Table 6.3 (1975: 260).

The 1975 sequence shows categories (which are all *macro*-categories) in capital letters, and foci in lower-case. Thus, WHITE includes, in Kay's words, 'white, very light shades of all colors, all warm colors', with a focus in either white, red or pink. BLACK 'includes black, some very dark browns and purples, all but the lightest blues and greens' and, probably, a variable focus in black and in dark greens and blues (Kay 1975: 260). RED indicates the acquisition of a new category which 'removes' the warm colours from the older WHITE category. At Stage III, a society may develop a GRUE category (Stage IIIa) or it may acquire a 'yellow' category instead (Stage IIIb). In either case, the second of these two categories is acquired at Stage IV. At Stage V, the single category GRUE splits into the two categories of 'green' and 'blue'.[8]

The 1975 sequence includes both categories (upper-case letters) and foci (lower-case), and this is confusing for the reasons discussed in Section 6.2. This means that Kay's 'BLACK' (full-size capitals) indicates the dark+cool macro-category while, elsewhere in colour semantics, BLACK (small capitals) indicates only the darkest extreme of the achromatic tone scale. The convention used in this book will consist of small capitals prefixed by M- to denote macro-categories (for example, M-BLACK), and the already established lower-case letters prefixed by f- to denote foci (for example, f-green).

In conclusion to this section, the 1975 sequence adopts the view that early macro-categories include between them the entire colour space, and successive sub-dividings of these large categories result in increasing numbers of single hue categories. This is a major change from the 1969 principle of the gradual naming of the colour space through the successive recognition of single hue foci. Unlike the 1975 sequence, the 1969 version implied that early stages involve large areas of colour which remain unnamed by any basic term, but Rosch Heider's work had shown this was unlikely.[9] The sub-division of macro-categories can be a lengthy process, sometimes involving several sub-divisions over many years or even centuries. However, not all societies feel a need to increase the number of their categories, and they may be content to use a small number of them until (and if) the motivation arises to acquire more.

6.4   The problem of grey

The later updates and revisions of the evolutionary sequence will only be presented here insofar as they impinge on historical studies. The first consideration is the revised sequence published by Witkowski and Brown (1977: 51). This involved some changes in labelling; for example, the 'WHITE', 'BLACK' and 'RED' labels at Stages I to II (Kay 1975: 260) were renamed 'MACRO-WHITE', 'MACRO-BLACK' and 'MACRO-RED' to better indicate firstly, that the Stage I categories were not LIGHT and DARK but LIGHT+WARM (M-WHITE) and DARK+COOL (M-BLACK) and, secondly, that Stage II represented the division of M-WHITE into WARM (M-RED) and LIGHT. However, the most important change was probably the 'exile' of 'grey' from the main sequence.

'Grey' had always been problematic. Berlin and Kay had expressed doubts from the beginning about the inclusion of f-grey in their Stage VII: 'The only systematic error, then, is the premature appearance of grey. If additional cases of this type are found the theory might have to be revised' (Berlin and Kay 1969: 45). By the time Kay published his revised sequence (Section 6.3, Table 6.3), several other cases of the premature appearance of 'grey' had been reported, either in print or by personal communication to him (Kay 1975: 261). Soon afterwards, Kay and McDaniel accepted that 'grey' should be a 'wild-card' which developed into a basic category at any point between the sequence's Stage III and Stage VII (1975: 33, as reported by Witkowski and Brown 1977: 54). In Witkowski and Brown's sequence, f-grey is removed from Stage VII and appears below the sequence with dotted arrows showing the range of its possible initial introduction point (page 51).

6.5 The role of the Hering primaries

Another milestone work on colour was published by Kay and McDaniel in 1978, and this marked an increased interest in the neuro- and psycho-physiology of vision, and also in the question of colour category boundaries. Kay and McDaniel summarized what was known at the time of the physiological and psychological processes involved in human colour perception (1978: 617–21). They suggested that recent experiments by De Valois and his colleagues, concerning the responses in macaque monkey brains to colour stimuli, provided the physiological basis for the perceptual *opponent process theory* of Hering (Section 7.2), whereby colours were said to be perceived by means of the three opposing pairs of red versus green, yellow versus blue, and black versus white being routed separately to the brain.[10] This theory appeared to tally nicely with the earliest categories of the evolutionary sequence. Today, the Kay and McDaniel article must be read with caution, and with a knowledge of later research. The main problem is the authors' suggestion that there is a direct connection between features of neurophysiology and language: 'the semantics of basic color terms in all languages directly reflect the existence of these pan-human neural response categories' (page 621). Although this connection was quite widely accepted at the time,[11] it results from insufficient consideration of cognitive processes (Biggam 2004: 24–5).[12] The remainder of this section will concentrate on two innovations in Kay and McDaniel's paper which remain important.

The stages of the evolutionary sequence were rethought by Kay and McDaniel so that, instead of portraying the acquisition of eleven universal categories, the sequence consists of the Hering primaries and a restricted number of their unions and intersections (see Section 3.2). In other words, the early stages of the sequence are shown as containing 'composite' categories (macro-categories) which each consist of more than one of the Hering primaries. These categories can be modelled as *fuzzy unions*. Composite categories have a tendency to sub-divide, one or more times, eventually creating individual primaries, modelled as *fuzzy identities*. Finally, new categories develop, called 'derived' categories, which are located at the intersections of two primaries, just as PURPLE evolves between RED and BLUE, and they can be modelled as *fuzzy intersections*.[13] Reflecting this new emphasis, the sequence was no longer presented as showing consecutive additions only, denoted by English words, but all the categories present at each stage were shown in full, and denoted by letters. For example, the composite category M-BLACK was shown as 'Bk *or*

G *or* Bu' (black *or* green *or* blue), the primary YELLOW was shown as 'Y', and the derived category ORANGE was shown as 'R+Y' (red plus yellow) (Kay and McDaniel 1978: 639, Fig. 13).

It is now time to consider a word which has appeared in the last few sentences, namely, *fuzzy*. This occurs in connection with Kay and McDaniel's use of set theory, the mathematical study of collections of items. In standard set theory, an item is judged to belong to one category or a different category but, in 1965, the mathematician Lotfi Zadeh introduced the idea of 'fuzzy sets' (1965; 1996). In fuzzy sets, items can be assigned *degrees* of membership of categories, ranging from zero to unity (best example) rather than a simple status of member or non-member. Kay and McDaniel quoted examples of linguistic forms which suggest that colour categories are best modelled as fuzzy sets rather than discrete categories. For example, English has the terms *slightly red, yellowish red, a good red, off-white* and so on, which indicate degrees of membership of the red and white categories (1978: 622). An approach like this means that the colour turquoise, for example, does not have to be assigned either to the blue category or the green category (a difficult decision) but can be regarded as having a certain degree of membership of each one.

Fuzzy set theory was clearly a most useful means of dealing with category boundaries. They had posed a long-lasting problem in colour semantics because of their variability, both within and between languages. Fuzzy set theory had much in common with aspects of Rosch's 'prototype theory' of categories, first presented in 1973, whereby certain items were considered to be typical, or best examples, of their categories while other items could be located anywhere on a range of better to poorer examples (1973: 112).[14] This is known as 'graded category membership' or 'family resemblance' (Rosch and Mervis 1975). For example, an informant may consider focal blue as prototypical of the blue category, while pale blue may be less so, bluish-grey less so again, and focal red has zero membership of the blue category.

6.6   The arrival of trajectories

The 1969 sequence had consisted of a very straightforward periodic addition of foci (representing categories) with only one built-in option. This was at Stage III, where a society might add a green category (Stage IIIa) or a yellow category (Stage IIIb).[15] As more research was carried out into various languages, it became clear that additional options, indicating different routes or 'trajectories' by which societies acquired new colour categories, needed to be incorporated into the sequence. Two major research projects in particular made available a considerable amount of data: firstly, the World Colour Survey (WCS), managed by Brent Berlin, Paul Kay and William Merrifield, began, in 1976, to study over one hundred languages spoken by peoples who had received minimal or no linguistic influence from the Western world; and secondly, the Mesoamerican Colour Survey (MCS), conducted by Robert MacLaury from 1978 to 1981, in which 900 speakers of 116 Mesoamerican languages were interviewed.[16] All this information was preliminarily processed and analysed in the 1980s with interesting results.

After an initial consideration of seventy-two of the WCS languages, a new form of the sequence was presented to the eighty-fourth meeting of the American Anthropological Association in 1985. Some terminology had changed: the two Stage I categories were called 'white-light' and 'black-dark', and the labels 'warm' and 'cool' appeared in Stages II ('warm') and III to V. However, much more significant was the proliferation of options: Stage III was now sub-divided into three parts, and Stages IV to VI all had two subdivisions (Berlin, Kay and Merrifield 1985: 384, Fig. 19). This proliferation had been driven by MacLaury's (1987) confirmation of a newly recognized macro-category of YELLOW+GREEN for which the classic case is his study of Shuswap, a language of British Columbia, Canada.[17] In addition, certain data had suggested that PURPLE and BROWN were sometimes distinguished before the partition of COOL, and this phenomenon contradicted the neat development from composite to primary to derived categories that Kay and McDaniel (1978) had suggested (Section 6.5). As Berlin, Kay and Merrifield stated: 'While the major outlines of our earlier understanding of the nature of color classification proposed by Berlin and Kay appear confirmed, it is clear that only part of the story has been told' (1985: 362).

When a new partial sequence appeared in 1991, Stage III boasted five subdivisions, and Stage IV had three (Kay, Berlin and Merrifield 1991: 19, Fig. 3).[18] This new sequence also indicated, by means of arrows, the routes known to have been taken by societies developing and naming additional colour categories. The evidence showed that, although not every language took the same route, there was a highly restricted number of options. So, for example, in 1991, two languages were known to be evolving from Stage II to a Stage IIIa system, while four other Stage II languages were expanding into a Stage IIIb system. The particular trajectory favoured by a society was ascertained from cases in which the WCS data showed some native speakers of a language to be using an older colour system while others employed a system belonging to the next stage (Section 5.7).

The 1991 article revealed a problem in the interpretation of some trajectories. Languages found to have a yellow+green category at Stage IIId or IIIe, appeared to have a system which had evolved from a Stage II in which yellow and green were *not* associated. The process of partition, whereby macro-categories gradually divide into smaller macro-categories and/or single hue categories, seemed not to work in the case of YELLOW+GREEN. As a result, Kay, Berlin and Merrifield's Figure 3 cannot suggest a source system for Stages

IIId and IIIe, and they struggle to interpret this part of their data. They suggest three possible explanations, but admit that 'none of them is particularly plausible' (1991: 20). They suggest firstly that, in some languages, the macro-categories at Stage II divided but may then have recombined in an unusual way. This process is referred to as *splitting and relumping* (or *recombining*) but there was no evidence for it in the WCS data. Their second suggestion is that, given the world-wide rarity of the yellow+green macro-category, the missing evidence for its origin does exist, but has simply not been encountered by field-workers. Their third suggestion is that Stages IIId and IIIe simply have no history, and do not evolve from systems such as those shown in Stages I and II. The authors comment that this 'seems more a confession of bewilderment than a solution to the mystery' (page 20) but, by the time the final WCS report was published, a better hypothesis had been developed (Section 7.5).

As work on the WCS data progressed, the researchers refined their trajectories and, in the process, developed a new form of notation and a shorter evolutionary sequence. In 1997, a further interim report was published by Kay, Berlin, Maffi and Merrifield. The authors agree with an earlier observation of MacLaury's that two processes were involved in the development of colour categories: firstly, the subdividing of macro-categories into primaries (which they call 'fundamentals'); and secondly, the combination of primaries to form derived categories, as when RED and WHITE combine to form the derived category, PINK. Kay and colleagues decided to refer to the first process as involving 'basic stages', and to remove from the sequence the stages representing derived categories (Stages VI and VII), since there was increasing evidence that they could be developed 'out of sequence', that is, prior to the last two stages. Derived categories could now be added to a stage number to denote the complete situation of any language; for example, it could be described as 'Stage V; purple, pink'. This would mean that the language was at Stage V, but also had BCTs for the derived categories of PURPLE and PINK (Kay *et al.* 1997: 29–30). From 1997, the evolutionary sequence has consisted of only five stages (see Table 6.4).

The new form of notation denoting position on the new sequence involves the stage number, plus sub-type (where applicable) added in subscript. For example, a Stage III language might belong to Stage $III_{Bk/G/Bu}$ or to Stage $III_{G/Bu}$, the sub-type being shown in bold (as in Table 6.4). The sub-type thus identifies the remaining cool macro-category in that position on the sequence. For societies or languages, as opposed to individuals, Kay and colleagues make the important point that some should be considered as transitional between stages. They quote the example of Candoshi, a language isolate spoken in Peru. This language could be denoted as '$IV_{G/Bu} \rightarrow V$' meaning it is transitional between a particular sub-type of Stage IV, and Stage V (Kay *et al.* 1997: 32).

Table 6.4 *The evolutionary sequence of colour category acquisition (1999)*

Stage I	Stage II	Stage III	Stage IV	Stage V
		W, R, Y, Bk/G/Bu ($III_{Bk/G/Bu}$) → or ↘	W, R, Y, G, Bk/Bu ($IV_{Bk/Bu}$) ↘	
W/R/Y → and Bk/G/Bu →	W, R/Y, Bk/G/Bu ↗ or →	W, R/Y, G/Bu, Bk ($III_{G/Bu}$) →	W, R, Y, G/Bu, Bk ($IV_{G/Bu}$) →	W, R, Y, G, Bu, Bk
		W, R, Y/G/Bu Bk ($III_{Y/G/Bu}$) ↗ or →	W, R, Y/G, Bu, Bk ($IV_{Y/G}$) ↗	

→ represents development towards the same-level set in the next column, while an up-arrow or down-arrow represents development towards the higher or lower sets in the next column. Options are indicated by the word *or*.

Kay and colleagues also point out certain constraints on the choice of trajectory. This involves two so-called 'channels' referred to as the 'white/warm channel' (or simply 'w'), and the 'black/cool channel' (or 'c'). These channels are concerned with the process of subdividing M-WHITE and M-BLACK respectively and, athough w-division and c-division are partially independent of each other, there exists a certain amount of interaction which results in the constraints. This was to be more fully developed in the next publication (Section 6.7).

6.7   The 1999 evolutionary sequence

At the time of writing, the full publication of the WCS data and its interpretation has just been published (Kay *et al.* 2009).[19] The evolutionary sequence remains unchanged from the version published in 1999 (Kay and Maffi), and the stages are shown in Table 6.4.

Kay and Maffi based their model on the WCS data, and on four principles.[20] Their first principle is partition (P), referring to the general tendency of societies to sub-divide and name various domains of cultural significance such as family relationships, animals, plants, colours and so on. In the case of colour, in which the sub-divisions overlap in several places, 'partition' should be understood as 'fuzzy partition' (1999: 745; Section 6.5). Kay and Maffi's remaining three

Table 6.5 *Trajectory A, the most common path for BCC acquisition (1999)*

Stage I	Stage II	Stage III	Stage IV	Stage V
W/R/Y and Bk/G/Bu	W, R/Y, Bk/G/Bu	W, R/Y, G/Bu, Bk (III$_{\text{G/Bu}}$)	W, R, Y, G/Bu, Bk (IV$_{\text{G/Bu}}$)	W, R, Y, G, Bu, Bk
→	6	3	41	23
	3 →	4 →	11 →	

Numbers without arrows represent the total WCS languages at each stage, while numbers with arrows represent the total WCS languages in transition towards the next stage.

principles concern the most frequently occurring human priorities in colour distinction, and they can be listed as follows:

1. Distinguish between black and white (Bk&W) (pages 746–7).
2. Distinguish the warm primaries (red and yellow) (Wa) from the cool primaries (green and blue) (C) (page 747).
3. Distinguish red (R) (pages 747–8).

The authors maintain that the interaction of the partition principle with the six Hering primaries, through the process of adding one basic category at each stage is the basis of their evolutionary sequence. When the three principles listed above are applied, in order, to each stage of the sequence, they indicate which will be the next basic category to be added. In other words, the authors have constructed a model which demonstrates (and predicts) the restricted number of routes by which the vast majority of societies add their colour categories, as can be seen in Table 6.4.

The WCS languages indicate five paths or trajectories towards Stage V, and these paths have been designated by the letters A to E. Trajectory A is particularly common, and is evidenced in 83 per cent of the WCS languages (Kay and Maffi 1999: 750, Figure 2). It is shown in Table 6.5. As the most common route taken by the WCS languages, this trajectory is worth explaining in detail, using the three principles listed above (pages 750–1). Stage I shows the two categories, M-WHITE (W/R/Y) and M-BLACK (Bk/G/Bu) which result from the application of Kay and Maffi's Principle 1, that is, that Bk and W must be in different composite categories. Next, the application of Principle 2, namely, the separation of warm and cool categories, dictates that R and Y must be in a different category from G and Bu. Principle 3 is not yet appropriate, since R should not be separated from its composite category before W. The WCS data have no example of a Stage I language so there are no numbers in this column. The arrow at Stage I indicates that the next step is Stage II, where Kay and Maffi's principles are again applied in order.

Stage II shows the results of having applied the principles to Stage I. Thus, Principle 1 requires the separation of either W or Bk from their respective composites, and the choice is determined by another of the principles. The application of Principle 2 is not yet relevant, but the application of Principle 3, namely, the separation of R from its composite category, means that W, rather than Bk, should first be distinguished, since that promotes the interests of R by reducing its composite. The numbers in the Stage II column show that there are six WCS languages at Stage II, and three which are in transition towards Stage III.

Stage III shows the results of having applied Kay and Maffi's principles to Stage II. Principle 1 leads to the separation of Bk from its composite, since this has already happened to W. Principles 2 and 3 are not relevant, since the first principle has already added one category at this stage (only one category is added per stage). The numbers at Stage III show that there are three WCS languages at this stage and four in transition towards Stage IV.

When the principles are applied to Stage III, in order to create Stage IV, we find that Principle 1 does not apply, since both W and Bk have already been separately distinguished, and Principle 2 does not help to produce a new category. Principle 3, however, leads to the separation of R from R/Y. The WCS data include forty-one languages at Stage IV and eleven in transition towards Stage V.

At Stage IV, only one composite category remains, G/Bu, so the application of the partition principle (P) is sufficient to separate the constituents of this last composite, and create Stage V.[21] The WCS data include twenty-three languages at Stage V.

The less commonly found trajectories, designated B, C, D and E, can be tracked from the arrows in Table 6.4, but they are also listed in Table 6.6, taken from Kay and Maffi's Table 1 (1999: 749). Trajectories D and E represent options which have been noted for the yellow+green category, and the question-marks at Stages I and II indicate the missing evidence for how these categories, observed from Stage III, have arisen (Sections 6.6, 7.5 and 11.4).

It is possible that further macro-categories may be authenticated in future, and a place found for them on the sequence. For example, McNeill reported on unusual categories in the language of the Ainu, a people of the northern Japanese island of Hokkaido and nearby Russian islands. In an Ainu dictionary, McNeill found evidence for the categories RED+GREEN and BLUE+YELLOW. Words containing *siwnin*, for example, denote 'blue mildew' and 'blue line' (a vein as on the forehead) as well as 'yellow butterfly' and 'jaundice'. Ainu *hu* was used of both red and green referents (1972: 30).[22] These two categories, if confirmed, break the 'rule' of *conjunctivity* whereby macro-categories can

Table 6.6 *Trajectories B to E for the acquisition of BCCs*

Trajectory	Stage I	Stage II	Stage III	Stage IV	Stage V
B	$I \rightarrow$	$II \rightarrow$	$III_{Bk/G/Bu} \rightarrow$	$IV_{G/Bu} \rightarrow$	V
C	$I \rightarrow$	$II \rightarrow$	$III_{Bk/G/Bu} \rightarrow$	$IV_{Bk/Bu} \rightarrow$	V
D	?	?	$III_{Y/G/Bu} \rightarrow$	$IV_{G/Bu} \rightarrow$	V
E	?	?	$III_{Y/G/Bu} \rightarrow$	$IV_{Y/G} \rightarrow$	V

only contain contiguous hues, with optional achromatics. Thus, green and blue are neighbours, but green and red are not, so, in the view of many linguists, they cannot form a macro-category (Witkowski and Brown 1978: 441). Bailey (2001) considered several suggested cases of disjunctive macro-categories and considered them all unacceptable. However, Bimler (2011: 23) points out that the WCS data include a category in Guaymi (Panama) which is focused in green but which extends into blue and a disconnected area of purple. In addition, Bimler finds a word in Vasavi (India) which is a yellow BCT but which also extends to pink and purple (Kay *et al.* 2009: 249, 539).

6.8   Criticism of early research methodology

The reader is likely to come across publications which criticize Berlin and Kay's 1969 findings on the basis of their research methodology. Their collection and interpretation of BCTs in many languages underlies the reliability, or otherwise, of their diachronic hypotheses, so must be considered here. Their book was greeted coolly by numbers of reviewers and commentators who were critical of what they could ascertain of the research techniques, and also of missing information in the published account of their work.[23] Durbin (1972: 258) points out that there is a lack of information about the interviewing of native-speaker informants who were consulted on twenty languages found in the San Francisco area. The reader is not told, for example, whether the locations of the experiments differed (important because of background colours, lighting levels and so on), whether the experimenters were acquainted with some or all of the informants, whether experimenters knew the languages they were investigating, and more.

Hickerson pointed out that the reader is not told how many informants were available for each language, although the authors admit that, in some cases, there was only one,[24] and, in addition, many of the informants were bilingual (Hickerson 1971: 260–1; Berlin and Kay 1969: 7).[25] Hickerson (1971: 260, 264) also criticizes the imbalance, in terms of both geography and language family, in the languages investigated. Other problems raised include: a lack of consideration of language acculturation (changes effected as a result of contact with another language) (pages 261–3); the extraction of data from outdated published sources (pages 263–4); apparent inconsistencies in decisions on basicness (pages 265–6); and an apparent simplification of the interpretations of colour terms to make them fit one of the stages of the sequence (pages 267–8; Saunders 1995: 24–6). Van Brakel gives an example of the last criticism from the WCS data in which the field-note 'dark weather' was later interpreted as describing a black BCT in the Kemtuik language of Indonesia (van Brakel 2004: 14). This process of standardization certainly took place but was, apparently, not totally subjective, as some writers seem to imply: 'In later analysis, we substituted our own judgements of basicness for those of the fieldworkers, taking account both of the fieldworkers' original judgements and of certain statistical summary information regarding the responses of the speakers, which was not available to the workers in the field' (Kay et al. 2009: 14).[26]

Finally, it is worth pointing out that while the presentation and details of Berlin and Kay's theories have changed considerably since 1969, two core principles have always remained stubbornly resistant to demolition. The first is that the Hering primaries (black, white, red, yellow, green and blue), either alone or in combination, appear to represent perceptual landmarks for humans, and play a substantial role in the cognitive colour systems of most of the world's societies (Section 7.2). The second core principle is that societies very commonly acquire basic colour categories in a partially fixed order, and they very rarely lose a category once it has become basic (Kay and Maffi 1999: 744, endorsed in Kay et al. 2009: 8).[27]

The evolutionary sequence has been interpreted in many ways. It has been said that it shows a transition from brightness to hue, from contextualized to abstract names, from single-dimensional to multi-dimensional description,[28] and that it is a mirror of human neurophysiology, and/or of increasing global westernization (Alvarado and Jameson 2002: 74–6). There is probably at least an element of truth in all of these. More fundamentally, the description of the sequence as 'evolutionary' has been interpreted as insulting to many world societies, and this will be discussed in Section 7.3.

7   Different approaches

7.1   Introduction

The 'Berlin and Kay school' or UE model of colour category acquisition, namely, the evolutionary sequence discussed in the previous chapter, is a classic case of a universalist hypothesis. It benefits greatly from two things. Firstly, it is so well known that no publication which touches even briefly upon the subject of colour categories can afford to omit some mention of it. Secondly, the 1969 sequence was so simple and neat that it entered every linguist's and anthropologist's consciousness with immense ease, and stuck like a limpet. Nonetheless, many researchers were immune to its charms. Some of them would proudly claim to be relativists, while others would prefer not to be labelled at all.[1] There is also an emerging view which combines aspects of both schools of thought and, since neither universalism nor relativism will, in their entirety, lie down and die, such a combination may indicate the way forward (Section 7.6).

The aim of this chapter is to describe criticisms of, and alternatives to, the UE model that fall into one or both of the following two categories: firstly, arguments and/or models which feature strongly in the literature, and which, therefore, need to be understood by historical researchers when they read about colour semantics in *modern* languages; and, secondly, those arguments and/or models which appear to offer useful techniques for the study of historical languages.

7.2   Barbara Saunders and Jaap van Brakel

Saunders, a British anthropologist, and van Brakel, a Dutch philosopher, have criticized, over many years, several aspects of the UE model, the WCS, and a number of current hypotheses concerning colour vision. They are not alone in their criticisms of the early Berlin and Kay methodology (Section 6.8) but much of that has now been improved. Dedrick makes the important distinction between *proving* a hypothesis, and setting up a hypothesis to inaugurate a research tradition aimed at testing it. If the latter is true of Berlin and Kay's

1969 book, criticisms should be levelled, not at that book, but, if necessary, at the research tradition that resulted from it (Dedrick 1998a: 181–4). Dedrick argues that criticisms of field methods, sampling, BCT definitions and prototypes are part of an ongoing dialogue which has resulted in improvements on earlier infelicities but has not swept away the UE model. While this is true, certain specific criticisms require some consideration here.

Saunders and van Brakel have challenged several assumptions about colour which are widespread among both linguists and anthropologists. They have argued, for example: that colour is not completely described by the features of hue, saturation and 'brightness'; that there is no incontrovertible evidence for four universally perceived elemental hues; that the opponent process theory is not proven; and that colour is not universally recognized as an autonomous and abstract phenomenon (1997: 167).

Let us consider their first criticism, namely, that colour impressions consist of more than hue, saturation and 'brightness'.[2] This concern is fundamental to Saunders and van Brakel's worries about the quality of the linguistic data which have been used to develop the evolutionary sequence and the criteria for BCT recognition. Central to this concern is the cultural neutrality (or otherwise) of standard colour charts such as the Munsell array and the chips based on it, as used in interviews with native speakers.[3] This particular criticism featured strongly in a 1988 paper by Saunders and van Brakel, published when they were both at the University of Utrecht in The Netherlands.[4] They discussed the usual fieldwork methodology of the early UE investigations, using Rosch Heider's work with the Dani of Papua New Guinea as an example (Section 6.3). Colour chips from the Munsell array were used to question the Dani but Saunders and van Brakel point out that these chips display only a limited number of the many possible features of colour. They mention sixteen such features, including softness, size, glossiness and fluctuation (1988: 364; Section 1.6) which all affect the quality of the colour impression and, in many societies, may also influence the choice of colour terms, but Munsell chips can only indicate hue, saturation and 'brightness'.

Saunders and van Brakel conclude about the Munsell colour chips that they 'may be useful for specific scientific purposes, but would be useless for checking the meaning of colour words' (1988: 364), and van Brakel describes them as 'villains . . . whose limitations are known' (2004: 12).[5] This is a valid criticism when the reader considers what we have learnt about Hanunóo and Yucatec colour semantics (Section 4.5). The effects of using the chips are, firstly, to ignore the fact that colour terms are used in different ways in different contexts and, secondly, to exclude all those (non-hue) features of colour naming which English speakers consider peripheral or irrelevant. This, of course, feeds the criticism of anglocentrism (Section 7.3) which is often made of the UE methodology. Saunders and van Brakel argue that the colour concepts of a particular society arise from general agreement within that society and, where we find 'surprising' concepts, such as YELLOW+GREEN (a macro-category), we should not seek for explanations as to how they could have evolved within the parameters of the evolutionary sequence, but we should simply conclude that such a society has different concepts from ours (1988: 368).

Saunders' doctoral thesis was entitled *The Invention of Basic Colour Terms* (1992) and it presents her view that basic categories have often been 'created' by researchers who ignore the cultural context in which colour terms are used. Saunders carried out fieldwork among the Lekwiltok Kwakiutl people of British Columbia, Canada, who speak the Kwak'wala language, and her report formed the second section of her thesis. When Saunders asked her informants to name colours, she used fruit and vegetables, pictures of plants and animals, beads and sequins, and, at the end of the exercise, the Munsell colour chart (pages 144–7). The responses of informants were most interesting. Saunders writes: 'While the plants, animals, beads and sequins were unproblematic, the introduction of the colour chart at the end of each interview caused discomfort, anxiety and agitation. All but one person was reluctant to continue' (page 147).

Saunders' interpretation of her informants' problems with the Munsell colour chart is that, while a concept such as RED FLOWER makes perfect sense to them, the abstract concept of REDNESS, to be mapped onto the restricted interpretation of redness offered by the chart, poses a serious problem. Although the colour chart is often thought by English speakers to be universally applicable and value-free, Saunders describes it as 'a device which transmutes indigenous meanings onto a single standard of what there is, a standard that decrees that American English abstract colour terms have absolute ontological independence' (1992: 188–9). There are several other recorded cases of informants being puzzled, embarrassed or startled by the colour chart (one researcher even refers to her subjects apparently experiencing 'colour shock'), and, since it is the aim of a linguist to study language as it occurs *naturally*, such a reaction should instantly prompt the abandonment of the colour chart experiment.[6] The researcher also needs to investigate the wider cultural context in which colour terms are used, as did Saunders in Canada.

Saunders' research into the Kwak'wala colour system included investigating the history of Kwakiutl contact with white cultures, their contacts with anthropologists before her visit, and early dictionaries and recorded texts in the language. She also considered aspects of Kwakiutl pre-contact (with Europeans) society which had any relevance to colour, such as their coloured blankets, natural dyes, paints and pigments, place-names using colour terms, and ceremonies involving coloured objects such as red bark. A detailed study like Saunders' on Kwakiutl society and their colour terms is the best way to uncover colour concepts and terminology *as they are used naturally*.[7] She writes: 'To abstract them [colour concepts] from the contexts of the traditions which they inform and which inform them, is to risk a damaging misunderstanding' (1992: 221). Elsewhere, Saunders makes the point that Third and Fourth World peoples can 'allow us a glimpse of what is denied when we use a Munsell colour chart'; in other words, studying their colour terms in context can reveal nuances of meaning which the use of colour chips would have obliterated (1999: 244).

The case against colour charts and samples in fieldwork impinges on historical research in two ways. Firstly, it warns the historical semanticist who considers modern comparative evidence that, depending on the researcher's methodology, such evidence may well represent a 'tidied up' version of a language's colour system. Secondly, where a modern-language study *has* taken the cultural context into consideration, the historical researcher is provided with valuable insights into the effects of certain socio-economic developments on colour concepts and vocabulary. Such developments, for example the arrival of new textile imports or the introduction of a new dyeing process, may also be discernible in a historical society.

Although Saunders and van Brakel are perfectly correct to say that colour is not limited to hue, saturation and 'brightness', the use of these and other features in historical research is not linked to a chart, but serves rather as a check-list to remind the researcher whose own language is hue-dominated that other features must also be sought (Chapter 1). Although historical researchers cannot impose their own biases on dead authors, there is a danger that they will overlook non-hue evidence.

It was mentioned above that Saunders and van Brakel (1997: 173–5) have also argued that there is no incontrovertible evidence for four universally perceived elemental hues (red, green, blue and yellow).[8] They argue that cross-cultural research would have confirmed their universality, were it to be true, but this has not happened. Instead, they point out that there are languages without terms for blue, or that split blue into pale and dark regions, or that do not distinguish between yellow and green.[9] They ask why, when such categories exist, do we consider that the innate elemental hues are those which conveniently coincide with the observed foci of English-speakers' categories. They conclude: 'before deciding there is *scientific* evidence for four unique hues . . . it is necessary to be sure one is not simply fitting one's data to modern English' (page 175; authors' italics).[10]

Saunders and van Brakel's concerns are considered unjustified by Broackes who suggests that hues such as lime and orange, for example, are unlikely to be considered elemental hues by anyone, regardless of their culture or language. Among other arguments, he points out that we readily see a red element in orange, but do not see an orange element in red, and this viewpoint is widespread (1997: 183). He concludes: 'The fears of Saunders & van Brakel will be justified if people prove to do as well with lime, purple, orange and teal as we do with red, yellow, green, and blue. But we should not underestimate the fact that such an outcome at the moment seems almost unimaginable' (page 184). In addition, it seems that the four elemental hues hypothesis is currently the best we have. What is probably the majority scientific view is summarized by Abramov and Gordon writing in response to Saunders and van Brakel (1997): 'We accept the four canonical fuzzy sets of red, yellow, green and blue' as a 'viable framework until something better replaces it' (Abramov and Gordon 1997: 180).

The third hypothesis about colour which is questioned by Saunders and van Brakel is the opponent process theory (Section 6.5). The story, in non-scientific terms, can be related as follows. The eye focuses an image onto the retina, a layer at the back of the eye which contains several types of photoreceptor cells with differing sensitivities to the various wavelengths of light. In humans, colour vision is normally trichromatic, and this is usually interpreted as resulting from the presence of three different types of receptors, probably cone cells (Abramov 1997: 90–5). From the receptors, and by mechanisms which are not fully understood, signals are sent to the brain for processing into a visual experience. Ewald Hering's opponent process theory was developed to try to explain certain visual phenomena, for example that although we can see reddish yellows and greenish blues, we do not see reddish greens or yellowish blues. Hering suggested that this phenomenon indicates the presence of three opponent channels: red versus green, yellow versus blue, and black versus white. Activation of one part of the opponent pair inhibits the other part, thus explaining why, for example, we cannot see red and green mixed (Saunders and van Brakel 1997: 170–3).

While the opponent process theory accounts for some observed phenomena, it does not account for others, and Saunders and van Brakel are not alone in questioning the three-channel hypothesis (see, for example, Jameson and D'Andrade 1997). Once again, the situation seems to be that this is the best we have, pending further research. Byrne and Hilbert provide a list of psychophysical phenomena which are explained by the opponent process theory, and conclude 'That is why it is reasonable to believe that it [the theory] is at least approximately correct' (1997: 185).

One of Saunders and van Brakel's concerns seems to be that some researchers assume all is resolved in vision science. They warn that 'the cautions and hesitancies of the neurophysiologist are frequently lost when adjacent disciplines adopt their findings' (1997: 173). It is certainly worthwhile to keep this warning in mind. Saunders and van Brakel's fourth major contention, namely, that colour is not universally recognized as an autonomous and abstract phenomenon, is also strongly argued by Wierzbicka, and will be discussed in Section 7.3. In effect, then, Saunders and van Brakel are correct that there is no proof of the four elemental hues or the opponent process theory, and, as a result, some conclusions in linguistic and anthropological colour studies are expressed too dogmatically. These matters, however, cannot be resolved until the neurophysiology of vision is better understood.

7.3   Natural Semantic Metalanguage

Anna Wierzbicka, a Polish-born linguist working in the Australian National University, argues that experimental methods such as the use of Munsell chips and hypotheses such as the evolutionary sequence are anglocentric. In other words, the English language and assumptions made by English speakers dominate anthropological linguistic colour studies, and result in the squeezing and squashing of colour concepts in other languages into an English-language mould. Wierzbicka writes: 'the whole Berlin and Kay . . . paradigm is based on the assumption that all languages can be legitimately described and compared in terms of such English words [the names of the basic categories in the evolutionary sequence]' (2006: 2). Wierzbicka, along with other researchers such as Saunders and van Brakel (Section 7.2), considers the UE model to suffer from anglocentrism and, therefore, elitism.[11] Are these reasonable criticisms?

At its most extreme, the accusation of elitism depicts the Berlin and Kay school as suggesting that the general state of intellectual and cultural development of a society can be assessed by its position on the evolutionary sequence, and that, as in the nineteenth-century tradition, those with few basic colour categories can be considered primitive. This reaction to the sequence seems to be triggered by a particular interpretation of the word *evolutionary*. This word has several senses, and one is the *biological* sense, especially with reference to the known development of modern humans from ape-like ancestors (*OED*, sense 8a). This has led some critics of the sequence to believe that it depicts steady and inexorable progress from a primitive state towards the heights of intellectual and technological achievement as exhibited by Western societies. Personally, I have always interpreted *evolutionary* in this context as 'A process of gradual change occurring in a system, institution, subject, artefact, product, etc . . . a gradual and natural development as opposed to a sudden or instigated change' (*OED*, sense 7a). In other words, the sequence can simply be understood as indicating that the acquisition of basic colour categories, where it happens at all, takes place gradually over time. There is no need for a value judgement to be made of any stage in the sequence, since a Stage I language is no less capable of serving the needs of its community than is a Stage VII language.

Critics of the sequence's 'elitism' have also pointed to certain statements which suggest that a correlation exists between the number of a society's basic colour categories and 'cultural complexity (and/or level of technological development)' (Berlin and Kay 1969: 16–17). Some readers have found such statements offensive but they often prove to be true. A society which lives in a predominantly natural environment, and manufactures artefacts from natural materials, has much less need to develop several abstract colour terms than a society which manufactures large quantities of items, including ranges of colour products like paints and dyes, and many items for which colour may be the only distinguishing feature, as with cars or clothes.[12] This latter society is said to be complex but it is not said to be superior. The situation is that societies which have to classify a wide variety of artefacts find colour-coding an indispensable tool, and this naturally encourages an abstract concept of colour categorization.[13]

Turning to the accusation of anglocentrism, as explained at the beginning of this section, there seems to be greater justification for this criticism. The problems of using the Munsell chart and chips as if they were universally familiar have been discussed in Section 7.2. The other aspect of the anglocentric accusation involves the nature and names of the basic colour categories. They are named with English words or, in the later versions of the evolutionary sequence, with codes such as 'W/R/Y' which use the initial letters of English words. Critics of this terminology suggest that it prejudices the full understanding of non-English categories by causing English categories to be always present in the mind of the researcher, thus excluding from consideration many potentially significant aspects of colour which are alien to the English colour system. Wierzbicka has worked tirelessly to develop an unbiased method of conveying the semantics of any language.

Wierzbicka and colleagues such as Cliff Goddard have worked for many years to gather a list of 'semantic primitives' (or 'primes' or 'atoms'), and they have now accumulated over sixty of them.[14] Two important things are claimed for these semantic atoms: firstly, that they are concepts which cannot be analysed into any smaller constituent parts; and, secondly, that they are universal. The English-language list of these elementary units of meaning includes, for example, I, YOU, ONE, TWO, GOOD, BAD, SAY, DO and so on.[15] It seems clear that, if a concept is expressed only by means of semantic atoms, it is unlikely to be moulded or distorted by any particular cultural bias, since these concepts are simple and common to all humans. Semantic atoms form the basis of Wierzbicka's *Natural Semantic Metalanguage* (NSM) which, among other uses, enables bias-free cross-linguistic comparisons (see, for example, Wierzbicka 2006). Concepts are conveyed by 'explications' which may consist of a few words or of several related clauses, and which express the concepts, in the simplest examples, in terms of atoms along with certain combinatory features. Explications are, in other words, reductive paraphrases which break down a meaning into elements which can be reduced no further. As an example, the explication for English *to lie* 'to make an intentionally false statement' is as follows:

someone X lied to someone Y:
someone X said something to someone else Y
this someone knew that it was not true
this someone said it because he/she wanted this other someone to think
    that it was true
people think that it is bad if someone does something like this.[16]

If this explication were expressed in, for example, the Korean language, using Korean terms for the semantic atoms expressed here in English, the meaning of the English verb *to lie* would be accurately conveyed to a Korean speaker. The reader may ask why a Korean speaker could not simply look in an English–Korean dictionary. This would simply provide a *translation* and it is well known that word-for-word translation is a blunt instrument which often provides only a rough equivalent in the target language. Wierzbicka is suggesting an *analysis* and the presentation of the results in universally recognized concepts. What may seem to us to be straightforward and unproblematic translations are often surprisingly nuanced by culture. For example, Uwe Durst presented examples of words from six languages which are all likely to be defined as 'angry' or 'anger' in dictionaries (2004: 184–7). The NSM explications for these words show that they all differ in subtle ways which represent their societies' particular understanding of anger and its consequences. To give two examples, English *angry/anger* involves a negative judgement of someone's action, and a desire to do something to him or her as a result, whereas Biblical Hebrew *qcp* involves no desire to do anything to the offender because of the belief that, without human intervention, s/he will suffer negative consequences. Such subtle differences emerge through the use of close analysis and explications but they are 'standardized' in an anglocentric manner when translated simply into English *angry/anger*.

In NSM, it can be shown that so-called 'semantic molecules' can be constructed from the universal semantic atoms, and molecules may or may not be universals themselves (Goddard 2007). Molecules can be reduced to smaller concepts (which is not true of atoms), they can function as units in explications of other concepts, and they can also contribute to even more complex meanings. This process of elaboration may continue for several levels or layers, and is referred to as *semantic nesting*. For example, the explication of CATS involves the semantic molecule ANIMALS ('animals$_{[M]}$ of one kind'), body-part molecules like EARS ('they have pointed$_{[M]}$ ears$_{[M]}$') and shape descriptors such as LONG ('they have a long$_{[M]}$ tail$_{[M]}$') (pages 10–11). For a complete semantic analysis of CATS, each semantic molecule would have to be broken down into semantic atoms. (Molecules are indicated in an explication by a subscript $_{[M]}$.)

How does NSM deal with colour concepts? Before progressing, it is important to understand that the word *colour* in an English-language NSM explication denotes only hue, thus excluding concepts restricted to vividness, dullness, paleness, darkness, aspects of brightness, and other visible surface effects such as texture which all affect the visible experience of colour (Chapter 1; Wierzbicka 2006, Note 2). These non-hue aspects of a colour impression, when required, are conveyed separately in NSM. Rather than retaining NSM *colour* unchanged so that it conflicts with the use of *colour* in this book, or substituting 'hue' for 'colour', which does not represent NSM usage, I will express this meaning in explications and some other contexts as COLOUR [HUE].

In her discussions of hue, Wierzbicka (2008) starts with the undeniable fact that many languages have no word equivalent to the English word *colour* (meaning 'hue') and, therefore, there can be no such thing as 'colour [hue] universals'. Hickerson (1975: 326) reports, for example, that the Zuni language of New Mexico, USA, has no generic word for 'hue', the nearest concept being denoted by the word *jeli* 'paint, clay'. John Lucy understandably wonders how Lenneberg and Roberts worded their questions about colour to Zuni informants (Lucy 1992: 154; Lenneberg and Roberts 1956: 21–32).[17] Wierzbicka questions how the hue terms of English can be directly compared with those of a language which does not label the concept of hue.

In NSM, COLOUR [HUE] is not a semantic atom, but it emerges in some societies as a semantic molecule built from the foundation of the atom SEE (Wierzbicka 2006: 6), since hue is a visible feature. The molecule COLOUR [HUE]$_{[M]}$ underlies the meaning, for example, of English *red*. The explication for *red*, involving three semantic molecules, is given as:

X is *red* =
a. people can think about X's colour [hue]$_{[M]}$ like this:
b.   'it is like the colour [hue]$_{[M]}$ of blood$_{[M]}$'
c. at the same time, they can think about it like this:
d.   'sometimes people can see something like this when they see fire$_{[M]}$' (Wierzbicka 2006: 9)

The starting point for this explication of English *red* is the establishment of the prototypes and exemplars of the English red category, and Wierzbicka believes these are BLOOD and FIRE. She explains that this does not imply that blood is always blood-red in English, or that fire is red rather than orange, but that some conceptual link exists between, for example, fire and redness, and this is indicated by expressions such as *red coals*, *red-hot* and *fiery red* (2006: 9–10). In an explication, the use of such prototypes as 'benchmarks' helps to activate the required concept.[18]

Wierzbicka also explains how the use of NSM can avoid the anglocentrism of the WCS classifications. She takes issue, for example, with the WCS definition of *miji-miji* in the Australian language of Martu Wangka. The WCS suggests that some speakers of Martu Wangka use *miji-miji* as an M-WHITE term (W/R/Y) at Stage I (Berlin, Maffi and Merrifield 1997: 37). Wierzbicka explains that Martu Wangka has no word for COLOUR [HUE], and its speakers have no apparent interest in the subject. Like many other languages without a word for this concept, Martu Wangka speakers have, nonetheless, a word for SEE. The significance of *miji-miji* appears to be high visibility, rather than a particular hue or group of hues, and its meaning is said to be not 'significantly different' from that of the Burarra word *-gungaltja* which has been closely studied (2006: 17–18).[19]

The Burarra language has been studied by Jones and Meehan (1978) who describe the range of *-gungaltja* as 'refers to light, brilliant and white colours, and also to highly saturated red'. They report that the 'true' *-gungaltja* colours 'require a touch of brilliance or "animation" as well as a high degree of brightness', and both hue and saturation appear to be of less importance than brightness. Thus, the researchers found that *-gungaltja* was considered appropriate to describe blue and deep orange plastic buckets, bottle-green plastic bags, and glossy, deep green mangrove leaves. Although some of these hues are dark in tone, all the items have shiny surfaces and, in Burarra, shininess predominates over tone and hue. The researchers also describe the use of *-gungaltja* in the context of the sea on a moonlit night when light glints on the water (page 27). English speakers would come close to an understanding of *-gungaltja* by thinking of English words and phrases such as *shining, flashing, glinting, dazzling* and/or *vivid red* (Section 11.4).

Wierzbicka proposes that, in order to understand a term such as *-gungaltja*, we must 'formulate the semantic components that we posit as constituting a given word's meaning in words which would be readily translatable into Burarra itself' (2006: 14). In other words, we must avoid terms like *white, warm colour* [hue] or *colour* [hue] because they have no counterparts in Burarra. The explication for *-gungaltja* is as follows:

X is *-gungaltja* =
a. some things are like this:
b.   when people see a place where these things are they can always see these things
c. the sun[M] is always like this
d. fire[M] is always like this
e. at some times, blood[M] is like this
f. X is like this. (Wierzbicka 2006: 15)

The reader will probably notice two problems immediately. The first is that many NSM explications are lengthy, even with the use of semantic molecules, and this presents practical difficulties, especially when dealing with more than one. It can be impossible for readers to retain in their minds several unfamiliar concepts which are, in addition, expressed in an unfamiliar way. The second problem concerns the difficulty of retrieving the correct meaning from explications. Judging from informal experiments with friends and acquaintances, only the shortest and simplest explications elicit the correct interpretation.[20] This has even been the experience of linguists, for example, Koptjevskaja-Tamm writes: 'In particular, long definitions are not only not immediately comprehensible, but remain cryptic for a long time' (Koptjevskaja-Tamm and Ahlgren 2004: 259).

The question which is important in the context of this book is whether NSM is useful in historical studies. To answer this question, it is necessary to investigate further. In any lexical semantic study, there is a need to gather data, and then analyse them. This is usually followed by the selection of a means of successfully conveying the results to those who are unfamiliar with the word and/or the concept it represents. Wierzbicka and colleagues would devise an NSM explication, aiming to produce a text in directly translatable words which carry no cultural baggage. Other researchers usually aim to devise a definition in words which are appropriate both to the concept involved and to the target readership. It seems to me that NSM explications often sacrifice comprehension for speakers of the target language, in favour of the undoubted value of a culturally neutral analysis of source-language concepts. On the other hand, a non-NSM lexicographer often sacrifices cultural neutrality for quick comprehension.[21] Certain attempts to explain Burarra -*gungundja* and -*gungaltja* illustrate this dilemma.

The NSM explication for Burarra -*gungundja* is as follows:

X is -*gungundja* =
a. some things are like this:
b.   when people see a place where these things are they can always see these things
c. many other things are not like this
d. X is like these other things. (Wierzbicka 2006: 16)

Without having read Wierzbicka's discussion of this word, I suspect a reader would interpret the explication as follows: some things are visible (line b); but many other things are *not* visible (line c); and so X means 'not visible' (line d). In fact, Wierzbicka describes this word as referring to the 'absence of conspicuous visibility (which is implied by -*gungaltja*)' (page 16). So -*gungundja* things *are* visible but not highly visible. Without Wierzbicka's explanation in normal English (that is, not restricted to semantic atoms), I believe a reader would not have fully and accurately comprehended this Burarra concept.

Semantic molecules present a further hindrance to reader comprehension. As an example, the reader may care to consider a line in the explication for Burarra -*gungaltja*: 'at some times, blood$_{[M]}$ is like this' (line e). The molecule BLOOD can itself be analysed into semantic atoms, representing, in this context, the Burarra concept of BLOOD. However, since there is no atom for COLOUR

[HUE], this molecule explication could not even hint that the task of 'blood$_{[M]}$' in the explication of *-gungaltja* is to indicate the vivid red hue which that word sometimes denotes. So the non-Burarra speaker reading the full explication would understand that a visible feature of blood is involved (because of line b: 'people...can...see these things'), but does not know *which* visible feature. Possibilities could include: its liquid appearance; its solid appearance (when a scab); its lack of shininess and so on. In other words, the Burarra concept may have been accurately analysed, but it has been ambiguously communicated.

Turning to non-NSM explanations, conventional dictionary definitions may be easily understood by their target readership but inaccurate in conveying the source-language meaning. Wierzbicka criticizes Kathleen Glasgow's dictionary because she defines *-gungaltja* as 'being white or warm-coloured, clean (as of clothes)'. Wierzbicka protests that Burarra has no concept of WHITE or of WARM COLOUR (2006: 14; Glasgow 1994). From what we now know about this interesting Burarra word, I imagine readers will see that, while dazzling white would, no doubt, be correctly described as *-gungaltja*, so would (I think) an object or entity of *any* colour that shone, glinted, flashed or dazzled. I also think that not *all* warm colours (unless they are a feature of some reflective material) are *-gungaltja*, and that the only non-shiny part of a hue which can be described with this word is vivid red. So, lacking the detailed analysis of *-gungaltja* from a Burarra point of view (which NSM can supply), Glasgow's readers will easily understand her dictionary definition and yet, unknown to them, still not comprehend this Burarra word.

My point about the NSM explication for *-gungundja* and Glasgow's definition of *-gungaltja* is that neither of them works well for *both* source- and target-languages, but I would argue that both types of lexical analysis have a contribution to make to a better conveyance of meaning from one society to another. Perhaps analysis of a word should be carried out in NSM, and a target-language definition constructed with minimal change, except to express it in terms considered normal and unambiguous in the target language. Wierzbicka, however, takes a firm line on dictionary definitions since she writes: 'To try to describe the meaning of Burarra words through English words and phrases which have no equivalents in Burarra would be to impose on the Burarra people English ways of thinking rather than trying to elucidate their own' (2006: 14). It is certainly true that poorly researched dictionary definitions exist but, if any imposition is going on, it is the imposition of a misleading definition on English speakers.

Would any of this help the *historical* semanticist? As I understand it, NSM explications are written on the basis of evidence usually derived from sources such as newspapers, popular songs, novels and corpora, and the result is then checked with a substitutability test. This involves asking native speakers whether the explication and the original word, or one sense of the word, both have exactly the same meaning. In other words, could one be substituted for the other without any semantic loss? (Yoon 2004: 2–3). The historical semanticist has two major problems, neither of which would be helped by NSM. Firstly, the basic historical evidence is usually non-representative of the former spoken language because of the random survival of texts, the bias of surviving texts in favour of the privileged and/or literate classes, and the rarity of evidence for natural language based on speech. This is an unavoidable problem which affects every aspect of historical semantic research, including dictionary definitions. The second problem in historical studies is equally unavoidable, namely, that the researcher has no native speakers with whom to conduct a substitutability test. The question is, therefore, is it sensible to express an incomplete and untestable historical concept in NSM when the whole ethos of this system is to 'get inside the head' of the (non-existent) native speaker? The danger of misrepresenting historical concepts is far higher than with modern concepts, so the precision of NSM would appear to be quite misplaced in the historical context. Researchers into very recent periods of history may find they have sufficient surviving evidence to construct NSM explications, but the crucial native-speaker test of substitutability can, of course, never be applied.[22]

Although I doubt the practical value of NSM as a mainstay of historical semantics, I believe that understanding its principles is of benefit. For example: semantic atoms have a role to play in prehistoric studies (Chapter 11); explications show a way of avoiding the researcher's cultural bias where sufficient historical evidence survives; the obvious importance of exemplars and prototypes in colour explications is salutary; and the dictionary problems discussed above emphasize the need for careful semantic analysis prior to reaching a semantic conclusion.

7.4   Vantage theory

Between 1978 and 1981, Robert MacLaury directed extensive research into the colour terms of 116 languages in Mesoamerica, principally in Mexico and Guatemala, and this huge project is known as the 'Mesoamerican Colour Survey' (MCS). As his research progressed, MacLaury became dissatisfied with the fact that contemporary models of categorization, such as Rosch Heider's prototype theory or Berlin and Kay's evolutionary sequence, did not account for observed diachronic changes and variations in language. He asks why, for example, the cool category divides into separate basic green and blue categories in some languages even though the colours of grass and sky are just the same before and after the division (1997a: 7).

MacLaury's dissatisfaction with the ability of then-existing models to cope with all aspects of the evidence he was finding in his field research led him towards what was then the relatively new discipline of cognitive linguistics

(Evans and Green 2006). Linguists developing this approach, including George Lakoff and Ronald Langacker, had abandoned the prevalent notion that language was an autonomous structure in which meaning results from the function of linguistic units within an interacting system of aspects such as phonology, morphology and syntax. This model reduces semantics to a dependency role. Taking a different view, *cognitive* linguists believe that meaning is of crucial importance since the purpose of language is to communicate concepts within a speech community, and such concepts are developed as a result of the needs and requirements of both individuals and their social groups. Categorization is vital in this process, since it represents the mind's attempts to shape and classify the massive range of entities, artefacts and phenomena which is perceived by the speaker in his or her environment. In other words, the minds of individuals and (collectively) of their societies develop cognitive categories which reduce perceptual overload to a manageable and memorable classification while also excluding unimportant and background 'noise'. The categories are labelled by language but they can, of course, vary from speaker to speaker (to a greater or lesser extent) and, over time, they can shift, change and add or subtract semantic features.

MacLaury was clearly drawn towards cognitive semantics with its interests in categorization, analogy, viewpoint and metaphor so, with acknowledgement to those theorists whose work nourished his own, and motivated by his research in Mesoamerica, he proceeded to design a model for the dynamics of colour categorization (1997a: 7–8). That model is known as 'vantage theory' (VT).[23]

The basic data of the Mesoamerican Colour Survey was collected through interviews with native speakers in their own environments. It is interesting that MacLaury's original plan was to assemble data from various written and printed sources, supplemented by investigations on his behalf made by missionaries and academics in Mesoamerica. His own field studies were intended simply to illuminate gaps in the evidence, but he discovered that 'the published sources had given no clue of the actual situation' (1997a: xx). This is both a salutary warning to linguistic anthropologists and a depressing message to *historical* linguists who are forced to rely on textual evidence alone.

In his interviews with native speakers, MacLaury used ten achromatic Munsell chips and 320 saturated hue chips (1976 issue) ranging in tone from dark to pale. This was the same set of chips as used by the WCS (1997a: 11), and a Munsell array (colour chart) of the same colours was also used.[24] Informants were asked to complete three tasks, named here in brackets. Firstly, they named all 330 chips, presented in random order ('Naming'), and this provided the researchers with 'head lexemes', that is, potential BCTs. Secondly, informants were shown the Munsell array and asked to point out the 'best example' of each head lexeme ('Focus selection'), thus providing category foci. Thirdly, for each head lexeme, informants were asked to place a grain of rice on every

Table 7.1 *Vantage theory model of the English red category*

Levels	Fixed coordinates	Mobile coordinates	Entailments
1	R	S	focus, range
2	S	D	breadth, margin

colour square of the array which could be named with that lexeme ('Mapping') (page 77). The result of this exercise was a collection of individual responses to the three exercises in each language studied. Making use of all three tasks, each response was then plotted on to a representation of the Munsell array to produce naming ranges and a focus or foci for each head lexeme. This provided the raw data for MacLaury's development of vantage theory.[25]

Vantage theory is a model of the way in which a person constructs a mental category, then uses, recalls and changes it over time. A category in VT must have at least one fixed coordinate, two mobile coordinates and at least one arrangement of the coordinates (MacLaury 2002: 505). A particular arrangement of the coordinates is a vantage, that is, a personal view of the category, which may differ from another person's view of the same category. The process is analogous to the way in which a person conceives of his or her position in space and time: s/he mentally plots or fixes that position in space by means of the fixed coordinates up–down, left–right and front–back. Position in time is assessed as a mobile coordinate on the dimension of motion.

In a similar way, a person may construct any other cognitive category by establishing a fixed mental landmark which is distinguishable from other landmarks, and then developing a category based on it by attending to the mobile coordinates of 'similarity' and 'difference' (or 'distinctiveness'). The mobility in the similarity and difference coordinates arises from the fact that the individual can mentally move to any position on a vast continuum ranging from maximum similarity (unity or identity) to maximum difference (total disparity) in relation to the fixed landmark. Similarity and difference have, of course, a reciprocal relationship; where similarity is strong, difference must be weak, and vice versa. The process of constructing and using categories is not conscious, but is a rapid and automatic process forming the foundation of thought and speech (MacLaury 2002: 494–5).

MacLaury provides a VT model of the English red category as a very simple example. It has the minimum of three coordinates: the fixed coordinate (landmark) is here the image of 'the purest red envisionable' (R) and it appears with the mobile coordinates of similarity (S) and difference (D) (2002: 495–6). The model is presented in Table 7.1. Starting on Level 1, R (red) is referred to as the 'primary fixed coordinate' and it provides the landmark concept of pure redness, the focus of the red category.[26] S (similarity) appears alongside R, indicating that shades of red which are not *pure* red can, nevertheless, be considered members of the red category. Essentially, S extends the range of the category outwards from the focus R.

In VT, it is believed that the human mind can only deal with one 'level of concentration' at a time.[27] The next phase of the category construction is, therefore, separately conceptualized on Level 2, involving a process known as 'zooming in'. This means that S is now considered to be established information (the breadth of the category), thus becoming the new fixed coordinate. In this position on Level 2, S is paired with a new mobile coordinate D (difference), and this has the effect of curtailing the extension of the category. In other words, after S on Level 1 has extended the category by including various non-pure reds, D on Level 2 denotes the margin of the category, beyond which the various shades of colour are not reds at all but members of a different colour category. The English red category can, therefore, be said to be constituted as R SS D (MacLaury 2002: 495–7).

The red category in Hungarian offers VT more of a challenge. There are two salient Hungarian terms for this category: *piros* which is a general term for red, and *vörös* which is used in sinister or passionate contexts. *Vörös* has a narrower range than *piros* and has a darker focus but it has more metaphorical and figurative uses. Both words, therefore, are salient (MacLaury 2002: 499). MacLaury models the Hungarian red category as having two vantages (viewpoints): a dominant vantage represented by *piros*, and a recessive vantage represented by *vörös*. The dominant vantage is constructed as R SS D, just like the English (entire) red category discussed above, but the recessive vantage in Hungarian RED is inverted and can be represented as R DD S. This means that the emphasis on similarity in the *piros* vantage results in a wider-ranging category than that for *vörös* (more shades of red are considered to have a similarity to the *piros* focus than to the *vörös* focus). The emphasis on difference in the *vörös* vantage indicates a narrower range (more shades of red are considered to be different from the *vörös* focus) (pages 499–502).[28] The VT model for the Hungarian red category appears in Table 7.2.

MacLaury also shows how values of category membership can be demonstrated by representing the coordinates on a curve. Taking the simple example of the English red category (R SS D), this can be depicted as a curve in which R (the focus) is at the top, D (the margin) is at the bottom, and S (Level 1) and S (Level 2) are on the slope of the curve between them. A vertical axis showing values of category membership runs from maximal membership (1.0) at the top to no membership (0.0) at the bottom, while S (Level 2) occurs at the mid-point (0.5). The peak and shoulder of the curve are established by R S on Level 1 while S on Level 2 adds breadth to the curve as it declines towards

Table 7.2 *Vantage theory model of the Hungarian red category*

Piros				Vörös		
Dominant vantage				Recessive vantage		
E	*F*	*M*	*L*	*F*	*M*	*E*
focus, range broad	R	S	1	R	D	focus, margin narrow, dark
literal, margin	S	D	2	D	S	figurative, range

E = Entailment, F = Fixed coordinate, M = Mobile coordinate, L = Level

D (2002: 497).[29] The membership value of any colour can be shown on the model by placing the colour (for example, crimson) between the fixed and mobile coordinates on any appropriate level of the VT model. The 'dynamic tension' between S and D will assign a membership value by means of the individual assessing how similar to or different from the fixed coordinate the colour crimson is (page 506).

There is much more to VT than I have presented here.[30] For example, degrees of strength of S and D can be represented by letter sizes so that a speaker pays more attention to similarity than difference in S D. This technique can be used to indicate category change manifested through the mobility of the S and D coordinates. For example, a broad category (SS D) may become narrower (SS D) (MacLaury 2002: 504–5). Diachronic aspects of VT will be discussed in Section 10.3.

The crucial problem with VT for the historical semanticist is that the means of gathering basic data requires the help of native speakers. This has become a common 'complaint' in this book but it is an unfortunate truth that methodologies designed for linguistic-anthropological research into present-day languages are unlikely to be of great use to the historical semanticist. A glance at MacLaury's three procedures for data-collection, that is, naming, focus selection and mapping, shows that each one requires the presence of informants. The historical researcher, however, may be able to substitute different techniques.

The aim of MacLaury's naming process is to collect colour terms from informants and ascertain the 'head lexemes'. In text-restricted studies, the researcher can collect colour terms from texts, select potential BCTs (such as frequently occurring terms), and test them for basicness by applying appropriate BCT criteria. MacLaury's focus selection procedure aims to identify category foci, and historical researchers may find a certain amount of evidence for foci from expressions such as similes and proverbs (Section 3.20), or useful statements comparing a 'most typical' colour with a familiar entity. MacLaury's mapping task would, however, pose particular problems and, unless the researcher has large quantities of data available, it is likely to be pointless. A colour term may have modifiers, such as *pale* or *dull* which would enable the category to be extended from the focus, but by how much? It should be noted, furthermore, that MacLaury produced mappings for each individual interviewee, involving people of both genders and all ages, while any map drawn by a historical researcher could, at best, roughly assess the usage of individual authors. In many cases, the mapping would have to refer to the whole language or, more accurately, to the surviving evidence of that language. In conclusion, VT is, by definition, geared to revealing the vantages or viewpoints of individuals, and historical research often suffers from a severe shortage of this commodity. However, VT may be applicable where considerable data is available, and it also has something to offer in diachronic studies, as will be seen in Section 10.3.

Finally, a little warning about all models may be in order. The researcher is advised to try and prevent a model taking charge of his or her data. Where the researcher believes a model is valuable, and has found it vindicated by his or her earlier projects, there is a distinct danger that s/he will interpret inconclusive data in a manner compatible with the model. In other words, the mere existence of a familiar model can result in a serious loss of objectivity. MacLaury, for example, is only too aware of this problem. When a model is being built, he warns that a somewhat circular argument is hard to avoid: 'Although behavior is said to be predicted from the cognitive model, the model can never be directly observed. Rather, it is inferred from the very behavior that it is assumed to predict' (2002: 498).[31] However, he expects a model to be tested and reassessed whenever 'previously unobserved behavior' is encountered. The equivalent of previously unobserved behaviour for the historical researcher is the discovery of new texts which, for earlier periods, is a relatively rare event, so undue interference from a model should be resisted.

7.5   The Emergence Hypothesis

Throughout most of the history of the evolutionary sequence associated with Berlin, Kay and their colleagues, it has been assumed that every language has a small number of BCTs which together cover every part of the colour space. Even a language with only two BCTs can refer to all colours because, the fewer the basic colour categories used by a particular society, the larger their size. As we have seen, the large early categories (macro-categories) divide over time to produce smaller categories, and this process is known as the Partition Principle (Section 6.7).

In the late 1990s, some researchers challenged the assumption that partition was a universal process, and they suggested that some languages spoken in non-industrialized societies may have a collection of salient colour terms which do *not* cover the entire colour space between them, and do not appear to have emerged from earlier macro-categories.[32] It has been surmised that such situations may pre-date the development of 'true' BCTs, or they may simply represent rare, anomalous variations from the norm.[33] Non-partition systems, which are still somewhat controversial, are considered to represent what is known as the Emergence Hypothesis (EH).[34]

Adherents of the UE model accept the existence of EH languages although the WCS data suggest they are rare. In the published report of that data, the authors point out that there are only ten known or suspected non-partition languages, and this rarity may indicate that such languages represent ancient and almost vanished colour systems (Kay *et al.* 2009: 35–41).[35]

By far the best researched EH (non-partition) language is Yélî Dnye (*dnye* means 'language'), an apparent language isolate spoken on Rossel Island (Yela) in Papua New Guinea. Stephen Levinson has been studying the language and culture of the island for several years, so his work on this society's salient colour terms is an example of the in-depth research into a language's colour vocabulary of which we need many more. Levinson (2000: 16) found that Yélî Dnye colour expressions could be classified into three types. Firstly, there are those which make no reference to colour at all but can be used to impart a colour sense. An example can be found in the two contrasting phrases meaning 'tree unripe leaf' (*yi kuu yââ*) and 'tree desiccating leaf' (*yi chii yââ*) which are used to indicate green and yellow (page 13). Secondly, there are expressions that apparently include colour information, such as the reduplicated form of *mgîdî* 'night', that is, *mgîdîmgîdî*, meaning 'black' or 'dark'. As with other such terms, *mgîdîmgîdî* is not exclusively a colour term, so is not a good candidate for basic status. Thirdly, there are expressions which refer exclusively to colour, so remain BCT candidates, and Levinson considers that the best example is *kpêdêkpêdê* 'black' (*kpêdê* is a tree species) (page 16).

Levinson (2000: 22) concluded that a small number of colour expressions in Yélî Dnye 'are the conventional expressions for a perceptually salient hue'. These expressions are: *kpaapîkpaapî* 'white' (*kpaapî* is a pure white cockatoo); *kpêdêkpêdê* 'black'; *mtyemtye* 'red' and *taataa* 'red' (*mtye* and *taa* are words, in different dialects, for a red parrot described as 'startling crimson'); and the phrase *yi kuu yââ* 'green [and other meanings]'. There was no consensus on the most salient yellow term, and, as regards blue, some informants could offer no expressions at all (page 22).[36] Levinson points out that this represents a cline of conventionalization, ranging from the established (such as the term for white) to the barely recognized (attempts to name blue).

Although Levinson's cline of conventionalization is compatible with the UE model's sequence of BCT acquisition, there appear to be serious differences from other aspects of the UE model. Firstly, the Yélî Dnye equivalent of 'black' should represent a macrocolour category including blue, and probably also green, with variable foci in black, blue or green. Levinson found that the Yélî Dnye black category is *not* a macro-category, and there was consensus among his informants that the category focus is located exclusively in pure black. Secondly, since the focus of the white category was agreed by informants to be located at pure white, this should mean (according to the UE model) that an earlier M-WHITE had split into WHITE and M-RED, the latter including yellow, so that the focus for some speakers would be in red and for others in yellow. The Yélî Dnye red category, however, does not include yellow and, although this means that its focus should be near elemental red, informants placed the focus in locations varying from pale orange (E4 on the Munsell array) to crimson (G1). Thirdly, the foci for all other colour expressions deviated 'surprisingly' from the perceptual landmarks or universal foci (2000: 26).[37] In addition to all these 'anomalies', Levinson found that, on average, about 40 per cent of the colour space remained undescribed or unnamed in Yélî Dnye, that is, between 30 and 60 per cent across the various informants (pages 29, 35).

When Levinson comes to consider how many BCTs exist in Yélî Dnye, the impossibility of fitting this language into the UE model becomes obvious. Although it is easy to suggest that Yélî Dnye may be at Stage II, with BCTs for WHITE, BLACK and RED, the descriptive phrase for GREEN looks better established than terms for RED, so Yélî Dnye could just as well be considered in transition between Stages II and III. However (and Levinson puts this crucial point in italics): '*there are no signs at all of any composite categories* [macro-categories]' (2000: 40; his italics). Levinson concludes that EH may be symptomatic of societies in which colour is not a distinct cognitive or semantic domain, nor does it have a significant functional role in the culture. He had explained earlier in his article that there is no word meaning 'colour' in Yélî Dnye (apart from the English loan-word *kala* used by those younger people who have lived on the mainland), and there is little interest in colourful arts and crafts, except for basketwork of natural colour, black and blue (pages 9–10).[38]

Kay and colleagues have searched the WCS languages for the EH type but they are hampered by the fact that the existence of such a type was not suspected when the WCS data were collected. They isolate four languages, however, which could be interpreted as cases of EH type: Culina, spoken in Peru and Brazil; Mundu, spoken in the Sudan; and two Australian languages, Kuku-Yalanji and Murrinh-Patha (Kay *et al.* 2009: 39–40).[39]

An explanation for EH languages which accommodates them in an expanded UE model was proposed by MacLaury. He suggests a model showing five evolutionary sequences feeding into or exiting from stages of the familiar

Berlin and Kay evolutionary sequence. Sequence 1 consists of the seven stages of the 1975 evolutionary sequence; Sequence 2 is concerned with desaturation; Sequence 3 with 'brightness'; and Sequence 4 with the yellow+green category. It is, however, MacLaury's Sequences 5 and 6 which concern the EH languages (2001: II.1232, Figure 90.3).[40] Both sequences are affected by *retraction*, that is, the reduction of the early macro-categories (M-WHITE, M-BLACK and M-RED) until they are no larger than the appropriate primary colours (WHITE, BLACK and RED), but this reduction does *not* happen by means of colours splitting off from their macro-categories: the macro-categories simply shrink. Later generations will name new categories which are also based on the primary colours but the names are not, at first, BCTs. MacLaury interprets Sequence 6 as pertaining to a period of stabilization for the emerging categories. In the light of this alternative (expanded) model, MacLaury interprets Yélî Dnye as being in the process of stabilizing categories for GREEN, YELLOW and BLUE (in that order) to add them to the older retracted categories of WHITE, BLACK and RED. It should be added that MacLaury gives other examples of languages which he interprets in this way (2001: II.1244).

In the final WCS report (Kay *et al.* 2009), Kay and colleagues present a hypothesis to explain both the mystery of Stages I and II in Trajectories D and E (see Chapter 6, Table 6.6) and the early history of EH languages. They suggest that speakers of EH languages prioritize BLACK, WHITE and RED so heavily that they develop single-colour categories for these colours rather than macro-categories, meanwhile neglecting other areas of the colour space. However, at Stage III, it is suggested that such societies adopt the partition principle (this is referred to as *delayed assertion* of partition). As a result, they develop a category for the so-far unnamed colour areas, resulting in a yellow+grue (Y/G/Bu) macro-category to add to their single-colour categories, thus creating a Stage III$_{Y/G/Bu}$ system. The partition process then takes over in the usual way, reducing the new macro-category in Stages IV and V (pages 38–9).

The researcher is, therefore, currently left with two possible interpretations of the origin and development of non-partition languages. MacLaury envisages the retraction of M-BLACK, M-WHITE and M-RED to BLACK, WHITE and RED, followed by the continuing development, in turn, of further single-hue categories. On the other hand, Kay and colleagues suggest an absence of macro-categories until the development of YELLOW+GRUE at Stage III, followed by its subsequent reduction to single hue categories. These are scenarios which the historical semanticist needs to bear in mind.

7.6   Universalism and relativism

As a closing thought for this chapter, I should like to provide an update on what Kay, Berlin and Merrifield (1991: 13) have called 'two opposing and unyielding dogmas', namely, relativism and universalism.[41] We have seen how relativism reigned supreme in anthropological linguistics until the emergence of the cognitive sciences resulted in a swing to universalism, especially from 1969 onwards (Sections 2.6–2.7). Relativism, however, was never totally eclipsed and, from the late 1980s, many researchers decided that, while certain aspects of colour looked universal, others differed from society to society. The more extreme forms of the two theories were not compatible but it became increasingly clear that the milder forms were. An early milestone in this realization was a Wenner-Gren Foundation international symposium entitled 'Rethinking Linguistic Relativity' which was held in Jamaica in 1991 as a forum to consider old ideas in the light of then-recent research in developmental psychology and other discipines. In the published report on the conference, it is clear that some scholars on both sides of the universalist–relativist divide were still taking quite a hard line but others took the view that elements from both stances were often compatible (Gumperz and Levinson 1991).[42]

The renewed interest in relativism has been called the 'Whorfian renaissance' but this should not be interpreted as another full swing of the pendulum, this time away from universalism, but rather as a move to bring relativism back into the discussion. Over the years, John Lucy (for example, 1992) in particular has argued for a correct reading of Whorf, divorced from the radical relativism which has become linked to his name, and for a sober reconsideration of his views.

Many scholars are now content to accept that neither universalist nor relativist tenets should be rejected in their entirety. Dedrick (1998a: 200), for example, expresses disapproval of what he calls 'the zero-sum game; only one 'side' can win', while Bornstein (2007: 8–21) devotes several pages to 'Universalist–Relativist Reconciliations'. He refers, for example, to experiments with pre-language infants that show they can already perceptually categorize hues, obviously uninfluenced by language (page 10) but, nonetheless, he observes that individual traditions 'can overlay and modulate this universalist foundation' since perceptual categories can be influenced by social forces, such as the number of categories encoded by a particular society (page 21). In other words, 'nature proposes and nurture disposes' (Kay and Regier 2006: 53).

Kay and Regier published an article in 2006 in which they considered the replies to two questions:
1. Is colour naming across languages largely a matter of arbitrary linguistic convention?
2. Do cross-language differences in colour naming cause corresponding differences in colour cognition?
They explain that, traditionally, a relativist answers 'yes' to both questions whereas a universalist answers 'no' to both. However, they also explain

that recent studies had complicated this straightforward situation (2006: 52).

A rethink began with the publication of an article by Roberson, Davies and Davidoff (2000) on the Berinmo language of Papua New Guinea. Crucial to the universalist stance for some decades had been the experimental work of Rosch Heider which had indicated that, regardless of the language spoken, people remembered focal colours better than other shades (for example, Rosch Heider 1972b). This, of course, suggested that focal colours were universals in both language and memory. Roberson and colleagues, however, failed to replicate Rosch Heider's results in experiments with English and Berinmo. Although their findings could offer no support to the theory that categories develop around universal foci, they did find evidence to suggest that categories develop from linguistically defined category *boundaries* (Roberson, Davies and Davidoff 2000: 395). Kay and Regier admit that, should these claims turn out to be well supported by future evidence, then the relativist position would have triumphed (2006: 52). However, the balance was redressed by Kay and Regier's (2003) own experiments which produced good statistical evidence for universal tendencies in colour naming across several languages. As a result of this research, Kay and Regier conclude that the two questions listed above should be answered with a 'no' for Question 1 and a 'yes' for Question 2, giving a partly universalist, partly relativist, result (2006: 52).

Three years later, following further experimentation and publication, the answers to the two questions have shifted again. In 2009, the current view of Regier and Kay is that Whorf was *partly* correct in his 'yes' answers to both questions. As regards Question 1 (whether colour terms affect colour perception), the answer is now 'yes' but mostly in the right visual field. As regards Question 2 (whether colour categories are determined by linguistic convention), both universal tendencies and local conventions have been detected (2009: 439). Regier and Kay point out that neither of these findings fits well in the old universalist versus relativist debate, and they may hint at new angles on the relations between language and perception (page 445). Perhaps the wisest comment comes from C. L. Hardin who writes: 'The real task is not to take up cudgels on behalf of biology on the one hand or culture on the other, but to trace the contributions of each and tease out the strands that connect them' (Foreword to Kay *et al.* 2009).

The historical semanticist is very much concerned with the shifts and changes in this discussion since, depending on his or her period of research, the amount of evidence available may be severely limited. Under these circumstances, s/he hopes to lean cautiously on what is known of perceptual and evolutionary universals, but this ground has a tendency to shift under the researcher's feet.

8   Historical projects: preliminaries

8.1   What is a 'historical' language?

The reader who has heroically read through the previous chapters of this book will now be familiar with some of the basic principles, methodologies and controversies of colour semantics. It is time to apply that knowledge to *historical* studies. This chapter is principally intended for those who are new to historical semantic research, although some points may be of interest for more experienced researchers.

As used in this book, 'historical' describes a form of language which is no longer spoken as anyone's native tongue. This includes a language such as Latin which is still written and spoken by enthusiasts but is not now (as far as I am aware) taught to infants as their mother tongue. Some would argue that Latin is still a living language because, in certain circles, it is being adapted to modern circumstances and is acquiring vocabulary for very modern concepts,[1] but with no native speakers, as defined above, this is a somewhat synthetic form of life.

Also considered 'historical' are the earlier forms of current, undeniably *living* languages. So, for example, Present-Day English is a living language, but Victorian English is not. The latter contained all manner of vocabulary and expressions which would be strange, comical or even incomprehensible to current speakers of the language, so it too is considered to be historical.[2] But where does one draw the line? Is 1950s English, for example, with its now equally obscure words and expressions also to be considered historical?[3] The individual researcher must decide where the boundary lies between historical and present-day forms of the language s/he is studying, since some languages are conservative and others are constantly innovative, but one possibility would be to classify as non-historical the language of all living native speakers which, as a rule of thumb, would create a boundary between dead and living languages at about one century before the present.

My definition of a historical language allows the inclusion of a great many languages under the historical umbrella. Some were spoken in powerful empires while others barely clung to life among small, marginal communities. Some languages produced multiple descendants while others totally disappeared, leaving no progeny. Each one is fascinating for what it can tell us about its people and their culture and, in many cases, for the beautiful and/or informative texts which survive. My main concern in this book is, of course, how to retrieve from these textual remains some information about the colour systems, if such existed, of past societies.[4]

8.2   A major problem

At the risk of boring the reader, I must reiterate a vital point before proceeding. The nature of historical semantic research is very different from that of modern-language semantics. It is not simply a difference in the quantity of the evidence, but also in its quality and bias. Anthropological linguists can gather data by means of interviews, questionnaires and audio recordings, they can observe vocabulary being used in its natural linguistic and cultural contexts, and they can appeal to native speakers when problems require elucidation. The anthropologist can make sure the data are representative of various groups of native speakers, by gender, age, occupation and status, or s/he can conduct a specialized study on one or more of these groups. If circumstances allow, s/he can learn to speak the language s/he is studying and gain all manner of insights into its everyday usage.

The *historical* semanticist would dearly love to proceed in the same manner but, of course, lacks the vital ingredient, namely, living native speakers. This situation results, not simply in less evidence than exists for a modern language, but also in less *representative* evidence since it has been selected by the chance survival of records rather than by project design. In addition, the evidence will often be biased towards a particular class or occupation, usually those who are literate and, therefore, well-educated for their time. Only for very recent periods of history will the historical researcher benefit from large numbers of varied texts, and from audio and/or video recordings of speech. As a result of this situation, the historical semanticist is usually forced to express his or her conclusions in broader, more general terms than s/he would like, pending that longed-for discovery of hidden hoards of previously unknown manuscripts.

8.3   The scope of the study

This section will be concerned with the types of research project which the colour semanticist may undertake. S/he may design a project to answer specific questions, or s/he may simply wish to know more about a particular colour system at a particular date or over a specific period of time. Projects may be large or small but researchers should be aware that the smallest, most specific projects are the most likely to produce unrepresentative and, perhaps, distorted results. Let us begin with the largest types of investigation and move towards the smallest. Leaving aside research that would take several lifetimes, such as the study of all extant historical texts in every language, the most ambitious and extensive type of study is likely to be the investigation of the full colour semantic system of a language family or a single language from its first surviving records to approximately one hundred years ago (Section 8.1). This may sound a daunting task, but it depends on the language or languages selected. If that language is, for example, a variety of Chinese then the researcher will indeed be embarking upon a massive task, since the first substantial records in Old Chinese date from the Shang Dynasty of (arguably) 1600 to 1046 BC. Alternatively, the researcher may have at his or her disposal only a few centuries of written records as, for example, in the case of Albanian for which the earliest surviving text dates to the late fifteenth century AD.

Bearing in mind that the larger the textual sample, the better the quality of the evidence is likely to be, the researcher is advised to work with as much data as is practical or possible within his or her time limits. Where a computer-searchable database of texts has been created for a particular language, the researcher can obviously manage a great deal more data than if s/he had to retrieve the information by reading. If, however, the complete historical records of a language are too extensive to manage efficiently, the investigator is likely to focus on a particular period of time. The period chosen will depend on the language and on the history of its speakers. Linguists may have already divided the history of a language into phases, in each one of which distinctive structural or lexical developments have been noted. Thus English evolved from Old English (spoken from about the mid fifth century to about 1100) to Middle English (spoken from about 1100 to about 1500) to Modern English. The dates are, of course, to be taken only as a rough indication, since languages do not change overnight. For those languages in which developmental changes are evident, a colour semantic study can be restricted to one phase. As in the case of English, however, the tendency is for the amount of surviving textual evidence to increase rapidly as the centuries pass, so that the modern phases of languages usually represent extremely data-rich periods. This situation may persuade the researcher whose main interest is recent history to reduce his or her period of interest still further, by individual centuries, or, depending on the history of the society or societies concerned, to any period which appears to be linguistically or culturally distinct, such as a period of unusual creativity, or of crisis, or of geographical expansion.

The researcher may, alternatively, decide to concentrate on a particular aspect of colour semantics. It may be important to know the colour system of a single dialect of the language concerned, and/or of a particular region. It is also possible to study the expression of colour in a single type of text or literary genre, such as newspapers, novels or historical chronicles. Then again, the researcher's interest may settle on the colour vocabulary of certain occupations, such as dyers, painters or weavers, or s/he may be curious about the colour usage of other groups such as women, children or the elderly. It is also of interest to investigate the colour terms used by a particular writer throughout his or her working life, or a group of writers. It may even be useful to analyse colour in a particular text or compilation, provided it is sufficiently lengthy to offer significant amounts of evidence.

It is obvious that the type and size of a potentially useful project will depend on the amount of material available for that project, and the questions to which the researcher wishes to find answers. These factors may cause the approaches mentioned in the above paragraph to be combined so that, for example, a region may be combined with a century, or a social group with a genre, or a period with an occupation. It should be noted that several of these projects need to develop into comparative studies to provide better quality information (Section 12.2). For example, it would be interesting to research the colour vocabulary of the French writer, Voltaire, but the results would mean so much more if compared with those from a broader sample of French colour terms. It would then be possible to answer a wider range of questions. Was Voltaire's colour vocabulary innovative for his time, or was it uninspired? Was it typically Parisian (he was born in Paris in 1694)? Was it influenced by his knowledge of other languages (such as English)? It is often the case that particularly valuable information derives from specific studies only when they are considered in a wider context and/or when their results are compared with those from other specific studies.

The reader may have already realized that a colour semantic study which is too small in scope is likely to yield misleading results. It is well known, for example, that the vocabulary of poetry is often different in nature to that of everyday usage or even to that of prose literature. Poetic vocabulary can be flowery, archaic and even pretentious. I rarely look out of my window and comment on the beauty of my *verdant* grass, but I might well describe it as very green. A researcher into English colour terms used in the poetry of a certain period may conclude that *verdant* was a highly salient term in the language but, without a prose study with which to compare his or her results, the conclusion drawn would probably be incorrect. Similarly, a study of Voltaire's colour usage in his poetry alone may be interesting, but it will be difficult to draw sensible conclusions without knowing whether such usage was typical of his other writings, or of early eighteenth-century French poetry in general. With such comparisons there is an opportunity to know a little more about Voltaire himself, such as whether he tried to be 'different', whether he embraced Classical influences, and whether he targeted a particular audience. If it is sparingly used by an author, colour vocabulary alone may not be able to answer such questions, but where it is used extensively and enthusiastically, it can offer valuable clues which may usefully support or contradict other evidence.

In historical studies, the research plan and methodology is, of course, heavily influenced by the amount of surviving evidence, that is to say, the number of records which can be found in manuscripts, transcriptions, editions, sound recordings and/or digital images. These resources will be found in libraries, archives, private collections, databases and on the internet. For practical purposes, there are three broad categories of textual quantity: firstly, some languages may have left so much material that it is impossible to retrieve a comprehensive list of colour terms: I refer to this category as *data-rich*. Secondly, some languages have left a small enough number of records for the researcher to be able to investigate the entire extant corpus, and I call these languages *data-restricted*. Thirdly, some languages have left no records at all and are only 'known' from linguistic reconstruction: I call these *data-constructed* (Section 10.4). The data-rich category will now be discussed further.

Languages which have left large amounts of textual evidence usually date to more recent times and/or they may have functioned as prestige languages in powerful civilizations. The reader can, no doubt, think of many examples of recent historical languages for which there is still ample evidence, such as nineteenth-century American English, eighteenth-century German and many more. The researcher into such subjects will be overwhelmed with texts ranging across the full gamut of types: creative literature, administrative documents, sacred texts and commentaries, recorded dialogues and interviews, newspapers and magazines, children's literature, ephemera of many types and much more. Similarly, certain languages of the more distant past may be well represented in the historical record because their speakers were politically and militarily powerful for long periods of time, as was the case with Latin. At various times and places in history, some languages became the vehicles of imperial administration, a role which produces large numbers of documents. The Civil Services of Imperial China and British India are famous cases of massive organizations in which written records played a vital role.

A researcher faced with such huge quantities of linguistic evidence must reduce his or her data to manageable proportions. The details of that decision will be dictated by the particular resources available, the form in which they are stored, and what the researcher wishes to learn from his or her material. The prime consideration in making this decision is that the reduced amount of material must remain representative of the total evidence, including examples of the various types of text.[5] This rule applies whether the planned study is concerned with the language as a whole or with one specific aspect of it. In an initially proposed general study of nineteenth-century American English colour terms, for example, the chronological scope might have to be reduced to the earlier or later part of the century or, alternatively, to balanced selections of texts from something like ten-year intervals across that century. If the researcher has a more specialized query about, for example, the use of colour terms in nineteenth-century American *newspapers*, s/he must consider the *types* of newspapers on sale in that period, and include examples from each, perhaps in addition to a reduction in the period under study. Thus, as the scope of the study is reduced, the representative nature of the sample is maintained.[6] It is hardly necessary to add that, where an appropriate computer database exists, the reduction of the scope of the study can be much less severe since a computer can efficiently manipulate huge quantities of data.

There is one more preliminary decision which the researcher has to make, and this will depend on the information s/he hopes to retrieve. A comprehensive search for *all* colour terms will include words and expressions denoting hues, saturation, tone and all forms of brightness (Chapter 1). The vast majority of language-specific colour semantic studies have been restricted to the investigation of hues but the reader has seen from the previous chapters of this book that many languages apportion equal or greater significance to *non-hue* visual features. This suggests that it would be advisable to include within the research plan the equivalents of English words such as *glittering, matt, dull, pale, shiny* and many more. Equally important to retrieve at an early stage are cases of suspected colour terms which include essential non-colour elements (Section 1.7). The reader may remember the non-colour features of colour terms occurring in Hanunóo and Yucatec (Section 4.5), and s/he may wonder how it would be possible to recognize them as *partly* colour words from text-restricted evidence alone. Would a non-native speaker of English, for example, wonder if the phrase *lush grass* involved a colour element? There is no easy answer to this problem, but it is suggested that, at the data retrieval stage (Sections 8.4–8.5), the researcher should include everything which *may* have a colour feature. Later stages of research may clarify the situation but, if not, dubious terms should be listed as such in the final report.

8.4   Vocabulary retrieval

With the intended scope of the study decided (Section 8.3), and a representative balance of texts selected, the researcher next needs to establish his or her basic data, namely, the occurrences of colour terms and their contexts as found in those selected texts. This section is concerned with the retrieval of colour vocabulary, that is, words, phrases and expressions, while Section 8.5 addresses the matter of their contexts. The reader should note from the previous sentence that the modifying elements of phrases and expressions are as important as the principal terms themselves since they alter the colour described. For example, the researcher must record *dirty blue*, not just *blue*, and, in Latin, *sub* (literally 'under') should not be omitted from *subrufus* 'reddish' in order to file it with other occurrences of *rufus* 'red'. Colour terms of all types should be collected, whether adjectives, nouns, verbal forms or any other part of speech. I would also recommend collecting words relating to patterns, such as the equivalents of *striped, spotted, speckled* and so on, at least until their significance in that society's colour system is understood (Wierzbicka 2008: 414–7). In some cultures, such words have colour connections. Morphological variation should also be recorded as it is encountered; for example, *black, blackish* and *blacken* need to be separately logged since they may represent valuable information. Corbett and Morgan (1988: 58), for example, found in their research into Russian colour terms that older terms have a larger number of derivatives and, where the morphology ranking is significantly lower than the frequency ranking in their system of assessment, it indicates a historical disturbance of the colour system.

Returning to practicalities, must the researcher read through page after page of editions and/or manuscripts to find colour vocabulary? The answer to this depends on how much work has already been done on his or her chosen language. If there has been no work done at all, or if the researcher does not trust certain editions and needs to work from the original manuscripts, there is no alternative but to read the texts and record the occurrences of colour terms in a card catalogue or computer database.

The researcher may find, however, that a certain amount of previous study on his or her chosen language has resulted in some helpful reference sources. S/he may discover that someone, probably a teacher, has produced a classified vocabulary list to help his or her pupils in their studies, and such lists may be found as separate publications or as appendices to grammars and dictionaries. With luck, one of these subject lists will be of colour terms but, if the researcher has gleefully discovered such a gem, s/he must not imagine that it is comprehensive. It will probably have been compiled, along with the other subject vocabularies, in order to provide a fairly minimal list of indispensable terms. The serious colour semantic researcher requires a *comprehensive* word-list from the textual sample to be studied.

The researcher may be lucky enough to find that his or her language has a *thesaurus* relating to at least some of the texts to be studied.[7] A thesaurus classifies the individual senses of a language's words and expressions in a subject scheme (a single word may have multiple senses).[8] If the researcher first consults the contents pages of the thesaurus, s/he may well find 'Colour' included in the list, as it is in the *Historical Thesaurus of the Oxford English Dictionary* (*HTOED*, xxix).[9] Such a section will certainly provide the researcher with the bulk of the required vocabulary, and s/he should record all the colour headings and synonyms s/he finds there. It is important to remember, however, that a thesaurus is organized by concepts or ideas, and even the most innocuous word can convey *several* concepts, each one of which will be classified in a

different place in the thesaurus. The 'Colour' section, while providing a valuable list of word- (or phrase-)*forms*, will provide only one word- (or phrase-)
meaning under the 'Colour' heading. It is very likely that almost all the words
listed in the 'Colour' section are *also* listed in at least one other section and, in
several cases, many other sections.

To gain a full appreciation of the functions and possible limitations of a
particular colour term in the language under study, the researcher needs to
consult the thesaurus' index for each of the terms s/he has found in the 'Colour'
section. S/he will find listed there all the additional concepts in which those
colour terms are involved, and they can then be individually checked, and
the concepts added to the researcher's records. In this way, more specialized
uses and meanings will be discovered, and contextual limitations probably
uncovered. To give one example, the researcher may have found English *red*
in the *HTOED* section on 'Colour', but the index will lead him or her to many
other places in the thesaurus to reveal the various roles of this word in English.
S/he will find, for example, one sense of *red* in a 'red' sub-category, numbered
01.02.05.11.04|05, of the adjectival section of the category 'Colour of hair'
(01.02.05.11.04).[10] Along with *red* in this section are listed several synonyms
for this hair-colour, including *auburn*, *Judas-coloured* and *Titian-tinted*. There
are over fifty concepts listed for the simple form *red* in the *HTOED* (quite
apart from phrases such as *in the red*) and they include various parts of speech
denoting highly disparate phenomena such as a type of potato, the stomach,
communism and many more.

If the researcher has chosen a topic which is restricted to a certain chronological period, social group or author, the scrutiny of a thesaurus in his or her
language of study may be just a first step in the data retrieval process. The
HTOED includes the dates of each word; that is, their first and last recorded
appearances in the language, or an indication that they are still in use.[11] This
information makes the *HTOED* a much-appreciated resource for those studying
a particular period but, for other types of research, such as one restricted to
poetry, the researcher will still have to check the texts. Nonetheless, s/he has
acquired what may be a comprehensive list of colour terms in the language
being investigated, and this can be used as a search-tool in any alphabetically
organized reference work which may be appropriate to the research topic. Such
a list is invaluable when we consider the minuscule likelihood of even a native
speaker thinking unaided of a term such as *Titian-tinted*.

In an ideal world, the researcher at this point would have a comprehensive
list of the colour terms in the language, and from the period which s/he is
investigating, and s/he could then turn to finding which of them occur in the
selected texts. For the researcher who has not found a printed or computerized
classified resource at all, or has found a resource which is unlikely to be
comprehensive, it is time to turn to *alphabetical* sources. In the case of a

smaller project, such as the works of a single author, the researcher may find a glossary of the author's principal vocabulary included in the standard edition, but a larger list is still necessary for the purposes of comparison. The researcher is most likely to seek out a good general dictionary, and to work through this compilation to produce a list of every likely candidate for his or her study.[12] It is important to choose a dictionary which is considered to be scholarly and well researched, and equally important to avoid the temptation of selecting the smallest possible dictionary with the largest print! It cannot be denied that only a minority of semanticists find manual data-retrieval exciting but the thoroughness of this work is crucial to the project.

8.5   Context retrieval

Having acquired a comprehensive list of colour vocabulary for the language and period being investigated, the researcher can now ascertain which terms occur in the texts to be investigated. S/he needs to seek out each occurrence of every colour term in the texts, along with their specific and broader contexts. In some older colour semantic studies, context was ignored, or was the subject of only minimal concern, and yet it is of the greatest importance. This is perhaps the point to consider the purpose of a colour semantic study. The researcher may be keen to explore literary texts and gain a 'colour sense' of individual poems and novels: are they bright and cheery, dark and dismal or pale with splashes of vivid hues? This sort of discussion is fascinating, and has the potential to reveal new insights into literary works (see Section 12.2), but the degree of speculation involved will be unnecessarily large if the semantic 'groundwork' has not been done.

Unless the researcher understands the most likely meaning of the colour terms in his or her texts, the way in which they were used at the period concerned, the cultural implications of certain expressions, and much more, his or her conclusions will be of limited value. It is advisable, therefore, to gather the data thoroughly, to consider the contexts both in detail and in broad scope, and to assess for oneself the meaning and role of each colour term within the scope of the research project. In many cases, this means ignoring dictionary definitions. This may seem perverse when it appears that someone has already done the work, but a general dictionary will not address the role of words within the specifically defined parameters of a research topic, while the particular problems of colour semantics may not have been considered.

Armed with a list of the colour terms occurring in the texts to be studied, the researcher now turns to the immediate and general contexts of each occurrence of each term. The immediate context involves, firstly, the referent of the colour term, and, secondly, any information in the same phrase or sentence which impinges on the colour term's meaning. The referent is here interpreted as the entity or phenomenon which has the literal or metaphorical colour conveyed by the colour term. In the sentence *The park was bright with beds of yellow tulips*, the referent of the colour word *yellow* is TULIPS, but the researcher will also be interested in the fact that the writer has applied the word *bright* to the overall effect of large numbers of these flowers. If the reader imagines this sentence in some historical language in which the equivalent of *yellow* is poorly understood, s/he will realize that the referent does not provide a great deal of help in clarifying the meaning of the *yellow* word, since tulips occur in a wide range of colours.[13] However, the nearby presence of *bright* suggests that dark-coloured tulips can be eliminated. At this stage, the researcher is only collecting information. It will be easier to interpret, as well as more informative, when all the immediate contexts of the *yellow* word can be reviewed together.

It is sometimes possible to gain valuable information from the way in which a colour statement is expressed. Cruse, for example, provides the following sentences:

1. It's a dog, but it's brown.
2. It's a dog, but it isn't brown.
3. It's a dog and it's brown (1986: 17).

Where the historical semanticist can ascertain the predominant colour of dogs in the historical society s/he is researching, the structure of any of these sentences will help to elucidate the meaning of *brown*. Sentence 1 implies that *brown* does not represent the typical dog-colour of this particular period and place, while Sentence 2 implies that *brown* does indeed represent the typical dog-colour. Sentence 3 implies that there is no typical dog-colour in this society but this particular dog's colour causes no surprise.

As regards the broader, more general context of the colour terms, this involves reading more of the texts in which they occur. It may involve no more than a paragraph but the ideal would be to know much more of the text so as not to miss any clues. The colour denoted by a particular term is often greatly affected by a piece of information which has been supplied for the whole context of the event, story or phenomenon. The reader has only to think of an example such as *From the hill-top the blue sea could just be seen*. If we again think of this sentence in a historical language in which the researcher is unsure about the extent of the blue colour denoted by the *blue* word, information about the wider context is essential. Is this the vivid blue of the sea around a coral island, or is it the mid-blue sea of a sunny day in southern England? Is it the grey-blue of a northern European sea on a dull day, or the sparkling blue of the Mediterranean? Is it the dark blue of the sea in the evening, or the blue-black colour of a stormy scene? If the reader thinks of the two Russian blues, s/he will understand that it cannot be assumed that the same *blue* word will be used to denote *all* the above contexts (Sections 3.21, 5.6). Then again, the sea can be green or grey (Minnaert 1993: 335–45), and we have seen that a grue macro-colour term occurs, or has occurred, in many languages so perhaps the blue word in this particular context should not be translated into English as *blue* at all (Section 5.5). The vital information which may clarify the scene for us may have been provided at some textual distance from the occurrence of the colour word, and it is this which makes the broader context important.

If the researcher is very fortunate, s/he may find a resource which will provide the immediate contexts of his or her vocabulary, namely, a computer database of texts which is appropriate for all or part of the research. This statement ushers the reader into the exciting and still quite new world of the linguistic *corpus*. A corpus (plural: *corpora*) is an electronic archive, typically of immense size, but with the invaluable facility of a search program which enables the enquirer to construct a particular search, retrieve the appropriate data, sort it into the desired order, and print it out or download it, to provide listings of basic data.[14] The English language is particularly blessed with corpora (Anderson and Corbett 2009: 183–7) but they also exist for other languages such as German, Swedish and Czech (Teubert and Čermáková 2007: 67), and more are being developed.

A more precise definition of a corpus is that it is a collection of spoken and/or written texts which have been brought together for a particular purpose. In other words, a corpus is designed as a representation of an even larger entity, such as an entire language, for the purposes of linguistic enquiry. Anderson and Corbett (2009: 4) raise the important point that the researcher must match his or her needs with the aims of the corpus designer in order to retrieve useful results. It is clearly inadvisable, for example, to search a corpus of newspaper articles with the intention of learning about children's language. It is therefore evident that the chosen research project may be unable to benefit from a corpus even when the language has several corpora available. The researcher needs to understand the strengths and limitations of any corpus s/he decides to use, in order to correctly interpret the results.

Where an appropriate corpus exists, the researcher can search on the colour terms s/he has found and retrieve the immediate contexts. The sentences or phrases retrieved are all taken from 'normal' speech or writing, that is, they do not represent responses to linguists' interviews and tests, nor have they been edited for factual or grammatical accuracy.

The final type of reference work to be considered here is the *concordance*. This has similarities, on a much more modest scale, to the results of a corpus search. The concordance is an alphabetical printed list of words from a particular text or texts, in which the immediate contexts of the words are given. Concordances have a long history, and were often produced from the works of a major author, such as Chaucer, or an important text such as the Bible. The Scottish classical and biblical scholar Alexander Cruden (1699–1770) compiled an early modern concordance to the Bible.[15] This work was first published in 1737 and has never been out of print. As an example of what the enquirer may find, a glance at the word *crimson* reveals four occurrences, two in II Chronicles, one in Isaiah and one in Jeremiah. They are presented within a very short immediate context, not always involving a complete phrase so, for example, the reader finds: 'though your sins be red like *c.* they shall be' (Isaiah 1.18). In other words, some concordances will include more of the context than others but all will provide a glimpse of it, as well as a reference to where the full context can be found. However, even with what appear to be straightforward reference works like this, there are pitfalls for the unwary. The researcher needs to know exactly what the concordance has analysed. In the case of Cruden, for example, which version of the Bible has been used? Has Cruden omitted some occurrences deliberately or by accident?[16]

The researcher may easily overlook another source of colour terms in context, and that is place-names. Where the origin of a place-name can be traced back to the researcher's period of interest, it may provide some particularly valuable clues. The semantic researcher wants, as far as possible, to access the normal language of historical native-speakers, and this is relatively easy for recent periods but is far more difficult for data-restricted periods. With considerable variations depending on the culture being researched, 'ordinary' (unaffected or unadorned) language is usually spoken by the poorest, least educated and lowest ranking people in a society, and yet they usually constitute the majority of speakers, and language change is likely to originate amongst them. Place-names can offer insights into such language because most of them originated in descriptions assigned by local people to specific villages, hills and fields to which they needed to refer. Dating (even roughly) the earliest use of a place-name may be an insuperable problem if there is a lack of early records but, where such information is available, as is often the case in the UK, dated place-names can be added to the list of colour vocabulary contexts.[17]

A qualification needs to be added to the colour semantic value of place-names, however, since certain name elements may have had a different sense in place-names to that of everyday language. In other words, a particular sense may belong to the *toponymicon* as opposed to the lexicon (Hough 2010). This situation may only be evident from a thorough review of all the evidence, such as Hough's survey of Old English colour terms in English and Scottish place-names. She found that only seventeen colour terms (broadly defined) were used in these place-names (2006: 192–5), and this is likely to indicate a classificatory, as opposed to a descriptive, usage (Section 3.18).[18] One of the important aspects of place-names for the historical semanticist is, of course, that they are easily and precisely located, and so augment dialectal and regional colour-term studies.[19]

As s/he reaches the end of this chapter, the reader may be wondering why it includes so much discussion of reference sources, first steps in the research process, and the acquisition of basic data. It may seem that this is the easiest stage of the work, but it contains a number of obstacles and a fair number of repetitive tasks. It is crucial for the researcher to understand, however, that getting this stage wrong often means compromising the quality of the remaining work. In the worst cases, the bulk of the time spent on later phases of research will be wasted. This first phase is all about deciding on an interesting, useful and viable project, assessing how much basic data can be retrieved from computer searches and/or printed reference sources, and ascertaining how much of the work must be done from scratch. The researcher may back away in horror from the thought of collecting data manually by reading but, if s/he finds there is no alternative to this, it is some comfort to realize that s/he is the first in the field and that his or her work is potentially ground-breaking.

8.6   Metalanguage

The researcher has now decided on a project and retrieved the basic data necessary to support the investigation. Before moving on to the next stage, which is likely to involve assessing the meanings of the colour terms in extant texts, the researcher may wish to consider how those meanings should be described. It is recommended that some type of metalanguage should be employed; that is, a controlled or conceptually standardized terminology. The linguist has a problem in conveying to readers the results of his or her research because s/he is enmeshed in the tricky situation of trying to describe one language, or one phase of a language, in the words of another. Without a form of control, such an endeavour is likely to result in ambiguity, creating confusion among readers, and obstructing comparisons within or between languages. This argument is very similar to that of Wierzbicka, who developed Natural Semantic Metalanguage to attempt to convey meaning in universally shared basic concepts (Section 7.3). The reader may remember that, whatever the merits of NSM, it was concluded that it was impractical for any but the most data-rich historical languages since it needs native-speaker informants to support the required degree of accuracy.

Some form of metalanguage, however, is certainly required in historical studies but it has to be constructed with sufficiently broad concepts to allow for the likelihood of missing evidence. Whether the amount of missing data is suspected to be severe or minimal, the fact remains that the researcher never knows its full extent. This is bad enough without the added confusion of related and alternative expressions being used in the reporting language. If an English-speaking researcher, for example, uses the terms *pale red*, *pink*, *unsaturated red* and *light red* at different places in his or her report, the reader will wonder if there is a difference between these colours or whether they are just alternative names for the same thing. The researcher needs to establish a terminology which s/he finds appropriate, make his or her usage clear to the reader, and then avoid straying from that terminology unless there is a good reason (which should be explained to the reader). The resulting style may sometimes seem bland and repetitive, but it is more likely that all readers will interpret the colour term in the same way.

I have constructed a metalanguage for colour descriptions in my own historical research (Biggam 2007: 183), and I shall describe it here in case it is of use to others. The aim and purpose of this particular metalinguistic system is to facilitate the description of those aspects of a historical colour term for which there is evidence, and to express that description in a standardized form which is not precise, because of the gaps in the evidence, but represents, nevertheless, an attempt to avoid ambiguity and uncontrolled imagination. These metalinguistic expressions represent the extent of the researcher's knowledge of individual historical colour terms, so they do not necessarily indicate the actual way in which they were used in the living language. Naturally, it is hoped that the researcher's conclusion is close to the 'truth', but it is more likely to represent just a part of the native speaker's understanding. The creation of this metalinguistic system was prompted by the discovery that the word *brightness* had been used differently by each of the three earliest writers on the colour terms of Old English, namely, Mead (1899), Lerner (1951) and Barley (1974) (Biggam 2007: 173–6), and that their work had prompted a steadily increasing interpretation of Old English colour terms as 'brightness' terms over the succeeding years, in which writers continued to interpret *brightness* in their own ways (pages 176–82).

To offset the potential for misunderstanding, it is recommended that any work on a historical language should include an appendix providing a guide to the author's colour terminology (see Appendix, Section 1). 'Red', 'yellow', 'green' and 'blue' can be assumed to denote categories based on the elemental hues (with or without further explanation) but other colour terms, especially if they have a significant role in the research project, need to be translated into metalanguage, either once in the appendix, or throughout the discussion. For example, a word equivalent to English *turquoise* could be explained as 'greenish-blue/bluish-green' (indicating a range of hues), an equivalent to *orange* as 'red-yellow' (indicating an apparently equal mix of the two hues), an equivalent to *violet* as 'bluish-purple' (indicating a mixture of blue and red in which blue predominates) and so on. If the researcher needs to describe a macro-category, a plus sign can be used; for example, 'green+blue'.

Mixed hues are perceived to consist of two hues (as in purple or orange) or one or more hues plus an achromatic (as in brown and pink), and they can be described according to the balance of their elements. To take purple as an example, in cases where blue predominates, I use the term *violet* or the description 'bluish-purple' and, in cases where red predominates, I use *red-purple* or the description 'reddish-purple'. Where the colour has an apparently equal measure of both constituent hues, I describe it as 'red-blue'. However, a much more likely scenario in historical studies is that the balance of the two hues cannot be ascertained, in which case I use *purple* which indicates 'reddish-blue/red-blue/bluish-red'. Similarly, orange can be described as 'reddish-yellow' (yellow being dominant), 'yellowish-red' (red being dominant), 'red-yellow' (neither being dominant) or 'orange' (no detailed information available).

If it is possible to identify a degree of saturation in a historical colour term or context, I select an appropriate term from the range 'vivid' – 'mid' (saturation) – 'dull' and combine it with the required hue name. Thus, 'vivid red' is fully saturated red, 'dull red' has a grey element which is stronger than the red hue, and 'mid red' is the same as 'grey-red', that is, a roughly equal mixture of grey and red.

The remaining mixed colours, brown and pink, present a special difficulty as regards saturation because their constituents include achromatics. Brown is generally understood as a mixture of red, yellow and black, and pink as a mixture of red and white.[20] Logically speaking, this means that neither colour can be vivid. This is because *vivid* does not mean 'bright' in this metalanguage but 'fully saturated', indicating the absence of any achromatic element which would make the hue dull, pale or dark. By definition, brown includes black and pink includes white, but the achromatic elements have to be ignored in a purely hue description. Thus, brown can be described as 'yellowish-brown', 'reddish-brown' or 'brown' (the last indicating a lack of more detailed information). In exclusively hue terms, pink can be indicated by 'pink' and 'strong pink', the latter referring to shades close to so-called 'shocking' pink (Section 9.3).

If it is possible to ascertain a tonal element in a colour term or context, I select from the range of 'pale' – 'medium' (tone) – 'dark', along with the hue name. Thus 'pale red' is whitish, 'dark red' is blackish and 'medium red' is neither pale nor dark. For achromatics, the range is: 'white' – 'pale grey' – 'medium grey' – 'dark grey' – 'black'.

We now turn to the problem of denoting brightness, a word which is used here as a superordinate term for the various aspects of this phenomenon. As used in everyday speech, and even in many colour semantic publications, this word has multiple meanings (Biggam 2007). One form of brightness is light-emission, that is, the visual impression caused by an object or entity, such as the sun, a fire or a lamp, which creates and transmits its own light. Light-emission can be expressed by the range 'dazzling' – 'shining' – 'glowing', and each word can be further described, if necessary, by 'intermittent' or 'constant'. 'Shining' denotes a middle category, indicating a light which is neither extremely bright nor faint, 'dazzling' is extremely bright, and 'glowing' is relatively faint. Thus, the appearance of the sun on a cloudless day in high summer could be described as 'dazzling (constant)' while the appearance of a lighthouse light, seen from a distance, could be described as 'shining (intermittent)'.

Table 8.1 *A metalanguage for historical colour-term meanings*

HUE	red	yellow	green	brown *etc.*
SATURATION	vivid	mid	dull	
TONE *achromatic*	white black	pale grey	mid grey	dark grey
TONE *chromatic*	pale	medium	dark	
BRIGHTNESS *light emission*	dazzling	shining	glowing	+intermittent? +constant?
BRIGHTNESS *reflectivity*	shiny	lustrous	matt	+intermittent? +constant?
BRIGHTNESS *surface illumination*	well-lit	poorly lit		
BRIGHTNESS *space illumination*	brilliant	dim	unlit	
TRANSPARENCY	transparent	translucent		

Another form of brightness is reflectivity which depends on the various abilities of surface materials to reflect the light produced elsewhere. Reflectivity can be described by means of the range 'shiny' – 'lustrous' – 'matt', with the addition of 'constant' or 'intermittent' if required. The middle category here is described as 'lustrous', while 'shiny' indicates an eye-catching effect, and 'matt' indicates the non-reflecting (non-shiny) quality.

Another form of brightness is surface illumination. This is described with the terms 'well-lit' or 'poorly lit', with medium illumination being taken as the norm. This range relates to entities which do not produce their own light, and are not made of reflective material, but their appearance may be significantly affected by the degree of illumination falling on their matt surfaces. For example, an object may appear vivid yellow in the daylight, but it will not have the same quality at dusk, so it can then be described as 'poorly-lit yellow'. This phrase conveys the fact that the saturation and tone of a hue are obscured in poor light.

Yet another form of brightness is space illumination. This can refer to daylight (or the lack of it) outdoors, or to an enclosed space such as a room illuminated by a fire or artificial light. The range for this description is 'brilliant' – 'dim' – 'unlit', in which a medium illumination is taken as the norm and does not require comment. 'Dim' indicates a low lighting level, and 'unlit' indicates darkness (a lack of both daylight and artificial light). Finally, the researcher may wish to comment on transparency, in which case s/he can use the terms 'transparent' or 'translucent'. Table 8.1 summarizes this section, while the Appendix, Section 2, provides more detail.

8.7   The separability of colour features

The researcher may choose to describe each occurrence of a particular colour term (Term X) in metalinguistic form so that the various descriptions can be easily compared. Thus Term X may apparently indicate 'pale blue and shiny' on some occasions, and 'dark blue and poorly lit' on others. In a list of the known occurrences of Term X, there are likely to be several different combinations of colour elements, as well as several cases for which the colour effects cannot be ascertained from the context. The variations may indicate the extent of hue coverage, so that Term X, for example, appears to be a blue term, unrestricted by tone. This sort of information will help the researcher to frame a general definition of Term X, based on all occurrences, for the place and time being investigated. Crucial to such a definition is any suggestion from the list of occurrences that certain colour features seem to be nearly always present, and never specifically excluded or contradicted. This may persuade the researcher to combine two or more colour features in the general definition of the colour term; for example, 'blue+shiny'. But exactly what does this imply?

A metalinguistic definition in the form of [colour element]+[colour element] indicates that both elements are essential and *inseparable* semantic elements in the meaning of Term X. In other words, 'blue+shiny' can only be used of referents which are *both* blue and shiny. It is important to stress the inseparable nature of the colour features in Term X because a different term (Term Y) could also be used to describe an object which is blue and shiny but, unlike Term X, it may be used on another occasion of an object which is blue and matt (in a well-illuminated context). This variability in reflectivity would strongly suggest that Term Y means 'blue' but not 'blue+shiny'.

Information on the various aspects of a historical colour meaning can usually only be garnered from its referents and their contexts. Contexts are very important here, as the researcher can be led astray by a list of referents without their full contexts (Section 9.2). To illustrate the dangers, I carried out a brief survey of the referents of ModE *grey* as represented in a random sample from the *British National Corpus* (Biggam 2007: 181–2). I was able to 'prove' that *grey* is a brightness word since it describes many reflective or light-emitting referents such as: human eyes, metal, wire, satin, sunlight, a river, horses and a car. Having come to this erroneous conclusion, I could easily interpret other referents in the sample in the same light, so that a chair and a wardrobe included in the list of referents could be interpreted as having been painted with gloss paint, an owl and a parrot 'must' have had a sheen on their feathers, and so on. I could conclude, therefore, that ModE *grey* always means 'grey+bright', but any native speaker knows that brightness is not an inseparable part of the meaning of *grey*.[21] This procedure, whereby referents are considered out of context, is the same as that used by earlier researchers such as Mead (1899) and Lerner (1951) to retrieve the colour features of Old English vocabulary, on the basis of which later writers declared the language to have only a minimal concept of hue (for example, Casson 1997: 224).

I have suggested that a colour feature should only be accepted as an inseparable element of a colour term under two circumstances (Biggam 2007: 184). The first is where the feature can be shown to occur in the majority of occurrences, and where the opposite feature does not occur more than once (allowing for a misunderstanding). Thus, if the majority of occurrences of a word clearly imply vividness, only one instance of dullness can be tolerated in accepting vividness as an inseparable element of the colour term. With data-restricted languages, of course, the number of occurrences may not be statistically significant, in which case the researcher should err on the side of caution, and merely make a suggestion that an extra colour feature may be always present. One possibility is to express the meaning as, for example, 'blue(+shiny?)'. The second criterion for accepting a particular colour element as an inseparable part of a colour term is when it occurs in a context as the only possible element present. In other words, if a colour term were used in a dazzling context which excluded the possibility of any other visible colour element, including hue, it is highly likely that some form of shininess represents an inseparable semantic element of that word. The reader should use the second criterion with caution, however, since the presence of macro-categories, for example, will render unsafe any hue judgements on this principle.

Non-appearance features can also be included in a definition, and such features are expressed freely rather than metalinguistically. The meaning of a contextually restricted colour term, for example, may be expressed in a form similar to the following: 'dark blue (dyes, textiles)'. At this point, the reader stands at the brink of the more interesting analytical work to be discussed in the following chapters. Hopefully, firm foundations have been laid in this present chapter for the valuable and exciting work ahead.

9   Synchronic studies

9.1   What is a synchronic study?

This chapter will be concerned with synchronic research projects. A *synchronic* study is concerned with a particular period of time, as opposed to a *diachronic* study which is concerned with the changes that occur across time. Although these two approaches are given separate chapters in this book, I very much regard them as being interdependent. As April McMahon (1994: 11) writes: 'if we do not accept, and reflect in our theories, that 'tall oaks from little acorns grow', how much can we really claim to know about trees?'.

In the case of ancient languages with few surviving texts and, no doubt, some insuperable dating problems, it may be difficult or impossible to follow diachronic change, so every project may have to be conducted as a synchronic study based on the entire surviving corpus. This may also be true of relatively recent languages which, for various reasons, were not often used for written records, or where large numbers of records have been destroyed; for example, as a result of war. Since varying circumstances surround the different languages, the period of time involved in a synchronic study is also highly variable. This chapter will attempt to address synchronic studies in data-rich and data-restricted languages (these terms are explained in Section 8.3).

9.2   Basic data

The opening of this chapter should find the researcher with his or her basic data complete (Sections 8.4 and 8.5). These data comprise at least four resources: firstly, a comprehensive list of the colour terms appearing in the chosen texts; secondly, an expanded list showing every occurrence of those colour terms in the texts (Section 8.4); thirdly, details of the immediate context of each colour term's occurrence; and, fourthly, notes describing the broader contexts in which each colour term and its referent had been found (Section 8.5). Ideally, the researcher will also have retrieved a larger colour term list, appropriate to the place and period of the research, which will facilitate comparison of the vocabulary of the specific project with the norms of the time.

127

To illustrate some of the approaches described in this chapter, I shall give examples from a poem by Geoffrey Chaucer (c.1342 to 1400).[1] Chaucer was born into a family of merchants, specifically vintners, who had moved to London from their native Ipswich in the time of Chaucer's grandparents. Chaucer himself had an extremely varied career with phases as a soldier, an esquire of the king's household, a diplomat, a senior customs official, a Justice of the Peace, a Member of Parliament and more (Crow and Leland 1988: xi). Somehow he also found time to write poetry, and he is considered one of the greatest poets who wrote in Middle English (ME) which dates from about 1100 to about 1500 (Barnickel 1975; Burnley 1976).

One of Chaucer's poems is *The Parliament of Fowls* in which a dream is recounted. The dreamer travels through a landscape to a temple of Venus, and then proceeds to a meeting of birds of various types which is presided over by Dame Nature. The birds have gathered to choose their mates, and the poem is a celebration of Saint Valentine's Day. This poem will be used to provide a very small example of the four types of resource which constitute the basic data of a research project in historical colour semantics.

The first resource of the basic data is a list of the colour terms occurring in each text included in the project. *The Parliament of Fowls* contains the following: *blāk, bleu, bright, clēr, derk, don, frostī, gōld, grei, grēne* (adjective), *grēne* (noun), *light, lightnesse, pāle, rēd, shēne, silver, whīt* and *yelwe*.[2] In the search process, the researcher should have added any further information which was considered useful; for example, the appropriate part of speech (the list above includes adjectives and nouns, but others can occur).

The second resource of the basic data is a list of all the occurrences of the colour terms in each text. In practice, this resouce is likely to be combined with the third resource, that is, the immediate contexts of the colour terms since, in most reference sources or databases, they will be found together. As an example, in Table 9.1, I list the four occurrences of ME *rēd* in *The Parliament of Fowls*. It is useful to record the actual spellings as found in the text in columns 2 and 5, rather than standardizing them to the form of a dictionary headword. The 'real' spellings may offer clues to information such as dialect, a change of scribe, morphological variation, the presence of homonyms and much more.[3] The researcher needs to be aware, however, of what these 'real' spellings represent, and to consider matters such as the number of surviving manuscripts of the text, whether some are obviously poor copies of others, whether any manuscripts are contemporary with the creation of the text, whether the scribe or copyist was familiar with the language of the text, whether the text has been well edited in modern times and so on. The form of a word is obviously less useful if it was changed at a later date, or is the result of a copying error.

Column 4 in Table 9.1 provides the immediate referents and/or context of the colour term, in other words, the entity or phenomenon which is described

Table 9.1 *Occurrences of ME* rēd *in Chaucer's* The Parliament of Fowls

Ref. no.	Spelling	Line no.	Referent	Associated terms
1	*rede*	186	flowers in a garden	*white, blewe, yelwe* (other flowers)
2	*rede*	189	fins of small fish in springs	*sylver bryghte* (the fishes' scales)
3	*rede*	442	1. rose 2. a bird (i.e. a human) (embarrassed)	1. *freshe, newe*
4	*red*	583	a turtledove (i.e. a human) (embarrassed)	

by the colour term. As can be seen from the example at line 442, there may be more than one simultaneous referent; in this case, ROSE and FACE. The researcher needs to record this information carefully as it is easy to generalize in error; for example, the reseacher might have given the referent at line 189 as FISH when it is precisely the *fins* of the fish which are *rēd*. Column 5 includes any further description of the referent which occurs in the immediate context, or any description of entities which are closely associated with the referent. The brief explanations in brackets clarify whether the descriptions are used of the referent itself or of entities connected with it. It is important at line 186, for example, to stress that it is not the *rēd* flowers which are also *whīt, bleu* and *yelwe* but *different* flowers. The researcher is also advised to add a column (Column 1 in Table 9.1) to provide a number for each occurrence. This is because, after a large amount of basic data has been compiled, it may be easier to refer to a specific occurrence as, for example, Red 1, Yelwe 2 and so on.

Having gathered the first three types of basic data, that is, the colour vocabulary in the selected texts, the individual occurrences of each term, and their immediate contexts, the researcher has only one more type to consider, namely, the broader contexts. This is likely to involve reading an entire text or, alternatively, the chapter, section or scene in which each colour term occurs. In the case of the *rēd* references in *The Parliament of Fowls*, the broad context notes might read as follows:

Red 1 (line 186): the garden in which the flowers are found is located in a meadow (*mede*) by a river (*ryver*) (line 184) and this, in turn, is situated in a tract of land (*park*) enclosed by a stone wall (line 122). The text is not conclusive on this point, but the flowers may be the blossom of trees. Certainly, the garden includes trees with 'blossoming boughs' (*blosmy bowes*) (line 183) but there may be other flowers in addition. The previous verse consists entirely of

a list of trees and their uses. However, since this landscape is seen
in a dream, the colours cannot be presumed to be realistic.

Red 2 (line 189): the fish are swimming in cold (*colde*) springs (*welle-
stremes*) which are described as 'not at all lifeless' (*nothyng dede*)
(line 187) which implies that the water is moving strongly and
quickly. The springs are located in the garden described under Red
1. As these fish occur in a dream, they may be an imaginary type.

Red 3 (line 442): the rose is described as 'ayeyn the somer sonne
coloured is' which could be translated in different ways but implies
that the colour of the rose is drawn out in the presence of the summer
sun. The rose-colour here refers to a female bird (*formel*) (almost
certainly an eagle) who blushes on hearing a declaration of love
for her from a high-ranking male eagle (*tersel*). As eagles do not
blush, and because the birds in this dream are anthropomorphized
(they speak, reason and make decisions), the second referent for
this colour term can be accepted as a blushing *human* face.

Red 4 (line 583): The colour refers to a turtledove (*turtle*) which is
blushing. This bird, symbolizing faithfulness,[4] has just been chosen
to speak for the seed-eating birds, and begins by exclaiming 'Nay,
God forbede a lovere shulde chaunge!' (line 582). The next line
describes the bird as 'for shame al red'. The blushing seems to
have been occasioned by embarrassment at stating so passionately
in public that lovers should remain together through both good and
hard times. As with Red 3 above, this context is best interpreted as
referring to a human face.

With all four types of basic data recorded, the researcher can consider what
to do next. This depends very much on the questions s/he would like to have
answered, and the quality of information which is already available to him or
her. For a language which has been only minimally studied, or for a language
with dictionary resources which pre-date computer databases and recent work
in colour semantics, the next step is to ascertain the meanings of the words as
closely as the evidence permits, and this is the concern of Sections 9.3 to 9.5.

9.3   Referents

In assessing the meaning of a colour term, the historical semanticist must be
as objective as the imperfect nature of the evidence allows. As has already
been mentioned, the researcher is advised not to assume that the meaning of a
historical word must be the same as that of a modern word of similar form as,
for example, in the case of ME *rēd* and ModE *red*.[5]

The subject of this section, namely, colour term referents, refers to anything
which is described by a colour term; for example, in the phrase, *the red robin*,

ROBIN is the referent of *red*. Here, another warning must be issued. The researcher should ignore the temptation to look at just a few referents, seizing upon those which can be observed today (such as a type of animal or flower), and then concluding that the meaning of the colour term has been established. S/he should bear in mind that the colours of a few referents may indicate only *part* of the colour term's coverage, and may not reveal a contextual restriction, quite apart from the problems of whether the referent has always looked the same. It adds immensely to the value of a colour term study if *all* the surviving referents are carefully considered. In fact, the researcher should proceed as if the colour terms in his or her project were totally alien (as, indeed, they may be), requiring the collection of every scrap of evidence. This last recommendation should be taken particularly seriously by a researcher working in a language closely related to his or her native speech, as in the case of an English-speaker working on Middle English. Only if Middle English is treated as if it were an exotic 'foreign' language will the researcher be able to attempt objectivity.

In the example investigation of *rēd* in *The Parliament of Fowls*, the researcher has a very small list of referents but even this includes items of interest. Red 1 involves flowers which may be the blossom of trees. There is clearly insufficient evidence here to provide a likely colour. Similarly, Red 2 involves the fins of small fish. They are freshwater fish which can be found in cold, swift-flowing water but this is not sufficiently diagnostic to identify the species. The researcher should not, at this stage, look in reference sources for a fish with red fins, since that is to assume s/he already knows the colour or colours denoted by ME *rēd*. Nonetheless, the fish should be investigated at a later stage when the colour of *rēd* has been at least partially established.

The remaining referents of *rēd* in *The Parliament of Fowls* are more promising. Red 3 and 4 both refer to an embarrassed bird, and these instances can be convincingly understood as evoking blushing human faces, for the reasons given in Section 9.2. The hue and tone involved in these two references can, therefore, be ascertained from the general knowledge of human beings that we all share, so it can be concluded that a blushing face, as found in mediaeval England, was pale red. Finally, the referent ROSE occurs in Red 3, described as *frēsh* 'unfaded, fresh' (*MED* 6a), and as *neue* 'recently grown [flowered]' (*MED* 1b). Unlike the flowers in Red 1, this names a particular *type* of flower which now needs to be researched. In the discussion that follows, the aim is not to produce a definitive report, but to indicate the potential and limitations of several subjects which the semanticist may have to explore.

The researcher should always begin with a definition of the name of the referent, even where it seems obvious. The definition of ME *rōse* is 'a plant of the genus Rosa; the flower of this plant' (*MED* 1a).[6] Armed with the name of a genus, the researcher should now turn to botanical sources. In the course of investigating referents and associated entities, the researcher should be prepared to explore subjects which are entirely new, or only vaguely known to him or her, such as plants, animals, rocks, weather, textiles, dyes and much more. How can s/he avoid making errors when working in an unfamiliar discipline? The golden rule is to find an up-to-date, authoritative reference book or books, and to make no statement which cannot be substantiated from such a source. Even if the information is controversial in that discipline, the semanticist can justifiably claim to be expressing the opinion of at least one expert in the field.[7] This type of investigative process can be time-consuming, but it is also one of the most productive research techniques for obtaining information.

Returning to the genus *Rosa*, I consulted Stace's *New Flora of the British Isles* (1997) and discovered a long list of species belonging to this genus. The reader, of course, will have seen modern roses of many different colours, but they are often the result of centuries of imports and hybridization while our concern is exclusively with the roses of fourteenth-century England. The first step is to retrieve those species which Stace labels as 'native'. There are differences between botanists as to precisely what 'native' should include but it always refers to plants that were growing in Britain at the end of the last glaciation (about 10,000 years ago) and sometimes includes those plants that were introduced into Britain by humans before the Neolithic period (beginning in Britain about 6,000 years ago). As far as medievalists are concerned, any plant labelled as 'native' which had not become extinct before the medieval period would have been known to some people, at least, of that period, depending on the extent of its habitat. In addition to native species, medievalists are also concerned with those non-native or 'introduced' plants which are classed as archaeophytes. This refers to plants which were introduced into Britain and became naturalized before 1500 AD. Over 150 species, or other taxa, have been identified as archaeophytes in Britain, and listed with the dates at which there is evidence for them (Preston, Pearman and Hall 2004: 264–70).

As regards Chaucer's rose, Stace labels twelve of the *Rosa* genus as 'native', and there are no members of this genus listed as archaeophytes.[8] If this list contained species of several different colours, the researcher would need to look for botanical information, such as location, habitat or rarity, which might permit the elimination of some species.[9] In the case of the twelve rose species listed here, however, their colours are restricted to white and/or various shades of pink. Since it is evident from the context of Red 3 that the colour of the rose is comparable to that of a human face blushing, white can be eliminated, and that means that the Field-rose (*Rosa arvensis* Huds.), which only has white flowers, can be removed from the list.[10] It would also be reasonable to remove the Burnet rose (*Rosa pimpinellifolia* L.) since Stace describes its flowers as 'white, rarely pale pink' (1997: 358). This is acceptable because Chaucer is using the rose as a colour exemplar, and that implies he is not referring to its rarest colour.

The ten remaining rose species are all members of the *Canina* group and, leaving aside the white flowers that some can also produce, their colours range from pale pink to strong pink.[11] The botanical evidence suggests, therefore, that the hue of Chaucer's rose was pink. Unfortunately, this appears to be contradicted by a piece of evidence from heraldry.

The Red Rose of Lancaster, also called the Apothecaries' Rose (*Rosa gallica* L.), a native of southern and central Europe and parts of Asia, has flowers which range from various pinks, including strong pink, to red and dark red. It is believed to be this rose which became the emblem of the House of Lancaster, an aristocratic English family which opposed the House of York in the civil wars later named the Wars of the Roses (hostilities occurred mostly between 1455 and 1485). The reason for believing that the Lancastrian rose was the *Rosa gallica* is that it is depicted with vivid red petals, not the pink of native roses. However, there are reasons for discounting the heraldic evidence. Firstly, motifs on badges and in heraldry did not have to be realistically coloured so, for example, the badge of King Edward I (reigned 1272–1307) was a golden rose (Boutell 1966: 163–4). Secondly, the heraldic colours (known as *tinctures*) were limited in number, and pink was not among them. The nearest available colour to pink would have been red (known as *gules*).[12]

If the heraldic evidence is discounted, the researcher may turn to contemporary literature for confirmation that Chaucer's rose is pink. It is relatively simple to find early references in the work of English authors to red roses but the contexts of such documents must be taken into consideration. To give one example, the English author Bartholomaeus Anglicus compiled an encyclopaedia in Latin at a date estimated to be about 1240, and he mentions red roses. However, Bartholomaeus, a Franciscan monk, spent the greater part of his life studying and teaching on the European mainland, firstly in Paris, and then in Magdeburg, Germany. Not only could he be describing continental roses but his encyclopaedia is a compilation made from many older works including those of southern European writers such as Pliny the Elder who had lived in an area where the *Rosa gallica* was native. Bartholomaeus, therefore, cannot be taken as providing evidence for the presence of the *Rosa gallica* in England at an early date.

Literary evidence cannot, however, be discounted so easily. A proximity search (*rēd* occurring near *rōse*) was carried out on the quotations appearing in the *MED*, and the results were clear, if surprising. A search restricted to texts dated to Chaucer's lifetime results in a close association between roses and the red to dark red colour of blood. To give one example, the text entitled *Meditations on the Life and Passion of Christ* is dated to *ante* (before) 1400, and it includes the following: 'Whan I loke on my sauyour; Þat is blod-red as rose-flour.'[13] The search was then extended beyond Chaucer's lifetime (to *ante* 1475) where further useful evidence was found in a text with the incipit (beginning): 'Holy berith beris' (Holly bears berries) which includes the line 'Holy hat berys as rede as any rose.'[14]

Without further research, it presently appears that the majority of roses seen by the population in fourteenth-century England were white and various shades of pink (botanical evidence) but a single species (the *Rosa gallica*), which had been introduced at an unknown date, could produce red flowers (literary evidence). Especially revealing is the phrase 'holly has berries as red as any rose' because this implies that the rose was considered an exemplar of typical redness, and it was the colour of holly berries, that is, vivid red and not pink. As a vivid red rose was a novelty in England, and was presumably admired, it was taken for a badge by an aristocratic family, and frequently mentioned by poets. A suspicion lingers, however, which will be mentioned only briefly. It should be remembered that fourteenth-century English people had no basic category for PINK so would, presumably, have referred to the rose-colour as *rēd*. If the introduced *Rosa gallica* was growing almost exclusively in aristocratic gardens as an ornamental species, it is possible that very few ordinary English folk had ever seen a vivid red rose. For them, the phrase 'rose-red' might have evoked the pink hue of hedgerow roses.

It should be emphasized that the discussion above has been based on a single poem and, were this a full research project, it would be essential to work with more data in order to confirm, contradict and/or extend the findings. An example will be given here of further interesting evidence which emerged from the proximity search. The amethyst gemstone is described as being like the colour of the red rose in the *Peterborough Lapidary*, a treatise on gemstones dating to the late fifteenth century. It states: 'Amatitus is a ston like to purpull red as . . . wyne or red rose in color' (Amethyst is a stone like purple red as . . . wine or red rose in colour) (Evans and Serjeantson 1933: 69).[15] The *Lapidary* later describes the amethyst as 'purpel red in color, & is medeled with þe color of violet, as it were a blasinge rose' (purple red in colour, and is mixed with the colour of the violet, like a brilliant rose) (1933: 70).

Provided the gemstone called 'amethyst' in the *Lapidary* is the same as that indicated by the name today (and this would have to be investigated), the hues involved are red-purple and violet (Schumann 1977: 118). The reader will remember that the *OED* definition of ModE *pink* includes 'sometimes with a slight purple tinge' (Chapter 8, Note 20) and colours such as strong pink, pale red-purple and pale violet can be very similar to each other. This reference appears to expand the hue coverage of ME *rēd* to include strong pink and certain purples. Although this scenario looks convincing, the origin of this text demands caution. The *Peterborough Lapidary* borrows its information from a number of sources, and much of the amethyst entry derives from the Latin text of the Spanish saint, bishop and encyclopaedist, Isidore of Seville (c.560–636) (Evans and Serjeantson 1933: 163). Isidore writes: 'Amethystus purpureus est permixto violacio colore; et quasi rosae nitor'[16] (Amethyst is purple with a violet colour mixed in; its brilliance is like that of a rose) (Barney *et al.* 2006: 324). In other words, the compiler of the *Peterborough Lapidary* is not the originator of the comparison between rose and amethyst, and this inevitably reduces the value of its evidence for Middle English semantics.

Another valuable lesson emerges from the proximity search. It involves the Middle English translation of the Latin poem *De viribus herbarum* (On the Powers of Plants), a herbal text which dates to the period between the late ninth century and c.1100. It is attributed to a certain 'Macer Floridus', a name which is generally considered to be a pseudonym, possibly of Odo de Meung (Odo Magdunensis) who lived in the early eleventh century and whose name appears on one of the surviving manuscripts. The herbal contains a section headed 'Popie' in the Middle English version, and its flower is said to be 'reed as is þe rose' (Frisk 1949: 122). At first sight, this reference appears to provide unambiguous evidence that the rose is being described as vivid red, the prototypical colour of the poppy in England. However, there are two problems with this conclusion. The first has been encountered already, namely, that this text is a translation of a continental work, but the second problem concerns the waywardness of common plant-names. In this case, ME *popie* does not always equate with ModE *poppy*.

Plant-names pose a serious problem for the historical semanticist. In modern times, we have botanical Latin names which aim to provide a unique international identifier for each species and sub-species, and we also have a list of recommended English names for plants in Britain which enable unambiguous discussion in the vernacular (Dony, Jury and Perring 1986). In the past, however, plants, animals and other elements of the natural world were classified and named according to unscientific and often extremely localized criteria. This form of categorization is known as a *folk taxonomy* and there are often *several* taxonomies in existence at the same time across a sizeable region. Folk classification and naming tends to class together different entities, in this case plants, according to their appearance, behaviour or value to humans, so a name might mean 'bell-shaped flower' or 'water-loving plant' or 'wound-healer'. The problem for modern researchers is that different plants were considered typical 'water-dwellers' or 'wound-healers' in different areas, as dictated by local tradition and plant availability. This results in a single plant having several different names across a country like Britain (in some cases, fifty names or more have been recorded) and, similarly, one name may be used of many different species. Thus, plants which botanists consider to be unrelated might bear the same name in different regions, and plants which are botanically closely related might be considered quite distinct because of their differing uses. In other words, a traditional plant-name should never be trusted.

Returning to ModE *poppy*, most Britons, on hearing this name, envisage the scarlet-flowered Common Poppy (*Papaver rhoeas* L.), and it would probably be a surprise to many of them to hear that this is not the only colour, nor even the only species, of native poppy. The Common Poppy flower is usually vivid red, but can also be 'white, pink, mauvish or variegated' (Stace 1997: 103). The researcher may be even more surprised when s/he consults the entry *popie* in the *MED* and finds that the prime sense of this Middle English word is the Opium Poppy (*Papaver somniferum* L.), the flowers of which are 'white to deep mauve, sometimes red or variegated' (page 102). Further senses listed in the *MED* are: *Papaver* species cultivated in gardens (not necessarily native); the *bleu popie* which is the cornflower (*Centaurea cyanus* L.) with blue flowers; the *wilde popie* which denotes the Common Poppy but can also be used of several unrelated species which may include Gorse (*Ulex europaeus* L.), Common Restharrow (*Ononis repens* L.), Red Star-thistle (*Centaurea calcitrapa* L.); Corncockle (*Agrostemma githago* L.); and possibly the woodruff.[17] This list explains why ME *popie*, and most other plant-names, require considerable investigation before their colour can be decided, although, in this case, the earlier comparison of the rose with holly berries strongly supports the interpretation of this *popie* as being vivid red. Thus, from a very small amount of evidence, it can be preliminarily suggested that ME *rēd* in *The Parliament of Fowls* probably indicates pale red (blushing), vivid red (the *Rosa gallica*) and strong pink (some native roses and some flowers of the *Rosa gallica*). It is also likely that the last two colours are in the focal region of the Middle English red category.

The researcher will, of course, discover references which include uncertain colour words and suspected metaphorical usages. An example occurs in *The Parliament of Fowls* where the many types of birds present at the meeting are listed, and sometimes characterized; for example, the raven is wise and the cormorant gluttonous (lines 362–3), but what should we make of the *frosty feldefare* (line 364)? Middle English *fēldefāre* is defined by the *MED* as 'A kind of large thrush (Turdus pilaris), the fieldfare'. This bird is a northern thrush which commonly flies south in the autumn to spend the winter in Britain. It has a grey head and rump, a dark reddish-brown back, dark spotted chest and a black tail. When seen on the ground, therefore, it looks like a dark-coloured bird but, when seen in flight, it looks much paler as it has large areas of white under the wings and on the lower part of the chest. This explains the note 'frosty: with a white chest' in the *Riverside Chaucer* (Chaucer 1988: 390, Footnote 364), which suggests the existence of a Middle English colour word *frostī* meaning 'white' which is, of course, perfectly logical. The difficulty is that, as this bird is only seen in England in the winter months, it is possible that *frostī* has a metaphorical use indicating 'seen in frosty weather'. Indeed, several translators refer to 'the wintry fieldfare'. What do we find in the *MED*?

The principal definition of ME *frostī* is 'cold, frosty, wintry' but the last (the fifth) sense in the list is 'hoary (beard)'. This suggests that *frostī* does indeed sometimes have a colour sense although the dictionary restricts its usage to beards. It is interesting that the *MED* includes '?wintry (bird)' in the third sense of *frostī*. The fieldfare reference is the only example given of a wintry bird, but the dictionary does not pretend to offer a comprehensive list of quotations. The researcher has to weigh the possibilities in a case like this, and s/he may prefer not to favour one explanation over the other since Chaucer may have been alluding to *both* meanings, namely, the whiteness of this bird in flight, and its apparent liking for British winters.

It is hoped that this section has given the reader a taste of the adventures which can befall the semantic researcher, especially where a relatively specific item is mentioned. A glimpse has been offered here of how Chaucer's mention of roses has led the researcher down various botanical, heraldic, literary and gemmological trails which, it is hoped, have usefully augmented the linguistic data. This approach to historical meaning has been called *interdisciplinary semantics* (Biggam 1997, 1998).

9.4   Translations

Information about the colour terms of a historical language can often be obtained from surviving translations between the language being researched (the first language) and another contemporary one (the second language). This approach is particularly helpful in studies of data-restricted languages, especially if the second language has been better researched. In cases where the colour terms of the second language have not been thoroughly studied, the researcher can find him- or herself in a quandary, since, ideally, it would be advisable to research the colour terms of *both* languages. For example, if a researcher were investigating an Old English colour term and found that it had been used to translate a Latin colour term, it could be argued that the use of the Latin term in Anglo-Saxon England is as much in need of research as is the Old English term, but this could open up a parallel research project of similar, or even larger, proportions than the original investigation. In practice, the researcher usually has to rely on a good dictionary of the second language or, where none exists, on a strictly limited, small-scale investigation of crucial terms in that language. Translation evidence is just one part of the data being collected, so any serious distortion of the overall evidence as a result of a problematic translation will be noticed at a later stage, and the specific problem can then be targeted for more detailed investigation.

Translation is a notoriously difficult activity to carry out with accuracy and style, and the researcher needs to consider several aspects of a translation in order to evaluate its real worth to the research. Generally speaking, there are varying degrees of confidence, according to the genre of the text, with which the researcher can retrieve a literal colour sense. Degree of confidence may range from poetical works, which are often more concerned with impressions, atmosphere and metaphorical meanings than with 'straightforward' colour senses, to historical dictionaries, glosses and glossaries in which it can usually be assumed that accuracy of translation was the aim. Between these extremes lie a huge range of literary works such as novels and plays, in which the translator may have aimed to produce pleasing and exciting prose rather than precise lexical equivalents, and another huge range of practical, often mundane records such as administrative and legal documents in which any colour vocabulary is likely to be basic and unadorned.

It is not only the type of text, however, which may affect the precision of colour translation. Where possible, the researcher may decide to investigate the translator. How well did s/he know both languages? Did s/he know a third language or more which could have affected the choice of colour terms? Was his or her knowledge of the second language academic or conversational or both? Was the translator working under pressure (perhaps with a deadline to consider) or was the work carried out at leisure with adequate reference resources? Was the translator a creative writer in his or her own language? The researcher should also bear in mind that more than one translator may have been involved, and/or a reviser from a later period may have made anachronistic alterations. Anything which may have affected the accuracy of the translation should be taken into consideration although, of course, many of the above questions may simply be impossible to answer in data-restricted studies.

The reader will now be presented with a small example of the management of translation evidence between Old English and Latin. Old English, the language of the Anglo-Saxons, was spoken in England from the arrival of these settlers (an event traditionally dated to the fifth century AD) to about 1100 when the language was in process of evolving into Middle English. The Old English word *grǣg*, which gives us ModE *grey*, can be found with eight translation equivalents in Latin: *cinereus, croceus, cycnēus, elbus, ferrūgineus, ferrūgō, fuscus* and *glaucus* (Biggam 1998: 36). From the seventh century, along with Christianity, the Anglo-Saxons were introduced to the reading and writing of manuscripts, and the translation of Latin texts brought from the European continent. This means that all the surviving instances of OE *grǣg* date to the period between c.600 and c.1100.[18]

The researcher also needs to know the phases and dates of the second language involved in his or her translated texts. It is likely that the first Latin dictionary which s/he finds on a library shelf will be a record of *Classical* Latin. This is the literary and 'educated' Latin of the late Roman Republic and early Roman Empire, a language which is generally considered to have reached its zenith in the oratory of Marcus Tullius Cicero (106–43 BC) and the epic poetry of Publius Vergilius Maro (Virgil) (70–19 BC). Naturally, even the educated register of a language is likely to change over approximately one thousand years, and the Latin of early mediaeval England is not the Latin of the Roman Republic. The researcher into the *grǣg* references is, therefore, concerned with what is now known as British Medieval Latin (BML), for which the most authoritative dictionary is the *Dictionary of Medieval Latin from British Sources* (*DMLBS*).

The *DMLBS* colour definitions of the eight Latin words translated by OE *grǣg* are as follows:

> *cinereus*: ash-grey, ashen
> *croceus*: saffron-coloured, yellow (or ruddy)
> *cycnēus*: swan-like (in whiteness)
> *elbus* [under *helvus*]: dull yellow, grey or brown
> *ferrūgineus*: rust-coloured, purple or black; iron-coloured, grey
> *ferrūgō*: colour of rust, purple or black; colour of iron, grey
> *fuscus*: dark-coloured; (of person) dark-skinned; grey; deprived of light (figurative); obfuscated, opaque
> *glaucus*: grey, greyish-blue, silvery-grey; (of horse) grey or (?)blue-eyed; (?)sparkling, shiny, brilliant; greyish-yellow, yellow or orange.

A full-scale investigation of OE *grǣg* would make use of all sorts of evidence apart from translations (Biggam 1998: 30–99) but, for the purposes of this chapter, the translations will be considered in isolation. We have a scenario in which Anglo-Saxons or, at least, individuals wanting to explain Latin words to Anglo-Saxons, chose OE *grǣg*, either by itself or in association with other words, to explain all the Latin terms listed above. This information has the potential to give the researcher an insight into early mediaeval translation techniques and, perhaps, to reveal cases of skill or misunderstanding in the attempts to interpret Romance words and concepts into Germanic equivalents.

The first consideration for the researcher is whether any of these Latin words indicates only one colour, since it would be reasonable to assume that such a colour was an essential element of the meaning of OE *grǣg*. There are three such words: *cinereus* 'pale grey',[19] *croceus* 'reddish-yellow',[20] and *cycnēus* 'white', and the *croceus* translation will be used here as a case study. These results may come as a shock to anyone expecting *grǣg* to simply mean 'grey' but, as with referents, the contexts are of crucial importance and require careful investigation.

The reader will be presented here with a fairly complex example of translation which requires a certain amount of 'unweaving' to understand the likely colour sense involved. Let us start with the question, how is the ancestor of ModE *grey* appropriate to translate a Latin word meaning 'reddish-yellow' (*croceus*)? To attempt to answer this question, the researcher needs to have or to acquire two areas of knowledge: saffron and glossaries.

Let us begin with saffron. The Latin noun *crocus* refers to the Saffron Crocus (*Crocus sativus* L.), a plant of unknown origin, which has been cultivated for centuries and, at various times, in areas ranging from England to China. The three red stigmas in the flower of this plant produce, in terms of weight, the most expensive spice in the world, a commodity which has been used as a medicine, a food flavouring, a perfume and, relevant to the present study, a dye. As in the case of many natural dyes, saffron produces a *range* of colours which result from several variables such as the nature of the material being dyed, whether it was first or last into the vat, and various other details of the dyeing process employed (Cardon 2007: 302–7). It is highly likely that saffron, as a product, was imported into Anglo-Saxon England, but less likely that the plant was cultivated there (Biggam 1996: 19–22). Although no saffron-dyed textile fragments have been found in Anglo-Saxon contexts (Walton Rogers 2007: 63), it can be shown that Latin texts known to the Anglo-Saxons refer to it as a dye, so it may have been used for this purpose in England (Biggam 1996: 24–5).[21] It would be reasonable, therefore, to assume that the results of saffron dyeing had been seen, at least by some people in Anglo-Saxon England, either on home-produced or imported textiles. This makes it at least possible that a translator in England, faced with the adjective *croceus*, could envisage the reddish-yellow colour range of saffron dyes.

It should be remembered that Old English had no basic term for ORANGE, so this hue was likely to have been divided between the basic terms for the red and yellow categories, depending on which constituent hue was perceived as dominant. To indicate these hues, the Anglo-Saxons resorted to phrases such as *geolu-rēad* and *geolu crog*, literally 'yellow-red' and 'saffron yellow' (Oliphant 1966: 187, line 420). Before proceeding to look at cases of *croceus*: *grǣg* translation in glossaries, the reader needs to consider the nature of such contexts.

Anglo-Saxon students and scholars learnt Latin as a foreign language, and it seems that, from the earliest days of the Christian missions, glossaries were compiled to help them understand Latin vocabulary.[22] These glossaries can be thought of as somewhat like a dictionary since they list Latin words (referred to, in the plural, as the *lemmata* of the glossary), which are explained by Latin or Old English (sometimes both) interpretations (known as *interpretamenta*). The *interpretamenta* are not true definitions of the *lemmata*, as would be expected from a modern dictionary, since they usually address a lemma's meaning in a particular context only. It is also fairly clear that some Old English words were invented in order to stand as equivalents of their Latin lemmata, and such words were unlikely to have been used in everyday speech even among educated people.

To someone accustomed to using a modern dictionary, the Anglo-Saxon glossaries appear to be muddled and awkward. This is because each entry has a unique history which can often be reconstructed by modern scholars. Some lemmata originated in the Latin texts of major authors such as the encyclopaedist Pliny the Elder (23–79 AD), or they originated in Latin-to-Latin or Greek-to-Latin continental glossaries, or they consisted of *glossae collectae* gathered in England from glossed Latin texts. *Glossae collectae* originated in the custom of writing either a continuous translation or occasional word translations in Old English into Latin texts. These glosses provided a resource for later scholars who selected Latin words and their Old English explanations from such manuscripts and listed them in a new compilation so as to create a glossary. This is the meaning of *glossae collectae* 'collected glosses'. At first, they retained the order in which they were taken from the original text, and this often enables the text to be identified. As the glossaries were copied several times, various scribes added to them, missed out words, confused different entries, 'corrected' earlier errors, and reorganized the entries into alphabetical or classified order, all of which was copied and possibly changed yet again by the next scribe. It is hoped that this limited explanation of the complexities of glossaries will help to make sense of the case study which follows.

One Latin-to-Old English glossary is the eleventh-century 'Harley Glossary' (manuscript London, British Library, Harley 3376) which includes the entry: 'Croceus .i. rubicundus, rubeus, geolu 1 græg' (Oliphant 1966: 114, line 2120). *Croceus* is the lemma for this entry, followed by *.i.* which is an abbreviation for *id est*, 'it is', a frequent introduction to interpretations. This glossary entry is likely to have begun life as a phrase in Isidore of Seville's encyclopaedic work, *Etymologiae sive origines* ('The Etymologies or Origins'), in a section on dyes. He writes 'Luteus color rubicundus, quod est croceus' (*Lūteus* is a reddish colour, that is, saffron-coloured) (Book XIX, section xxviii.8). If this suggestion is correct, an early glossary entry was constructed which aimed to explain the word *croceus*. The simple entry probably first appeared as: 'Croceus .i. rubicundus' (*Croceus*, it is reddish) which makes good sense.

At unknown dates in glossaries pre-dating the Harley Glossary, further helpful words were added to this entry. One was Latin *rūbeus*. The basic term for RED in Latin is *ruber*, so *rūbeus* differs in some way. In Classical Latin, it indicated the reddish colour of some animals, for example oxen and chickens (*Oxford Latin Dictionary* (*OLD*), under *rōbeus*) but, in the Late Middle Ages, it also acquired a more general meaning of 'red' (Latham 1965: 412).[23] Elsewhere in the Harley Glossary, *rūbeus* appears in an entry with the lemma *flāvus*. The lemma is followed by Latin *fulvus* and then by *rūbeus* (Oliphant 1966: 187, line 420). In British Medieval Latin, *flāvus* has the primary sense of 'pale yellow, golden; (with reference to person) golden-haired', and BML *fulvus* has the primary sense of 'tawny (from dull yellow to reddish brown), golden-yellow' (*DMLBS*). This second entry suggests that *rūbeus* in the Harley Glossary was thought of as 'reddish' rather than 'red', and the prevalence of the colour yellow in the meanings of both *flāvus* and *fulvus* suggests that this particular form of reddish was reddish-yellow. This is confirmed by the Old English interpretation of *geole read* 'yellow red' which follows *rūbeus* in the *flāvus* entry.

Returning to the *croceus* entry, it is now believed to be interpreted by Latin terms which can indicate 'reddish' and 'reddish-yellow', but how was this hue translated into Old English? The first Old English interpretation is *geolu* followed by the letter *l*, an abbreviation for *vel* 'or', and then the second Old English word *grǣg*. Old English *geolu* is usually defined by its modern descendant 'yellow', but the *Dictionary of Old English* (*DOE*) definition includes a considerable colour range: 'golden, saffron-coloured, reddish- or orange-yellow, amber-coloured, yellowish brown, yellowish grey, dun-coloured etc.'. It is reasonable to assume that the reddish senses of *rubicundus* and *rūbeus* would have been clear, in general terms, to the Anglo-Saxon translator because of their similarity to *ruber*. The translator who added *geolu* may have understood *rūbeus* to mean exclusively 'reddish-yellow', or s/he may have noticed the yellowish words involved with *rūbeus* in the *flāvus* entry, or s/he may have read about saffron dye in another Latin text, or perhaps had actually seen saffron-dyed cloth. The reader will remember that the Anglo-Saxon yellow category almost certainly extended into reddish-yellow because of the lack of an orange basic category.

This case study began with the question of how a word meaning 'reddish-yellow' (*croceus*) could possibly be translated by a word meaning (apparently) 'grey' (*grǣg*). The reader may be aware from earlier chapters that historical colour terms tend to have broader coverage than many modern ones, and s/he may already suspect that OE *grǣg* is likely to mean more than just 'grey'. If it is assumed for the moment that the addition of *grǣg* to this glossary entry was not just an error, then there must be an explanation for its presence in such company. It is suggested here (on a minimum of research) that this particular glossary entry can be interpreted as follows:

> Reddish-yellow (*croceus*) =
>> reddish (*rubicundus*), reddish-yellow (*rūbeus*),
>> reddish-yellow (*geolu*), dull reddish-yellow (*grǣg*).

The meanings given above for the Old English words are certainly not their only colour senses. These particular senses have been selected from the ranges covered by these two words because they are compatible, both with each other and with the lemma *croceus*. The sense selected for OE *grǣg* in this context is derived from a full study of this word which concluded that its range was 'grey (greyish hue)' (Biggam 1998: 89). In other words, $græg$ could denote achromatic grey but also a greyish or dull variety of any hue. This means that it functioned as a saturation term, denoting low saturation.[24]

If the Harley Glossary entry preserves the order in which the four interpretations were added, it is possible to see how the meaning of *croceus* shifted slightly with the final addition ($græg$). 'Dull reddish-yellow' may seem like a rather downbeat description of the beautiful saffron colour, but it may indicate that *croceus*-colour had not been seen in vivid form in England. The degree of vividness obtained from saffron dye depends on the amount used in the dye-bath and, given the enormous expense of this substance, it may have been used sparingly in England, producing mostly pale and unsaturated oranges and yellows (Cardon 2007: 304), and any imported textiles may have been just a pale reflection of the best southern European and Asian products. This is speculation but, in a full word-study, as opposed to a consideration of the translation evidence in isolation, there would be further information available from other collected data.

The purpose of discussing the saffron case is to stress yet again the importance of context, since even a brief and sometimes distorted glossary entry has a context. Indeed, there may be two contexts, firstly, the original glossed text and, secondly, the one or more interpretations following the lemma in the glossary which, unless they have been misplaced, all have a semantic relationship with each other and the lemma. This case study also demonstrates something of the complexities of translation evidence. Not all cases will be so complicated but even simple ones may involve hidden traps. For example, every language learner is familiar with the concept of the 'false friend', namely, a foreign word which resembles a familiar word in form, and yet has a different meaning (see, for example, Rothwell 1993). An example is ModE *actual* 'existing in fact' and Modern French *actuel* 'in the present time'. A false friend is sometimes the explanation for a mistranslation in historical texts.

All aspects of language contact, including translation, confirm the need for the researcher to understand the social, cultural and political context of the historical period with which s/he is involved (Section 4.6). Many readers will know of societies today in which two or more languages are used in everyday speech, and are spoken fluently by almost every member of that society. This may result in one or both languages acquiring considerable vocabulary from the other (*code-mixing*) or it may result in people changing back and forth from one language to another in a single conversation (*code-switching*).[25] Code-mixing indicates an extensive use of foreign vocabulary in a context of such complete familiarity with both (or more) languages that speakers may appear to have a hybrid native tongue.

Code-mixing and switching must have been widespread in England, in certain social classes, after the Norman Conquest had introduced French as a prestige language. The progress of French in England, however, acts as a warning to a researcher who thinks of political and linguistic conquest as having a rather straightforward relationship. The military and political conquest of England by the Normans in 1066 introduced Norman-French, a variety of Old Northern French and, from the conquest to the early thirteenth century, this was the source of a somewhat restricted number of loanwords into English, mostly concerned with government, the law, estate management and other concerns of the new ruling class. It is likely that the vast majority of the native population was, in that period, unacquainted with such terms. Coleman has shown, however, that it was the late thirteenth century, two hundred years after the conquest, that saw the most active period of borrowing from French into English (1995: 107). The delay from the date of the conquest may seem surprising but, by the late thirteenth century, linguistic divisions between English and 'Normans' were less marked, and certain privileged and/or educated classes were bilingual. Bilingualism provided a conduit for vocabulary to pass in quantity between the two languages, and the effects can be clearly seen in the colour terms of Middle English. Many non-basic terms were borrowed from French, at various late medieval dates, into all the colour categories which had developed and retained English BCTs, but the blue category had not been firmly established in Old English, and its 'weakness' permitted French to take control. The Old English nearly basic blue term, *hǣwen*, was replaced by the French term, *bleu* (Biggam 2006c), and a host of non-basic blue terms arrived from French to populate the Middle English blue category: *asur*, *inde*, *pers*, *plunket*, *violet* and *wachet*. No other Middle English colour category is so French (pages 174–5).

Code-*switching* can occur when speakers are familiar, not just with individual words and phrases in a second language or language variety, but also with its grammatical structures. Such speakers are, of course, bilingual or multilingual and are perfectly at ease with two or more languages but, instead of keeping their languages separate, perhaps using them for different occasions or in different company, they mix them within a single conversation or text. The results, often described as *macaronic*, are surprising, and even comical to monoglots who usually regard different languages as inhabiting quite separate boxes. One medieval example will suffice to illustrate this phenomenon. The following quotation is taken from a mid-fifteenth-century English sermon in which the principal language is Latin but with frequent English 'intrusions' (shown in bold):

Dixi eciam quod venit in hominem et **doith** omni die **by grace of þe godhede**. Karissimi, debetis intelligere quod **it farith** per graciam Dei **as it doith** per solem. Videtis bene ad oculum quod quando sol splendet **bryȝte**, splendet ita prompte in loco qui est inmundus sicut in loco qui est mundus . . . set si aliquis defectus sit, **it is of mennys wicked hertis** qui possent recipere graciam Dei et nolunt. (Wenzel 1994: 125–6, taken from Schendl 2002: 59–60)

*I have further said that he comes to people and **does [so]** every day **through the grace of his godhead**. Beloved, you must understand that **it goes** with the grace of God **as it does** with the sun. You see well with your eyes that when the sun shines **brightly**, it shines as readily on a place that is unclean as on one that is clean . . . But if there is any fault, **it rests in people's wicked hearts**, who could receive God's grace and do not wish to.*

This situation, in cases where sufficient evidence survives, has the potential to identify social groupings, since the various forms of code-switching act as a means of expressing a sense of identity, providing the group with a feeling of common support, and separation from other unrelated, hostile and/or 'inferior' groups (Gardner-Chloros 2009: 5). For example, French words in English speech or writing appear to have functioned as a badge of superior status, suggesting a connection with the elite of the culturally important area centred on Paris (Smith 1999: 120–1), and most effectively distinguishing their users from the monoglot English-speaking peasants. Other types of information may also be obtained from macaronic texts. The sermon quoted above is obviously the work of an educated person familiar with Latin, the respected language of the Church, authority and the great authors of the past, but why should 'brightly' be better expressed in English? What overtones does it carry? Such questions could only be answered from more extensive textual sampling.

Among the literate and educated class in late medieval England, it would have been common, perhaps normal, to find trilingual individuals who were skilled or competent in English, French and Latin (or, more precisely, Middle English, Anglo-French and British Medieval Latin) (Rothwell 1994). Scholars of the period are coming to the conclusion that, in many cases, it is pointless to attempt to keep these three languages strictly separate since contemporary scribes and authors moved easily from one to the other, anglicizing French and Latin words, Latinizing English words and so on.[26] Trotter (1996: 31) writes that we should 'think in terms of a fluid, complicated and (to us) sometimes downright muddled situation'. He believes that people of this period would have been unaware of the origins of particular words, and unconcerned about using words from different languages in the same sentence. This situation means, firstly, that historical knowledge of past social and economic conditions is important for the semanticist and, secondly, that s/he should not be too strict about consulting the 'correct' dictionary but should consult all those which are appropriate.[27] In a code-switching society, lexical forms and meanings are regularly stirred together in a linguistic melting-pot.

9.5   Contrasts and comparisons

There remain further sources of information, some of which, it must be admitted, often prove to be of limited value. However, particularly in data-restricted projects, the researcher cannot afford to ignore any means of augmenting sparse evidence. The basis for much of this section is John Lyons' work on meaning- or sense-relations, in which meaning is extracted from the relations between members of lexical sets. The section on referents (Section 9.3) was concerned with the relations between words and extra-linguistic reality (the world), whereas sense-relations are concerned with the relations between linguistic units.

Lyons first applied his theories to a group of semantically related words, roughly concerned with KNOWLEDGE and WISDOM, in the Ancient Greek texts of the philosopher Plato. He investigated potentially revealing semantic phenomena such as incompatibility, antonymy, hyponymy, synonymy and others (1963: 59–78). A study of Plato's works certainly does not fall at the more deprived end of the data-restricted scale, since two thousand printed pages of text were available for analysis (page 93). Turning specifically to colour semantics, many research projects lacking the amount of surviving evidence that was available to Lyons, are likely to find that sense-relations are not easy to establish but, nevertheless, they should not be ignored. Those relations which are potentially useful in colour semantics are discussed below.

Several sense-relations involve some form of oppositeness, and this is often referred to as *antonymy* although the reader will find that this term is used in different ways by linguists. To some semanticists, antonyms are simply pairs of words with opposite meanings, such as *high : low, left : right* and so on. Lyons (1977: I.279) stressed the difference between gradable and non-gradable opposites, and restricted his use of *antonym* to the former, a preference which will be followed in this book. *Gradable antonyms* are concerned with a variable property such as length or temperature, which can be envisaged as a scale, for example: *long : short* or *hot : cold*. In the sentence *Today is hot*, the temperature is (linguistically) gradable because it could also be expressed as *very hot, extremely hot, rather hot* and so on.

Colour is another variable property, but antonymic relations require a scale, so tone, saturation and forms of brightness are amenable but hues are not, since they form a spectrum. Antonyms involve comparison, which may be explicit or implicit; for example, *The room is dark* implies that it is dark compared with the normally expected level of light, while *The sitting-room is darker than the kitchen* is an explicit comparison.[28] In historical studies, antonyms are not particularly helpful in establishing the meaning range of a colour term. For example, a sentence such as *His hair is darker than hers* is not tonally explicit unless we know the female's hair colour. The researcher must also remember that, because antonyms are gradable, a negative statement such as *John's hair is not dark* does not automatically imply that his hair is blonde because there are other alternatives, such as *red, pale brown, grey* and so on.

Turning to non-gradable opposites (also called *complementaries*), they divide the entire domain appropriate to them into two, without allowing for gradations.

An example is *open : shut*. It would be nonsensical to say **This door is more shut than that one*, because a door is either open or shut.[29] Complementaries only exist in the domain of colour where the referent is restricted to two varieties. For example, the sentence *The wheat in the field is not yellow* implies that the wheat must be green since growing wheat only occurs in these hues.

Another sense-relation which is oppositional in a different way is *converseness*. This refers to: word-pairs (or sometimes larger groups) such as *husband : wife*; pairs of antonyms in comparative form such as *bigger : smaller*; and corresponding active and passive forms of transitive verbs such as *killed : was killed*. Converseness is demonstrated by the acceptability of statements such as 'X is the husband of Y so Y is the wife of X'; 'X is bigger than Y so Y is smaller than X'; and 'X killed Y so Y was killed by X'. With regard to colour, the comparative forms of adjectives belonging to scales can usually be described as being in a converse relation; for example, *The girl's clothes were paler than the boy's* has a converse, namely, *The boy's clothes were darker than the girl's*.

Lyons suggests that the relation of *antipodal opposition* may be observed in some languages. This sense-relation refers to a group of words in which there is an antipodal (diametric) opposition. Among the primary English BCTs, *black* and *white* are regarded as opposites, and some speakers also regard *green* and *red* as opposites, as well as *blue* and *yellow*. This situation suggests that antipodal opposition is partially recognized in English basic colour vocabulary (1977: I.283). It is possible that this relation could be ascertained from textual evidence in a historical language and, if so, it might provide corroborating evidence for basicness.

Lyons' sense-relation *incompatibility* is described in logical terms as a condition whereby a particular property ascribed to a person or object excludes any possibility of ascribing a different, incompatible property to the same person or object at the same time (1963: 59–60). In a later book, Lyons provides a colour example of incompatibility: *Mary was wearing a red hat* is a sentence which implicity denies that Mary was wearing a yellow hat, or a blue one (1968: 458).[30] While the logic of this argument is undeniable, its value depends on the researcher understanding something of the colour system s/he is studying *before* considering incompatibility evidence. S/he must know, for example, whether the *red*-equivalent word in the language being investigated denotes a macro-category. If Mary were wearing a so-called 'red' hat in a language with a macro-red category, her hat could indeed be yellow. Similarly, if the historical-language equivalent of *red* was not a BCT, then not only would blue and green (and others) be incompatible, but so would several shades of red itself.

Cruse makes the point that the person or object described with a certain colour term may not be *entirely* of that colour, so that true incompatibility could only be claimed in connection with a precise area of the person or object.

He points out, for example, that one can have both blue eyes and red eyes at the same time because the iris may be blue but the sclera (the white of the eye) may be red and bloodshot (1986: 94). In historical studies, this sense-relation could only provide corroborative evidence in a language study which was already well advanced. The above oppositional sense-relations may prove useful in projects which have somewhat formulaic and/or data-rich evidence. For data-restricted studies, especially those with particularly sparse evidence, it may be difficult or impossible to ascertain whether any of these specific relations are operating.

In data-restricted studies of non-formulaic type, I have used *contrast* as a 'catch-all' label for a linguistic structure which indicates that two colour terms must have different meanings (Biggam 1997: 34). This classification is not recommended as an improvement on Lyons' suggestions, far from it, but simply to indicate that nothing more specific than a semantic contrast can be ascertained from the evidence available. For example, in the sentence *John brought her a red rose while James brought her a pink one*, the sentence makes it clear that, whatever *red* may mean, it is different from the meaning of *pink*. The problem for the historical semanticist is that s/he does not know *in what way* these two words differ: is it by hue, tone, saturation, texture, a completely unsuspected feature, and/or more than one of these features? However, a colour contrast such as this may be useful as corroborative evidence.

There are two more sense-relations which are of use in colour semantics. *Hyponymy* has been discussed in relation to basicness (Section 3.4), and it involves the 'containment' of one colour meaning within another. Thus the meaning of the hyponym *scarlet* is contained within the meaning of its super-ordinate term (hyperonym) *red*. Lyons defines this relationship in terms of *unilateral implication*, whereby *X is crimson* implies *X is red* (1977: I.292), but not vice-versa. In data-restricted studies where hyponymy may be difficult to establish because of the small amount of evidence, I have used the term *containment* to indicate suspected hyponymy (Biggam 1997: 35).

Lyons also included in his list the well-known sense-relation of *synonymy*, a term which refers to at least two lexemes having the 'same' meaning. This is a notoriously difficult area, and he deals with it by suggesting various types of synonymy (1995b: 60–64). The first type is *absolute synonymy* which Lyons strictly defines as the presence of identical meaning in all contexts, both descriptive and non-descriptive (page 61). The second type of synonymy is *partial synonymy* in which the terms or expressions satisfy part of the requirement for absolute synonymy but not all of it. The third type is *near-synonymy* which simply refers to terms which are very similar but not identical in meaning; for example, *fog : mist*. Finally, the fourth type is *descriptive synonymy* which requires that two propositions, each containing one of two synonymous expressions in otherwise identical constructions, and both applied to the same referent, must mean the same. For example, if this statement is true, *The house next-door to us is big*, then the truth of the following statement cannot be denied: *The house next-door to us is large* (page 63).

For the historical semanticist, the synonymous relations amount to putting the cart before the horse. To suspect any type of synonymy, the researcher must first establish the meanings of his or her colour terms. In other words, their meanings cannot be ascertained by the possible presence of synonymy. In any case, Christian Kay makes the point that the rise of cognitive semantics (Section 7.4) has effectively swept away the tendency to agonize over synonymy. Numbers of words and expressions simply have semantic connections of various types, exhibiting various degrees of synonymy (2000: 63).

In most historical research, even near-synonymy is difficult or impossible to ascertain unless clear statements, either direct or implied, are available in contemporary manuscripts or publications. The researcher needs to take care with such sources, however, and first evaluate their methodology and background. The Anglo-Saxon glossaries described earlier (Section 9.4), for example, in which Latin words are explained by another word or words, cannot be thought of as words explained by synonyms unless this is shown to be the case. It must be remembered that glossary entries may represent the work of several glossators working at different times and with different standards and purposes. While one may have supplied an intended synonym for an entry, others may have added extensions to its meaning, an approximate translation, a partial description or an error. The researcher can only consider glossary entries as a source of *potential* synonyms, requiring further investigation. In data-restricted studies, I have found it helpful to use the term *identification* indicating a potentially synonymous relationship of one term with another, which cannot be satisfactorily confirmed as yet (Biggam 1997: 34).

I have also used *association* in cases where two words or expressions appear to fulfil a similar semantic function but a synonymous relationship cannot be satisfactorily established (Biggam 1997: 84). Association often occurs in the formulaic context of a glossary entry where, for example, two Old English words may occur in a single entry, so that both appear to be interpretations of the Latin lemma. They may, however, represent different senses of the Latin word, in which case they are neither synonyms of the Latin lemma nor of each other. Association, therefore, refers to a proximity of two words on the page in a context which may suggest synonymy but cannot be shown to do so. It is a sign that the historical researcher is lacking information.

This section will conclude with some further considerations which may prove helpful in certain projects. Firstly, in a data-restricted study in particular, the researcher is entitled to stray outside the geographical and chronological limits of his or her project to a nearby time and place for which more evidence is available. This 'external' information should always be stated as such and presented as providing clues for the project, but not true evidence. It may be of use for the researcher, for example, to consider the definitions of cognate terms in related languages although s/he cannot be sure, of course, that both words developed in the same way after their separation. The researcher may also consider the evidence of concepts in an unrelated but contact language. In addition, it may be useful to look at the role of a particularly puzzling colour word at a later period of the same language, in order to observe its function in a larger sample of texts, but all this information needs to be handled with care, and not assigned too much importance.

A second potentially helpful consideration is the information which may arise from the role of certain colour terms in alliterative, or other formulaic structures found in poetry. It is sensible to consider the possibility, for example, that a particular colour word had been chosen because it alliterates with other words in the same line of a poem. It is unlikely to be completely inappropriate semantically in such a position but its meaning may be weakened or slightly shifted. If evidence from such a context were to contradict a conclusion drawn from all other evidence, it would be reasonable to give it less weight.

Finally, the researcher may care to give some consideration to what I have called *related citations* (Biggam 1997: 85). It can be seriously misleading to consider the frequency of occurrence of colour terms in surviving evidence without bearing in mind the history of the texts involved. The researcher might, for example, conclude that s/he has twelve occurrences of a particular colour term in legal documents, three in poetry and six in herbal (medical) texts. Before discussing the role of the colour term in the society which produced the texts, the researcher needs to ask whether any of them were copied, excerpted, edited or emended from other texts in his or her sample. S/he may find, for example, that seven of the legal documents are copies made for distribution to various interested parties, so that the *true* surviving total of the colour term's occurrences in this genre is five. Thus, the apparent importance of the term in the law is reduced to a more general function.

When the researcher has completed all the word-studies involved in the project, s/he will have a fair idea, at least, of some or all of the BCTs that occur in it. S/he may have found sentences which include colour terms functioning in a clearly superordinate role as in, for example, *The green ones were emerald and olive in colour*, or s/he may have found cases of similes and sayings using long-established colour terms, as in *The little boy's clothes were as black as a sweep's*. Any such evidence coupled with a look at the word-frequency lists from the project will provide a preliminary assessment of basicness. The researcher can then apply those tests described in Chapter 3 which are appropriate to the language under scrutiny, in order to confirm or negate his or her early impressions.

This chapter is all about establishing colour meanings and status for words and expressions in use in a particular place and time-span. Having established, or at least narrowed down, the meanings of colour terms at a particular time, the semanticist will often wonder how such a colour system arose and/or how it changed in a later period. The next chapter will advise on how to explore these questions.

10   Diachronic studies

10.1   What is a diachronic study?

As explained in Section 9.1, diachronic studies are concerned with the changes that occur in languages over time. For example, although Italian is a 'descendant' of Latin, the two languages are now mutually incomprehensible, and this is largely due to the initially tiny alterations made by native speakers which, over the centuries, have evolved into ever-increasing divergences from the earlier language. Thus, a linguist who studies the forms and meanings of the Vulgar Latin of Late Roman Italy is conducting a synchronic study, as is a linguist who studies Modern Italian, but the linguist who investigates how Italian Vulgar Latin developed into Modern Italian is conducting a *diachronic* study.

Generally speaking, the researcher who is involved in diachronic colour semantics is most likely to investigate changes in morphological and lexical forms and meanings, and/or various developments in semantic fields and cognitive categories. The semanticist may need to research, for example, the expansion or contraction of colour vocabulary over time, the changing distribution of lexical affixes, word loss and replacement, shifts in lexical semantics, the coining of new terms and so on. In any language, colour terms comprise an interactive set so that, where one term is lost or changes its meaning, another term is likely to take over its former role, and will itself be changed in the process. Such an event may trigger a small chain-reaction, changing the meanings and functions of several terms to accommodate the initial movement.

Diachronic studies of colour terms in the work of particular authors or in particular genres are less common, since the former involves a relatively short period of time (the author's working life) and, for the latter, it is usually difficult to ascribe changes specifically to the development of a genre, as opposed to general changes in the language or to the varying individual styles of writers working in that genre. As for categories, it has been seen in Chapter 6 that, whether or not the reader agrees with the specifics of the evolutionary sequence, languages increase the number of their abstract colour categories over time if their societies so require, and/or as contact with other languages may encourage.

Where there are sufficient data, these developments can provide a useful relative chronology.

A diachronic study can involve the investigation of a relatively short or a long period of time, and it can be restricted to a single phase of a language (such as Modern English), can cross phases (such as Middle to Modern English) or can cross languages (such as Latin to Italian). The amount of data available to particular projects will vary enormously, and this chapter will present some preliminary considerations, ranging from data-rich to prehistoric languages, and including both lexical and cognitive considerations.

10.2   Colour lexemes and semantic change

The value of good quality reference sources has been discussed in Section 8.4, and many such sources also provide varying amounts of diachronic evidence. A large dictionary which provides a selection of quotations showing how a word was used at different dates is likely to include its earliest known occurrence and the latest, if the word has disappeared from the current language. Similar information may be available for morphological variants such as the English examples of *reddish* and *redden*. These data provide the researcher with chronological boundaries for the recorded history of a particular word.[1] However, the first recorded appearance of a word may be a very long time after it was actually coined or adopted into the language, and allowance should be made for this, as also for the fact that its last recorded appearance may be similarly misleading for the *spoken* language. The historical researcher must deal with the data available but never imagine s/he has the full picture.

Let us consider an example project concerned with the changes in colour vocabulary which took place in English across the Stuart period (in precise terms, from 1603 to 1714).[2] This period saw several great events in English history, including a (failed) plot to blow up the Houses of Parliament, a civil war, a brief period as a republic, a terrible plague, the destruction of much of London by fire, and the union of England with Scotland, to mention but a few. The semanticist of Stuart English may have a number of questions in mind, such as the following: Did any of these events and their aftermaths have an effect on English colour vocabulary? Was the rejection of hue in clothing and church adornments by groups like the Puritans mirrored in their texts? Did contact with and settlement in the New World result in hitherto unknown items such as specific dyes, textiles, plants or gemstones prompting new colour words? Did union with Scotland affect the everyday colour vocabulary of Scots and/or of English under conditions of closer contact and cooperation?

As discussed in Section 8.3, a study of a relatively recent and data-rich period such as the seventeenth century would, ideally, have good quality reference sources to help the investigator but, where such sources are unavailable, s/he would need to work from representative selections of texts from the early and later years of the period. Where semantic changes are detected in the meanings of particular terms, the researcher can then investigate the course of that change across the years. In the present example, however, good reference sources *are* available.

Let us imagine that our researcher into seventeenth-century colour terms is interested in the vocabulary of YELLOW in England. By using a combination of thesaurus, dictionary, corpus and texts, s/he can tackle interesting questions such as the following: Do the words change their colour emphases over time? Are some initially restricted to particular referents and/or functions but later extend their roles? Are some more inclined to be used by poets, or courtiers, or ecclesiastics, and does this pattern change? Can any of them be seen to become fashionable, and then, perhaps, to become mundane, unpopular or even pejorative? How are new coinings treated; for example, are some at first considered pretentious but later appear to be ordinary? Why do some terms have a short life, and others become embedded in the language? Reference sources alone will not answer all these questions, of course, but they will provide some of the basic data which the researcher needs in order to investigate selections of texts. Almost invariably, that basic data will bring surprises, even to the native speaker researching his or her own language.

Starting with a thesaurus, the classified order of the *HTOED* enables a complete list of seventeenth-century yellow words to be retrieved, and this reveals an amazing plethora of terms which are familiar, almost familiar, unfamiliar, mysterious and downright bizarre.[3] The reader may be familiar with *flaxen* (hair) but probably less so with *flaxed*, *flaxy* or *flaxenish*; *sandy* is familiar but *sanded* (colour) probably not, while *flave* and *flavous* are likely to be entirely novel. But there is more: pale yellow can be described as *palew*, *festucine* or *sulphureous*; pale reddish-yellow as *fulvid*, *fulve* or *fulvous*; greenish-yellow as *subcitrine*; golden yellow as *pactolian* or *brazen*; 'deep' reddish-yellow as *crocean*, *croceal or croceous*; brownish-yellow as *och(e)ry* or *shammy*; greyish-yellow as *Isabella-coloured*; and orangey-yellow as *vitelline* or *luteous*.[4]

The *HTOED* also provides chronological information for each entry, and this enables our researcher to form an initial impression of which yellow words were contemporary with each other, which were newly coined (as far as the records suggest) in the Stuart period, and which words apparently went out of use during that time. For example, it can be ascertained that the pale yellow terms *flaxen*, *palew* and *straw-coloured* were all available to the writer in the first quarter of the seventeenth century but, by the last quarter of the century, *palew* had disappeared, while *sulphureous* and *strawy* had joined *flaxen* and *straw-coloured*, probably along with several other terms whose date-ranges are not so clear. As far as the *OED* records are concerned, *jaundiced*, *saffrony* and *pactolian* first appeared in the Stuart period, and the same period saw the demise of *saffronish*, *sanded* and *croceous*.

The researcher can now turn from thesaurus to dictionary, namely, the *OED*, to gain some idea of the usage of the seventeenth-century yellow words.[5] This will provide a valuable lesson for any researcher who imagines poets or playwrights freely selecting a yellow term from the more than fifty recorded by the *HTOED* for the Stuart period. It will become clear that some of these terms had minor and/or restricted roles in the language. For example, *sanded* was probably restricted to animal colours, although a reference to the sanded 'hair' of the sun requires closer investigation. Also, *palew* appears to have been restricted to describing the colour of urine. The practice of uroscopy, or the diagnosing of a patient's illness by means of visually examining a urine sample was widely practised in earlier times, and colour charts called 'urine wheels' were produced so that the colour of the sample could be matched to one of the colours on the chart, and the diagnosis thereby made.[6] The occurrences of *palew* listed in the *OED* suggest this contextual restriction, and this will prompt the researcher to investigate further.

If the researcher can access an appropriate corpus, it would be helpful to acquire more citations from that source.[7] For example, the *Helsinki Corpus of English Texts* has a diachronic section which covers the period from c.750 to c.1700. In fact, the table of sub-periods published in the manual to the diachronic part of the corpus provides an end-date of 1710. This is satisfyingly close to the end-date of 1714 for the Stuart period. The researcher will be interested in two sub-periods of the corpus: Early Modern English (British) II (1570–1640) and III (1640–1710), and will also be happy to read that 'the selection [of texts] strives for a representative coverage of language written in a specific period' (Kytö 1996).[8] In this particular project, the researcher clearly has available an appropriate corpus for his or her requirements, although the number of texts involved for each sub-period is not extensive, so s/he may well consider adding further textual research without disturbing the balance of text types. In addition, s/he will probably want to look up the broad contexts of at least certain citations.

Although this example of seventeenth-century yellow words has been restricted to adjectives, the researcher is advised to include all available parts of speech, as well as morphological variations, metaphorical uses, expressions and sayings, and any other relevant information. Each word will have a different history as the seventeenth century progresses, ranging from a complete absence of change to disappearance from the language, and every shift of meaning will suggest wider semantic and, perhaps, cultural movement.

It is highly likely that colour categories do not disappear in a society after they have been developed, but colour *terms* are less stable. As has been shown above, non-basic terms come and go (and sometimes stay) on an apparently random basis, and BCTs, although much more persistent, are occasionally replaced or demoted to a non-basic function. It is sometimes difficult in historical contexts to know whether the replaced term had been basic, but possible examples of replaced BCTs or near-BCTs include the demise of OE *hǣwen* in favour of *bleu* (to be discussed below), of OE *sweart* in favour of *blæc*, and of Medieval Welsh *rhudd* in favour of *coch* (Winward 2002: 238–47). In some cases, the researcher may encounter what looks like a replacement in progress, as is probably the case with Modern French *brun* being overtaken by *marron*, both brown words. Forbes has shown that there are clear age-related differences between the two with, for example, 18- to 30-year-olds using *brun* for only 10 per cent of the total of *marron* uses, while 61- to 65-year-olds use *brun* for 52 per cent of *marron* uses (2006: 105).

Diachronic studies can involve an extensive period, and this raises another matter which the researcher needs to consider. There may be a considerable difference in the quantity and variety of surviving texts at the beginning and the end of a long time-period so that the results of a diachronic survey across several centuries may suggest that a colour term had only a few, restricted roles in the earlier period but extended its use to many more functions and subtle distinctions in the later period. This may indeed be true, but it may also simply reflect the differences between a data-restricted and a data-rich period. There is little the researcher can do to compensate for this mismatch but one possibility is to pay special attention to the same genres in the later period which occur in the earlier one. If, for example, a data-restricted period has textual evidence almost exclusively from poetry and historical chronicles, the researcher may wish to study the same genres in the data-rich period particularly carefully.

In contrast with data-rich projects, a data-*restricted* study may produce insufficient evidence to answer the researcher's queries so it may be enlightening to examine the colour vocabulary of one or more contact languages, especially if more documents survive in such languages. A particularly unfortunate lack of data appears in the history of English after the Norman Conquest of 1066. Before this date, in Anglo-Saxon England, the vernacular was widely used for both record-keeping and creative literature, although Latin was also used by scholars. After the Conquest, the Norman rulers used Latin for administration and Church affairs, and Norman French, soon to become Anglo-French (AF) as the everyday language of the aristocracy and the royal court.[9] Although English remained, of course, the spoken language of the majority in England, its use in all forms of written record severely declined. For a century and a half after the Conquest, there are very few extant records in the English language, so its development at this crucial period in its history is sadly obscured.

The difficulties of tracing the history of colour terms through a phase of sparse records, and the value of considering evidence from contact languages, can be illustrated by a study of the rise of the word *blue* in English (Biggam 2006c).

This case also illustrates the relatively quick alterations in a society's colour system which can be occasioned by traumatic events such as foreign conquest. The modern word *blue* is descended from Norman-French *bloi* (in various spellings) which was clearly introduced by French-speaking immigrants to England. How can the history of its introduction to and naturalization in English be elucidated when so few records in that language survive from this period? The answer may not be ideal but it is better than nothing. In a bilingual or multilingual context, the researcher must make use of records of the appropriate date in all the languages available. This will provide a less than perfect picture of the situation in English but it offers more clues than could otherwise be expected, especially in a society in which code-mixing and/or code-switching takes place (Section 9.4). In the case of English *blue*, it was found that the earliest records of this word in England occurred in the names of Normans; for example, *Radulfus Bloiet* is mentioned as a land-owner in the *Domesday Book* of 1086, written in Latin (Munby 1982: Section 32.4), and *Rotbert Bloet*, Bishop of Lincoln, who died in 1123, is recorded in the *Peterborough Chronicle*, written in English (Plummer and Earle 1892–9: I.251). Perhaps the reader is thinking that this surname originates in some ancestor's liking for blue clothing, but this is not the case.

It soon becomes clear from other contexts that AF *bleu* did not always mean 'blue'. For example, King William II of England (surnamed Rufus) was described by the Anglo-Norman historian Geffrei Gaimar in 1139 as 'barbe aveit russe e crine bloie' (he had a red beard and *bleu* hair) (1960: 198). Since contemporaries describe the king's hair as red or blonde (Barlow 1983: 11–12) it can safely be assumed that it was not blue. Several other occurrences of *bleu* in twelfth-century Anglo-French texts lend support to the (perhaps surprising) conclusion that *bleu* indicated PALE, BLONDE or DARK when it was first imported into England. The *Anglo-Norman Dictionary* (*AND*) defines *bleu* as having three principal senses in the period up to the end of the thirteenth century: firstly, 'discoloured, livid, bluish'; secondly, 'fair, golden'; and thirdly, 'dark'. The first sense does not indicate an unrestricted use of 'bluish' since it refers to the appearance of people who are sick, bruised or harmed in other ways (Biggam 2006c: 164).

It is reasonably clear from the above (and other) information that any connection of the Anglo-French word *bleu* with the colour blue before 1300 was minimal and contextually restricted, so a question arises as to the nature of its role when adopted into Middle English. Turning to the *MED*, the researcher finds that ME *bleu* in texts dating up to the end of the thirteenth century is defined as: firstly, 'blue; esp[ecially], sky-blue, azure'; and secondly, as 'dark-skinned, ?bluish black'. This definition for ME *bleu* is much bluer than that for AF *bleu*, and it suggests what may have happened during the time of sparse records in English. Even though the BLONDE sense of AF *bleu* can still be found at the end of the thirteenth century, examples of *bleu*, quite clearly meaning 'blue', occur in Middle English texts at the same period (Biggam 2006c: 163–5). Although Old English had a principal blue word in *hæwen*, it was probably not a BCT, so it appears that the minimal BLUE sense of AF *bleu* was seized upon as useful for indicating BLUE in English while the BLONDE sense of the Anglo-French word was not required. The lack of records in English after the Conquest means that it can never be certain that *bleu* was never used in English with a BLONDE sense, but it would seem unlikely. The case study partially described above indicates the value of taking a long view of historical colour vocabulary, and of involving contact languages where sensible. This particular case shows some drastic changes, including the eventual total replacement of OE *hæwen* by ME *bleu*, and the apparently considerable semantic shift occasioned by the adoption of this word into English.[10]

The pre-Conquest situation of OE *hæwen* introduces the subject of *relative basicness*, whereby a colour term is assessed on a scale of basicness from zero to full basic status. A potential BCT will be located between these two points. Kerttula has devised a method for assessing the degree of relative basicness, or 'RB value' as she calls it, first used for English colour terms (2002: 84–92). The assessment is based on assigning values for the following: the primacy of colour meaning as given in three dictionaries;[11] the frequency of colour-use occurrences in the *British National Corpus* (*BNC*); the extent of the present 'application' of colour terms in the *BNC* as shown by types of referents; and derivational productivity. The last consideration concerns the number of morphological variants and compound forms exhibited by an individual colour term. Kerttula's experiments suggest that the more established colour terms have a longer list of derived and compound forms (pages 89–90).

Kerttula's suggestion of calculating an RB value for particular colour terms is a distinct possibility for data-rich studies, although the four criteria she uses for English may not be appropriate for all languages.[12] However, when assessing the relative basicness of colour terms in a data-*restricted* study, the precision of a numerical score for basicness is unavoidably inappropriate for use with what may be a considerable lack of data. My own recommendation would be for the researcher, having decided which of the BCT criteria were appropriate for his or her language of study, to simply record the number of criteria failed by a particular term. Failure on a single criterion would suggest a term just falling short of full basic status, while failure on several criteria would suggest, at best, a long delay before the achievement of BCT status. Even this rougher estimate of relative basicness rests, of course, on the shifting foundations of unrepresentative surviving evidence.

A colour term which fails on more than one BCT criterion may simply be a hyponym of an established BCT, in which case that particular colour category is already established among speakers of the language. Alternatively, if the

colour term is a potential BCT for a *new* colour category, and assuming there is
no other better-placed candidate, then its degree of relative basicness provides
a rough idea of whether and how the new category is evolving. For example, the
researcher may find evidence to show that the term was basic for *some* native
speakers but not others, that is, that it occurred in abstract usage in some types
of text only. This would mean that it was not a BCT, since a basic term must
be known as such by all native speakers but, if all other criteria were fulfilled,
basicness, and the general recognition of the new category, would probably be
very close.

10.3   Colour categories and cognitive change

This section is concerned with the diachronic study of colour *categories*, and
will build on the information to which the reader has already been introduced,
namely, the recognition of BCTs (Chapter 3), the structure of the basic categories they represent (Chapter 5), and the theory of the evolutionary sequence
(Chapter 6). Section 6.7 describes the current (2010) version of the evolutionary sequence, with the five trajectories along the sequence which have been
followed by the WCS languages (Table 6.4), and any future reference to the
evolutionary sequence in this book will refer to this model, unless otherwise
specified.

The evolutionary sequence is essentially a diachronic model. Readers may
be more familiar with its use in synchronic studies where, for example, the
position of a particular language on the sequence is assessed but, in diachronic
studies, the main interest lies in whether and how a language 'moves' along the
sequence. Although the development of new colour categories is a cognitive
process, it can only be revealed to the historical researcher through the function
of lexical items, namely, BCTs and potential BCTs. Potential BCTs are colour
terms which are, apparently, developing towards basicness since they exhibit
some of the basicness requirements appropriate to their language, but they do
not satisfy *all* those requirements.[13]

One important feature of the evolutionary sequence is that, as long as one
accepts its implicational universals, it provides a relative chronology for the
basic categories of a society. There are two types of chronology: relative and
absolute, and, unlike the latter, a relative chronology can only indicate whether
a particular event or entity is dated before or after a different event or entity.
Greater precision is impossible (Trask 2000). For those semanticists who accept
the evolutionary sequence as credible, therefore, it implies that, for example,
the development of a basic category for RED must pre-date a basic category for
BLUE. This implication even has the potential to be helpful in dating texts, but
its use requires great caution, for it is rather daring to suggest that a society
had no blue basic category at a particular date simply because no blue BCT

occurs in the texts available. The safety of such a statement would depend very much on the quantity and nature of the extant texts, and the presence of clear attempts to express the colour blue by alternative means, such as descriptive phrases and/or similes.

The colour semanticist has another diachronic tool, for use in assessing the break-up of macro-categories, and this is the diachronic continuum which MacLaury modelled in vantage theory (VT) (Section 7.4). VT is compatible with the evolutionary sequence since, in its diachronic function, it concentrates on the transitional steps between the stages of the sequence, and models how the categories change. Winters expresses the diachronic aspect of VT succinctly: 'what is being considered is the way in which alterations in human attention become linguistic change' (2002: 627).

Vantage theory can model several semantic relational types which, it is suggested, may occur in sequence before, during and after the splitting of a macro-category. The mobile and reciprocal nature of 'similarity' and 'difference', coupled with an apparently universal tendency, over time, to concentrate increasingly on difference, explains category change. In other words, people change their categories over time through an increasing tendency to create and name smaller and smaller colour areas (that is, they pay more attention to the *differences* between colours than to the similarities between them).

MacLaury presents a diachronic continuum of relational types which model the gradual break-up of macro-categories as represented in his Mesoamerican data. The reader is reminded that MacLaury is describing language change from the perspective of multiple mappings (on a colour chart) of the basic categories of many individual speakers for each language. The first phase is *near-synonymy* in which a category has two vantages (named by two colour terms) of almost identical extent and with closely positioned foci (1997a: 122–6). One term is dominant, showing a strong attention to similarity, and the other is recessive, showing a slight concern with difference and a correspondingly lower attention to similarity (MacLaury 2002: 516, Figure 15). Near-synonymy between the vantages of a macro-category can develop into a relation of *coextension* in which both vantages share the category in one of several coextensive types (MacLaury 1997a: 113–22, 153–79). A coextensive category is named with two terms (occasionally more), and the meaning of each one is centred on a different elemental hue. The focus of the recessive vantage is usually towards the margin of the category. The mapping, however, shows that the range of each term includes not only its own focus but that of the other term as well, and the ranges overlap considerably (page 113). The dominant vantage pays more attention to similarity (although not strongly) which causes its range to be larger than that of the recessive vantage which maintains, for its part, a medium-strength interest in difference (MacLaury 2002: 516, Figure 15).[14]

Coextensive vantages may develop into a relation of *inclusion* in which there is a strong attention to difference that indicates an approaching separation of the two hues. The recessive range retracts to the area surrounding its focus while the dominant range maintains its size and continues to include both foci. In lexical terms, the word denoting the recessive vantage is a hyponym of that denoting the dominant vantage. Inclusion may then develop into *complementation* in which there is a very strong attention to difference in both vantages resulting in both ranges retracting to their separate foci, and the category splitting (MacLaury 1997a: 150–2; 2002: 516, Figure 15). Stanlaw (2010: 211–13) interprets the two Japanese blue categories, named by *ao* 'blue' and *kon* 'dark blue' as having a complementary relationship.

MacLaury also describes a process which he often found to operate in Mesoamerican cool categories. The changes begin with *skewing*, which may occur in a non-coextensive cool category with one colour term, and one focus located in either the green or blue areas. Skewing involves an increasing emphasis on the focal hue, in the context of increasing attention to difference. The process eventually causes a split from the other hue, and the latter then acquires a new colour term (1997a: 223–32). It was observed that skewing results in *darkening* of the hue which had contained the focus of the macro-category, and the darkening increases as division is achieved, and continues afterwards (pages 243–6). In MacLaury's survey, he found that at least three times as many cool categories were skewed towards green as towards blue, and yet evidence from the earliest phase of the skewing and division process showed more cool categories skewed towards blue. He suggests that skewing towards green may be a 'panhuman proclivity', and that some societies carry out *transference*, that is, in the process of dividing the cool category, the focus is transferred from blue to green (pages 252–63).

For the historical semanticist, MacLaury's theories on the dividing of macro-categories offer the chance of ascertaining the position of a language on the evolutionary sequence with greater precision than was hitherto possible. Instead of regarding a language as simply being in transition from one stage to another, it may be possible to decide how far advanced it is in that transitional process. MacLaury's data-collection methods are, of course, only applicable to living languages, but the historical researcher may, in some cases, have sufficient textual evidence to attempt an assessment.[15]

Other methods have been suggested for judging the relative age of colour categories in a particular society. For example, those categories denoted by opaque terms are, as a general rule, older than those denoted by transparent terms. Thus, ordinary speakers of English have no idea what the derivation of the opaque term *red* may be, but they understand perfectly well the derivation of the transparent term *orange* (which is a much later BCT than *red*). This criterion is helpful to the historical researcher provided s/he knows that any transparent term is not a relatively recent replacement of an older BCT, but it may be difficult to know whether terms are opaque or transparent without a contemporary statement on the matter. Some further suggestions for relative dating have already been discussed in another context. For example, Hays and colleagues suggest that dating assessments could be made from the expression length of colour terms (Section 3.14), and from their frequency of occurrence (Section 3.15).

In his or her attempts to provide a relative dating for a society's colour categories, the historical researcher needs to be wary of unexpected disturbances. It is often the case that, when the gradual development of a colour system, category by category, appears to be lexically or cognitively disrupted or to be impractically complex, the explanation may be found in recent traumatic events such as foreign conquest, as with the case of Anglo-Saxon BLUE (Section 10.2), or some other form of social stress. MacLaury provides an extreme example in the case of a Tzotzil-speaking community in Chiapas, Mexico. This society, the inhabitants of the village of Navenchauc, live in a mountain valley which was once relatively isolated but this isolation was shattered, both socially and linguistically, by the construction of the Pan-American highway through the village in the early 1950s (1991: 45). The colour system of the Navenchauc Tzotzil was studied by MacLaury in 1980 and revealed immense intra-linguistic variation. For example, MacLaury's Speakers A and B were both middle-aged and had known each other all their lives but A had three BCTs and B had ten (page 36). MacLaury interprets this as the clash of a strong attachment to the traditional system with immense pressure to cognitively conform to the Spanish system now constantly visiting from the outside world (pages 45–6).

For reasons not entirely understood, the blue category in many societies appears to be particularly susceptible to disruption, confusion or neglect. For example, Andres Kristol describes the roller-coaster career of Latin *caerul(e)us* which he considers 'the basic "blue" term' in Classical Latin, although many would disagree with this assessment. He suggests that the 'original' Roman category it named was PALE BLUE but, under the influence of the Greek colour system, it expanded to include dark blue, black and blue-green. *Caeruleus* was present throughout the period of Classical Latin but then disappeared in Late Latin, and Italian developed quite different blue terms, especially *blu* and *azzurro* (Kristol 1980: 138).[16] Kristol found that early twentieth-century records of southern Italian dialects apparently showed that four dialects had no blue category at all, and, for thirteen others, *verde* 'green' included blue (pages 142–3). The Roman blue category, whether basic or not, therefore appears to have expanded and then drastically regressed in many of its dialectal Italian descendants.[17]

10.4   Linguistic genealogy

The reader will have encountered the terms *data-rich* and *data-restricted* many times in this book, but s/he has perhaps forgotten that there was a third category, namely, *data-constructed*, and this type of approach will be considered next. A project which relies on data-construction is qualitatively different from historical projects because it is concerned with prehistory. A prehistoric period is a range of time for which we have no written records from a particular society, either because that society did not use writing, or because none of their early written records have survived.[18] Since different societies developed writing systems at different times, their prehistoric phases have widely differing date-ranges. There are societies *today* which are prehistoric in the sense that they do not produce their own written records, while in the regions of the great early civilizations such as China, Egypt and Mesopotamia, prehistory ended several thousand years ago.

There are also cultural phases which, for various reasons, can be described as 'protohistoric'. In some societies, for example, symbols may have been used in certain highly restricted contexts such as indicating ownership or recording quantities, while more extensive texts were absent. A society may also be described as protohistoric when it has no writing system at all but has been mentioned in the records of another society which knows of it. To the colour semanticist, the distinction between prehistoric and protohistoric societies is only rarely significant, since minimal records and brief mentions of neighbouring groups are unlikely to involve a range of colour terms. For the purposes of this present book, therefore, *prehistoric* will refer to both prehistoric and protohistoric societies.

This brings us to the obvious question: if there are no extant records in a language, how can we discuss its colour system? Prehistoric languages can only be discussed after they have been (re)constructed by comparative linguists, hence the term data-*constructed*. This may sound like a highly suspect activity, and it is certainly true that the further back in time the reconstruction extends, the more tenuous its association with evidence becomes, but the methodology is based on rules established through extensive analysis and comparison of recorded languages. Leaving colour aside for the moment, let us consider the process of this reconstruction. The reader is probably aware that, since the eighteenth century, historical linguists have been establishing the relationships (or lack of them) between languages by means of the *comparative method*.[19] This process begins with known languages, and works backwards in time. The researcher is guided by a list of basic concepts which are likely to be lexicalized very early in all languages, thus reducing the danger of including words borrowed from elsewhere.[20] The basic words for these concepts in various languages are then listed and compared. For example, the word for 'father' is *père* in French, *padre* in Spanish and *pare* in Catalan. These words look similar because French, Spanish and Catalan are all 'sister' languages belonging to the Romance group.[21] If the Romance languages are all sisters, they must have the same parent, and we know that that parent is Latin. Thus the comparative method can establish sibling languages, but it can also take us a step back in time, in this case from modern languages to a historical one. The 'father' words are all *cognate*, that is, they all have the same origin, and we know that origin is the Latin word for 'father', namely, *pater*. It is clear that these Romance languages have all changed *pater* in slightly different ways to produce their own versions.

The survival of copious Latin textual evidence means that formulating sound-change rules for the Romance languages is relatively straightforward, but what if we had no surviving records in the parent language at all? Would it be possible to reconstruct the language from its Romance 'children'? Use of the comparative method by skilled historical linguists would indeed result in an acceptable reconstruction of Latin, because it has been found that languages change in regular ways, unless disturbed by out-of-the-ordinary events and contacts. Phonological change (sound-change) has proved particularly regular over time.[22] Thus, it can be shown that the sound-changes exhibited by the various words for 'father' above are repeated in other words: Latin *māter* 'mother' has produced French *mère*, Spanish *madre* and Catalan *mare*, while Latin *prātum* 'meadow' has produced French *pré*, Spanish *prado* and Catalan *prada*. From just three words in three languages, a distinct impression is building up that Spanish has changed Latin /t/ to /d/ while French has deleted Latin /t/ altogether.[23] But do these changes *always* happen, and why has Catalan deleted Latin /t/ in *pare* and *mare* but changed it to /d/ in *prada*? Even with this apparent irregularity, applying the comparative method may look easy, but readers are warned that this brief illustration of the method is an extreme simplification. Historical linguists have to work with many linguistic features in many languages in order to establish relationships and ancestry, and they must take into account all sorts of complicating factors such as the various phonological environments of a particular sound, the tendency towards conservatism or innovation shown by different languages, and much more.

When historical linguists have established a group of related or cognate languages, such as the Romance group, and they have ascertained that the group's parent is Latin, they can then legitimately ask whether this process can take us back even further; for example, did Latin itself belong to a group of cognate languages? The answer is in the affirmative. Latin, made important in

Italy by the military and political dominance of Rome, became the principal language of the Italic sub-family but it had several 'sisters' such as Faliscan and Umbrian. Having tracked back to this stage, we find that all the languages are historical, and we have left behind the comforting presence of living native speakers.

Languages of the Italic sub-family belong to an even larger group, the Indo-European (IE) language family whose relationships have been ascertained by means of the comparative method. The languages and sub-families, some modern and some historical, which make up this family are: Albanian, Anatolian, Armenian, Baltic, Celtic, Germanic, Greek, Indo-Aryan, Iranian, Italic, Slavic, Tocharian and some other poorly attested languages such as Dacian and Thracian (Mallory and Adams 2006: 12–37; for the fragmentary languages, see Fortson 2010: 459–71). Lexical relationships across this huge family are less obvious to the non-linguist since sounds have had longer to diversify than in a small group like Romance. Turning to 'father' words again, we have seen that the Italic language, Latin, has *pater*. Related to this word are, for example, Sanskrit (an Indo-Aryan language) *pitā*, Old English (a Germanic language) *fæder* and Old Irish (a Celtic language) *athair*. It becomes clear that all the Indo-European languages derive from a single parent, which is most often referred to as 'Proto-Indo-European' (PIE). We have now moved backwards from historical languages into the realms of prehistory.

There are no written records in PIE, and it is an entirely (re)constructed language, although this has been done on the basis of great erudition and many years of work. Looking once again at the 'father' words, we can now, by means of known sound-changes, trace a Romance route backwards in time from Spanish *padre* to Latin *pater* to PIE *$ph_at\acute{e}r$* (*pət\acute{e}r*) or, alternatively, we can trace a Germanic route back from ModE *father* to Proto-Germanic **fadēr* to PIE *$ph_at\acute{e}r$*.[24] We can also trace back the pathways of the other Indo-European languages, and find that they all end with the PIE form. The two forms supplied here for the PIE 'father' term illustrate reconstructions which post- and pre-date respectively the acceptance of the laryngeal theory. This theory, first proposed by the Swiss linguist Ferdinand de Saussure in 1879, suggested a way in which two apparently separate systems of PIE root-vowel change (ablaut) could be shown to belong to one system. The suggestion involved the reconstruction of former laryngeal sounds which do not survive in living languages nor in most Indo-European historical languages. De Saussure's suggestion was later vindicated through analysis of the Hittite language, a member of the Anatolian sub-family, for which cuneiform texts and inscriptions survive. This language, which has the oldest records of any Indo-European language, preserved some laryngeals. These sounds are now usually indicated in PIE reconstructed forms by *h* with subscript numbers. Linguists differ on the number of laryngeals involved, but three or four is the most commonly accepted number, denoted by h_1, h_2, h_3 and h_4. Their pronunciation is also a matter of controversy.[25]

The initial sound of the Germanic 'father' words represents the change from PIE /p/ to Proto-Germanic /f/ which is one feature of a set of sound-changes known as the First Germanic Sound Shift (also known as Grimm's Law). According to the First Sound Shift, for example, PIE /p, t, k/ changed in Germanic to /f, θ, x/[26] but because this law does not apply to Romance languages, PIE /p/ was retained in that group, hence the different initial sound in Spanish *padre* and English *father*. The First Sound Shift suggests that the /t/ in PIE *$ph_a t\acute{e}r$ should have changed to Germanic /θ/ rather than /d/, but this was prevented by another sound-change known as the Second Germanic Sound Shift (or Verner's Law), whereby a voiceless stop, such as /t/, between vowels and following an unaccented vowel, becomes a voiced stop or fricative, such as /d/. The discovery and formulation of these regularities in Germanic by Jacob Grimm and Karl Verner was crucial to understanding why Proto-Germanic differed from PIE, and the brief and partial description given here enables the reader to glimpse the sort of research which is being carried out in all the historical languages. The reconstructed PIE lexical forms are intended to represent the most recent phase of PIE, just before it split into various 'daughter' languages.[27]

Proto-Indo-European is a prehistoric language but it has been reconstructed from many historical languages; in other words, it has a relatively firm foundation on which historical linguists have built a structure which is not wildly speculative. There is, however, a natural tendency to ask whether we can go back still further in time. What was spoken before PIE evolved? Some scholars have indeed taken that further step, but they face considerable scepticism from other linguists because, of course, they are reconstructing from the reconstructed, not from written records, and the more steps one takes back from attested forms, the greater potential there is for error. Nonetheless, the continuing story will be briefly recounted here.

Some historical linguists recognize a language *macrofamily* which has been named *Nostratic*, and research in this area is heavily indebted to Russian scholarship, in the persons of Vladislav Illich-Svitych, who died in 1966, and Aharon Dolgopolsky who is now based in Israel.[28] Dolgopolsky considers that the Nostratic macrofamily includes the following families: Indo-European, Afroasiatic (also known as Hamito-Semitic), Dravidian, Altaic, Kartvelian (also known as South Caucasian) and Uralic (2008: 7). As Renfrew comments, 'This offers an astonishing and breathtaking perspective – a vast linguistic panorama' (1998: xi). The Nostratic macro-family, according to Dolgopolsky, extended across Europe, most of Asia, and northern Africa, but he suspects that the following families may also prove to be Nostratic after further research:

Chukchi-Kamchatkan, Eskimo-Aleut, Gilyak, Elamic and possibly Etruscan (2008: 7). The same principle used earlier can now be applied again: if the members of the Nostratic macrofamily are all related, they must have a common parent, and this language is known as *Proto-Nostratic*.

The reader may be somewhat lost in time as no dates have so far been mentioned. If s/he looks for dates in published works, s/he will find considerable variation, often differing by thousands of years. This apparently cavalier approach to chronology represents both the difficulty of assessing such dates, and the different things being dated. To begin with the obvious, the reader should take careful note of the letters or phrases which follow the numbers, since a date may be quoted as 10,000 BC (Before Christ) or 10,000 BCE (Before the Common Era) or 12,000 BP (Before Present) or 12,000 years ago.[29] Needless to say, there is no intention to suggest a precise point in time with dates like this, but merely to offer an approximation.

The reader needs to consider too just what is being dated. It can be seen above that a proto-language such as Proto-Nostratic, which had first to develop from its parent language, is usually assigned a date relating to the period just before it produced distinct daughter languages. Such daughter languages had, no doubt, existed as dialects of the proto-language before they diverged more drastically from each other. After some time, Proto-Nostratic itself will have disappeared, leaving several languages belonging to the Nostratic macrofamily. When a rough date-range is given for 'Nostratic', the reader must ascertain whether this estimate relates to the parent language or to the developed macrofamily or to both. In addition to this, the reader needs to be aware of the geographical area involved in the date. If a language spread westwards, for example, in the distant past, it could have taken thousands of years of migration and/or language contact to spread from Asia to western Europe. While these points about dates merely advise the reader to remain alert, there are also considerable differences of opinion among scholars of prehistoric languages as to the current best assessment of their date-ranges. Indeed, the view has been expressed that, until the quality of the data, and of the methodology for the interpretation of various patterns, have both been substantially improved, attempts at dating will be 'unfalsifiable, ungeneralizable and counterproductive' (McMahon and McMahon 2006: 160).

It is not surprising, given the difficulties of dating prehistoric languages, that many linguists who make the attempt prefer to deal in expansive date-ranges. An example can be seen in Hegedüs' schema, based on that of Gyula Décsy. Hegedüs refers to *protolinguistics* as the study of 'well-established and extensively reconstructed proto-languages' such as PIE, which he dates to the period from about 13,000 BC to about 5,000 BC. He refers to *palaeolinguistics* as the study of the macro-families (he uses *macrophyla*) such as Nostratic, which are ancestral to the better established proto-languages, and which he dates to the period from about 25,000 BC to about 13,000 BC. Hegedüs has an even earlier phase, the concern of *archaeolinguistics*, which is the study of *superfamilies* (or *superphyla*) recovered through comparison of macro-families, and this phase is dated to between about 40,000 BC and about 25,000 BC (1997: 67).[30]

The final step is a language which has been called *Proto-World*, Proto-Human or Proto-Sapiens. If one believes in *monogenesis*, that is, a single original human language, then Proto-World is the final form of that language before it divided into two or more languages. Hegedüs includes a very early phase in his schema which is appropriate for the study of *glossogenetics*. This phase, dating to before about 40,000 BC, is concerned with the emergence of speech in our species, *Homo sapiens sapiens*, and Hegedüs regards linguistic reconstruction techniques as unsuitable at this date (1997: 67, 70). Monogenesis is a subject which divides historical linguists into two camps: some would argue either that it is an unlikely hypothesis and/or that we cannot, in any case, reconstruct linguistic relationships over such a time-depth, while others are convinced and optimistic. Note, for example, the confidence displayed by Bengtson and Ruhlen (1994: 292): 'In the long run we expect the evidence for monogenesis of extant languages to become so compelling that the question will be not whether all the world's languages are related, but why it took the linguistic community so long to recognize this obvious fact.'

11   Prehistoric colour studies

11.1   Introduction

The previous chapter briefly showed how phonological change, in particular, can be tracked back through time and extended into prehistory but it has been stressed many times already in this book that the *form* of a word does not have a stable relationship with its meaning. Although certain areas of language exhibit a degree of regularity in their semantic development (Traugott and Dasher 2002), this is not necessarily linked with changes in phonology. Indeed, meaning may not change at all over a long period of time.

In attempting to retrieve meaning from data-*constructed* (prehistoric) languages, the researcher is forced into using a greater element of subjectivity than s/he would ideally like but this limitation can be somewhat reduced by considering the latest linguistic and archaeological research, including such factors as the likely prototypes of colour categories, the major economic and technological developments in human prehistory, and the natural environment in which prehistoric languages were spoken. The 'prehistorical' semanticist is obliged to press into service any or all of the disciplines which may be appropriate to the investigation of a particular word-root because, where evidence is sparse, each little piece should be prized. The discipline of palaeobotany, for example, may eliminate a particular fruit as the likely prototype of a colour category because the plant could not have grown in the area where the prehistoric language was spoken. This chapter will aim to present the difficulties of prehistoric colour research, but also to offer some examples of how clues can be followed up.

11.2   Modern and historical comparative evidence

One way of estimating how a prehistoric speech community expressed colour is to consider widely occurring general trends in a large number of those modern and historical languages which have very few BCTs. Such languages provide useful insights into colour systems which are almost certainly alien to the researcher. Also of great interest to the semanticist are those historical descendants of the prehistoric language s/he is researching which have very early records, even though they are unlikely to be close in date to the last period of their prehistoric ancestor. If certain trends and patterns can be discerned in surviving records, it is reasonable to 'track back' the process of development and acquisition of categories according to the priorities known to be extremely common around the world.

The semanticist is fortunate that a considerable amount of colour evidence from modern and historical languages has already been retrieved and processed in the form of the UE model's evolutionary sequence (Chapter 6), coupled with diachronic vantage theory (Section 10.3). The sequence offers a set of predictions that certain basic colour categories will be developed before others. It is not necessary to believe that the sequence is a linguistic universal, only to believe that its principal findings are commonly found in all language families. Those principal findings can be listed as: firstly, all societies appear to distinguish between DARK and LIGHT; secondly, if they distinguish any hue at all, it is most likely to involve RED; and thirdly, if they have a second hue category, it is most likely to involve GREEN or YELLOW or both. If the reader is uneasy about referring to the sequence for guidance, it may help to know that the combination of prototypes with the relative chronology of crucial socio-economic developments, appears to support the order of acquisition suggested by the sequence (Biggam 2004: 28–32; 2010: 239–49; Section 11.4).

Although this section may seem concerned solely with *basic* categories, it involves non-basics by implication. It should be remembered that, before a colour concept becomes basic, the researcher can be confident that it has passed through a period of development towards basicness, provided it was not a relatively sudden introduction from another society.

11.3   Category development

The reader will remember that Wierzbicka's research has shown that COLOUR [HUE] is not a universal primary concept. She believes it was constructed on the foundation of the truly universal primary concept of SEE (Section 7.3). In other words, the first step on the path to a colour vocabulary is simply human visual perception. However, humans have colour vision for a reason, and that reason is bound up with the various techniques and processes that humans and their ancestors employed to survive.

If the reader imagines him- or herself in an entirely natural environment, in which all his or her artefacts are also made from natural substances, s/he can imagine how colours would be mostly taken for granted. Everyone would know what grass looks like, or the sky, or the sea, so there would be no need to verbally describe their appearance.[1] But what if one's very survival depended on finding specific plants to eat or avoiding a particularly dangerous animal? Under such circumstances, the human brain registers, or mentally fixes, the features of these vital objects for future recognition. In the case of a bear, for example, the brain may register its size, behaviour, shape and colour. At this point, these phenomena have moved from perception to cognition, and, while this state involves an *element* of colour cognition, it is just a feature of bear-recognition, not an independent colour concept.

Given time, however, people may start to use phrases such as 'like a bear' in contexts which indicate its colouring, and this may encourage the development of a non-basic colour category, namely, BEAR-COLOURED. It is necessary to remember, however, that a prototype such as BEAR will have evolved in a particular society located in a particular region, and that implies a certain type or types of bear. The BEAR prototype in the mind of a modern researcher may be quite a different colour from the appropriate prehistoric species. Zoological and archaeozoological sources must be consulted. This scenario, however, refers to the *origin* of the BEAR prototype, and does not preclude later changes since, perhaps as a result of migration, a society's concept of BEAR may alter, expand or become an imperfect memory.

The majority of colour concepts will remain tied to particular entities, as in the case of BEAR-COLOURED, and they are likely to have been labelled with words which, at least initially, have transparent meanings relating to the entity. However, a few colour concepts may be found to be so important, and used so frequently, that they eventually free themselves from their object-prototypes and become applicable to any appropriately coloured entity. A few of these will become independent colour concepts or basic categories (Chapter 5).

I suggest that the motivation for the development of contextually free colour categories in early societies is simply their practical value, based on the need to refer to dangerous, socially important and/or exotic entities. Let us assume that BEAR-COLOURED in our hypothetical society indicates a reddish-brown colour. Frequent use of this concept may encourage the formation of a new category by, for example, removing a reddish-brown area from an existing RED+ macro-category.[2] Vantage theory interprets such a development as an increasing attention to difference, that is, the difference of brown shades from red ones is increasingly noted, but an entity or phenomenon of importance surely triggers that observation.[3] Once a category has divided, the new one may expand by drawing in other shades on the basis of similarity. Thus the reddish-brown bear-colour may expand into, for example, dark brown, yellowish-brown and other areas. If the category acquires a wider range of related hues, it is less identifiable with the more specific bear-colour, and this mismatch, I suggest, encourages the increasing abstractness of the category and, in a few cases, eventual basicness. An essential quality of a basic category is that its coverage must be sufficiently large for its BCT to function as a superordinate term.[4] A category with an entity origin, such as BEAR-COLOURED, may change to BROWN if it becomes basic, whereupon, as part of the same gradual process, its prototype will change from BEAR-COLOURED to (FOCAL) BROWN.[5] The BCT naming such a category, provided it has not been replaced, is likely to be cognate with the word meaning 'bear'.

The transparency of a colour term denoting an abstract category, especially that of a frequently used basic category, is likely to fade over time until the obvious connection with the old object-prototype is obscured, especially if the forms of the colour word and the object-word diverge. Eventually, the transparency of the term may be completely lost to native-speakers, in the way that no modern English speaker can guess the original prototype of *yellow*, for example, from the form of the word. A fully saturated yellow colour is the effective modern prototype of this now-abstract colour category. I suggest that prototypes are crucial to the origins of the *early* colour categories, although later-established categories, and sub-divisions of categories referring to small areas of the colour space, can develop as a result of other processes. A later category can be triggered by a contrast judgement such as, for example, purple being noted as 'not blue' and 'not red', thus making it separate from both. As regards sub-divisions of categories, a society which names various small areas of GREEN, for example, such as *olive green*, *grass green*, *emerald* and others, is more likely to notice gaps in the coverage and coin new terms to deal with them.

I agree with MacLaury that the *reduction* of macro-categories is driven by the increasing recognition of difference within the category, and I suspect that the 'different' area of the category is first registered when a new (or newly important) entity of that colour is recognized. One could speculate, for example, that a macro-red category, based on a FIRE prototype, split in two as the cultural significance of a new yellow entity grew in importance.[6] On the other hand, the *expansion* of categories from a specific prototype such as BEAR-COLOURED (after it had split from RED+) is driven by the recognition of 'similarity', since shades of colour once outside the BEAR-COLOURED category were later interpreted as being so similar to it that the boundary was extended to embrace them all. In category expansion, newly acquired boundary shades may differ from the colour of the old object-prototype sufficiently to weaken its position and encourage the development of an abstract prototype consisting of the focal shade.

11.4   Prototypes

Colour category prototypes exist in the context of particular societies so that, for example, SNOW could not be a white prototype for a society living in a tropical climate. Nonetheless, the most ancient categories were formed at such early dates that they may be considered prehistoric universals. Wierzbicka proposes that the origin of colour concepts lies in the universal concept of SEE (Section 7.3), but humans have a tendency to conceptualize opposing pairs, such as BAD and GOOD or FAT and THIN, so it is very likely that the earliest human species had the concepts for SEE and NOT SEE, indicating high versus low visibility. The prototypes for such concepts seem to be obvious; they are DAY and NIGHT, the time of seeing and the time of not seeing. I have suggested that early humans needed, above all, to quickly and effectively understand anything that aided or threatened their survival (Biggam 2010: 232). The contrast between day and night could hardly be of greater importance in this regard. Daylight was essential for gathering and hunting food, for making tools and shelters, for noticing various dangers, for travelling safely, and much more. Darkness has always been a time of danger for humans, and was, no doubt, feared by them. The linguistic significance of such a crucial daily contrast is that light and darkness, being so important, were likely to have been frequent topics of communication (pages 234–9).

The evidence from those modern languages with three BCTs is that the next colour category to emerge in a society, after LIGHT and DARK have been established, is M-RED which forms by splitting off from the larger LIGHT category (also known as M-WHITE) (Biggam 2010: 239–41).[7] The evidence for this new stage (Stage II in the evolutionary sequence) is derived from twenty-one languages reported in Berlin and Kay (1969: 52), a further six languages investigated for the World Colour Survey (WCS), and a further five WCS languages which are in transition between Stages II and III.[8] All these languages have only one basic *hue* term, namely, that denoting M-RED, so it seems reasonable to suppose that a macro-red category developed after LIGHT and DARK in prehistoric languages too.

Wierzbicka suggests that the prototype for M-RED was probably FIRE.[9] The most salient hues in M-RED are red and yellow, but the category usually contains, in addition, all the other warm hues. Fire contains elements of them all, since flames are orange and yellow, glowing wood is red, and cooked meat is brown. More than this, the new category would have emerged from LIGHT and so would have carried with it certain brightness elements typical of its parental concept and also, of course, typical of fire. If FIRE was indeed the usual prototype for M-RED, semanticists should also expect BRIGHTNESS to be involved in such categories, to a greater or lesser extent, for long periods of time.[10] This is most likely to be the explanation of cases such as Burarra *-gungaltja* (Section 7.3), Old English *brun* and many others.[11]

In terms of human survival, fire was absolutely crucial, providing warmth in winter, and protection from dangerous wild animals at night. In addition, fire made food like meat more palatable, and enabled humans to expand into colder regions. It was also, no doubt, the subject of some awe because of its power to turn a little bit of night into day, to inflict pain on humans, and to utterly destroy certain materials. The ability to create and manage fire was probably the earliest technological breakthrough in human history, and it is impossible to avoid the conclusion that it must have been the subject of discussion, instruction and warning in early human groups, requiring a relatively extensive vocabulary.

No doubt, the skills of fire management were learnt at different times by the various human groups but, in some cases, this took place at an extremely early date. Archaeologists in Israel, for example, believe they have found evidence for the control of fire which dates back to almost 790,000 years ago (Alperson-Afil and Goren-Inbar 2010). It would, therefore, be reasonable to expect 'fire-words' to be part of the earliest human language. This is certainly suggested by Bomhard and Kerns' reconstructed Proto-Nostratic word-roots, albeit for a much later period (1994; for Proto-Nostratic, see Section 10.4). I am not putting forward their suggestions as hard evidence, of course, but, if I had access to a time-machine, I would expect to find just the colour situation which Bomhard and Kerns present. If my trawling of their book is accurate, I find that they have no word-roots for RED or any other hue. There are, however, ten reconstructions related to LIGHT and BRIGHT, thirteen related to FIRE and BURNING, and six indicating both BRIGHT and BURNING. There are also eleven word-roots concerned with BLACK and DARK.[12] This scenario indicates strong concerns with light, darkness and fire which is entirely compatible with the evolutionary sequence and the suggested colour category prototypes. It suggests a society with perhaps basic LIGHT and DARK categories but without a fully developed basic M-RED category (Biggam 2010: 241–3). The interest in fire and burning suggests the social importance of fire, making it a likely future colour prototype, but this is very uncertain territory.[13]

Only the crudest dating is possible in the earliest periods envisaged for the development of Stages I and II of the sequence. Since day and night have always been with us, and since the management of fire apparently dates to a very early period, it is clear that non-basic, partial- and pseudo-colour concepts centred on the prototypes of DAY, NIGHT and FIRE are extremely ancient. It is impossible to know when such concepts may have become abstract categories, although I have suggested that the development of the human brain may offer some guidance on this (Biggam 2010: 238–9). A basic colour category must have the capacity to function as an abstract concept applicable to any phenomenon of the appropriate colour, and this may have been impossible for the earliest periods of human development if certain hypotheses about the brain are correct.

Steven Mithen (1996) has suggested that the most primitive human mind operated on the basis of a small number of modules which were concerned with vital aspects of prehistoric human life.[14] The modules would have included concerns such as social intelligence (interaction with fellow humans), natural history intelligence (interpretation of the environment), technological intelligence (the making and use of tools) and, possibly, a separate linguistic intelligence. It is likely that these modules operated separately at first but, over long periods of time, connections were forged between them so that knowledge acquired in one module could be applied in another. This facility to communicate between modules is known as *cognitive fluidity*, and it would have enabled invention and creativity to advance at a much quicker pace (1996: 66–72). If this scenario for brain development is correct (and not all evolutionary psychologists would agree that it is), it seems to me that the achievement of cognitive fluidity would be an essential precondition for abstract colour concepts, that is, concepts operating in any formerly separate module of the brain.

Mithen dates the development of cognitive fluidity to between 60,000 and 30,000 years ago, depending on the area of the world. He refers to a 'series of cultural sparks' starting in Australia, occurring in the Near East between 50,000 and 45,000 years ago, and occurring in Europe around 40,000 years ago (1996: 152–4). It is likely that this development of the brain coincided with a transition between two cultural phases known to archaeologists as the Middle and Upper Palaeolithic, and this transition is marked by improved tool-making techniques in stone, new varieties of stone tools, the use of new materials like bone, and artistic innovations such as cave paintings (Mithen 1994).[15] Linguistically speaking, this period belongs in Hegedüs' archaeolinguistic phase which pre-dates the Nostratic languages (Section 10.4). I would argue that it is unlikely that any society had abstract colour concepts before the Middle to Upper Palaeolithic transition had taken place in their culture, although they could have had non-basic 'visual impression terms' relating to daylight, darkness and fire long before. The practice of artistic techniques such as cave-painting, which is a feature of the Upper Palaeolithic, must have prompted discussion of pigments using, presumably, pigment-names rather than colour terms proper. Most importantly, this would have directed attention to colour as a separate commodity.

The next phase of prehistory, the Mesolithic, is a slippery customer. It is said to represent the various adaptations made by humans to cope with climate warming at the end of the last glacial period, and it lasted, for each prehistoric society, until they developed a Neolithic way of life. As Mithen states, 'Both of these time boundaries are extremely fuzzy' (2001: 79). As the northern ice sheets retreated around the world, they did not do so at a uniform and steady rate. There were warmer periods known as *glacial interstadials* when humans began their process of adaptation, only to suffer set-backs when extremely cold weather set in once more. The later interstadials are dated to about 13,000 to 12,000 years ago, and the usual rough date quoted for the last major retreat of the ice sheet which has, so far, not been reversed, is about 10,000 years ago. The reader will, therefore, find the start of the Mesolithic dated anywhere between 15,000 and 10,000 years ago.

Culturally, characteristics of Mesolithic life included microlithic technology (the manufacture of small stone tools) and the exploitation of coastal resources, but these phenomena have also been found in the later Upper Palaeolithic and in the Neolithic. The Mesolithic is sometimes referred to as the *Epipalaeolithic* since it represents a transition phase rather than a truly distinctive period.

The appearance of Proto-Nostratic or, speaking less specifically, a language ancestral to PIE and other proto-languages, is dated to the Mesolithic or the late Upper Palaeolithic, coinciding with the most recent period of Hegedüs' palaeolinguistic phase (Section 10.4). Kerns associates the spread of Mesolithic cultural traits with the spread of the Nostratic languages descended from Proto-Nostratic (Bomhard and Kerns 1994: 154). As discussed above, Proto-Nostratic may have had basic categories for LIGHT and DARK, and a developing M-RED category which could have become basic in the Nostratic family or later.

While the prototypes of the light and dark categories, and probably that of M-RED, can be considered universal, the prototypes which developed later cannot. The evidence from modern and historical languages suggests that the basic category which develops after M-RED is YELLOW or GRUE or YELLOW+GRUE. From the earliest version of the evolutionary sequence, Berlin and Kay (1969) found an especially close relationship between green and yellow, and divided their Stage III into two options: the acquisition of green before yellow, or the acquisition of yellow before green (Stages IIIa and IIIb). No other stage was divided in the first evolutionary sequence. The category or category focus labelled 'green' on the earliest versions of the sequence turned out, in several cases, to be more accurately described as 'grue' ('green' with 'blue'), so it became clear that the area of yellow, green and blue had not always been conceptualized as three distinct categories. The routes taken by the World Colour Survey languages from Stage II to IV were found to follow one of five trajectories, of which the most popular (Trajectory A) was to develop a Stage III basic category for GRUE from part of DARK (M-BLACK). This was followed in Stage IV by the emergence of a yellow category from the former M-RED (Section 6.7, Table 6.5). A less frequently attested trajectory (Trajectory B) in the WCS languages develops the same categories in reverse order, namely, a category for yellow at Stage III from M-RED, and then one for grue at Stage IV from M-BLACK. Also rarer than Trajectory A is Trajectory C which acquires a category for YELLOW at Stage III, and for GREEN at Stage IV. Rarest of all are Trajectories D and E, which acquire categories for YELLOW+GRUE then YELLOW, and YELLOW+GRUE then BLUE respectively. As can be seen from the trajectories (Table 6.6), the principal developments at these stages of all the WCS languages involve YELLOW and GREEN or GRUE, with some small concern for BLUE (Kay and Maffi 1999: 748–54; Kay *et al.* 2009: 33–9). Is there a prototype which explains this close relationship of yellow and green (and/or grue)?

The cultural phase which followed the Mesolithic is the Neolithic, a way of life which is characterized by an increasing tendency towards a settled life growing crops and raising animals, as opposed to a more nomadic existence based exclusively on hunting and gathering. The spread of this new way of life across Europe was, of course, gradual, beginning in the south-east around 9,000 years ago and arriving in Britain around 6,000 years ago. Not everyone would have adopted the new ways, so the Mesolithic way of life persisted in various regions. Some prehistorians, for example Colin Renfrew, have suggested that the PIE language was spread in conjunction with the new farming techniques.[16] This hypothesis contradicts the more traditional view, suggested by Marija Gimbutas, that PIE spread into Europe with the expansion of the Kurgan culture from its homeland in Russia from about 6,000 years ago (Gimbutas 1973a; 1973b). There is currently no resolution to this difference of opinion.[17] Linguistically, Hegedüs' protolinguistic phase arrives with the development of proto-languages (Section 10.4), that is, languages such as PIE which are constructed from later records.

Something can now be said about a likely prototype for Stages III to IV of the evolutionary sequence. It has been suggested that the prototype was CEREAL CROPS (Biggam 2010: 244). It should be remembered that the growing of cereal crops, as the Neolithic way of life spread across western Asia and Europe, was a novelty worthy of comment. It was also a means by which survival was more secure. Instead of relying on finding food-plants growing in the wild, people had, close to their homes, a supply of the raw material for crucial food items such as porridge and bread. Of course, there were problems, not least with the weather, grazing wild animals and marauding enemies but, generally speaking, agriculture enabled the land to support a larger population, and resulted in settled habitation which, in turn, encouraged aspects of what is called civilization.

Where a settled community has invested much of its potential for survival in a successful harvest, it waits and watches for a change of colour in the crop, namely, the change from green (unripe) to yellow (ripe, and ready for harvesting). As the crop ripens, each field (or small patch of ground) consists of a green-yellow mixture, in which yellow gradually comes to predominate. It is suggested that this is why green and yellow appear to be so closely related in the evolutionary sequence. Unlike the earlier prototypes of DAY, NIGHT and FIRE, however, it is not suggested that CEREAL CROPS was universal, since not every society began to grow cereal crops, or even to adopt agriculture at all.[18]

Later colour prototypes, whether belonging to basic or non-basic categories, tend to be more specific to their cultures. They may represent dyes, animals, fruit or other distinctively coloured objects, and etymology is often a useful guide to a likely prototype, as can be seen in the next section of this chapter.

11.5   Etymology and prototype change

It is sometimes possible for the colour semanticist to suggest the most likely prototype of a prehistoric category, or other aspects of a category's past, by means of etymology, that is, the study of lexical origins and meanings. To take a Modern English example, a monoglot English speaker may be familiar with the colour term *cerise* and will understand that it is a type of red or pink,[19] but the etymology of the word is not transparent and, therefore, the prototype is not obvious. A little research reveals that *cerise* is French for 'cherry', so this establishes the original prototype of this hue, and suggests its original shade. In the case of prehistoric reconstructed words, the etymology has to be suggested from a range of cognate terms in related historic languages. To take a hypothetical example, the researcher may be interested in a collection of cognate words in various languages which all have some connection with reddish colours and/or reddish objects. If the etymological origin of these words is found to be concerned with the fox, a reddish-coloured animal, it would be a reasonable assumption that the proto-language parent had an evolving colour concept based on a FOX prototype. This reasoning would apply whether or not the term was a later BCT.

Etymology can also offer guidance on other aspects of prehistoric languages, even to the extent of solving quandaries. Let us take as an example the development of Stages III and IV of the evolutionary sequence in PIE and its daughter languages (Section 11.4). The reader may remember that the sequence includes five trajectories, or optional pathways, by which the WCS languages developed their categories (Section 6.7, Tables 6.5 and 6.6). Which route was taken by PIE, or did it follow a different, previously unrecorded trajectory?[20] Starting with Stage III, the WCS languages were found to acquire a category for YELLOW (Y) or GRUE (G/Bu) or YELLOW+GRUE (Y/G/Bu). Is there any evidence for assigning one of these categories to Stage III in PIE?

Crucial to Stage III of the sequence in several Indo-European languages is PIE **ĝhel-* and **ghel-* (**ĝhel-* and **ghel-*?).[21] Mallory and Adams (2006: 474–5) define **ĝhel-* as 'yellow' and **ghel-* as 'shine, yellow', while Pokorny (1959–69: I.429) assigns both forms the principal definition of 'to shine, to glitter' (Ger. *glänzen*, *schimmern*).[22] This word-root, which seems to have survived from one of the earliest registered visual impressions, namely, LIGHT with BRIGHT, was apparently evolving an additional sense of YELLOW. Pokorny lists a large number of words in PIE daughter languages which are descended from **ĝhel-* / **ghel-*, and many of them indicate YELLOW or GOLDEN in some form; for example, words in Sanskrit, Avestan, Latin, Old Icelandic, Old English, Polish and others. This widespread agreement across language groups initially suggests that the yellow basic category had been developing (or had even become basic) *before* the break-up of the PIE language.

The basic green words, on the other hand, are more varied in the Indo-European languages so that, for example, Germanic languages use terms cognate with English *green*, Romance languages use terms cognate with French *vert*, and Slavic languages use terms related to Polish *zielony*. This variety indicates that the green basic category developed *after* the break-up of PIE, and this in turn suggests that YELLOW is more ancient in Indo-European languages than GREEN. This scenario would lead us to believe that PIE adopted YELLOW at Stage III. Or would it? What has *actually* been shown here is that certain colour words descended from PIE *$\hat{g}hel$- / *$ghel$- are found to denote YELLOW, centuries after PIE had disappeared. This certainly suggests some sort of connection between PIE *$\hat{g}hel$- / *$ghel$- and YELLOW but is this the full story?

It is true that PIE *$\hat{g}hel$- / *$ghel$- produced descendants which denoted YELLOW, or broadly yellow, objects such as gold and bile, but yellow is not the only hue which is strongly involved in the history of this word-root. Among the cognates denoting yellow entities and shades, Pokorny lists Sanskrit *hári*- which means 'yellow' but also 'green-yellow' (Ger. *grüngelb*). Monier-Williams (2008) records *hári* as denoting varieties of brown and yellow but he also defines it as 'green, greenish'. He defines Sanskrit *hárita* as 'greens, vegetables', and quotes an unspecified scholiast (early commentator) who defines it as 'unripe grain'.[23] Returning to Pokorny, he includes the following under PIE *$\hat{g}hel$- / *$ghel$-: Greek *chlōros* 'pale green, green-yellow'; Latin *(h)olus* 'greens, vegetables, cabbage'; Latin *galbinus* 'green-yellow'; Lithuanian *želiù* 'to (be or become) green' (Ger. *grünen*); Latvian *zâle* 'grass, herb or plant'; Old Church Slavonic *zelije* 'vegetables'; Russian *zelje* 'plant, herb'; Russian *zlak* 'grass' and others (1959–69: I.429–30). The cognates show that GREEN too features strongly in the meanings of *$\hat{g}hel$- / *$ghel$- descendants, including potentially early examples such as those in Sanskrit and Greek,[24] and that there are several cases of a close association or mixture of YELLOW and GREEN. Should the researcher, therefore, conclude that PIE had an early yellow+green category? The current trajectories of the evolutionary sequence offer this possibility only at Stage IV ($IV_{Y/G}$) where there is also an independent blue category. The scenario of a blue basic category predating independent GREEN and YELLOW is so unlikely for PIE that it should be discounted.[25] Where can the hapless researcher go from here?

The researcher will keep in mind the possibility that the evolutionary sequence may not accommodate his or her findings, but first, let us consider the Stage III options currently offered by the sequence: they are YELLOW, GRUE or YELLOW+GRUE. Firstly, the strong GREEN element which is frequently associated with YELLOW in PIE *$\hat{g}hel$- / *$ghel$- suggests that these word-roots denoted a macro-category, not a single-hue category such as YELLOW. The second option, that of acquiring GRUE at Stage III, involves the continuation of a macro-red category, that is, YELLOW must be associated with RED, not

GREEN, and there is no later evidence for this. That leaves the last option currently offered by the sequence, namely, the development of a yellow+grue macro-category.[26]

GRUE, of course, includes BLUE so is there any evidence for this hue in the Indo-European descendants of PIE *ĝhel- / *ghel-? Pokorny (1959–69: I.429) gives a principal definition of this PIE word-root as 'to shine, to glitter' as mentioned above, but he adds a further definition: 'as a colour adjective: yellow, green, grey or blue'. He was not, however, able to instance many cases of words with a BLUE element in their meanings. He gives the following: Latvian *zils* 'blue'; Russian *gołubój* and Old Prussian *golimban* 'blue'; Lithuanian *gelumbẽ* 'blue cloth' [although translated elsewhere as 'green cloth']; Irish *glass* 'green, grey, blue';[27] Welsh *glas* 'blue'; Gaulish *glastum* 'woad'; and Middle Irish *glaisīn* 'woad'.[28] These words constitute an almost insignificant presence of BLUE compared with the strong evidence for LIGHT / BRIGHT, YELLOW and GREEN, so this situation suggests that PIE had a Stage III macro-category consisting of YELLOW+GRUE (III$_{Y/G/Bu}$) which retained brightness elements from Stage I, but in which YELLOW and GREEN dominated, and BLUE was little more than an accompanying presence.[29]

The above speculations concerning Stage III in PIE have implications for the current evolutionary sequence. If PIE had a Stage III yellow+grue category, this would place it in the sequence's Trajectory D or E. These are the trajectories for which the UE model once had no known predecessors at Stages I and II, since, in order to make a yellow+grue category, YELLOW would have to have been taken from M-RED, and GRUE from DARK, whereas, in the 'normal' evolutionary process, new categories derive from only one parental category.

Kay and colleagues, however, found an explanation for the origin of the yellow+grue category, thanks to the emergence hypothesis (EH) (Section 7.5) (Kay *et al.* 2009: 37–9). Their suggestion is that speakers of EH languages develop categories and BCTs for BLACK, WHITE and RED, that is, not for the *macro*-categories of DARK, LIGHT and M-RED. In other words, EH-language speakers do not divide up the entire colour space at Stages I and II as speakers of partition languages do. Kay and colleagues suggest, however, that this situation changes at Stage III when EH-language speakers belatedly turn to the partition principle (Section 6.7), and develop a macro-category for YELLOW+GRUE, that is, for the thus-far unnamed hues. What would cause this change to partition? Kay and colleagues use expressions which suggest that partition is an irresistible force: 'then Partition exerts itself' (Kay *et al.* 2009: 38, 39) but the model itself has no motivating power, whereas social and cognitive pressures do.

My own view concerning the earliest stages of Trajectories D and E is that prototype change and, perhaps, greater time-depth, may combine to offer an explanation. It has already been suggested that the change from a non-basic colour concept, centred on a concrete prototype, to an abstract concept, occurs when attention shifts from a coloured object to the colour itself (Section 11.3), and a new prototype (a focal colour area) is triggered. It is likely that such shifts were not the first or only prototype changes in the long history of a developing category. For example, it has been plausibly suggested that the prototype of the M-RED category was FIRE, but this is not an appropriate prototype for RED, that is, the single hue which emerges at Stage III or IV with a prototype of FOCAL RED.[30] What was its prototype between FIRE and FOCAL RED? It was probably not the same in all societies, and the etymologies of the red BCTs in various languages may offer guidance, but likely candidates are BLOOD, (RED) BERRIES, (RED) OCHRE and COPPER.[31]

It is suggested then that the cognition, social importance and discussion of a new or newly significant entity establishes a prototype which often motivates the development of a new category, either *de novo* or from part of an existing category. This does not contradict the vantage theory explanation of new categories arising from an attention to difference, as it simply offers a reason as to why a difference is noticed.[32] In other words, prototypes change, and may change more often than we suspect. It is suggested, therefore, that the 'splitting and relumping' that has apparently happened at Stage III of trajectories D and E may indeed represent a 'jolt' in the sequence, but that this can happen where a new prototype is sufficiently important in a society to cause a cognitive realignment of its colour system.[33]

Where does this leave us with Stage III of PIE? If we follow the UE model without question, the conclusion would have to be that PIE Stage III was III$_{Y/G/Bu}$ which had emerged from an EH phase. I have suggested, however, that PIE Stage III may indeed have been III$_{Y/G/Bu}$ but it is not necessary to derive that stage from an EH history. There are also two other possibilities which, I must admit, I favour. The much later evidence for BLUE in related languages is so slight that it could be attributed to a development in some languages which post-dated PIE. This would indicate that PIE Stage III included a Y/G category rather than Y/G/Bu. This is not an option on the UE model. Finally, the indication, mentioned above, that YELLOW appears to pre-date GREEN in Indo-European languages (based again on much later data) could be taken to suggest a PIE Stage III with a separate single-hue YELLOW (as occurs in III$_{Bk/G/Bu}$) with a possible prototype of RIPE CEREAL CROPS.

This struggle to comprehend PIE Stage III is not presented as a completed argument, but an illustration of some of the considerations and limitations of working with the few clues and models available for the semantic prehistory of languages. However, even as the reader attempts to fit fragments of information into a diachronic framework, another force is at work to complicate matters, namely, semantic shift.

11.6   Semantic shift

In following the various semantic trails back from historically attested cognates to their prehistoric ancestor, the researcher is often astonished at the extent of semantic change over the centuries, and the widely differing paths pursued by related languages. Changes which can seem quite drastic are often the cumulative result of many very small semantic shifts. A shift occurs, for example, when the meaning of a word shifts from one already existing cognitive category to another or extends its meaning in order to take on an additional role in a second category. Thus, if a word for WHEAT should shift its meaning to BREAD, for example, its semantics will have shifted from the category of PLANTS to that of FOOD or, if the original sense is retained, its semantics will have extended to have roles in both PLANTS and FOOD. Campbell refers to this 'semantic promiscuity' as 'one of the most common and most serious [problems] in long-range proposals' (2003: 272).

When a proto-language bequeaths words to its daughter languages, they may develop further semantically, either through a process of independent evolution and/or through the influence of contact languages. The process of change usually takes place through the accumulation of small semantic shifts, often a gradual and lengthy process but, occasionally, a relatively sudden change is occasioned by an unusual or traumatic event (Biggam 2006c). Each individual shift, when it occurs, has a clear connection with the older meaning but, if further shifts occur, they are increasingly likely to obscure or supersede the earlier meanings. Thus, the shift from WHEAT to BREAD might represent the first in a chain of shifts, for example, BREAD might shift to LOAF and then to BLOCK. The last shift assumes a society in which the traditional shape of a loaf is a rectangular cuboid. The reader can see how each semantic shift is logical and has an obvious link with the previous meaning but, if earlier meanings are not preserved in the records, the researcher will be faced with the puzzle of why a word whose etymology suggests a connection with wheat appears to denote BLOCK in the historical records.

To make a difficult situation worse, the researcher may find that, while one descendant of a prehistoric language may have travelled the path from WHEAT to BLOCK, the other descendants have made many and varied other journeys. The semanticist, looking at all the descendants of the proto-language, may be faced with a selection of meanings which have diverged, not only from that of their proto-language, but also from those of each other. The meaning in the proto-language is not, of course, attested and has to be reconstructed from the apparently unrelated and puzzling concepts in the daughter languages. The reader has already seen how a word in Latin meaning 'cabbage' and a cognate word in Middle Irish meaning 'woad' are descended from a PIE word-root meaning 'to shine, to glitter'.

Changes of meaning in early languages can rarely be closely dated, and certainly not in prehistoric languages. It must be remembered that a semantic shift may take place over several generations, and it may occur in the language of *some* native speakers only. It is sometimes possible to estimate how many shifts are likely to have taken place, although this can usually indicate little more than a short versus a long period. For example, a shift from TIMBER to BUILDING could easily take place with no intermediate shift, whereas a shift from TIMBER to WHEAT would, if it were to happen at all, require a number of semantic shifts and, probably, a longer period of time. This gives only the roughest quality of information in a single language, but is a little more helpful where several cognate words in various languages are considered. In other words, semantic connections between cognate words in sister languages may be, at first sight, unfathomable, but they must all track back via small shifts of meaning to a single meaning, or a closely connected group of meanings, in the parental language.

11.7   From the known to the unknown

At this point, I fear my surviving readers may be wondering how the various points of advice and warning which they have encountered so far can be applied in a practical way. It is hoped that this section will provide a helpful example of how the colour semantics of an unknown (prehistoric) language can be constructed with the minimum of unfounded imaginings. The main principle involved in this research is to gain a thorough understanding of the earliest surviving records of a language family, so that suggestions about the colour semantics of the parent language lead convincingly towards the historical situation. The discussion which follows centres on one of the earliest colour categories normally recognized, namely RED, and how it could be reasonably reconstructed in Proto-Indo-European (PIE).

If a researcher aims to assess or re-assess the colour system of a prehistoric language, it is advisable to begin with the red category. This is because red is highly likely to have been the first hue to have been established and labelled in the Indo-European languages (and others), and, as a result, there is a good chance of encountering numbers of cognates in the records of the descendant languages. These cognates suggest a principal (and perhaps basic) ancestral colour term, and the meanings of the cognates will form the basis of a retro-spective semantic history. When the researcher has assessed the red situation in the prehistoric language as a benchmark study, s/he can then make a reasonable judgement as to whether s/he is likely to find further principal or basic concepts.

The initial step in assessing the semantics of a potential PIE red category is to collect the red, reddish and red-like word-roots which have been reconstructed by historical phonologists. With the help of Mallory and Adams' English-to-PIE index, it can be ascertained that four reconstructions can indicate this hue (2006: 551). They are: *h_1ei- (*ei-); *h_1elu- (*el-); *h_1reudh- (*reudh-); and *$\hat{k}ounos$ (*$\hat{k}ou$-no-s).[34] The researcher then needs to look at the languages which are descendants of the proto-language, especially those with the earliest surviving records, and collect from them those red words which are considered by phonologists to be descendants of the four PIE word-roots given above. Pokorny's dictionary is a good source of such information, and it can be seen, for example, that many Indo-European languages have terms which are cognate with PIE *$h_1$reudh-, including Sanskrit róhita- 'red, reddish', Latin rūbidus 'dark red', Old Irish ruad 'red' and Old Icelandic roðra 'blood' (1959–69: I.872–3).

For each word-root retrieved, the researcher now needs to investigate the earliest available texts, and collect as many examples of uses of the descendant-words as is possible. Textual examples may be given in the most authoritative dictionaries for those languages but the researcher will still have to investigate the texts him- or herself, in order to understand the wider context, to find more examples and to assess the context. If the researcher finds only sparse examples of the crucial words in the earliest records, s/he may decide to consider later records too, but the later the evidence, the greater the chance that semantic change has occurred since the date of the prehistoric language. Having gathered a collection of early textual uses of each red word, the researcher needs to study the types and dates of the texts involved, the referents described by the red terms, whether they could be loan-words, any metaphorical and symbolic usages, and anything else which may have influenced their meanings and usage. In other words, the study should be conducted like any other data-restricted research. When this phase of the research is complete, the researcher will, almost certainly, be faced with some 'eccentric' meanings which may represent late historical developments or fading semantic elements from the prehistoric language. At this point, the researcher is ready to assess the meaning of the ancestral PIE terms that preceded the early historical situation.

It is impossible to describe all the twists and turns in the research process which the prehistorical semanticist is likely to encounter, since every investigation is unique. One of the PIE word-roots with a red connection (*$h_1$elu-) will be briefly discussed here to indicate both the depth of analysis and the variety of subjects which can elucidate the situation.

Pokorny defines PIE *$h_1$elu- as 'red, brown' when used in animal- and tree-names, but as 'white, shining' (Ger. weiss, glänzend) when used in the names of various aquatic birds (1959–69: I.302). As has been pointed out earlier (Section 11.5, Note 29), Pokorny's definitions represent summations of the various meanings of the many lexical descendants of PIE word-roots. In other words, a PIE definition is an estimate of what is compatible with the majority of the disparate attested meanings in descendant languages. Considering the extent of colour semantic research that has taken place since the publication of Pokorny's dictionary, not to mention progress in the linguistic analysis and lexicography of ancient Indo-European languages such as Hittite, the colour semanticist should be wary of accepting Pokorny's definitions without question. What follows is a partial reassessment of the meaning of PIE *h_1elu- as an illustration of various research possibilities which the prehistorical colour semanticist might care to consider.

The investigation starts with a consideration of Pokorny's *h_1elu- cognates which he divides into four main groups: colour adjectives, tree-names, mammal-names and bird-names. It is clear from his definition that he believes a prehistoric colour root (*Farbwurzel*) gave rise to names for certain trees and animals of the same colour. But why has he dismissed the reverse possibility, namely, that animals and trees exhibiting certain colours gave rise to colour adjectives? There are two reasons why the reverse possibility is unlikely in this case. Firstly, the name of a red-brown animal would be a convincing source for a colour term meaning 'red-brown', but certainly not for a term meaning 'white', yet both meanings are involved with this PIE root. The second reason why the colour sense is likely to be earlier than the animal and tree senses is that two of the earliest attested Indo-European languages, Sanskrit and Avestan, have colour adjectives derived from this PIE root, but minimal or no involvement with animal- or tree-names.

When the researcher turns to historical instances of *h_1elu- descendants, it is necessary to take care with the dates of particular languages, and always ask *what* is being dated. Mallory and Adams provide a table of the Indo-European languages in order of their earliest attestation but they also caution the reader that the earliest records may only comprise a few inscriptions, with full textual evidence surviving from, perhaps, centuries later (2006: 13–14). Furthermore, for the colour semanticist, the earliest date of interest is the first attestation of *colour* terms specifically, so s/he needs to ascertain the dates of the earliest texts in which they appear, as far as possible.

Pokorny provides two Sanskrit and one Avestan descendant of PIE *h_1elu- and these represent the earliest known examples of descendants of this word-root. Bearing in mind what was said about dates in the previous paragraph, it must be pointed out that both Sanskrit and Avestan exhibit earlier and later forms of the languages, although the dating, in both cases, can only be approximate. The older Vedic (or Ancient) Sanskrit is known from a number of poems which were collected together in ten books around 1,000 BC although they may have been orally transmitted for up to five hundred years before that date. Old Avestan, which survives in the ancient sacred texts of the Zoroastrian faith, is also dated to roughly 1,000 BC.[35]

The descendants of PIE *h_1elu- in Sanskrit are *aruṣa* and *aruṇa*. This is a clear case of how sound-changes can obliterate any obvious connection between words, but the change of PIE -*l*- in certain circumstances to -*r*- explains how the PIE root can be discerned at the beginning of these Sanskrit words (Fortson 2010: 204, 211). Both *aruṣa* and *aruṇa* occur in the *Rigveda*, written in Vedic Sanskrit. While this is encouraging, the researcher needs to investigate the latest scholarly research on this text, since it was revised and altered in antiquity, and some books were added to it at a much later date. Leaving such detailed considerations aside for present purposes, let us proceed to dictionary definitions. Pokorny defines Sanskrit *aruṣa* as 'fire-coloured' (Ger. *feuerfarben*), and it is immediately clear from a major Sanskrit dictionary (Monier-Williams 2008) why he did so. The word is heavily involved in describing Agni, the Hindu personification of fire, who has three forms: fire, lightning and the sun. He is depicted as red in appearance. The dictionary shows that *aruṣa* is used of Agni himself, his horses and cows, the sun and the dawn. The compound term *aruṣastupa* is also used of Agni and means 'having a fiery tuft [of hair]' (Monier-Williams 2008).[36] It would appear that this particular word is quite narrowly restricted to Agni and his attributes and possessions.

Pokorny defines Sanskrit *aruṇa* as 'reddish, golden yellow' while Monier-Williams (2008) describes the primary sense as 'reddish-brown, tawny, red, ruddy (the colour of the morning as opposed to the darkness of night)'. As can be seen, Monier-Williams commits to the pure hue sense 'red', and he offers ample justification for this, instancing cognate nouns for 'red colour', 'ruby' and 'a kind of leprosy (with red spots)'. In addition, *aruṇa* is a noun for Indian Madder (*Rubia manjith* Roxb. ex Fleming), a plant which produces a red dye, and also for a plant which is sometimes called Dyer's Rottleria (*Rottleria tinctoria* Roxb.) which can produce a red or yellow dye, depending on the mordant used (a substance that fixes the dye in the cloth). It can also be seen from the Monier-Williams entry that *aruṇa* is a noun for 'the sun', 'a red cow (in the Vedic myths)' and 'the dawn', all of which suggest a close relationship with *aruṣa*.

The Avestan cognate with Sanskrit *aruṣa* and *aruṇa* is *auruša-*, defined by Pokorny, and by Bartholomae (1961) as 'white'. In this case, I have consulted the Avestan texts directly and propose to give two contexts in which *auruša-* appears, as examples of a particular dilemma. The first concerns the Zoroastrian angel named Sraosha (the name occurs in various spellings) who is the personification of obedience to the divine word of the supreme god, Ahura Mazda. Sraosha drives a chariot drawn by four horses which are described as *auruša* (Yasna 57.27).[37] This word is translated as 'white' by L. H. Mills but the intended visual effect is perhaps more impressive. The four horses are described as swifter than the wind, the falling raindrop or the arrow in flight, and these supernatural qualities should be considered alongside a further detail of their appearance, namely, that they are shining. The presence of light in connection with Sraosha can be taken even further, since he is said to inhabit a palace which is 'self-lighted from within, star-studded from without' (Yasna 57.21).

The second example of the use of Avestan *auruša-* occurs in the *Hadhokht Nask* (The Fate of the Soul after Death).[38] In this text, Zarathustra (the founder of Zoroastrianism) asks Ahura Mazda what happens to the soul after death, and he is told that, after dawn on the fourth day, the dead soul may see a beautiful young maiden approaching him. She is fair, bright, tall and noble and (crucially for present considerations) 'white-armed', a phrase which includes *auruša-* (Section 2, verse 9).[39] The maiden explains that she is the personification of the dead soul himself, since this particular soul has led a good, noble and religious life.

It is necessary to pursue a small diversion here. The reader is advised to be a little suspicious of the definitions 'black' and 'white' when applied to languages with early records and/or only a small number of abstract colour terms. The concepts of BLACK and WHITE in societies which have a set of abstract hue categories are located exclusively at the extreme ends of the tone scale. In such a system, BLACK and WHITE become 'honorary' hues, indicating only the most extreme forms of darkness and paleness. In early texts, the researcher can expect that words translated as 'black' and 'white' are likely to indicate larger categories, such as DARK+BLACK and PALE+WHITE+BRIGHT. The two Avestan contexts described above are, perhaps, really intended to indicate only WHITE (the colour of snow) but both contexts are supernatural and full of brightness. Furthermore, when white is well-illuminated it can itself be regarded as bright. The researcher needs to take the suspicion that these contexts may indicate WHITE+BRIGHT or even BRIGHT alone to an expert in the language.

In considering the earliest known descendants of PIE *h_1elu-, the researcher may wonder why they appear to contradict each other, that is, why the Sanskrit terms have a 'red/reddish/yellowish' emphasis while the cognate Avestan term is defined as 'white', and probably indicates 'white, bright'. A single ancestor of these cognates, however, could indeed include both concepts. The reader will remember that the Burarra language (Section 7.3) exhibits a comparable situation to that suggested for the common ancestor of the Sanskrit and Avestan terms discussed in this section. Burarra *-gungaltja* can be used of various reflective qualities and shiny effects, and also of vivid red. It can, perhaps, be summarized as denoting those visual effects which catch the eye, and I have argued that this is the loosely interpreted equivalent of M-WHITE in the evolutionary sequence. The most commonly observed future development of M-WHITE is for M-RED and the BRIGHT+WHITE concepts to separate, and the apparently contradictory situation observed in Sanskrit and Avestan suggests that such a separation had taken place before the time of their surviving records. This in turn suggests that the PIE word-root *h_1elu- would have indicated M-WHITE, comprising a combination of pale, bright, white and eye-catching warm colours.[40]

As has been mentioned above, Pokorny also detects the PIE *h_1elu- root (his version is *el-*) in a number of tree-, animal- and bird-names and, in fact, these roles of *h_1elu- are far more widespread than colour in the descendant languages. The bird-names appear to show continuity from the BRIGHT | WHITE sense of this PIE root, since descendants of *h_1elu-, in various Indo-European languages, denote birds which are either white, or black and white. The pre-eminent white bird is the swan, and this is denoted by cognate terms such as Latin *olor*, Old Irish *elae* (*ela*), Welsh *alarch* and Old Cornish *elerhc*. Black and white birds include the male long-tailed duck (*Clangula hyemalis*) which is named in Old Swedish and dialectal Swedish as *alle*, *al(l)a* or *al(l)*, and in dialectal Norwegian as *haval* or *havella* (in which *hav* means 'sea'). Also black and white are the razorbill (*Alca torda*) and penguins, which are named *alka* in Old Norse. Pokorny includes another black and white bird, the black-winged stilt (*Himantopus himantopus*) which is called *elōrios* in Greek, but he states that the form of the word is uncertain (1959–69: I.304). These bird names are compatible with the cognate Avestan word defined as 'white', and with the apparent origins of this word-root in concepts such as WHITE+BRIGHT. Another possibility which the researcher can explore is that, if brightness, in the sense of shining and reflectivity, had been a significant element in PIE, as suggested by Avestan *auruša*-, it would appear to have become a subordinate element to whiteness in these later languages.

It looks, however, as if the M-RED sense of the *h_1elu- word-root was also productive in languages descended from PIE, given its widespread applications to trees and mammals. The most commonly encountered tree-name cognates refer to the alder (*Alnus* genus), but Mallory and Adams suggest caution with the reconstructed PIE word-root for the alder-names since it depends on Hittite *alanza(n)* 'type of tree' being cognate, and that is currently uncertain, as a more precise meaning of the word cannot yet be ascertained (2006: 158).[41] Whether or not the tree sense which is apparent in certain descendants of PIE *h_1elu- developed as early as PIE itself, the semanticist will want to find a convincing reason why a semantic shift from the domain of COLOUR to that of TREE apparently occurred. Is or was the alder in any way bright, white or red?

The alder has a number of characteristics which make it a convincing candidate for an epithet such as 'the red tree'. First of all, the male catkins of this tree are red, and the female catkins are red-brown. Miles writes 'A riverbank lined with alders covered in dark red male catkins is quite something to behold' (1999: 205). The semanticist, however, needs, in addition, to consider those attributes and features of the tree which are not immediately visible. For example, alder-wood is reddish. Step writes that when the wood is cut 'it becomes red; finally, on drying, it changes to a pinkish tint' (Step n.d.: 30). There is no doubt that alder-wood has always been of considerable value to people since it is highly resistant to rot when entirely submerged. It has been used for piles driven into wet places to provide a secure foundation for buildings, and for the construction of bridges, quays, sluice-gates and drain-pipes (Howard 1947: 6–7). Prehistoric European peoples would have found this characteristic of alder wood invaluable for their lake dwellings and timber causeways across marshy areas. Another strong connection of the alder with the red hue concerns the dye which is obtainable from the bark and young shoots of this tree. The dye can be combined with various mordants to produce yellowish hues but, without a mordant at all, the bark dyes reddish, a hue known as Aldine Red, and, depending on the process used, the shoots can dye 'cinnamon' (orangey-brown) or 'tawny' (yellowish- or orangey-brown). The fresh wood can also yield a 'pinkish-fawn' dye (Grieve 1973: 17). The alder, therefore, has a strong connection with red and reddish hues.

Other descendants of PIE *h_1elu- came to denote tree species which are less amenable to explanation, including terms for the elm (*Ulmus* genus) in Latin, Celtic and Germanic, and for a group of trees with needle-like leaves. These include the juniper (*Juniperus* genus) in Baltic and Slavic, the cedar (*Cedrus* genus) in Armenian, and possibly the spruce (*Picea* genus) or fir (*Abies* genus) in Greek. In a detailed study of this PIE word-root, the semanticist would investigate further, in particular to establish as much dating evidence as possible, since these tree species may represent additional semantic shifts from ALDER (TREE) or ALDER (WOOD). In other words, while ALDER may represent a shift from a reddish hue, ELM may represent a shift from ALDER which is based on a non-colour connection between the trees. The small group of needle-leaved trees may represent a further shift, although, without dating evidence, the researcher needs, for the moment, to remain cautious. The juniper, cedar, spruce and fir are all evergreens, and all produce cones and needle-shaped leaves. It is clear, therefore, why they could have been classified together, but the link with alders and elms is not immediately obvious.

The PIE *h_1elu- root also provided animal names in the Indo-European languages, which Pokorny groups together under the heading 'Deer and similar animals' (Ger. *Hirsch und ähnliche Tier*) (1959–69: I.303–4). Most of the cognates are defined with the generic term 'deer', although some terms in Germanic, Slavic, Latin and Greek are defined more specifically as '(European) elk' (Ger. *Elch, Elentier*). Old Irish has a cognate defined as 'roe-deer' (Ger. *Reh*), and Sanskrit has a term meaning 'antelope' (Ger. *Antilopenbock*).[42] These animals are not white, but they could all be described as brown.[43] However, a brown hue is hardly a distinguishing feature among mammals, so it would be reasonable to suppose that a particular type of brown is intended, and reddish or yellowish are suggested by the meanings of the cognates discussed above. It should not be assumed, however, that all cognates denote the same hue variety.

So far, three of Pokorny's four sections relating to descendants of PIE *h_1elu-, namely, trees, mammals and birds, have been briefly discussed. The fourth section is concerned with *h_1elu- descendants which function *primarily* as colour adjectives and, as has been mentioned above, this function appears to pre-date the plant and animal names. Pokorny found cognate colour adjectives in two early languages, Sanskrit and Avestan, which have been discussed above. There are also examples in Old and Middle High German for which Pokorny constructs the Proto-Germanic root *elwa- which he interprets as 'brown, yellow'.[44] Now that Pokorny's four sections have been discussed, it is appropriate to recap and consider future work.

The reader will see from this study of PIE *h_1elu- that there are multiple problems which a thorough study of this word-root would need to address. Firstly, for the non-German speaker, there is an initial problem in interpreting Pokorny's German definitions of PIE word-roots and descendant cognates. A brief translating dictionary can be too generic when dealing with plant- or animal-names, and a larger dictionary can offer alternatives which may be misleading. Thus Ger. *Hirsch* can, according to my dictionary, be interpreted as 'stag, hart; (red) deer'. A *hart* is 'an adult male deer, especially a red deer over five years old'; and a *stag* is 'a fully adult male deer'.[45] Did Pokorny intend to imply that the *h_1elu- cognates refer specifically to male deer, and/or red deer, or is this a German to English translation problem? If this were a thorough piece of research, it would be necessary to probe more deeply. The *crucial* questions, of course, are not concerned with the best English interpretation of Ger. *Hirsch*, but with the meanings of colour terms in the original sources, the opinions of experts in particular languages, the definitions appearing in the best modern dictionaries, and the arguments presented in research publications.

Another obvious problem with this type of research is that it involves plants and animals, and it is assumed that few semanticists are also qualified botanists and zoologists. The researcher needs to consult reference works in these subjects, but must also consider the geography and chronology involved. It is quite possible that a deer species named by early Indic speakers in the Indus valley around 1,000 BC would not be the same species as that named by Gothic speakers in eastern Europe in 400 AD, and yet the words used by these two groups of speakers may be related.

My recommendation to the colour semantic researcher would be to draw up a working hypothesis at this stage, based on research to this point, and then to investigate various specific queries more thoroughly. My present interim hypothesis for the meaning of PIE *h_1elu- and the directions of its descendants' semantic shifts would be something like this:

1. BRIGHT+WHITE+ (eye-catching) RED/YELLOW in PIE is ancestral to:
   a. WHITE (+BRIGHT?) in Avestan,
   b. BRIGHT (specifically LIGHT-EMISSION?)+ RED/YELLOW in Sanskrit (*aruṣa*),
   c. M-RED and BRIGHT (specifically LIGHT-EMISSION?) in Sanskrit (*aruṇa*),
   d. WHITE, RED (one or both) in several other language groups.

2. WHITE gave rise to bird names in Greek, Italic, Celtic, Germanic.
3. M-RED gave rise to:
   a. ALDER ('red tree') in Italic, Celtic, Germanic, Slavic and Baltic,
   b. DEER ('reddish-?/yellowish-? brown animal') in Indic, Greek, Italic, Celtic, Germanic, Armenian, Slavic and Baltic.
4. ALDER linked with ELM (reason unknown) in Italic, Celtic, Germanic.
5. ALDER and/or ELM linked with (reasons unknown): JUNIPER in Slavic and Baltic; CEDAR in Armenian; and possibly SPRUCE/FIR in Greek (all evergreens with needle-shaped leaves).
6. DEER gave rise to BROWN (specifically YELLOWISH-BROWN?) in Germanic.

The reader is reminded that this study of PIE *h_1elu- is incomplete, since it has been used only to illustrate a suggested methodology. Even if the study were complete, the evidence retrieved needs to be considered alongside that from similar studies of the other three PIE word-roots (given above) which indicate a red connection. With these caveats, it looks at present as if Pokorny's definition of PIE *h_1elu- ('reddish, yellow, bright, white and brown' (colours); 'red, brown' (animals and trees); 'white, shiny' (swans and sea-birds), has been provisionally revised to 'white+bright+ (eye-catching) red/yellow'. How has this interim conclusion been reached?

The starting point is the earliest surviving evidence, namely, the Sanskrit and Avestan usages. These languages differ, to the extent that Avestan chose to emphasize whiteness and, probably, brightness, while Sanskrit chose to emphasize redness but without totally discarding brightness. However, we know that the Avestan and Sanskrit words derive from the same parent, in terms of their form, so the parent must have had a meaning which can be explained as ancestral to all three later words. The interim suggestion of 'bright+white+ (eye-catching) red/yellow' provides an origin for both the white and/or bright theme, and the macro-red theme evidenced in later languages. Furthermore, there is good prototypical support for this suggestion, since the eye-catching phenomenon of FIRE must have played a crucial role in social, perceptual and cognitive aspects of prehistoric life, and PIE *h_1elu- looks very much like a fire-related word. In addition, we have evidence that 'bundles' of eye-catching appearances comprise the meaning of certain words in some *modern* languages, of which Burarra is an excellent example (Section 7.3). The 'reddish brown' and 'tawny' hues which are said to be possible definitions of a Sanskrit descendant of PIE *h_1elu- suggest that, having emphasized redness, it became possible to extend the meaning of *aruṇa*- to reds of lower visibility, such as reddish-brown.

As regards basicness, the widespread connection of certain later cognates with plant- and animal-names suggests that they were unlikely to have been BCTs, since there is a strong suspicion that they were contextually restricted.

In addition, if it is correct that PIE was a Stage III language (Section 11.4), its BCT for RED+ would, presumably, have had little concern with whiteness and, therefore, been unable to bequeath this emphasis to its Avestan descendant. Studies of the other red word-roots would help to clarify this situation.

The reader may find a lot to disagree with in the above investigation and interim conclusion for PIE *h_1elu-* and its descendants but the importance of this section is to suggest that Pokorny's colour definitions often relate, not to PIE, but to a period long after its demise. This is inevitable because of the date at which Pokorny worked, but I hope to have persuaded the reader that it is now possible to target, however roughly, the colour semantics of PIE itself.

12 Applications and potential

12.1 Introduction

The purpose of this book has been to investigate how much colour semantic information can be retrieved from the records and/or the descendants of dead languages or phases of languages. In particular, the aim was to leave no stone unturned in the hunt for clues, and then to evaluate the evidence uncovered. The emphasis has been on *literal* colour meaning since that must come first before more eccentric uses of colour terms can be noticed by means of their deviation from the norm. Since the aim has been to investigate how the colour senses of past vocabulary can be assessed, there has been no real attempt to tackle the potential next step, namely, applying improved colour semantic understanding to the surviving artefacts of particular societies, whether literary, linguistic or artistic. It is not the purpose of this book to take that extra step but this chapter will briefly discuss two case studies which reveal the potential (and limitations) of what may be called 'applied historical colour semantics'.

12.2 Robert Edgeworth and the *Aeneid*

Robert Edgeworth studied the colour vocabulary of the *Aeneid*, an epic poem by the first-century BC Roman poet Virgil. At the beginning of his book, Edgeworth makes an important observation which could be applied to almost any literary study of pre-modern texts. He writes: 'I offer it [his research] for publication because misconceptions about ancient color terms are so widespread as to interfere substantially with our understanding of the actual meaning of many ancient texts.' On his specific subject, he writes: 'Without an understanding of Vergil's color strategies, our appreciation of the *Aeneid* is incomplete' (1992: xiii).

The value of Edgeworth's book lies in the combination of his sensitivity to literary considerations, his deep knowledge of Classical texts, and, not least, his compilation of detailed semantic data. The reader of his book will find a list of all the colour terms in the *Aeneid* with their distribution across the twelve books of the poem (1992: 169–72), and another table showing the relative frequency of colour terms per book (page 21). Edgeworth then presents all the colour terms in alphabetical order with their occurrences in the poem in order of appearance, together with a description of their contexts (pages 65–168). This detailed work results in the richest possible basic data for more conventional literary studies. But Edgeworth does not stop at investigating the detailed context of each colour term in the *Aeneid*, he also considers the broader context, involving the colour usage of seven of Virgil's predecessors in Greek and Latin literature (pages 3–17). This leads him to recognizing six major ways in which colour is used in Classical literature.[1]

If anyone should doubt the value of such meticulous work, Edgeworth's conclusions on Virgil's use of colour should dispel their concerns. He shows how the notable lack of colour terms in Book Two of the *Aeneid* is linked with an 'atmosphere of terror, of utter devastation' (1992: 21), while other books show colour changes which follow and enhance the moods of the narrative. Thus, Book Five opens, after the death of Dido, with a few dark colours only but it is followed by a riot of colour in the account of the funeral games dedicated to Anchises, the father of Aeneas, and then, as events turn against the Trojans, the instance of colour terms drops with at least half of them denoting black. With considerable supporting data, Edgeworth shows that the relative frequency of colour terms is directly comparable with fluctuations in the poem's mood, and that colour term frequency lends the poem a certain symmetry. In the final book, Book Twelve, he notes the plunging decrease in colour term frequency, unrelieved at the end by any glorious or triumphant injection of hues. Edgeworth writes: 'The final scenes of the *Aeneid* were "filmed" not in heroic technicolor but in cold, clear black and white' (page 24).

There is much more in Edgeworth's book, about colours used as motifs, colours that cross-reference episodes, and the intriguing use of thematic colour clusters, but it has been included here as an excellent example of how an initial colour semantic study can credibly encourage new and valuable literary insights. A semantic approach would, hopefully, avoid the initial difficulties mentioned by Irwin. Writing about Ancient Greek poetry, Irwin admits that the use of colour terms can be very puzzling, but she concludes 'they make perfectly good sense when we broaden our vision to focus on qualities other than hue' (1974: 203).

12.3   Literary limitations

The role of colour in the *Aeneid* appears to be central and crucial to its frequently changing atmosphere but, in this Section, some caveats will be considered. Firstly, not all societies are equally interested in colour, and the researcher may find that the literature which s/he is studying rarely uses colour terms. Duncan wrote about medieval Spanish literature that it 'seemed to require little use of color terms' (1975: 57). It would be interesting to know, however, whether this situation in the literature simply reflected the concerns of that society in general or whether it was a matter of literary tradition or the preferred style. It has been shown that two societies which are comparable in every way; for example, they live in the same or similar environments at the same period of history, may yet differ widely in the extent of their colour usage. To take a modern example, Davies and colleagues found that 5-year-old children who spoke Damara (a language of Namibia) named most of the colours correctly, whereas 5-year-old Setswana speakers in neighbouring Botswana made many mistakes, and the under-fives appeared to know no colour terms at all. Setswana has fewer BCTs than Damara, and Setswana speakers also exhibit lower consensus on the meanings of their colour terms than Damara speakers. The researchers came to the conclusion that colour simply has greater salience for Damara speakers (Davies *et al.* 1997: 204). It would have been interesting to know if this difference in colour interest between the two societies was reflected in their folk-tales, clothing and other artefacts. Suffice it to say that the specialist in historical literature may or may not have illuminating colour data available.

Another phenomenon which may, to a degree, falsify the results of a literary colour project is deliberate archaism, that is, the preference or cultural necessity on the part of authors to use intentionally archaic vocabulary. Kirsten Wolf, for example, suggests this as a distinct possibility in Sturluson's *Gylfaginning*. Snorri Sturluson (1178/9–1241) was an Icelandic scholar, poet and politician who wrote the prose *Edda* in about 1220. This manual of poetics contains a section known as the *Gylfaginning* which is our principal source for Norse mythology, and helps to explain various mythological allusions in the poetry. Wolf refers to this text's 'extraordinarily limited use of color terms' (2007: 1), which she concludes is deliberate, and represents the author's efforts to help his readers view the world of their pagan ancestors (pages 8–9). For the researcher who is considering a literary work against the background of a thorough colour semantic study, it will be easier to notice deliberate archaism, to assess a relative dating, and to evaluate changes in this aspect of literary style.

Lexical familiarity is an aspect of literary impact which may have greatly changed from the date of the work's creation to the time it is read by the modern literary scholar. The frequent use of a language's BCTs in a poem may seem unimaginative or hackneyed to the modern reader but, at the time of writing, some of those BCTs may have been quite novel in their abstract condition, and the poem may, in fact, have been innovative. Similarly, a historical writer may use newly coined non-basic terms which would have seized the attention of his or her readers but which are boringly familiar to modern readers. Thus, to describe someone as having *mousy* hair in the late nineteenth century would grab the attention, but the phrase has lost much of its force today.[2]

Studies of poetry involve distinct semantic considerations. Colour terms may appear, not for the specifics of their meaning, but because of their alliterative or rhyming value. In order to recognize what may be an eccentric function, the poetry specialist needs to have to hand a thorough study of the 'normal' colour semantics of the language involved. The reverse is also true, namely, that a colour semanticist should treat evidence from poetry with caution.[3] The first studies of Old English colour vocabulary were restricted to poetic usage only and, as a result, the conclusions are insecure (Mead 1899; Willms 1902).

It would also seem that the genre of poetry encourages the use of colour terms more than prose, making poetry unrepresentative of less ornamental language. For example, Moskovič studied four authors who had written both poetic and prose texts on similar topics in Russian, and found that colour terms occurred four times more frequently in the poetic texts (Moskovič 1969, cited in Corbett and Morgan 1988: 49).

12.4   Comparative literary studies

Many literary and sociological colour studies will be concerned with comparative projects, such as the comparison of colour expressions in two or more distinct periods of time, of languages, dialects, genres, authors or works. Some of these studies present the researcher with almost insuperable problems. If, for example, two periods of literary output are compared, the researcher must be sure the comparison is a fair one. For example, the medievalist will have read many times that Anglo-Saxon poetry is dull-coloured and dark compared with the lively hues of Middle English poetry, but this is hardly a balanced comparison. Firstly, there are many more lines of poetry surviving from Middle English than Old English, and, secondly, heraldry, tournaments and knights with their coats-of-arms had a deep influence on literary colour in the later period. The researcher, therefore, in order to conduct a meaningful study must consider how s/he can compensate for one period having less data than the other, and for changes in society which impinge on colour sensitivities. This is not an easy matter to resolve, but it is clear that the reseacher should not make a free choice of texts for comparison from either period.

Comparative studies *within* languages and dialects are similarly problematic and require research projects to be carefully designed. Sometimes the lucky survival of manuscripts coupled with a later scribe's eagerness to update the text provides an excellent source for a diachronic study of literary colour terms. One such case was investigated by Heidi Lazar-Meyn who studied the Irish legend *Táin bó Cúailnge*, usually translated as 'The Cattle-Raid of Cooley'. This pre-Christian tale was recorded in much later medieval manuscripts which span the transition from Old to Middle Irish, thus providing an opportunity to investigate whether and how colour terms and their usage had altered from one phase of the language to another within the strictly delimited circumstances of the same text. In the case of the *Táin*, Lazar-Meyn found there had been no change in colour vocabulary except where passages had been added or expanded (1994: 201–2). Although the possibilities of lexical conservatism and/or deliberate archaizing in the Middle Irish version need to be considered, the addition and expansion of certain passages suggests 'editing' was acceptable. This makes it more likely that the Old Irish colour terms were still current for speakers of Middle Irish.

12.5   John Baines and Ancient Egypt

Turning from literary applications of colour semantics to artistic ones, it is tempting to expect a certain degree of interaction between the material culture of a particular society and its cognitive colour categories, as revealed by a semantic survey. Archaeologists are also interested in colour, and increasingly make observations about the appearance of artefacts and structures, noting hues, shininess, patterns, colour changes and colour mixtures (Jones and MacGregor 2002). It would currently appear, however, that there is no simple correlation between the colours of art and artefacts, and cognitive categories. Baines' study of the painting and colour terminology of Ancient Egypt is illuminating in this regard.

Egyptian studies, of course, benefit from centuries of both textual and material remains. Baines assessed the position of the Ancient Egyptian language on the evolutionary sequence, and concluded that it was at Stage IIIa (2007: 253), with BCTs for black, white, red and grue (page 242). What is surprising is the stability of this colour system, which remained the same from the third millennium BC to the Middle Ages (page 241). While the BCTs remained unchanged, however, the use and, presumably, the naming of pigments steadily expanded over time. Baines explains that, if the pigments had motivated the establishment of basic cognitive categories, Ancient Egyptian would have steadily expanded its colour system so that, according to the evolutionary sequence, it would have been at Stage V in the Old Kingdom (c.2575–2150 BC), perhaps Stage VI in the Middle Kingdom (c.1980–1630 BC), and partially Stage VII in the New Kingdom (c.1540–1070 BC) (page 253). It is clear from the Ancient Egyptian language, however, that the pigments increasingly available to Egyptian artists did not motivate the development of new basic cognitive categories. As Baines rightly says, 'colour is more easily seen and painted than talked about' (page 254).

Baines' results show that while a pigment can provide a category prototype, it appears that something more is required to develop a new basic category. Indeed, if this were not the case, the Palaeolithic cave artists would have had several basic categories long before the rise of Ancient Egypt but this seems most unlikely given the later situation in Europe. The explanation is probably that painting and colour-related crafts were and are specialized occupations, and the knowledge of pigments was likely to have been jealously guarded by artists and craftsmen, so this may be the reason why the extensive Egyptian palette did not prompt basic cognitive categories or widely known BCTs. By definition, basic colour terms must be known to the entire speech community. It would appear, therefore, that we cannot postulate a simple connection between the number and range of colours available in a society and the basic categories enshrined in the language.

12.6   Conclusion

It is to be hoped that a cogent argument and workable methodology for the pursuit of historical colour semantic information has been presented in this book. The aim has been to show that colour semantics can, at its most helpful, open windows into the minds of past individuals through their remarks on exotic imports, their comments on features of the natural world, their discussions of colouring materials for their creative arts, their expressions of admiration for beauty, their mockery of ugliness and so much more. We have briefly considered the application of historical colour studies to a literary and an art-historical topic, but the subject is also of value to social and cultural historians, and to psychologists working in areas such as colour metaphors and symbolism (see, for example, Jacobs and Jacobs 1958); folklore (for example, Popovic 2007); colour associations (for example, Prado-León, Ávila-Chaurand and Rosales-Cinco 2006) and colour connotations (for example, Allan 2009).

Historical colour semantics can also help with the understanding of *modern* colour systems. It has been recognized by several colour specialists (for example, Jameson 2005: 194–6) that the historical dimension to the cognition of colour categories and the role of colour terms in languages is crucial for our understanding of the still-dynamic, present-day situation. In conclusion, although colour terms may seem to be just a minor element of language, their involvement in all aspects of human life lends them the potential to reveal multiple aspects of historical culture far beyond their apparent significance.

Appendix: Metalanguage, signs and conventions

1. COLOUR METALANGUAGE (AS USED IN THIS BOOK)

1.1 HUE

The chromatic primaries: **red, yellow, green, blue**
    The researcher can specify areas on named colour charts if required.
Mixed hues: **brown, purple, orange, pink, turquoise, chartreuse** etc.
    The researcher may prefer to use conventions such as 'red-yellow' instead of
    'orange' (see Appendix, Section 2 below). If the more unusual mixed-hue
    terms are used, e.g. *chartreuse*, it is helpful to provide an explanation.
Ranges and macro-categories: see Appendix, Section 2.

1.2 SATURATION

Saturation range: **vivid – mid – dull**
    Ranging from a fully-saturated hue (vivid), through a saturation level which
    is neither vivid nor noticeably dull (mid saturation), to a distinctly greyish
    hue (dull).

1.3 TONE

Achromatic tone range: **white – pale grey – medium grey – dark grey – black**
    A tone range which has no hue element. If required (and justified by the
    evidence) greater precision can be added in the greys with the addition of
    very pale grey and *palish grey* or *darkish grey* and *very dark grey*. (See
    Section 1.4.)
Chromatic tone range: **pale – medium – dark**
    Ranging from a pale hue through a tone level which is neither noticeably pale
    or dark (medium tone) to a dark hue. Greater precision can be employed if
    required, as described under the achromatic tone range above.

1.4 BRIGHTNESS

Light-emission: **dazzling – shining – glowing**
    Ranging from a 'blinding' level of light (dazzling), through a strong but
    comfortable light level (shining), to a low light level (glowing). Light-
    emission can be further described by its constancy: intermittent or constant.

Reflectivity: **shiny – lustrous – matt**
> Ranging from high reflectivity (shiny), through low reflectivity (lustrous), to a lack of reflectivity (matt). Shininess and lustre can be further described by their constancy: whether reflecting light intermittently or constantly.

Surface illumination: **well-lit** or **poorly lit**
> A medium level of illumination is taken as the norm.

Space illumination: **brilliant – dim – unlit**
> Referring to daylight or the light levels in a space such as a room. A medium level of illumination is taken as the norm.

1.5 TRANSPARENCY

Transparency: **transparent – translucent**
> Ranging from complete transparency to less than complete transparency (translucency).

2. SIGNS AND CONVENTIONS (AS USED IN THIS BOOK)

SMALL CAPITALS: e.g. GREEN, indicate a semantic feature, that is, a concept (as opposed to a word-*form*) as manifested in a particular society.

italics: 1. e.g. *jaune*, indicates a specific word-form in a specific speech community, in this case, French-speakers' standard word for YELLOW.
> 2. Indicates emphasis.

- (hyphen): e.g. yellow-green, indicates a roughly equal mixture of both hues.

- (hyphen): e.g. yellowish-green (a primary hue qualified by a hue with modifier such as *-ish*), indicates a mixture of both hues but with the non-modified element predominating.

- (hyphen): e.g. bluish-purple (a non-primary hue qualified by a hue with modifier such as *-ish*), indicates the predominance of one element (the modified element) over the other element in the hue, e.g. purple is a mixture of blue and red but in bluish-purple, blue predominates over red.

/ (slash): e.g. blue/green, indicates a range of colours (in this case, blues, shades of turquoise and greens) which do not necessarily comprise a macro-category. (Note that slashes with colour-term *abbreviations*, e.g. R/Y, as used in the evolutionary sequence, indicate mixed colours, in this case, orange).

+ (plus):[1] e.g. green+blue, indicates a combined (inseparable) colour category (a macro-category).

+ (plus): e.g. grey+shiny, indicates a combined (inseparable) colour category consisting of two features which are unlikely to form a macro-category.

(+?) (plus and query in round brackets): e.g. blue(+shiny?), indicates a case where shininess is suspected to be inseparable, but the evidence is not clear.

'and': e.g. grey and shiny, indicates a colour in which the two elements are not inseparable, or in which their relationship is unknown.

(entity or entities) (round brackets): e.g. dark blue (dyes, textiles), indicates a colour which is contextually restricted to the entities in the round brackets.

*(asterisk): e.g. *furnitures*, indicates a word or expression which is not attested in a particular language.

Þ, þ ('thorn'): a letter used in Old English to indicate a voiced or unvoiced dental fricative, i.e. the sounds now represented in English by 'th'. In Modern Icelandic, thorn represents the voiceless sound.

Ð, ð ('eth'): a letter used in Old English to indicate a voiced or unvoiced dental fricative, i.e. the sounds now represented in English by 'th'. In Modern Icelandic, eth represents the voiced sound.

ʔ: indicates a glottal stop (see Glossary).

// (double slash): the symbols between the slashes indicate phonemes (see Glossary).

Glossary

Ablaut: an alternation of sounds within words which indicates a change of grammatical function, for example *man : men*.

Absolute chronology: a set of dates which are independently established by fixed means such as a year or a reign. See also 'Relative chronology'. See Section 10.3.

Acculturation: changes occurring in one language or society as a result of contact with another language or society.

Achromatic: without hue, that is, white, black or grey. See Section 1.4.

Adopted (as used in this book): referring to a term or expression which has been accepted into, and become established in, another language. See also 'Borrowed'.

Affix: a morpheme added to a simplex term; for example, English *unknown* consists of a simplex term (*known*) with the affix (in this case, a prefix) of *un*-. English *slowly*, for example, consists of a simplex term (*slow*) with a suffix (*-ly*).

Alliteration: the occurrence of the same sound in the first syllables of at least two words or expressions, as in *dark, damp dungeon*.

Allomorph: a morphemic variant, such as *rud*- for *red*- in English.

Analogy: a comparison made by transferring a concept from one entity or phenomenon to another, for example comparing the heart with a (mechanical) pump.

Antipodal opposition: a sense-relation denoting diametric oppositeness, as in BLACK versus WHITE. See Section 9.5.

Antonymy: a sense-relation denoting oppositeness. See Section 9.5.

Association: a situation whereby two or more words or expressions occur together in a text with, apparently, the same explanatory function, as in a glossary entry. See Section 9.5.

Atoms, semantic: in Natural Semantic Metalanguage, universal and irreducible concepts. Also known as 'semantic primitives' or 'semantic primes'. See Section 7.3. See also 'Molecules, semantic'.

Attributive usage: see 'Descriptive usage'.

Basic Colour Category (BCC): a cognitively salient colour concept, linguistically labelled by a Basic Colour Term. See Chapter 5.

Basic Colour Term (BCT): a colour term which denotes one of the most salient colour concepts in a society. See Chapter 3.

Bilingualism: the use of two languages in speech or text.

Borrowed (as used in this book): referring to a term or expression from one language which is temporarily used by another. See also 'Adopted'.

Brightness (as used in this book): perceived light at various strengths, and of various types, such as: emission, reflection, surface illumination and space illumination. See Section 1.5.

Category, colour: a cognitive division of the colour space as used by a particular society. See also 'Basic Colour Category'.

Centroid: the focal area of a category, delimited by mapping the various foci of individual native speakers.

Chromatic: see 'Hue'. See also 'Achromatic'.

Chronology: see 'Absolute chronology' and 'Relative chronology'.

Codability: the ease (or otherwise) of naming concepts in a language. See Section 2.6.

Code-mixing: the acquisition of considerable vocabulary from one language or dialect into another, or between two or more languages or dialects, as a result of high speaker-familiarity with the languages or dialects involved. See Section 9.4.

Code-switching: the use of two or more languages or dialects, including their syntax, within a single conversation or text. See Section 9.4.

Coextension: in vantage theory, a category with two overlapping vantages, each of which includes the other's focus in its range, although one is dominant and the other recessive. See Section 10.3.

Cognate: having the same etymological origin.

Cognition (as used in this book): the knowledge of particular concepts.

Cognitive fluidity: the ability of the human brain to apply knowledge acquired in one field of activity (for example, hunting) to another field of activity (for example, tool-making). See Section 11.4.

Cognitive linguistics: an approach to the study of language which assigns prime importance to meaning and concepts.

Coining: the invention of new words.

Collocation: the common co-occurrence of certain words; for example, *blonde* commonly collocates with *hair*.

Colour (as used in this book): 1. a visual effect which involves more than one of the colour elements discussed in Chapter 1; 2. a visual effect, the exact colour elements of which are not known. *Colour* is not used as a synonym for *hue*.

Colour space (as used in this book): the range of colours visible to the normal human eye.

Combinability: in connection with contextual restriction, the ability (or inability) of a colour term to combine with terms for natural phenomena as well as those for artefacts. See Section 3.5.

Comparative method: a means of investigating relationships between languages by comparing various linguistic features.

Complementation: in vantage theory, a category with two vantages which have both retracted to their own foci and are about to separate. See Section 10.3.

Composite category: see 'Macro-category'.

Compound term: a term which can be analysed as consisting of two or more words, such as *motorway.*

Concordance: a reference work which provides an organized list of words occurring in a particular text or texts along with short contexts for each occurrence. See Section 8.5.

Conjunctive senses: two senses of a word or expression which are both always present when the word is used. See also 'Disjunctive senses'.

Conjunctivity, category: the principle by which the constituent hues of a macro-category are contiguous on the hue spectrum. See also 'Disjunctivity, category'.

Consensus (as used in this book): the extent of agreement among a group of native-speaker informants as to the choice of colour term to name a particular colour sample. See Section 3.7.

Consistency (as used in this book): the naming of a particular colour sample with the same colour term on at least two separate occasions. See Section 3.8.

Containment: a meaning-relation, used in historical studies, which indicates *suspected* hyponymy in cases where the evidence is inconclusive. See Section 9.5.

Contextual restriction: the use of a word or expression, only or predominantly in a particular context, just as *blonde* is (usually) restricted to the context of human hair. See Section 3.5.

Contrast: a meaning-relation, used in historical studies, which indicates that two or more words or statements must denote different colours, but the exact details cannot be ascertained. See Section 9.5.

Controlled language: see 'Metalanguage'.

Converseness: a sense-relation denoting a form of oppositeness in which one word or statement must imply a converse word or statement; for example, *He is her husband* must indicate *She is his wife*. See Section 9.5.

Cool colours: all the colours and shades involving a perceived predominance of blue or green. See also 'Warm colours'.

Corpus (plural: corpora): a collection of texts, now usually a large, searchable database, consisting of samples of natural language taken from speech and/or written texts. It is often designed to be a representative sample of a particular date, type or use of a language. See Section 8.5.

Countable noun: a noun which can indicate more than one of an entity, as in, for example, *apples* or *six apples*. See also 'Uncountable noun'.

Cuneiform: an early form of writing, originating in Mesopotamia, and consisting of wedge-shaped impressions made in wet clay.

Data-constructed: referring to prehistoric languages for which the lexical data has been (re)constructed from descendant languages.

Data-restricted: referring to historical languages or projects with surviving data which are insufficient to enable the retrieval of comprehensive lexical data.

Data-rich: referring to historical languages or projects with so much surviving data that a comprehensive lexical study is considered practical.

Dental sound: a sound in human speech which involves contact between the tongue and the teeth, as with *th* in English *thin*.

Derivational morphology: the potential for certain attested morphemes to be added to other (colour) words, just as *ish* in English *reddish* can also be added to *green*. See Section 3.10.

Derived category: a colour category located at the intersection of two primary colours; for example, PURPLE is located between the red and blue categories. 'Intersection-based' has been suggested as a more accurate term. See Section 6.5.

Descriptive usage (as used in this book): the use of a colour term, not in an abstract sense, but to describe a particular object. See also 'Referential usage'. See Section 5.6.

Determinism, linguistic: the belief that languages not only influence the world-views of their speakers, but actually *determine* them. See Section 2.6.

Diachronic: across periods of time, as opposed to within a particular period of time. See also 'Synchronic'. See Section 10.1.

Disjunctive senses: two senses of a word or expression which can be used independently of each other, as in ORANGE (fruit) and ORANGE (hue). See also 'Conjunctive senses'.

Disjunctivity, category: the principle by which the constituent hues of a macro-category are *not* contiguous on the hue spectrum. See also 'Conjunctivity, category'.

Dispersion: the extent of distribution of a particular linguistic feature, such as a word, in a text or corpus. See Section 3.15.

Distributional potential: see 'Derivational morphology'.

Dominant vantage: in vantage theory, the dominant (more wide-ranging) vantage of a macro-category. See also 'Recessive vantage'. See Section 7.4.

Elemental colours (as used in this book): the purest areas of the four primary hues (red, green, yellow and blue) and the achromatics (white and black). Sometimes also referred to as 'unique colours' or 'fundamental colours'. See also 'Primary colours'.

Embedded expression (as used in this book): a 'fossilized' expression in a language, such as a well-established simile, metaphor or proverb. See Section 3.20.

Emergence hypothesis (EH): EH languages develop single-hue categories (as opposed to macro-categories) in the earliest stages of the evolutionary sequence, leaving certain areas of the colour space unnamed. See Section 7.5.

Entailment: a logical implication that, given the truth of a particular proposition, a second proposition must be true; for example, if *John bought a cup of tea in this café* is true, then *This café sold a cup of tea to John* must be true.

Evolutionary sequence: the suggested universal (or near-universal) order of acquisition of colour categories by societies. See Chapter 6.

Exemplar: an entity which is considered a typical example of a particular concept, just as snow is considered to be an exemplar of whiteness.

Explication: an explanation of a concept in Natural Semantic Metalanguage. See Section 7.3.

Extended category: see 'Macro-category'.

Focus (plural: foci): the area of a colour which is considered the best, or most typical example of that colour. Also known as a 'focal colour'.

Fricative sound: a sound which involves the air passing between two closely-positioned parts of the mouth so as to cause friction, as in the case of *f* in English *fish* (involving friction between the lower lip and upper teeth).

Fuzzy set: a collection of items (a set) in which the items have varying degrees of membership (graded category membership), as opposed to an either/or status of member or non-member. See Section 6.5.

Glossae collectae: glosses which have been added to a text to explain difficult words, and which are then collected together, usually with the purpose of compiling a glossary. See Section 9.4.

Glossary: a list of words relating to a particular subject or text/s.

Glottal stop: a voiceless stop made in the throat. In British English, for example, it replaces the usual sound of /t/ in some dialects or in fast speech. See also 'Stop sound'.

Graded category membership: see 'Fuzzy set'.

Grue: a linguistic term for a macro-category consisting of GREEN+BLUE and, sometimes, including GREY.

Headword: a dictionary entry, followed by a definition or translation, and sometimes other information too.

Hedge: a linguistic means of lessening the force or bluntness of a statement, as in the first part of *You may disagree, but I think we should leave.*

Hering primaries: the six primary colours (red, blue, green, yellow, black and white) involved in the colour opponency theory of Ewald Hering. See also 'Opponency'. See Section 7.2.

Heterogeneity, linguistic: a situation in which grammatical, phonological and/or semantic variations occur in the speech of contemporary native speakers. See also 'Homogeneity, linguistic'. See Section 5.7.

Homogeneity, linguistic: a situation in which all contemporary native-speakers of a language or dialect use the same grammar, phonology and semantics. This is now known to be an unlikely situation. See also 'Heterogeneity, linguistic'.

Homonymy: the phenomenon whereby a word has the same form as another, but a completely unrelated meaning. See Section 3.11.

Hue: the chromatic element of colour such as red, green and blue. See Section 1.2.

Hyperonymy: the phenomenon whereby the meaning of a higher-level, superordinate term includes the meanings of other, lower-level terms, just as *flower* includes the meaning of *tulip*. See Section 3.4. See also 'Hyponymy'.

Hyponymy: the phenomenon whereby the meaning of a lower-level word or expression is totally included in the meaning of a higher-level, superordinate term, just as *tulip* is included in the meaning of *flower*. See Section 3.4. See also 'Hyperonymy'.

Identification: a meaning-relation, used in historical studies, which indicates *suspected* synonymy in cases where the evidence is inconclusive. See Section 9.5.

Idiolect: the distinctive elements of speech belonging to an individual, as opposed to a group of speakers. See Section 3.9.

Idiom: a commonly understood expression which means something other than its literal meaning, such as *room to swing a cat.*

Inclusion: in vantage theory, a category with two vantages in which the recessive vantage has shrunk to its focal area, but the range of the dominant vantage includes the foci of both vantages. See Section 10.3. For general semantic usage, see 'Hyponymy'.

Incompatibility: a sense-relation in which a particular property assigned to a person or object excludes the possibility of a different property being assigned to the same person or object at the same time; for example, the statement *My hair is dark* is incompatible with the statement *My hair is blonde.* See Section 9.5.

Informant: one who provides information on their language or culture. Also known as a 'subject', particularly in the context of experiments.

Interdisciplinary semantics: semantic research which also involves non-linguistic evidence such as botanical information in the investigation of plant-names.

Interpretamentum: in glossaries, the explanation provided for a lemma. See also 'Lemma'.

Intransitive verb: a verb which does not require an object or objects, as in *The water evaporated* (the verb *evaporated* has a subject (*water*) but no object). See also 'Transitive verb'.

Isolate: a language which has no known relative, such as Basque (France and Spain).

Laryngeal sound: a sound made in the larynx (voice-box). In Proto-Indo-European linguistics, a number of consonantal sounds, the precise nature of which is not understood, are referred to as laryngeals.

Lemma (plural: lemmata): in glossaries and dictionaries, the initial word (headword) of an entry.

Lexeme: an uninflected word functioning as an abstraction which subsumes inflected forms. For example, the lexeme *walk* includes inflected lexical items such as *walks*, *walking* and *walked*.

Lexical item (also known as a lexical unit): a word or group of words conveying a single meaning in a given context, for example *grass* or *one-way street*.

Lexicon: all words and expressions found in a particular language or dialect.

Loan-word: see 'Adopted' and 'Borrowed'.

Macaronic language: speech or a text which mixes words, phrases and sentences from more than one language. See Section 9.4.

Macro-category: a colour category consisting of more than one hue. Also known as a 'composite' or 'union-based' category. See Sections 5.5 and 6.5. See also 'Grue'.

Mean: average.

Memorability: the ease (or otherwise) of concepts being remembered (recognized).

Metalanguage: standardized terminology, as used within a particular discipline, which has strictly controlled meanings that aim to avoid ambiguity.

Metaphor: a comparison of one thing with another, in which the subject is described in terms of another entity or phenomenon from a different, literally inappropriate, area of meaning, for example *she's a wizard in the kitchen*. See Section 4.3.

Metonymy: the phenomenon whereby the name of an entity is replaced with a term or expression used for another entity with which it has close links, for example the replacement of 'the American government' with *Washington*.

Micro-category: a colour category consisting of less than a complete hue. See Section 5.6.

Model, colour (as used in this book): a generally applied colour system, used in a particular society, which is based on the colours exhibited by an entity which is well-known to that society, such as cattle. See Section 4.2.

Modifier: a morpheme, word or expression which alters the standard meaning of a term, just as *sailing* modifies the meaning of *boat* in the phrase *sailing-boat*.

Molecules, semantic: in Natural Semantic Metalanguage, a concept which can be reduced to constituent semantic atoms. See Section 7.3. See also 'Atoms, semantic'.

Monogenesis: the theory that all human languages descend from a single ancient ancestor.

Monoglot: a person who speaks only one language fluently.

Monolexemic: meaning literally 'consisting of one lexeme or lexical item'. There is a degree of confusion over this term in colour semantics. See Section 3.3.

Monolingualism: the use of only one language in speech or text.

Morpheme: the smallest lexical unit capable of conveying meaning. It can be a word, such as *blue*, or a word-element such as *ish* in *greenish*.

Morphological complexity: the number of morphemes in a word or expression. Its use in colour semantics is sometimes unclear. See Section 3.13.

Morphology: in linguistics, the study of morphemes.

Multilingualism: the use of several languages in speech or text.

Munsell array: a one-dimensional chart produced from the Munsell colour solid.

Munsell colour solid: the three-dimensional Munsell colour system consisting of tone and saturation ranges and the hue spectrum.

Natural Semantic Metalanguage (NSM): a metalanguage developed by Anna Wierzbicka in order to explain concepts cross-linguistically without the interference of cultural influences from the defining language. See Section 7.3.

Nesting, semantic: in Natural Semantic Metalanguage, the process of combining semantic molecules to build up complex meanings. See Section 7.3.

Opponency: Ewald Hering's theory that the brain interprets colours by means of the three opponent processes: red versus green; blue versus yellow; and black versus white. Also known as the 'opponent process theory'.

Outlier: a language which is geographically distant from other members of its language family, and surrounded by unrelated languages.

Partition: the dividing of a macro-category into two separate colour categories. See Section 6.7.

Phoneme: a sound which, in a particular language, can be used to form a meaningful contrast with other sounds, thus distinguishing between otherwise identical utterances like English *cap* and *cat*.

Phonology: in linguistics, the study of sound systems.

Pidgin: a simple form of language constructed for communication purposes between societies who have no common (standard) language. A pidgin is usually a mixture of two or more languages, is often used in a particular context such as trade, and is not learnt by anyone as their first language.

Polysemy: the phenomenon whereby a word or expression has more than one meaning.

Prefix: see 'Affix'.

Primary colours (as used in this book): the six primaries are red, green, blue, yellow, black and white. This phrase does not necessarily imply the purest areas of the hues. See also 'Elemental colours'.

Proto-language: the common ancestral language of a language family.

Proto-Nostratic: a (re)constructed prehistoric language ancestral to several proto-languages (the Nostratic language family). Also known as 'Boreic' and 'Eurasiatic'. See Section 10.4.

Prototype (as used in this book): the entity or phenomenon which prompts the development of a new concept, just as the orange fruit is the prototype of the orange colour category. After the formation of a category, its members have varying degrees of prototypicality (quality of membership) so that a daisy would normally have a higher degree of prototypicality in the FLOWER category than does moss.

Recessive vantage: in vantage theory, the smaller element of a macro-category. See also 'Dominant vantage'. See Section 7.4.

Reduplication: a feature of some languages by which words and/or morphemes can be repeated to create new words, as in Samoan *mū* 'red hot, to burn', *mūmū* 'red'. See Section 3.3.

Referent: the person, object or phenomenon being referred to or described, for example, by a colour adjective.

Referential restriction: see 'Contextual restriction'.

Referential usage (as used in this book): the use of a colour term as an independent abstract concept, as in *I don't like brown*, as opposed to the description of a particular object. See also 'Descriptive usage'. See Section 5.6.

Register: a type of usage of a particular language, as used by social groups and/or in particular social situations, for example the educated register.

Related citations: the occurrence of a colour term in two or more sources where each occurrence originates in the same position in the same text. If not omitted from the statistics, they give a false impression of a term's popularity. See Section 9.5.

Relative basicness: the degree of basicness (salience) exhibited by a basic colour term or a *potential* basic colour term, ranging from zero to full basicness, according to the number of appropriate BCT criteria which are met. See Section 10.2.

Relative chronology: a set of dates which are estimated by means of their relation to more securely dated events or objects; for example, before or after a particular event. See also 'Absolute chronology'. See Section 10.3.

Relativity, linguistic: the belief that languages differ arbitrarily from one another in the way they classify and communicate aspects of the real world. This can be reflected in vocabulary. See also: 'Universality, linguistic' and 'Determinism, linguistic'. See Section 2.6.

Retraction: the shrinking of a macro-category over time, as single-hue categories are developed.

Salience (as used in this book): the state of being foremost in the mind.

Salience, cognitive: see 'Salience, psychological'.

Salience, psychological: a quality possessed by a concept which causes it to come immediately to mind when a certain subject is mentioned. See Section 3.6.

Sapir–Whorf hypothesis: the theory that the various world-views of societies are influenced or even determined by their languages. See also 'Relativity, linguistic' and 'Determinism, linguistic'. See Section 2.6.

Saturation (as used in this book): an element of colour which refers to the degree of purity of a hue, in relation to the amount of grey present. A fully saturated hue can be described as vivid, while a hue with low saturation is dull or greyish. See Section 1.3.

Secondary basic colour term (as used in this book): a basic colour term which is not a primary basic colour term, that is, it does not denote those categories named in English as: *red, green, yellow, blue, black* or *white*. *Secondary* is not used in this book to mean 'non-basic'.

Semantics: in linguistics, the study of how language conveys meaning.

Sense modification: see 'Type modification'.

Sense-relation: a relation (such as hyponymy or synonymy) between linguistic units, involving a semantic comparison. Also known as a 'meaning-relation'. See Section 9.5.

Simile: a comparison of one thing with another, such as *he is as strong as an ox*.

Simplex term: a word which is not part of a compound term, and which has no affixes; for example, *blue* is a simplex term while *sky-blue* and *bluish* are not.

Skewed: in vantage theory, in a grue category with a single focus, skewing involves increasing attention to the focal hue (either green or blue) eventually causing the category to split into two. See Section 10.3.

Source language (as used in this book): a language which is the source of borrowings into, or influences on, another language (the target language).

Spectrum: the various hues seen together. They do not, strictly speaking, comprise a range since they do not lie between two extremes, as do tonal and saturation variants.

Stain: in heraldry, a term for a non-primary, later colour, not accepted by all heraldry experts. See also 'Tincture'.

Stability of reference across informants: see 'Consensus'.

Stability of reference across occasions of use: see 'Consistency'.

Stop sound: a sound in human speech which involves stopping the airflow in the mouth, and then releasing it 'explosively', as in *p* in English *pan*. Also known (some would say inaccurately) as a 'plosive sound'.

Subject: see 'Informant'.

Sub-set (as used in this book): a group of colour terms, or senses of colour terms, which are only or predominantly used within a particular context, such as horse-colour terms. See Section 4.2.

Suffix: see 'Affix'.

Superordinate term: see 'Hyperonymy'.

Syllable: a group of sounds forming a whole word, or part of a word. It has one vowel, and may also have initial and/or final consonants.

Synchronic: within a particular period of time, as opposed to across time-periods. See also 'Diachronic'. See Section 9.1.

Synonymy: a sense-relation denoting 'sameness' (more often denoting great similarity) of meaning. Various types of synonymy can be distinguished: absolute; partial; near; and descriptive. See Section 9.5.

Synonymy, near-: 1. as a sub-division of John Lyons' definition of the sense-relation of synonymy, near-synonymy refers to terms with meanings which are very similar but not exactly the same, such as the pair *fog : mist*. See Section 9.5. 2. In vantage theory, near-synonymy refers to a category with two vantages of almost equal extent and closely positioned foci. See Section 10.3.

Syntax: in linguistics, the rules by which a language combines linguistic units to construct an expression or sentence.

Target language (as used in this book): a language which receives borrowings or influences from another language (the source language).

Taxonomy: a classification, especially of plants or animals. A *folk* taxonomy is a popular, non-scientific classification.

Tetrachromacy: the condition of possessing four types of light-sensitive pigments in the cone cells of the retina (in humans, this occurs only in some women). See also 'Trichromacy'.

Text (in this book): this generally refers to written or printed language, as opposed to speech.

Thesaurus: a reference work which classifies the individual senses of words and expressions in a subject scheme. See Section 8.4.

Tincture: in heraldry, a term for any of the primary colours, metals and furs used in coats-of-arms. See also 'Stain'.

Tone (as used in this book): an element of colour which refers to the amount of white or black combined with a hue. This results in hues which can be described as pale or dark. See Section 1.4.

Toponymicon: the specialized vocabulary of place-names in a language.

Trajectory: one of five 'routes' along the evolutionary sequence which a society may choose to follow by developing new colour categories. See Sections 6.6 and 6.7.

Transference: in vantage theory, the transference of a grue category focus from blue to green, in the process of category division. See Section 10.3.

Transitive verb: a verb which requires an object or objects, as in *He gives a present* (*present* is the object of *gives*). See also 'Intransitive verb'.

Trichromacy: the condition of possessing three types of light-sensitive pigments in the cone cells of the retina (this is normal for humans). See also 'Tetrachromacy'.

Trilingualism: the use of three languages in speech or text.

Type modification: in colour semantics, a classificatory, rather than descriptive, use of a colour term which modifies the 'standard' meaning of the term. So white wine is actually yellow but its function in this context is to separate 'white' wines from red. See Section 3.18.

UE model: the model of colour category acquisition, originated by Brent Berlin and Paul Kay (1969) but now considerably revised. 'UE' stands for 'universals' and 'evolution'. See Section 6.1.

Uncountable noun: a noun which denotes an entity or phenomenon which is regarded as an indivisible whole, such as *furniture*. In English, it is not acceptable to say **furnitures* or **six furnitures*. See also 'Countable noun'.

Unique colours: see 'Elemental colours'.

Universality, linguistic: the belief that certain aspects of language are common to all (or nearly all) researched languages. See also 'Relativity, linguistic'.

Vantage theory: a theory developed by Robert MacLaury which models how a person constructs a cognitive category by means of fixed and mobile coordinates. The model also explains category uses and changes. See Section 7.4.

Velar sound: a sound in human speech which involves contact between the back of the tongue and the soft palate (the back section of the roof of the mouth), as in the case of *k* in English *king*.

Warm colours: all the colours and shades based on red or yellow, such as pink, brown, red-purple and others. See also 'Cool colours'.

Notes

NOTES ON CHAPTER 1

1 I am, of course, referring here to the use of these terms in a technical sense, in what is known as *controlled language* or *metalanguage*, not in everyday speech. Technical usage is essential to achieve some degree of objectivity, and to facilitate semantic discussion (Section 8.6). In this book, technical terms will be introduced as they arise, but the reader can consult the Glossary and/or Appendix at any point.

2 A tripartite division into hue, saturation and brightness is more common in publications on colour.

3 Note that the difficulty or ease of distinguishing colours refers here to *language*. It is not suggested that such a society cannot *visually* distinguish certain colour varieties. See Section 2.4 for the abandonment of this formerly held belief.

4 Lucy concedes, however, that some form of metalanguage is essential in linguistic research (1992: 156).

5 See also the metalanguage, signs and conventions listed in the Appendix: Sections 1 and 2.

NOTES ON CHAPTER 2

1 For more information on semantics in general, see, for example, Saeed (2009).

2 The difficulties of translating colour terms are amply demonstrated in Oja's study of how Estonian colour terms are translated in dictionaries into English, Finnish, German and Russian (2002).

3 This statement refers to interest in the colour terms of *natural* languages, not in the various attempts to standardize colour terminology for scientific, technological or artistic purposes. In standardized terminology, words or phrases which may not be used at all in everyday language are linked with particular colour shades, usually on charts or other graphic representations of the colour space. A great deal of information on these systems can be found in Kuehni and Schwarz (2008).

4 *Colour* for Gladstone means 'hue': 'dark derives its force from a relation to light, and not to colour' (1858: III.465).

5 Gladstone's phrase, 'the organ of colour' relates to the study of phrenology, a popular science of the period, in which the brain was 'mapped' to indicate around thirty separate 'organs' with particular functions, such as acquisitiveness, conscientiousness, form, time, number and colour (Hickerson 1983: 37).

6 Magnus was not alone in proposing an evolutionary sequence of colour perception at this time. For further information, see Section 2.5.

7 This is not entirely true. Colour vision among New World monkeys, for example, is variable, with some seeing only blues and greens, but other primates can see red. (Information from 'Primate Color Vision' by Dennis O'Neil at anthro.palomar.edu/primate/color.htm.) With thanks to Christian Kay for pointing this out.

8 I would like to thank the Australian Institute of Aboriginal and Torres Strait Islander Studies for assisting my work on this section.

9 Lazarus Geiger was a German philosopher and philologist of the mid nineteenth century.

10 Some writers include both relativism and determinism under the phrase *linguistic relativism*, as did Benjamin Whorf himself (1956: 221). This occurs in an article entitled 'Linguistics as an exact science', originally published in 1940 in *Technology Review* 43: 61–3, 80–3.

11 For much more detail on Whorf's contribution, see Lucy (1992: 25–68).

12 'Both Sapir and Whorf were wont to suggest in certain sweeping and dramatic passages a kind of absolute linguistic determinism and linguistic relativity that elsewhere each qualified considerably' (Kay and Kempton 1984: 76).

13 This quotation comes from an article entitled 'Language, mind and reality' written in 1941 and originally published in *Theosophist* (Madras), January and April issues (1942).

14 MacLaury (1997a: 19) lists over twenty studies published between 1924 and 1971 (the last having been written in 1966) which feature linguistic relativity and/or determinism.

15 An example is Brown and Lenneberg's study of hue codability and memorability in Modern American English (1954).

16 Lenneberg later referred to codability as 'name-determinacy'.

17 Lenneberg and Roberts had reported on this work to a meeting of the Linguistic Society of America as early as 1953 (1954: 462).

18 For the reader who is interested in how the interpretation of colour semantics has been affected by the various trends and hypotheses which have held influence in linguistics over the years, the introduction in Taylor (2003: 1–18) is recommended. Trends such as arbitrariness, structuralism, generative-transformationalism and cognitive linguistics are all discussed in the context of colour categorization.

NOTES ON CHAPTER 3

1 A summary of the history of basic terms can be found in Saunders (1993: 37–9).

2 'Secondary' is often used by semanticists to denote what I refer to as 'non-basic' terms. I reserve 'secondary' for non-primary BCTs.

3 Personal communication, 14 December 2002. Berlin and Kay write 'the expression basic color term does not have a unique operational definition' (1969: 6), and they then proceed to explain the criteria *they* have used, but not in a prescriptive fashion. Kay wrote, much later, 'B&K offered what they unfortunately called a definition of basic color term (bct). Their intent was not to postulate and define a new theoretical

entity but to operationalize, insofar as possible, a tacit concept that was already in general use' (2001: 2250).

4 Several of these publications have predecessors and/or later revisions, not always by exactly the same authors, and these will only be mentioned insofar as they are appropriate to the historical emphasis of this book.

5 BCTs need not be restricted to adjectives. For example, although Berlin and Kay show a preference for adjectival BCTs in Somali, Maffi finds that this excludes two likely BCTs which are nouns (Maffi 1990: 319, 327; Berlin and Kay 1969: 66–7).

6 This has also been called the 'non-compositional' criterion, and the 'monomorphemic' requirement.

7 A morpheme is the smallest meaningful element in a language. For example, in English, the words *speaks* and *speaking* include the morphemes *-s* (meaning he, she or it is doing the speaking) and *-ing* (usually meaning 'happening now'). *Speaks* and *speaking* are inflected forms of the same lexeme, namely, the uninflected or 'unadorned' form *speak*, which is also a morpheme. Thus, *speaks* consists of two morphemes, while *speak* consists of one, and they are both forms of the same lexeme.

8 Some writers have replaced *monolexemic* with *monomorphemic*, which is more accurate.

9 Snow does not give the meaning of *uli*, but I have added this from *Solo ole va*, the website of a Samoan speaker, Pen Fiatola, at solo.manuatele.net.

10 This may not represent the current situation in Samoan, since Snow reports that *lanumeamata* was becoming the main term for green at the time he was writing (1971: 387).

11 MacLaury describes this criterion as the 'simplest expression applicable to color' (personal communication, 14 December 2002). Obviously, 'simplest' should be interpreted according to the structure of the language being investigated.

12 Kay and colleagues have suggested that where a reduplicative term is an encoding idiom, it can be considered non-predictable from its parts. An English example of an encoding idiom is 'as light as a feather' which can be easily understood by any English speaker but, nonetheless, s/he has to learn that a feather is the correct conventional epitome of lightness in English (Kay *et al.* 2009: 36).

13 This opinion is also applicable to recent loan words (Section 3.12), morphological complexity (Section 3.13) and expression length (Section 3.14).

14 This is also known as 'referential restriction'.

15 There has to be a certain amount of tolerance here, as *blonde* has been used to describe a type of port (drink), pine furniture and, in Glasgow, estate agents often describe the local pale sandstone as 'blonde'. These cases, however, have all occurred in the world of advertising in which there is a constant search for lexical novelty, some examples of which can be very short-lived.

16 The initial asterisk is used in linguistics to indicate a linguistic unit (such as a word or phrase) for which there is no recorded evidence in the language under discussion.

17 An early example of this search for measurability is the work of the anthropologist Ralph Bolton (for example, 1978a).

18 Information on this experiment was taken from Corbett and Davies (1995: 301–57).

19 Not all experimenters use a deadline but allow subjects to list all the terms they know (for example, Uusküla 2007: 372). See Section 3.16 for Urmas Sutrop's

cognitive salience calculation based on elicited lists and frequency of occurrence in speech.

20 There is a considerable literature on the Russian blues, supporting both one and two BCTs. See also Sections 3.21 and 5.6.

21 Other researchers have uncovered the same phenomenon and offered the same explanation, for example Bolton (1978a: 308).

22 It should be noted that one of the subjects in the 1987 study deliberately restricted his responses to BCTs only. This was a co-author of the paper, Conrad X. Olson. Furthermore, it is not clear from the two papers mentioned here what explanation of *monolexemic* was given to the subjects (see Section 3.3).

23 I have omitted *hai* 'grey', *momo* 'pink' and *daidai* 'orange' from these results since, because many Japanese speakers now use the English words for these colours, their given percentages represent a combination of the scores obtained for the Japanese and English words. While this combination is reasonable for indicating the informants' use of their colour *categories*, it is misleading as an indication of the use of their colour *terms*.

24 These were *mizu* 'water' (90 per cent consensus) and *hada* 'skin' (80 per cent consensus) (Uchikawa and Boynton 1987: 1829).

25 It is now customary to keep the two approaches separate by grouping psychological tests together under a heading such as 'Behavioural aspects'. See, for example, Corbett and Davies (1997: 200 and 204). Dedrick (1996) discusses the difficulties of reconciling evidence on colour categories from the linguistic, psychological and physiological domains.

26 The matter of likely phonological constraint with *orangish* is also mentioned by Steinvall (2002: 85).

27 Such a phenomenon may, however, indicate degrees of *relative* basicness (Section 10.2).

28 The reader will find it stated elsewhere that a BCT *can* be polysemous, but this usually indicates that no distinction has been made between homonyms and polysemes.

29 A number of these can be found in the second edition of Berlin and Kay's *Basic Color Terms*, which is a reprint of the text with a new bibliography compiled by Luisa Maffi (Berlin and Kay 1991: 173–89).

30 A synchronic study is concerned with the linguistic situation at a particular time (Chapter 9) while a diachronic study is concerned with changes and developments *across* time (Chapter 10).

31 A phoneme is a distinct sound which, in a particular language, can distinguish words which are otherwise identical; for example, only the sound represented by *t* distinguishes English *mat* from *mad*.

32 Comparisons of expression length should be carried out *within* languages, not between them. The differing lexical and phrasal structures of various languages render this procedure inappropriate for cross-language comparison. Lucy points out this misunderstanding in Brown and Lenneberg (Brown and Lenneberg 1954; Lucy 1992: 160: 455).

33 For extensive frequency tables in written and spoken Modern English, derived from the *British National Corpus*, and an introduction to such investigations, see Leech, Rayson and Wilson (2001).

34 In their Russian colour-term studies, Corbett and Morgan consider frequency across a range of texts to be an excellent predictor of basicness, even to the extent that 'It

is tempting to suggest that this should be the only test' (Corbett and Morgan 1988: 55). It is always inadvisable, however, to use only one test.

35 Much of this work was first published by Corbett and Morgan (1988).

36 While Corbett and Davies have likely explanations for the unexpectedly low score of *koričnevyj* 'brown' and the unexpectedly high score of *seryj*, the low score for *želtyj* is a mystery, albeit one that occurs in other languages too (1997: 206–7). Steinvall believes the low frequency of yellow BCTs is because of the relatively high frequency of certain other yellow terms, represented in English by *golden* and *blonde* (2002: 68–9).

37 See note 33 above.

38 Details of Sutrop's cognitive salience index can be found in Sutrop (2001).

39 Steinvall (2002: 99) traces the classification of adjectives back to Jespersen's restrictive and non-restrictive adjuncts (for example, Jespersen 1924: 108–44).

40 The *Bank of English* is a corpus jointly owned by HarperCollins Publishers and the University of Birmingham, UK.

41 For more detailed information on the rituals, see Bolton and Bolton (1976).

42 Linguists will also be wary of Bolton and Crisp's (1979) study of colour terms in the folktales of forty cultures around the world. This massive piece of work is marred by the fact that all its evidence was retrieved from English translations, a fact which the authors acknowledge to be regrettable but which they believe to be ameliorated by a number of considerations (page 240). Nonetheless, it is almost certain that subtle considerations of both colour and culture will have been lost in translation.

43 My understanding of Waszakowa's Polish-language article comes chiefly from an English translation kindly suppied by the author.

44 Derrig suggests that the development of metaphorical uses of colour terms mirrors Berlin and Kay's evolutionary sequence (Section 6.2) (Derrig 1978: 87) but other researchers deny this (Kikuchi and Lichtenberk 1983: 42).

45 The sentence *The sheets were as white as snow* indicates both that the colour of the sheets belonged to the white category, and also that they exhibited focal whiteness (the whitest part of that category).

46 A useful summary of the work on this subject, covering Russian, American and British research by both linguists and psychologists, can be found in Paramei (2005: 15–27; 2007). See also Sections 3.6 and 5.6.

47 References to Frumkina's Russian-language publications on this subject are given in Paramei (2005: 35).

48 Certain suggestions for basicness criteria have been omitted. The first is Bolton's criterion that colour terms used in dreams are more likely to be BCTs than non-basics. I am particularly wary of the lack of explanation as to how Bolton's investigations were carried out, and the difficulty with which many people try to remember dream conversations (Bolton 1978b: 299–300). The second is Wescott's suggestion of 'polylexicity', involving counting the number of colour terms which fall into each colour category. This would seem to be a test of the salience of a *category* rather than a term (1970: 354–5). The third omitted criterion is Wescott's suggestion of 'polymorphy' which involves counting the allomorphs (morphemic variants) exhibited by each colour term, and he gives the example of English *red* which can appear as *ret-*, *rad-*, *rud-* and so on (mostly in place-names). Since many of these forms are dialectal, they would be covered by idiolectal evidence (Section 3.9). The fourth criterion is also concerned with the basicness of *categories* rather than terms, and

was based on fuzzy-set logic (Kay and MacDaniel 1978: 636) but was shown to be inadequate for its purpose by Mervis and Roth (1981: 397–8). For fuzzy set logic, see Section 6.5.

49 I have not seen MacLaury (1982) which is an unpublished manuscript. This information about it is taken from Maffi and Hardin (1997: 350).

50 Bini, also known as Edo, is a tonal language, and Wescott uses International Phonetic Alphabet (IPA) diacritics to indicate this: the acute accent (´) denotes a high tone, and the grave accent (`) a low tone. He also uses IPA symbols for various sounds which are not suited to the standard alphabet (such as ɛ in *ìyélò*). For further information on the IPA, see www.langsci.ucl.ac.uk/ipa/.

NOTES ON CHAPTER 4

1 Although a BCT may form an *element* of a non-basic term, like *-blue* in *sky-blue*, the colour expression as a whole is non-basic.

2 See Chapter 3, Note 15.

3 My sources for British English horse-colour names and the colours they represent are Packer and Ali (1985) and Weatherbys (2008). My source for the Icelandic horse and its colours is 'Icelandic horses at Langhús Farm', the website of Arnþrúður 'Lukka' Heimisdóttir, at www.icelandichorse.is. The farm, on the north coast of the country, breeds, trains and sells Icelandic horses. I am grateful to Lukka and to Helen Carron for answering my queries.

4 Heimisdóttir provides the variant forms of the Icelandic colour terms on her website (see Note 3).

5 Both face- and limb-markings are mentioned as acceptable in Britain (Packer and Ali 1985: 10) but I have only found face-markings mentioned in this context for Icelandic horses.

6 Heimisdóttir (see Note 3) lists *brúnn* and its variants under the English horse-colour term *black* together with *svartur*.

7 See Note 3.

8 Packer and Ali mention that, officially, these terms should be discontinued. The British veterinary authorities point out that these colours can simply represent seasonal variations (Weatherbys 2008: 4).

9 I have not included any terms which refer to the patterns sometimes found on a horse's coat, such as the spotted *appaloosa* or the patches of, for example, the *pinto*, *skewbald* or *piebald*.

10 Packer and Ali (1985: 14) recommend that this colour should be referred to as 'dark chestnut'.

11 A golden-brown colour, very similar to that of the palomino horse, can be seen at the boiling mud sites of Iceland, such as Námaskarð. This may be the origin of 'mud-pale'.

12 For an introduction to metaphor, see Kövecses (2002: 3–13). Kövecses, and many others, are indebted to the seminal work on metaphors by Lakoff and Johnson (1980).

13 There is a certain amount of cross-cultural agreement on colour metaphors. The use of greenness to indicate immaturity and/or inexperience can also be found, for example, in German, Spanish, Russian, Ancient Greek and Hungarian (Kikuchi and

Lichtenberk 1983: 53–5). The authors provide an appendix of the figurative uses of colour terms in many languages (pages 42–61).

14 For further information on metonyms, see Lakoff and Johnson (1980: 35–40) or Kövecses (2002: 143–62).

15 Majuro is the capital of the Republic of the Marshall Islands, and was picked at random from a list of capitals.

16 This section on metonyms is concerned with entities which stand for colours, not those metonyms which consist of a colour word or phrase standing for a non-colour concept as in, for example, *blue moon* which stands for 'a rare event'.

17 Casson uses a dataset of 136 simplex hue terms (1994: 8) and he uses the word *secondary* to indicate *non-basic*. For comment on the use of *secondary* in this context, see Chapter 3, Note 2.

18 Casson's typology formed the basis of a more comprehensive scheme for all English colour terms devised by Smith *et al.* (1995: 207–9).

19 Hazlegrove's website is at www.hazlegrove.com.

20 Single examples of colour words in these categories are as follows: plants (*fuchsia*); animals (*salmon*); minerals (*bronze*); food and drink (*chocolate*, *coffee*); and artefacts (*navy*).

21 The traditional date for this discovery is 1704 but dates up to 1710 have also been suggested (Eastaugh *et al.* 2004: 309, quoting Harley 1982).

22 Obtained from the website of OregonWines.com, an information source for the wines and wineries of Oregon, USA. See www.oregonwines.com. Rosé wines (referred to as *blush* wines) and red wines are also subdivided into six types each.

23 Conklin (1955: 341) explains that the Hanunóo words can either be used as attributes of an entity with *ma-* 'exhibiting, having' or as what he calls 'free words (abstracts)'.

24 The symbol ʔ indicates a glottal stop.

25 See my Section 1.5.

26 Conklin does not explain why he had expected *mararaʔ* to be used of the cut bamboo. After all, brown is included in his quoted range for *malatuy*. I assume it must be the wrong shade of brown for this referent.

27 See also Note 13 above.

28 The language is also known as 'Yucatec Maya' but speakers simply refer to it as 'Maya' (Bricker 1999: 297, Note 1).

29 See, for example, Clarke's discussion of Ancient Greek *chlōros* (χλωρός) often translated as 'green' or 'yellowish-green' and used to describe referents such as rose-flowers, plants and honey. Clarke (2004: 135) concludes that, regardless of their colour, they are 'full of a flourishing richness that oozes and invigorates'. Wolf (2010: 121) finds that Old Norse-Icelandic *grænn*, cognate with English *green*, often functions without its colour sense to indicate fertility or freshness, as in 'green' fish.

30 The adoption of a new BCT (or a term destined to become a BCT) usually involves the establishment in the target language of a new colour category (a new concept) in addition to the new term. Colour *categories* will be considered in Chapter 5. However, an existing BCT or near-BCT is occasionally replaced by a different word, as with the replacement of Old English (OE) *hǣwen* by Anglo-French (AF) *bleu* in the English blue category (Section 10.3).

31 Note that *recent* adoptions into a language are unlikely to be BCTs (Section 3.12). I follow the *OED* principle of using *borrowing* for words which enter the language temporarily, and *adoption* for those taken into regular and long-term use.

NOTES ON CHAPTER 5

1 Taylor also warns that colour categories do not always operate in this 'neatly orga-
nize[d]' fashion, nor can relations between them be always understood simply in
terms of hyponymy (2003: 55).

2 The Standard Welsh and Ibo categories of GREEN+BLUE+GREY are macro-
categories (Section 5.5).

3 I would like to thank Galina Paramei (2005; 2007) of Liverpool Hope University,
UK, for help with this section. Her own publications on the Russian blues include
useful summaries of other research in this subject, including Russian-language
publications.

4 The test involved subjects using only their primary basic hue-names to describe the
colours presented. Russians did not usually select *goluboj* for focal blue (Abramov
et al. 1997).

5 Taylor, Mondry and MacLaury disagree with this interpretation and regard only *sinij*
as basic since, in the terminology of vantage theory, *sinij* is the dominant vantage of
the Russian blue category. This means that *goluboj* denotes a recessive vantage so
it cannot be a basic category (1997: 426, 429). For vantage theory, see Section 7.4.

6 Micro-categories appear to be particularly common in the blue region. Modern
Greek is believed to have two BCTs in this area (*blé* (μπλε) 'blue' and *yalázjo*
(γαλάζιο) 'pale blue') (Androulaki *et al.* 2006: 36), and Turkish has a blue BCT
(*mavi*) and a *potential* micro-category named by *lacivert* 'dark blue' (Rätsep 2011).

7 Kay (1975: 262) writes that the idea of the homogeneous speech community 'has
been found to be not just an idealization but a myth'.

8 It seems safe to assume that the informants were all speakers of American English,
but this is not stated.

9 This classification was later extended to seven categories by Simpson and Tarrant:
Basic, Modified Basic, Basic-Basic, Qualified Basic, Elaborate, Idiosyncratic and
Unnamed (1991: 59).

10 A study of sex-related differences in the colour vocabulary of Chinese university students (from the Northwest Normal University, Lanzhou) revealed, however, broadly
similar results to those reported for English speakers. Females scored higher than
males in the use of 'elaborate' terms, they left fewer colour samples unidentified,
and they were more accurate in their colour identification (Yang 1996: 210–11). In
this society, too, men had significantly fewer colour-related hobbies (page 215).

11 One of the adults was unclassifiable (Dougherty 1977: 103).

12 Kay published comparative statistics, showing mean ages against stages of the
evolutionary sequence for Aguaruna, 'Futuna' (his term) and Binumarien. Apart
from the West Futunese 'blip' all three languages showed higher mean ages for the
earlier stages (1975: 268, Table 1).

13 The meanings of some West Futunese colour terms from the yellow category
onwards vary from group to group. They also function both as BCTs and non-
basic terms, depending on the group context.

NOTES ON CHAPTER 6

1 Dedrick comments that Berlin and Kay found an interesting, and perhaps significant,
set of generalizations but mistook them for universals (2002: 54).

2 It now seems very likely that Russian has not only twelve BCTs but also twelve basic categories, including two for BLUE (Section 5.6). Furthermore, Stanlaw has expressed the belief that a twelfth category exists (or very nearly exists) in Japanese. It is *kon* 'dark blue' and Japanese already has *ao* 'blue' (Stanlaw 2010: 213). MacLaury disagrees with these interpretations (see Section 5.5 and Chapter 5, Note 5).

3 The Munsell system, one of the several available methods of indicating the colour solid and an array (chart) derived from it, was originally developed by Albert Munsell, an American art teacher and artist who died in 1918 (Kuehni and Schwarz 2008: 114–5, 160–1).

4 Informants were asked, firstly, to mark all the chips which could be described as *x* (*x* being one of the informants' colour terms) and, secondly, to mark the best examples of *x*.

5 It should be noted, however, that Kay's summary is a very rough description of Rosch Heider's results. Briefly, *mili* and *mola* can *both* denote dark and pale hues, and can *both* denote pale cool hues although *mola* is preferred for *very* pale hues. The distinctive difference between them appears to be in the areas of DARK COOL (*mili*) and DARK WARM (*mola*) (Rosch Heider 1972a: 462).

6 They described f-black, for example, as the focus of '*black* plus most dark hues' (Berlin and Kay 1969: 17). See also Section 5.4.

7 The existence of grue categories was not a new discovery. Brown and Lenneberg (1954: 458) mention such a category in Yakut, a Turkic language of the Russian Federation, and the existence of grue categories in the Celtic languages was recognized in the UK and Ireland. It was becoming clear, however, that such categories were more common than was once thought.

8 Grue categories may also extend into areas such as grey (as in Welsh *glas*) and bluish-purple, as in the Aguaruna 'blue purples' (Berlin and Berlin 1975: 71). See also Section 6.7.

9 However, in recent years, a few societies have been found which do indeed appear to leave areas of the colour space unnamed (Section 7.5).

10 Because perception of the six Hering primaries appears to reflect features of pan-human neurophysiology, they are often said to be 'hard-wired'. More detailed and technical accounts can be found in Wooten and Miller (1997: 65–72) and Abramov (1997: 99–109), while Bimler (2005) provides a useful summary of the various hypotheses. There is a large literature on the nature and extent of the role played by human neurophysiology in colour categorization, and a wide range of opinions can be seen in a special issue of the *Journal of Cognition and Culture* (2005: 5.3–4), admirably summarized by Dedrick (2005). Jameson and D'Andrade (1997), among others, argue against the opponent process theory.

11 Saunders lists publications dated to between 1976 and 1991 in which this direct connection is accepted (1992: 94, Note 236). It should be noted, however, that this may not represent these authors' current views.

12 It was also later found that De Valois and colleagues had not, after all, located the sites of the opponent hue responses, and this misunderstanding may have contributed to Kay and McDaniel referring to the sensations of red, green, blue and yellow as 'fundamental neural response categories' which they thought were directly reflected in the semantics of BCTs (Kay 2006: 118–9, Note 6).

13 Kay and McDaniel modelled the derived categories as, psychologically speaking, mixtures of two primaries, but doctoral research by Gokhan Malkoc has found that

derived-category foci do not correlate with the foci of the relevant primary hues (Malkoc 2003; Kay 2006: 118, Note 5). The terms 'union-based' and 'intersection-based' are now preferred for composite and derived categories respectively (Kay *et al.* 2009: 4).

14 Eleanor Rosch's earlier publications bore the name of Eleanor Rosch Heider (see both Rosch and Rosch Heider in the Bibliography).

15 The labels 'IIIa' and 'IIIb' did not, at this date, appear on the sequence, but they were used in the catalogue of individual languages (Berlin and Kay 1969: 63–73).

16 The interviews consisted of: the naming of colour chips; the selection of foci; and the mapping of the extent of categories on a Munsell array. Full details can be found in MacLaury (1997a: 76–81).

17 MacLaury was following up reports of likely yellow+green categories among the Muscogean and Salishan languages by Mary Haas and Dale Kinkade.

18 MacLaury refers to this as the 'baroque version' of the sequence (1999: 31).

19 The copyright date is 2009, and publication occurred in 2010.

20 Two sub-types in Stage III ($III_{Bk/Bu}$ and $III_{Y/G}$) which had appeared in Kay, Berlin, Maffi and Merrifield (1997: 33, Table 2.4) were deleted from the 1999 sequence because there were no WCS data to support their existence. It should be noted that Kay and Maffi (1999: 749) mistakenly refer to $III_{G/Bu}$ as one of those deleted.

21 It should be noted that there is increasing evidence for the retention of a GRUE category, even when separate BCTs for GREEN and BLUE have been developed.

22 MacLaury (1999: 31) states that the Ainu have a blue+green+yellow category with a probable blue bias, based on information in Hattori (1964).

23 An overview of the reception of Berlin and Kay's book can be found in Saunders (1992: 43–55).

24 It was later made clear that 'most languages' among the twenty for which native speakers were found were represented by only one speaker (Kay and Regier 2003: 9085).

25 All the informants spoke English to some extent (Kay and Regier 2003: 9085). Berlin and Kay foresee the objection concerning bilingualism, and inform the reader that inter-individual differences in their forty Tzeltal informants, for example, were found to be as great as inter-language differences, which weakens the objection to the use of bilinguals (1969: 12).

26 The full criteria for assessing basicness in the WCS data is given in Kay *et al.* (2009: 21). For more detail on Saunders' and van Brakel's criticisms, see Section 7.2.

27 Notice that this second core principle concerns cognitive *categories*, not basic *terms*. The loss and replacement of BCTs can certainly happen, although the reader will find this fairly frequently denied in print, presumably because of the confusion of terms with categories.

28 This refers to the constituents of a colour impression, namely, hue, saturation, tone and brightness (Chapter 1).

NOTES ON CHAPTER 7

1 Saunders, for example, does not consider herself a relativist (in 1992) just because she is critical of the Berlin and Kay approach to colour semantics. She writes that 'non-universalist' does not necessarily imply 'relativist' (1992: 2).

2 The inverted commas around *brightness* indicate that this word is not conveying the meaning it normally has in this book (Section 1.5).

3 The Munsell array is a one-dimensional chart which depicts the surface of the three-dimensional Munsell colour solid, just as a one-dimensional world map depicts the surface of planet Earth. The Munsell solid consists of a central vertical axis in which the achromatics are ranged in a tone scale from white at the top to black at the bottom. The hues are situated in different but mutually blending portions around the colour solid (rather like the segments of an orange), and their tone varies from pale at the top to dark at the bottom. Horizontal saturation scales are positioned for each hue at each tonal level (like the branches of a tree extending horizontally out from the trunk on all sides) and each 'branch' ends with a fully saturated hue at the outer edge of the solid (Munsell 1981: 16–20).

4 Saunders (1999) later wrote in more detail about the Munsell chart and linguistic experiments.

5 Henselmans (2002: 39) discusses how 'Munsell colour' is not the same thing as, for example, Dani colour or English colour, and refers to the Munsell system as 'the very tool that eliminated the influence of Dani color language' in Rosch's research.

6 Saunders (1992: 188, Note 489) provides several examples of confusion caused by the colour chart. Van Laar (1997: 210) points out that developmental psychologists working with children have had to address the problems of subjects misunderstanding their experimental methods, and similar consideration should be given to subjects whose cultural background differs greatly from that of the experimenter.

7 The importance of the cultural context was accepted by Maffi (1990: 316), a leading member of the Berlin and Kay school. Jameson (2005: 170–3) showed how cultural features could even be included in a model, namely, the 'interpoint-distance model' (IDM), for analysing composite categories.

8 In this book 'elemental hues' refers to the purest areas of red, green, yellow and blue. Saunders and van Brakel (and others) use the term 'unique hues' for the same concept. If black and white are included, all six are, in this book, referred to as 'elemental *colours*'. For terminology in this area, see Biggam (2004: 22).

9 They list many more 'anomalies' recorded from languages and individual speakers in reports by the WCS (Saunders and van Brakel 1999: 728).

10 Responses to this article of Saunders and van Brakel, however, often stress that vocabulary is not a reliable reflection of biological features (for example, Miller 1997: 205). Nonetheless, the innateness of colour categories is by no means beyond doubt (Bimler 2005).

11 The *OED* defines *anglocentric* as referring to England or Britain, but the term has often been used in colour semantics with reference to the English language in general and, in particular, to American English.

12 Narrol found a significant association between number of BCTs and Marsh's scale of societal complexity (Marsh 1967; Narrol 1970: 1278). On the importance of colour for distinguishing between items which are otherwise identical, see Kay and Maffi (1999: 744).

13 I have no idea whether my interpretations of the word *evolutionary* and the phrase *cultural complexity* are as Berlin and Kay intended them to be understood in 1969, but I see no reason to accuse them of prejudices which they may not have held. They have certainly vigorously denied all such bias (Kay and Berlin 1997).

14 A list can be found on Goddards's 'NSM Homepage' (click on 'NSM in brief'), www.une.edu.au/bcss/linguistics/nsm/. None of these semantic atoms are colour terms. For a thorough consideration of most of the atoms, see Wierzbicka (1996: 35–111).

15 The words used by languages to denote semantic atoms may be polysemous, but the atom represents only one of the meanings that such words can indicate.

16 Taken from Goddard's 'NSM Homepage' (click on 'Semantic explications'), www. une.edu.au/bcss/linguistics/nsm/.

17 The answer may be that eight of the twelve Zuni informants were bilingual (Lenneberg and Roberts 1956: 21). Wierzbicka (2006: 4) gives other examples of languages with no word for 'colour [hue]', namely, Burarra (Australia) and Karam, also known as Kalam (Papua New Guinea). It should be noted, however, that the lack of such a superordinate term does not prevent a language from having BCTs.

18 This view has been challenged, especially for abstract BCTs. Kay, for example, quotes the explication for English *green* that Wierzbicka published in 1990. It includes the line 'in some places things grow out of the ground' because green has the 'benchmark' of plants for English speakers. Kay (2004: 240) comments that it seems to him he is not thinking about things growing out of the ground when he sees a green car.

19 Martu Wangka is a language of the Western Desert of Australia, and Burarra (also known as Anbarra) is spoken in the Northern Territory. Burarra colour terms, such as *-gungaltja*, are presented here with initial dashes because they are used with prefixes indicating, for example, 'male', 'female', 'edible', 'inedible' and other features.

20 It may be that Wierzbicka considers a certain amount of training is necessary in order to interpret explications, but I do not recall this caveat having been expressed by her. Certainly, Durst (2004: 162) believes that the NSM method 'aims at semantic representations which are as simple as possible and thus immediately comprehensible'.

21 When referring to non-NSM definitions, I have in mind well-researched and detailed definitions as found in major dictionaries such as the *Oxford English Dictionary*. Wierzbicka and Goddard often compare dictionary definitions unfavourably with their explications by using 'pocket' or concise dictionaries in which the available space for individual explanations is limited (Section 2.2).

22 By 'native speaker' I refer, not just to someone who learnt the language as a child, but to someone who is also native to that historical society which spoke the language. For example, a person living in 1920s England spoke English, just as I do, but I am not familiar with the culture of the time.

23 VT no longer provides a model for colour categorization alone. It has been used in several areas, for example, discourse analysis, urban growth, Japanese orthography and more (MacLaury 2002: 493–4; Głaz and Allan 2010: 153–4). For a discussion of VT's potential and problems in non-colour usage, see Głaz (2006).

24 For details of the Munsell chart and solid, see Note 3 in this chapter.

25 MacLaury's data-gathering procedures differed from those of the WCS. Details of the latter's procedures can be found in Kay *et al.* (2009: 13–14).

26 MacLaury locates the pure (focal) achromatics and hues on the Munsell array at chips AØ (white), JØ (black), G1 (red), F17 (green), C9 (yellow) and F29 (blue). These chips represent the densest clusters of foci in responses from 2,476 speakers

of 107 languages (WCS data) (2002: 498). Further details of how these focal chips were established can be found in MacLaury (1997b). The fixed coordinate does not have to be the same as an individual person's 'best example' of that hue (MacLaury 2002: 514–5).

27 This refers to the numbered levels on a VT category model. Each level is the equivalent of a 'ground-figure' relationship (a fixed-mobile relationship) in Langacker's Cognitive Grammar. Głaz (2009) shows that Cognitive Grammar and VT, in spite of their differences, are compatible.

28 For more detail on the Hungarian RED category, see MacLaury, Almási and Kövecses (1997).

29 MacLaury explains that the nature of VT curves differs from those which occur in fuzzy set logic. The latter describes categorical operations, whereas VT not only describes, but also explains (2002: 520).

30 The VT website is at klio.umcs.lublin.pl/~adglaz/vt.html. It is hosted by Maria Curie-Skłodowska University in Lublin, Poland, and maintained by Adam Głaz of the University's Department of English, who researches into the linguistic applications of VT. The reader should also be aware of Dennis Preston's modifications to VT which include, for example, vantage chains (1994); VT2, an offshoot of 'classic' VT (but now really a new theory) developed by Keith Allan (for example, 2002); and Extended VT (EVT) (to facilitate non-colour modelling) developed by Adam Głaz (for example, 2010).

31 MacLaury (2002: 506) points out that the only parts of a VT model which can be directly observed are the entailments.

32 For references to publications which first questioned the universal nature of the partition principle, see Kay et al. (2009: 9).

33 For a third possibility, see MacLaury's retraction theory at the end of this section.

34 The term was coined by Paul Kay (1999: 76).

35 Kay and colleagues list the languages as: Yélî Dnye (Papua New Guinea), Arrernte (Australia), Proto-Salishan (North America), Cree (Canada), Culina (Peru and Brazil), Karajá (Brazil), Lele (Chad), Mundu (Sudan), Kuku-Yalanji (Australia) and Murrinh-Patha (Australia).

36 Discussion of the colours described by these terms can be found in Levinson (2000: 10–14).

37 Kay (2005: 50) later indicated that Yélî Dnye colour *centroids* (the focal area of a category, indicated by the varying foci selected by native-speaking informants) were not separated from the elemental hues by a statistically significant distance.

38 Levinson lists the likely 'symptoms' of an EH language (2000: 43). Apart from features already discussed, the list includes: a lack of sense relations such as clear hyponyms or antonymic pairs of expressions; tension between perceptually focal hues and the colours of prototypes; salient colour expressions which cannot be defined as BCTs; considerable variation in colour naming between individuals, and also by the same individual on different occasions; and a low frequency of colour expressions in texts.

39 Records for the individual languages are presented in Kay et al. (2009) on pages 207–10 (Culina); 413–16 (Mundu); 327–33 (Kuku-Yalanji); and 423–30 (Murrinh-Patha).

40 Sequence 5 is labelled 'Composite hue-stage by-passing' and Sequence 6 is 'Primary hue after retraction'.

41 An account of the history of the controversy up to Berlin and Kay (1969) can be found in Bornstein (1975: 777–82).

42 A book on the same theme followed a few years later (Gumperz and Levinson 1996). It should be noted that certain scholars had long been pointing out that a universal theory could include localized variations, for example Rosch (1977: 1), Witkowski and Brown (1982: 419), Maffi (1990: 328) and others.

NOTES ON CHAPTER 8

1 Latin has found a new home on the internet where, for example, it is the language of a newspaper (*Ephemeris*), a Latin-language email facility based at the *Grex Latine Loquentium* website, and a chat-room (*Locutorium Latinum*).

2 Queen Victoria's reign dates from 1837 to 1901, so 'Victorian English' refers here to the language of mid to late nineteenth-century Britain.

3 It included, for example, expressions such as *drainpipe trousers*, *teddy boy* and 'See you later alligator'.

4 It is not possible, of course, to discuss here the minutiae of historical languages around the world, even if I were competent to do so. The investigative approaches suggested here have been developed through working mainly with Indo-European languages, but it is hoped that specialists in other language families will also find them useful.

5 Owing to the nature of the evidence in historical studies, the word *representative* in this context does not mean, unfortunately, representative of the texts written by a particular society at a particular date. It merely denotes those texts which are representative of the *surviving* records.

6 It is not suggested that representativeness is easy to achieve. Some of the difficulties are briefly discussed by Anderson and Corbett (2009: 5–6, 22–8) in connection with corpora (Section 8.5).

7 Only one language, English, has a historical thesaurus which includes every period of the language's history and close to every word in the language: the *Historical Thesaurus of the Oxford English Dictionary* (*HTOED*), published in 2009 (page ix). A researcher into any other language will not, therefore, encounter such a massive resource but thesauri of *parts* of such languages may have been compiled.

8 The thesauri described here are concerned with the classification of concepts as denoted by natural language. Less useful, or not at all useful, to the semanticist, are prescriptive thesauri. These lists indicate the recommended standard terms for concepts that occur in a particular discipline or in a particular classification scheme. Their prime purpose is to avoid ambiguity by restricting word choice and thus facilitating indexing and information retrieval, but this type of thesaurus does not represent natural language.

9 Systems of classification differ, so 'Colour' will not appear in the contents lists of *all* thesauri.

10 The 'Colour' section, as opposed to 'Colour of hair', is at 01.04.09, and the two sections are separated by some 350 pages. Even in a much smaller thesaurus, therefore, the researcher cannot depend on browsing but must make use of the index.

11 The dates in the *HTOED* are based on information provided in the second edition of the *OED* (*HTOED*, xxii). The online version of the *OED* has links from its headwords to concepts in the *HTOED*. In this way, if the *OED* entry for *taupe* is consulted, the reader can click on 'Thesaurus' and open a window containing terms expressing the same or similar concept, such as *stone-colour*, *moleskin colour*, *nut-grey* and others.

12 The choice of a single-language dictionary in which each word is defined in its own language, or a bilingual dictionary in which each word is defined in the researcher's (or other) language, will depend entirely on the researcher's competence in the language s/he is studying.

13 Part of the research required in cases like this involves the investigation of the referent. In this example, the researcher needs to know the tulip species which were available at the time and place in which the text is set. If any habitual preference for certain tulip colours in this particular park could be revealed from historical records, that would be invaluable.

14 Introductions to corpora include Teubert and Čermáková (2007) and, specifically for English online corpora, Anderson and Corbett (2009), among many others.

15 Cruden himself gave credit for the first biblical concordance to Hugo de Sancto Charo (Hugh of St Cher), a Dominican friar who died in 1262 (Cruden 1769: vii).

16 Other biblical concordances list *five* occurrences of *crimson*, not four. Cruden or, more specifically, the third edition of Cruden (the last published in his lifetime), omits II Chronicles 2.14. This fact should encourage the researcher to read about Cruden's stated aims and methods.

17 The best information on the dates of English place-names can be found in the county surveys of the English Place-Name Society. The Survey of English Place-Names has published eighty volumes since 1924, and the research is continuing. There is also a Scottish Place-Name Society, founded in 1996, which is developing a database of Scottish place-names. See www.spns.org.uk. For dating problems in connection with English place-names, see Hough (2006: 185–6).

18 The situation with place-names needs to be assessed separately in each part of the world. There are obvious problems where there has been large-scale naming or renaming by modern colonizers, as in North America.

19 Personal names can also be based on colour terms, as in the family names Greene, Black, Gray and others. Generally speaking, these are of less use than place-names but may be helpful with matters of early dating (see English *blue* in Section 10.2).

20 The *OED* defines *brown* as 'a composite colour produced by a mixture of orange and black (or of red, yellow and black) and varying greatly in shade according to the proportion of the constituents' (adj., sense 2.a.). *Pink* is defined as 'A colour intermediate between red and white; a pale red, sometimes with a slight purple tinge' (adj.^{2}, sense III, 5.a.).

21 The erroneous description 'grey+bright' includes 'bright' rather than 'shiny' because it includes both light-emission and reflectivity.

NOTES ON CHAPTER 9

 1 For a discussion of aspects of Chaucer's hue terms, see Biggam (1993).

 2 The forms (spellings) of words for Middle English in this book are taken from the headwords of the *Middle English Dictionary* (*MED*). This valuable resource is freely

available on the internet at quod.lib.umich.edu/m/med/, hosted by the University of Michigan. The reader can probably guess at the Modern English descendants of the colour terms listed above but their meanings are not always the same.

3 As regards homonyms, *rēd* (colour term) occurs in *The Parliament of Fowls* only three lines above *rēd* 'advice' in line 586. If the researcher is unsure which meaning is intended, the doubtful occurrence can be recorded pending further work.

4 *The wedded turtil, with hire herte trewe,* 'the wedded turtle-dove with her faithful heart' (line 355).

5 The reader should note that the *MED* definition of ME *rēd* includes, for example, 'purple', 'pink' and 'brown'.

6 Dictionary definitions are not necessarily quoted in full in this book.

7 Great care should be taken in retrieving information from internet web-sites. Where the web-site is managed by obvious experts such as (in the case of plants) the Royal Botanic Gardens at Kew, there is no problem, but information taken from any less authoritative, unrevised and/or anonymous sources requires corroboration.

8 The twelve species are: Burnet rose (*Rosa pimpinellifolia* L.); Dog-rose (*R. canina* L.); Field-rose (*R. arvensis* Huds.); Hairy Dog-rose (*R. caesia* Sm.); Harsh Downy-rose (*R. tomentosa* Sm.); Round-leaved Dog-rose (*R. obtusifolia* Desv.); Sherard's Downy-rose (*R. sherardii* Davies); Short-styled Field-rose (*R. stylosa* Desv.); Small-flowered Sweet-briar (*R. micrantha* Borrer ex Sm.); Small-leaved Sweet-briar (*R. agrestis* Savi); Soft Downy-rose (*R. mollis* Sm.); and Sweet-briar (*R. rubiginosa* L.). The English names are those used in Dony, Jury and Perring (1986).

9 The researcher needs to remember that the information in a botanical flora refers to the *modern* situation, so further checks for the historical position are likely to be necessary.

10 The names or abbreviations following a plant's Latin designation (usually) indicate the botanist who classified it in the stated form; for example, 'L.' denotes the Swedish botanist Carl Linnaeus.

11 As explained in Section 8.6, pink is not considered to have a fully saturated form because it is perceived as an intrinsically pale hue, so this precludes a metalinguistic description of 'vivid pink'. 'Strong pink' is used here to indicate the eye-catching colour close to the shade described as 'shocking pink'. For those unfamiliar with this colour, it is recommended that they search on the internet under 'shocking pink images'.

12 Heraldry can also make use of so-called 'stains', of which *murrey* and *sanguine* are reds. The two terms have sometimes been used as synonyms but, in modern times, *murrey* is dark reddish-brown and *sanguine* is brownish-red, but there is no pink stain (Fox-Davies 1985: 60).

13 'When I look on my saviour who is blood-red as rose-flower' (Lines 421–2; D'Evelyn 1921: 12). The letter Þ (lower case: þ) denotes a sound spelt 'th' in Modern English.

14 'Holly has berries as red as any rose' (Verse 4; Greene 1977: 82).

15 The dots denote an illegible section in the manuscript (Cambridge, Cambridge University Library, Peterborough 33) but the comparison with the colour of a red rose remains clear.

16 *Etymologiae sive origines* XVI.ix.1 (Isidore of Seville 1911, unpaginated).

17 Some of the English names in the *MED* differ from those given here. I have used the English names recommended by Dony, Jury and Perring (1986) for the Latin

botanical names provided by the dictionary. Gorse, Common Restharrow and Red Star-thistle are queried in the dictionary, as is 'woodruff' which is not there assigned a Latin botanical name. 'Woodruff' in Dony, Jury and Perring refers to the *Galium odoratum* (L.) Scop.

18 This is a long period for a synchronic study but the small amount of evidence, and the difficulty of dating the origins of several of the texts involved warrants an initial synchronic treatment. Evidence for diachronic change may sometimes emerge from such sparse evidence but this can be considered later. The number of independent surviving examples of *grǣg* across the five hundred years of Old English texts is just over forty (Biggam 1998: 30). This includes a place-name, personal name and the compound colour term *grǣghǣwe*. ('Independent' refers to what is left after the removal of references which are believed to have originated from the same position in the same text as an already included reference.)

19 Dictionary definitions will now be transferred into my historical-language meta-language (Section 8.6). The *OED* defines *ashen* (as in the *DMLBS* definition) as 'Ash-coloured, whitish-grey, deadly pale' (*ashen* adj.[2]. 2).

20 Saffron colour (as in the *DMLBS* definition) is described as 'orange-yellow' (*OED*, *saffron* n. 3), and *ruddy* as 'red or reddish' (*OED* adj. 2.a.).

21 Walton Rogers explains that yellow dyes on archaeological textiles are difficult to scientifically identify (2007: 63), so the records of analysed dyes on surviving textiles may be particularly unrepresentative of this colour.

22 For a useful introduction to Anglo-Saxon glossaries, see Lendinara (1999).

23 The *DMLBS* is in process of publication, and has not yet reached 'R'. Latham (1965) is a valuable resource for the letters not yet covered by the *DMLBS*.

24 The *DOE* came to a similar conclusion, defining *grǣg* as 'grey', but also as 'light grey, dark grey, ?blueish-, ?brownish, ?reddish-, ?yellowish-grey'.

25 This sentence explains how these two terms are used in this book, but they are sometimes used interchangeably in linguistics publications. An introduction to the phenomenon can be found in Gardner-Chloros (2009). See also Bullock and Toribio (2009).

26 Laura Wright has made the point that the heavy abbreviation often found in late medieval manuscripts adds to the difficulties of distinguishing the three languages (Trotter 1996: 34, Note 18, verbal communication to the author). Presumably, this would be equally difficult for medieval readers (if they were at all concerned) as it is for modern researchers.

27 The principal dictionaries for the late medieval English context are the *Middle English Dictionary* (*MED*), the *Anglo-Norman Dictionary* (*AND*) and the *Dictionary of Medieval Latin from British Sources* (*DMLBS*).

28 Lyons points out that languages may have various ways of expressing comparison, and the researcher should not restrict his or her attention to comparative adjectives (1977: I.273).

29 Cruse points out that the meaning of one member of such a word-pair often seems less absolute than the other. For example, it could be argued that a door can be slightly open whereas it cannot be slightly shut (1986: 202–3).

30 This sense-relation is found in sets of lexemes with more than two members (Lyons 1977: I.288).

NOTES ON CHAPTER 10

1 The researcher, of course, should always check in the preliminary pages of the reference source to be sure of the compilers' policy concerning the details of their entries.

2 The dates refer to the reigns of the Stuart monarchs: James I and VI (of England and of Scotland respectively), Charles I, Charles II, James II, William III and Mary II, and Anne.

3 This is not to suggest, of course, that only YELLOW has large numbers of lexemes. For an introduction to the use of thesauri, see Section 8.4.

4 These examples are confined to adjectives, and pay no attention to dialectal or contextual restrictions.

5 For an introduction to the use of dictionaries, see Section 8.4.

6 Some examples of urine wheels in Latin manuscripts held by the Royal Library of Copenhagen have been published on the internet by Kirsten Jungersen under the title 'The Relation Between Text and Colours in Medieval Urine Wheels', at www.museion.ku.dk/upload/urinposter.pdf. I am grateful to David Bimler for bringing these web-pages to my attention.

7 For an introduction to the use of corpora, see Section 8.5.

8 The *Helsinki Corpus of English Texts: Diachronic and Dialectal* is the result of a project directed by Matti Rissanen of the Department of English, University of Helsinki. Details can be found at www.helsinki.fi/varieng/CoRD/corpora/HelsinkiCorpus/.

9 The editors of the *Anglo-Norman Dictionary* regard 'Anglo-French' as preferable to 'Anglo-Norman', bearing in mind that *Norman* French was only one form of the language spoken in England. The term 'Anglo-Norman' is retained in the title of the dictionary for purposes of continuity with an earlier edition (*AND*, A–C.v).

10 Stanlaw (2010: 208) shows a similarly dramatic influence of English colour terms on Modern Japanese, whereby the naturalized words adopted from English, namely, *pinku* (from *pink*), *orenji* (from *orange*) and *gurē* (from *grey*) appear to be replacing the native Japanese equivalents.

11 This refers to the order of the senses as given in the dictionary entries.

12 Kerttula (2007) has also used her methodology on the Finnish colour vocabulary with satisfactory results.

13 See the discussion on relative basicness in Section 10.2.

14 In Section 7.4, Table 7.2, the reader will find an example of coextensive vantages comprising the Hungarian red category.

15 Winters (2002: 632–5) assessed the potential of VT in further diachronic uses such as lexical disappearance, and analogical and morphological change.

16 Late Latin is dated from about 200 to about 600 AD, but opinions vary.

17 Kristol admits a certain 'precariousness in the interpretation of the records' (1980: 143, Footnote 12). Anderson (2003: 113–15) regards the loss of *caeruleus* as unremarkable, since he considers it only 'peripheral' in Classical Latin.

18 It is also possible for a society with surviving records to be 'prehistoric' as regards its colour terminology; in other words, the sparse extant records include no colour terms.

19 An introduction to the comparative method and its limitations, as applied to Indo European languages, can be found in Mallory and Adams (2006: 39–53), a more

extensive discussion of the limitations is presented by Harrison (2003), and Campbell (2003) summarizes the various methods which have been used to show distant language relationships.

20 Linguists tend to use the 100- or 200-word lists of 'items of meaning' drawn up by Morris Swadesh (1952: 456–7). However, Wierzbicka's list of over sixty semantic primitives is better researched (see Section 7.3). Swadesh's inclusion of, for example, GREEN and YELLOW is dubious.

21 The reader is warned that related words are not always similar in appearance; for example, it is not immediately obvious that Welsh *pen* 'head' and Scots Gaelic *ceann* 'head' have the same 'parent'. The converse is also true, namely, that words which look very similar are not necessarily related. Decisions on the relatedness of lexemes and morphemes in different languages should be made by those with an expertise in phonological change.

22 The reader is reminded that the spellings of a historical language are important because, before the era of standardized spellings, they provide evidence for pronunciation. Speech, where evidence for it can be found, is of primary importance in language studies.

23 The symbols within slashes, such as /t/, denote phonemes, that is, the smallest unit of sound in a language which can make a meaningful distinction. Thus, in English, the phoneme /t/ is vital to the meaning of *cat*, distinguishing it from *cab, can* and so on.

24 PIE forms in this book will, when first encountered, be given in two versions: the first is from the PIE indexes in Mallory and Adams (2006: 523–64), and the second bracketed form is from Pokorny (1959–69). Thereafter, the Mallory and Adams form alone will be used. Pokorny's (1959–69) is the most complete PIE dictionary currently available, while the forms in Mallory and Adams (2006) incorporate later research, in particular the laryngeal theory. A revised, updated but abbreviated edition of Pokorny has been made available by Gerhard Köbler at www.koeblergerhard.de/idgwbhin.html. In the Pokorny form, **pə́tēr*, the second letter is a *schwa* which, in the context of PIE, is one way of denoting a laryngeal sound (made in the larynx) of unknown quality. The macron (ˉ) over the -*e*- indicates a long vowel, and the acute accent indicates the syllable which carries the main stress. The Mallory and Adams form is explained in Note 25 below.

25 For a clear explanation of PIE laryngeal theory, see Fortson (2010: 62–4). The symbols in the non-bracketed form of the PIE word for 'father' can now be explained. This form contains the symbol $h̥$ which represents a vocalized laryngeal, and the subscript a indicates a possible h_2 or h_4 laryngeal.

26 The symbols θ and x represent a voiceless dental fricative (*th* as in *pith*) and a voiceless velar fricative (*ch* as in *loch*) respectively.

27 It is convenient to refer to the PIE 'language' as if it consisted of a single standard speech, but this name must be interpreted as encompassing many dialects.

28 Nostratic is also known as 'Boreic' and 'Eurasiatic'.

29 By international agreement the 'present' in a BP date is taken to be 1950 AD.

30 Even Hegedüs' date-ranges, as broad as they are, are too precise for many prehistorical linguists. Clackson, for example, concludes a review of attempts to date PIE with the statement that the matter cannot be resolved 'in any really meaningful or helpful way' (2000: 451).

NOTES ON CHAPTER 11

1 I differ in this opinion from Wierzbicka who considers that the background colours of the natural environment would have provided the most likely colour category prototypes in the form of benchmarks against which hue shades could be judged (1996: 289). We are in agreement, however, on certain other prototypes, in particular those for LIGHT, DARK and M-RED (Biggam 2010: 237, 240).

2 While the reader will be familiar with M-RED (as R/Y in the present UE model) and RED (a single-hue category), RED+ is my own terminology. It refers to a red-centred category which has lost YELLOW, so is no longer a M-RED category, but is larger than RED because it includes areas such as orange and pink which have, as yet, no basic categories.

3 The belief that a category can be prompted by a prototype is not shared by all colour specialists. For the view that categories develop from the demarcation between them, see Roberson, Davies and Davidoff (2000: 395).

4 Some more recently developed basic categories have not expanded a great deal beyond the colour of their prototypes, but their extent has, nonetheless, grown somewhat. An example is the category denoted by ModE *orange*. The scope for expansion for 'mixed' hues (orange is a mixture of red and yellow), such as orange, pink and purple is naturally restricted by the extent of their single-hue neighbours, and also by a more restricted range of objects with such colours.

5 Prototype change is not an original suggestion. Taylor writes 'there can be little doubt that the prototype representations of many categories may change dramatically over time'. He gives the undeniable example of how the typical automobile has changed over the years, but he adds: 'Possibly, more abstract concepts, like love and beauty, have undergone even more dramatic changes' (2003: 59–60).

6 See Section 11.4, concerning the suggested CEREAL CROPS prototype.

7 The reader will notice that I have not used the dark+cool and light+warm categories suggested by Rosch Heider (Section 6.3). This is not to deny her findings for the Dani language, but I prefer not to extrapolate these results to a generality, leave alone a universal.

8 Stage II languages in the WCS are Bété, Wobé and Yacouba (all Ivory Coast), Ejagham (Nigeria and Cameroon) and Nafaanra (Ghana). Gunu (Cameroon) has been classified as Stage II but is not a straightforward case. Languages in transition from Stage II to III are: Abidji (Ivory Coast), Campa (Peru), Konkomba (Ghana), Kwerba (Indonesia) and Tifal (Papua-New Guinea). Mundu (Sudan) is also classed as Stage II but is considered to be an EH language with a category for RED, not M-RED (Kay *et al.* 2009: languages in alphabetical order). For EH languages, see Section 7.5.

9 Many palaeobiologists and others consider that colour vision evolved as a food-finding mechanism in the ancestors of humans, and that the salience of red (and yellow) may be concerned with spying out fruit, berries or leaves against green backgrounds (Summer and Mollon 2003). This, and other theories, have their context in the biological evolution of primates which may, even now, play a role in our colour cognition and preferences, but which dates to millions of years before the specific prehistory of *Homo sapiens sapiens* which is the concern of this chapter. Dedrick suggests that primate colour discrimination may have been cognitively adapted by humans to suit their changing requirements (2002: 63).

10 Non-visual aspects of fire-words are also likely to have been closely connected with a macro-red category (as they sometimes still are), for example WARMTH, DANGER and others. Clarke interprets certain Ancient Greek concepts as emerging from a similar multi-sensorial history, describing the case of the cognates *xanthos* (ξανθός) 'yellow, reddish, brown' and *xouthos* (ξουθός) 'rapidly moving: golden yellow' as 'the fragments, not yet quite isolated, of what was once a single semantic range centred on a prototype which combined colour, light and movement' (2004: 137).

11 Old English *brun* has puzzled generations of Anglo-Saxonists because it can indicate 'brown, dark', and probably other warm colours, as well as 'shining, gleaming, burnished'. For further discussion, see Biggam (2010: 256–9).

12 Some of the word-roots have additional senses, such as COOK and BOIL which have not been discussed here.

13 The importance of fire to early humans is clearly demonstated by Pyne (2001).

14 Mithen recognizes that his ideas owe much to the work of other scholars, such as Jerry Fodor and Annette Karmiloff-Smith, but he is particularly adept at interpreting complex scientific evidence for the general reader.

15 *Palaeolithic* means 'Old Stone Age', and later phases are the Mesolithic (Middle Stone Age) and the Neolithic (New Stone Age). These are not fixed periods of time around the world, but refer to certain types of social, economic and technological development which were espoused at different times by various human groups.

16 This argument was made in Renfrew (1987), and a reconsideration, with revision of certain points, was published in Renfrew (2000). A review of the evidence appeared in Bellwood and Renfrew (2002).

17 For a summary of the controversy and the problems involved, see Mallory and Adams (2006: 460–63) or Fortson (2010: 39–49).

18 Wierzbicka suggests that the yellow prototype is the SUN but I find this hard to accept since the sun would have been so closely connected with DAY and/or FIRE, two previously used prototypes. New prototypes arise where a significant and important *difference* has been noted from existing categories and their prototypes. The sun would also be a strange prototype for those societies whose new categories involved GRUE at this stage, and it does not explain the close relationship of early yellow and green categories.

19 The *OED* describes it as 'a light bright clear red'.

20 The current evolutionary sequence is based on the 110 languages of the World Colour Survey, so it is possible that there are other trajectories yet to be discovered.

21 For an explanation of the bracketed forms, see Note 24 in Section 10.4.

22 Pokorny's definitions are in German, and are translated into English in this book. His dictionary (1959–69) does not include the Tocharian or Hittite languages, now known to be Indo-European.

23 Note the interest of this comment in view of the suggested prototype of CEREAL CROPS for Stage III in PIE (Section 11.4).

24 A thorough study of the green element in PIE *ĝhel-/*ghel- would require consideration of the dates of specific texts in these languages, including copying errors, later emendments and so on.

25 See Biggam (1997: 254–6) who shows that the principal Old English blue term (*hǣwen*) was probably not a fully developed BCT. If this was the situation in a historical language, it is unlikely that Proto-Germanic, still less its PIE parent, had a basic blue category. Unlike BLUE, Old English had basic single-hue categories for both YELLOW and GREEN.

26 MacLaury found a 'yellow-green-blue' category in Karuk (USA) and suggested that a similar category had once existed in Indo-European languages (1992b: 8).

27 Grey is often included in grue categories.

28 Woad is a plant (*Isatis tinctoria* L.) which produces a blue dye of the same name. Whereas the yellow and green words mentioned above are only a sample from Pokorny's list under PIE *ĝhel-/*ghel-, the blue words listed here represent every instance of this meaning that I could find, both under *ĝhel-/*ghel- and related roots (1959–69: I.429–34). The word-forms and definitions given here are as they appear in Pokorny. It should be noted that Welsh *glas*, like its Irish cognate, is a grue term.

29 It can be seen from Pokorny's definition of *ĝhel-/*ghel- that his semantic method-ology is to summarize the individual meanings of extant cognate terms. In most cases, there is little alternative to this method, but, in the case of colour vocabulary, so much more is now known about colour systems than when Pokorny compiled his dictionary that it is reasonable to reassess his definitions. For example, his suggestion that *ĝhel-/*ghel- could have indicated a separate 'blue' is unlikely.

30 Wierzbicka (2006: 9) interprets the Modern English red category as having two simultaneous prototypes (FIRE and BLOOD) but this does not preclude one being used long before the other, as I would argue.

31 Anderson (2000) suggests an early prototype of OCHRE, perhaps changing to COPPER with the introduction of metalworking, and perhaps changing again to BLOOD.

32 MacLaury discusses 'novelty' as the motivation for colour category evolution (1997a: 93–6), but he does not consider prototypes as an adequate explanation for features of category change that can be modelled in vantage theory. How-ever, he interprets *prototypes* as indicating Rosch's natural prototypes, rather than Wierzbicka's 'cultural artifacts' (page 193).

33 The UE model does not currently allow for splitting and relumping. See also Section 6.6.

34 The reader is reminded that the bracketed forms are from Pokorny's dictio-nary (1959–69) while the non-bracketed forms are from Mallory and Adams' index (2006). For further explanations, see Section 10.4. Although four word-roots are given for 'red' in Mallory and Adams' index, their section on 'Colour' states that there are three (2006: 332), *$h_1$ei-* having been excluded. Douglas Adams has confirmed (personal communication, 12 October 2010) that, although *$h_1$ei-* is less well established, it does meet the fairly generous criteria for inclusion.

35 Information on these languages has been taken from the website of the Linguistics Research Center of the University of Texas at Austin at www.utexas.edu/cola/centers/lrc. The web-pages consulted were 'Ancient Sanskrit Online' by Karen Thomson and Jonathan Slocum, and 'Old Iranian Online' by Scott L. Harvey and Jonathan Slocum.

36 Monier-Williams' dictionary of 1899 has been digitized and revised at the Institute for Indology and Tamil Studies, University of Cologne (see Monier-Williams 2008 in the Bibliography).

37 Included in the Avesta, the sacred scriptures of Zoroastrianism, is the Yasna, the liturgy and hymns of this religion. Chapter 57, entitled 'The Srosh Yasht', concerns Sraosha. I have consulted the Avestan texts at the 'Avesta: Zoroastrian archives' website at www.avesta.org/. The website provides an English (and sometimes German) translation, and the English version of 'The Srosh Yasht' is by L. H. Mills (1887).

38 This text can be found on the website cited in Note 37 above, listed under 'Avesta: Fragments'.

39 The Avestan word used here for 'bright' is the feminine form of *xšaēta-*, defined as 'light, beaming, gleaming, glorious' (Ger. *licht, strahlend, glänzend, herrlich*) (Bartholomae 1961).

40 Although I have used category names, such as M-WHITE, which are familiar from the evolutionary sequence, I am not suggesting that PIE *h_1elu*- and its descendants were or were not BCTs.

41 Friedrich (1970) is a source of much information on PIE and Indo-European tree-names but the researcher is advised to double-check with more recent sources.

42 Pokorny also gives a word in a Pamir dialect (belonging to the Iranian language group) which is defined as 'wild mountain sheep' (Ger. *wildes bergschaf*). Regarding colours, see the following note.

43 The animal-names descended from PIE *h_1elu*- hold a salutary lesson for the semanticist who ignores zoology (and other subjects). Some Germanic languages, such as Gothic and Old High German, have probable cognates meaning 'lamb' or 'sheep'. Although modern British readers will think of sheep as white, in earlier times it was normal for them to have fleeces in various colours including grey, brown and black. White sheep have been preferred, and favoured in breeding programmes, as their wool can be dyed any colour, but the variety of their older colours can be seen in the Icelandic sheep, for example (a Northern European short-tailed variety). See 'Gallery' at the website of the British Icelandic Sheep Breeders Group at www.icelandicsheepbreedersofbritain.co.uk/index.php.

44 PIE *h_1elu*- may also feature in *Helvetii*, the name of a presumably Celtic-speaking tribe, located in the area of modern Switzerland, and known from the second century BC to the first century AD (Pokorny 1959–69: I.302).

45 These definitions have been taken from the tenth edition of *The Concise Oxford Dictionary*, edited by Judy Pearsall (Oxford: Oxford University Press, 1999).

NOTES ON CHAPTER 12

1 The colour usages are: formulaic (as part of a repeated phrase); functional (expressing an element which is essential to the narrative); allusive (suggesting a similar usage in an earlier author); decorative (adding a striking or attractive detail); cumulative (as part of colour term clusters used at climactic moments); and associative (linking episodes in the poem) (Edgeworth 1992: 1–2).

2 Previously used of general appearance and smell, the *OED* (2010 draft revision) records the first use of *mousy* of hair colour in 1888.

3 Lehmann, for example, writes that the love of alliteration in the Irish language 'makes it unlikely that any aberrant use of a color term that alliterates should be taken very seriously in determining meaning' (1969: 74).

NOTE ON APPENDIX

1 The plus sign in this book is not to be interpreted as representing the +-features of componential analysis.

Bibliography

Abramov, Isaac. 1997. 'Physiological mechanisms of color vision', in Hardin and Maffi (eds.), pp. 89–117.

Abramov, Isaac and J. Gordon. 1997. 'Constraining color categories: the problem of the baby and the bath water'. *Behavioral and brain sciences* 20.2: 179–80.

Abramov, Isaac, J. Gordon, V. Akilov, *et al.* 1997. 'Color appearance: singing the Russian blues'. *Investigative ophthalmology and visual science* 38.4: S899 (Conference presentation abstract).

Aerts, Diederik, Ernest Mathijs and Bert Mosselmans (eds.) 1999. *Science and art: the red book of 'Einstein meets Magritte'.* Einstein Meets Magritte: an Interdisciplinary Reflection on Science, Nature, Art, Human Action and Society 2. Brussels: Vrije Universiteit Brussel, and Dordrecht, Boston and London: Kluwer Academic.

Allan, Keith. 2002. 'Vantage theory, VT2, and number'. *Language sciences* 24.5–6: 679–703.

2009. 'The connotations of English colour terms: colour-based X-phemisms'. *Journal of pragmatics* 41.3: 626–37.

Allen, Charles Grant B. 1879. *The colour-sense, its orgin and development: an essay in comparative psychology.* English and Foreign Philosophical Library 10. London: Trübner.

Alperson-Afil, Nira and Naama Goren-Inbar. 2010. *The Acheulian site of Gesher Benot Ya'aqov, volume 2: Ancient flames and controlled use of fire.* Dordrecht and London: Springer.

Alvarado, Nancy and Kimberly A. Jameson. 2002. 'The use of modifying terms in the naming and categorization of color appearances in Vietnamese and English'. *Journal of cognition and culture* 2.1: 53–80.

Amery, Heather. 1979. *The first thousand words in English.* London: Usborne.

Anderson, Earl. 2000. 'The semantic puzzle of "red gold"'. *English studies* 81: 1–13.

2003. *Folk-taxonomies in early English.* Madison: Fairleigh Dickinson University Press; London: Associated University Presses.

Anderson, Wendy and John Corbett. 2009. *Exploring English with online corpora: an introduction.* Basingstoke: Palgrave Macmillan.

Androulaki, Anna, Natalia Gômez-Pestaña, Christos Mitsakis, Julio Lillo Jover, Kenny Coventry and Ian Davies. 2006. 'Basic colour terms in Modern Greek'. *Journal of Greek linguistics* 7: 3–47.

Anglo-Norman dictionary, general editor, William Rothwell; edited by Stewart Gregory, William Rothwell and David Trotter. 2005–. 2nd edn. London: Maney.

Ardener, Edwin. 1971a. 'Introductory essay: social anthropology and language', in Ardener (ed.), pp. ix–cii.

Ardener, Edwin (ed.) 1971b. *Social anthropology and language*. London: Tavistock.

Atwood, E. Bagby and Archibald A. Hill (eds.) 1969. *Studies in language, literature, and culture of the Middle Ages and later*. Austin: University of Texas at Austin.

Bailey, Ashlee C. 2001. 'On the non-existence of blue-yellow and red-green color terms'. *Studies in language* 25.2: 185–215.

Baines, John. 2007. *Visual and written culture in Ancient Egypt*. Oxford University Press.

Barley, Nigel F. 1974. 'Old English colour classification: where do matters stand?' *Anglo-Saxon England* 3: 15–28.

Barlow, Frank. 1983. *William Rufus*. London: Methuen.

Barney, Stephen A., W. J. Lewis, J. A. Beach and Oliver Berghof. 2006. *The* Etymologies *of Isidore of Seville*. Cambridge University Press.

Barnickel, Klaus-Dieter. 1975. *Farbe, Helligkeit und Glanz im Mittelenglischen: Bedeutungsstruktur und literarische Erscheinungsform eines Wortschatzbereichs*. Düsseldorfer Hochschulreihe 1. Düsseldorf: Stern-Verlag Janssen.

Bartholomae, Christian. 1961. *Altiranisches Wörterbuch*. 2nd edn. Berlin: Walter de Gruyter.

Beardsley, Theodore S., Mary E. Brooks, Alan Deyermond, *et al.* (eds.) 1975. *Studies in honor of Lloyd A. Kasten*. Madison: Hispanic Seminary of Medieval Studies.

Bellmer, Elizabeth Henry. 1999. 'The statesman and the ophthalmologist: Gladstone and Magnus on the evolution of human colour vision, one small episode of the nineteenth-century Darwinian debate'. *Annals of science* 56: 25–45.

Bellwood, Peter and Colin Renfrew (eds.) 2002. *Examining the farming/language dispersal hypothesis*. Cambridge: McDonald Institute for Archaeological Research.

Bengtson, John D. and Merritt Ruhlen. 1994. 'Global etymologies', in Ruhlen, pp. 277–366.

Berlin, Brent and Elois Ann Berlin. 1975. 'Aguaruna color categories'. *American ethnologist* 2: 61–87.

Berlin, Brent and Paul Kay. 1969. *Basic color terms: their universality and evolution*. Berkeley and Los Angeles: University of California Press. (Second edition, 1991, with a bibliography by Luisa Maffi.)

Berlin, Brent, Paul Kay and William R. Merrifield. 1985. 'Color term evolution: recent evidence from the World Color Survey'. A paper presented to the 84th meeting of the American Anthropological Association, Washington DC, 1985.

Biggam, C. P. 1993. 'Aspects of Chaucer's adjectives of hue'. *Chaucer review* 28.1: 41–53.

   1995. 'Sociolinguistic aspects of Old English colour lexemes'. *Anglo-Saxon England* 24: 51–65.

   1996. 'Saffron in Anglo-Saxon England'. *Dyes in History and Archaeology* 14: 19–32.

   1997. *Blue in Old English: an interdisciplinary semantic study*. Costerus New Series 110. Amsterdam and Atlanta: Rodopi.

   1998. *Grey in Old English: an interdisciplinary semantic study*. London: Runetree Press.

2001. '*Ualdenegi* and the concept of strange eyes', in Kay and Sylvester (eds.), pp. 31–43.

2004. 'Prototypes and foci in the encoding of colour', in Kay and Smith (eds.), pp. 19–40.

2006a. 'Knowledge of whelk dyes and pigments in Anglo-Saxon England'. *Anglo-Saxon England* 35: 23–55.

2006b. 'Old English colour lexemes used of textiles in Anglo-Saxon England', in Caie, Hough and Wotherspoon (eds.), pp. 1–21.

2006c. 'Political upheaval and a disturbance in the colour vocabulary of early English', in Biggam and Kay (eds.), pp. 159–79.

2007. 'The ambiguity of *brightness* (with special reference to Old English) and a new model for color description in semantics', in MacLaury, Paramei and Dedrick (eds.), pp. 171–87.

2010. 'The development of the Basic Colour Terms of English', in Hall, Timofeeva, Kiricsi and Fox (eds.), pp. 231–66.

Biggam, C. P., Carole Hough, Christian J. Kay and David R. Simmons (eds.) 2011. *New directions in colour studies*. Amsterdam and Philadelphia: John Benjamins.

Biggam, C. P. and C. J. Kay (eds.) 2006. *Progress in colour studies, volume I: Language and culture*. Amsterdam and Philadelphia: John Benjamins.

Bimler, David. 2005. 'Are color categories innate or internalized? Hypotheses and implications'. *Journal of Cognition and Culture* 5.3/4: 293–347.

2011. 'Universal trends and specific deviations: multidimensional scaling of colour terms from the World Color Survey', in Biggam, Hough, Kay and Simmons (eds.), pp. 13–26.

Blench, Roger and Matthew Spriggs (eds.) 1997. *Archaeology and language I: Theoretical and methodological orientations*. London and New York: Routledge.

Blount, Ben G. and Mary Sanches (eds.) 1977. *Sociocultural dimensions of language change*. New York, San Francisco and London: Academic Press.

Bolton, C. and R. Bolton. 1976. 'Rites of retribution and restoration in Canchis'. *Journal of Latin American lore* 2: 97–114.

Bolton, Ralph. 1978a. 'Black, white and red all over: the riddle of color term salience'. *Ethnology* 17.3: 287–311.

1978b. 'Salience of color terms in the dreams of Peruvian Mestizos and Qolla Indians'. *Journal of social psychology* 105: 299–300.

Bolton, Ralph and Diane Crisp. 1979. 'Color terms in folk tales: a cross-cultural study'. *Cross-cultural research* 14: 231–53.

Bomhard, Allan R. and John C. Kerns. 1994. *The Nostratic macrofamily: a study in distant linguistic relationship*. Trends in Linguistics: Studies and Monographs 74. Berlin and New York: Mouton de Gruyter.

Borg, Alexander (ed.) 1999. *The language of color in the Mediterranean: an anthology on linguistic and ethnographic aspects of color terms*. Acta Universitatis Stockholmiensis, Stockholm Oriental Studies 16. Stockholm: Almqvist and Wiksell.

2007. 'Towards a history and typology of color categorization in colloquial Arabic', in MacLaury, Paramei and Dedrick (eds.), pp. 263–93.

Bornstein, Marc H. 1975. 'The influence of visual perception on culture'. *American anthropologist* 77.4: 774–98.

2006. 'Hue categorization and color naming: physics to sensation to perception', in Pitchford and Biggam (eds.), pp. 35–68.

2007. 'Hue categorization and color naming: cognition to language to culture', in MacLaury, Paramei and Dedrick (eds.), pp. 3–27.

Boutell, Charles. 1966. *Boutell's heraldry*, revised by C. W. Scott-Giles and J. P. Brooke-Little. London and New York: Frederick Warne.

Boynton, Robert M. and Conrad X. Olson. 1987. 'Locating basic colors in the OSA space'. *Color research and application* 12.2: 94–105.

1990. 'Salience of chromatic basic color terms confirmed by three measures'. *Vision research* 30.9: 1311–17.

Bricker, Victoria R. 1999. 'Color and texture in the Maya language of Yucatan'. *Anthropological linguistics* 41.3: 283–307.

Broackes, Justin. 1997. 'Could we take lime, purple, orange, and teal as unique hues?' *Behavioral and brain sciences* 20.2: 183–4.

Brown, Roger W. and Eric H. Lenneberg. 1954. 'A study in language and cognition'. *Journal of abnormal and social psychology* 49.3: 454–62.

Bullock, Barbara E. and Almeida Jacqueline Toribio. 2009. *The Cambridge handbook of linguistic code-switching*. Cambridge University Press.

Burgess, Don, Willett Kempton and Robert E. MacLaury. 1985. 'Tarahumara color modifiers: individual variation and evolutionary change', in Dougherty (ed.), pp. 49–72.

Burnley, J. D. 1976. 'Middle English colour terminology and lexical structure'. *Linguistische Berichte* 41: 39–49.

Byrne, Alex and David R. Hilbert. 1997. 'Unique hues'. *Behavioral and brain sciences* 20.2: 184–5.

Caie, Graham D., Carole Hough and Irené Wotherspoon (eds.) 2006. *The power of words: essays in lexicography, lexicology and semantics in honour of Christian J. Kay*. Costerus New Series 163. Amsterdam and New York: Rodopi.

Campbell, Lyle. 2003. 'How to show languages are related: methods for distant genetic relationship', in Joseph and Janda (eds.), pp. 262–82.

Cardon, Dominique. 2007. *Natural dyes: sources, tradition, technology and science*. London: Archetype.

Caskey-Sirmons, Leigh A. and Nancy P. Hickerson. 1977. 'Semantic shift and bilingualism: variation in the color terms of five languages'. *Anthropological linguistics* 19: 358–67.

Casson, Ronald W. 1994. 'Russett, rose, and raspberry: the development of English secondary color terms'. *Journal of linguistic anthropology* 4.1: 5–22.

1997. 'Color shift: evolution of English color terms from brightness to hue', in Hardin and Maffi (eds.), pp. 224–39.

Chaucer, Geoffrey. 1988. *The Riverside Chaucer*. 3rd edn by Larry D. Benson, based on *The works of Geoffrey Chaucer* ed. by F. N. Robinson. Oxford University Press.

Clackson, James. 2000. 'Time depth in Indo-European', in Renfrew, McMahon and Trask (eds.), vol. II, pp. 441–54.

Clarke, Michael. 2004. 'The semantics of colour in the early Greek word-hoard', in Cleland and Stears (eds.), pp. 131–9.

Cleland, Liza and Karen Stears with Glenys Davies. 2004. *Colour in the ancient Mediterranean world*. British Archaeological Report, International Series 1267. Oxford: John and Erica Hedges.

Coleman, Julie. 1995. 'The chronology of French and Latin loan words in English'. *Transactions of the Philological Society* 93.2: 95–124.

Coleman, Julie and Christian J. Kay (eds.) 2000. *Lexicology, semantics and lexicography: selected papers from the Fourth G. L. Brook Symposium, Manchester, August 1998*. Amsterdam Studies in the Theory and History of Linguistic Science 4: Current Issues in Linguistic Theory 194. Amsterdam and Philadelphia: John Benjamins.

Conklin, Harold C. 1955. 'Hanunóo color categories'. *Southwestern journal of anthropology* 11.4: 339–44.

Corbett, Greville G. and Ian R. L. Davies. 1995. 'Linguistic and behavioural measures for ranking basic colour terms'. *Studies in language* 19.2: 301–57.

　　1997. 'Establishing basic color terms: measures and techniques', in Hardin and Maffi (eds.), pp. 197–223.

Corbett, Greville G. and Gerry Morgan. 1988. 'Colour terms in Russian: reflections of typological constraints in a single language'. *Journal of linguistics* 24.1: 31–64.

Crawford, T. D. 1982. 'Defining "Basic Color Term"'. *Anthropological linguistics* 24.3: 338–43.

Crow, Martin M. and Virginia E. Leland. 1988. 'Chaucer's life', in Chaucer, pp. xi–xxii.

Cruden, Alexander. 1769. *A complete concordance to the Old and New Testament: or a dictionary and alphabetical index to the Bible*. London and New York: Frederick Warne.

Cruse, Alan [D. A. Cruse]. 1986. *Lexical semantics*. Cambridge University Press.

　　2006. *A glossary of semantics and pragmatics*. Edinburgh University Press.

Cunliffe, Barry (ed.) 2001. *The Oxford illustrated history of prehistoric Europe*. Oxford University Press.

Darwin, Charles. 1859. *On the origin of species by means of natural selection, or, The preservation of favoured races in the struggle for life*. London: John Murray.

Davies, Ian R. L. and Greville G. Corbett. 1994. 'A statistical approach to determining basic color terms: an account of Xhosa'. *Journal of linguistic anthropology* 4.2: 175–93.

Davies, Ian R. L., Penny Roling, Greville G. Corbett, Fritz Xoagub and Jomo Xoagub. 1997. 'Color terms and color term acquisition in Damara'. *Journal of linguistic anthropology* 7.2: 181–207.

Dedrick, Don. 1996. 'Color language universality and evolution: on the explanation for basic color terms'. *Philosophical psychology* 9.4: 497–524.

　　1998a. 'The foundations of the universalist tradition in color-naming research (and their supposed refutation)'. *Philosophy of the social sciences* 28: 179–204.

　　1998b. *Naming the rainbow: colour language, colour science and culture*. Synthese Library 274. Dordrecht and London: Kluwer Academic.

　　2002. 'The roots / routes of color term reference', in Saunders and van Brakel (eds.), pp. 53–68.

　　2005. 'Color, color terms, categorization, cognition, culture: an afterword'. *Journal of cognition and culture* 5.3–4: 487–95.

Derrig, Sandra. 1978. 'Metaphor in the color lexicon', in Farkas, Jacobsen and Todrys (eds.), pp. 85–96.

D'Evelyn, Charlotte. 1921. *Meditations on the life and passion of Christ from British Museum Addit. MS 11307*. Early English Text Society, Original Series 158. London: Oxford University Press.

Dictionary of Medieval Latin from British sources. 1975. Prepared by R. E. Latham and D. R. Howlett. Oxford University Press.

Dictionary of Old English: A to G. 2008. Edited by Angus Cameron, Ashley Crandell Amos, Antonette diPaolo Healey *et al*. Toronto: Pontifical Institute of Mediaeval Studies.

Dolgopolsky, Aharon. 1998. *The Nostratic macrofamily and linguistic palaeontology*. Cambridge: McDonald Institute for Archaeological Research.

2008. *The Nostratic dictionary*. Cambridge: McDonald Institute for Archaeological Research. (Internet: www.dspace.cam.ac.uk/handle/1810/196512.)

Dony, John G., Stephen L. Jury and Franklyn Perring. 1986. *English names of wild flowers: a list recommended by the Botanical Society of the British Isles*. 2nd edn. [London]: Botanical Society of the British Isles.

Dougherty, Janet Wynne Dixon. 1974. 'Color categorization in West Futuna: variation and change'. Paper presented to the American Anthropological Association Annual Meeting.

1977. 'Color categorization in West Futunese: variability and change', in Blount and Sanches (eds.), pp. 103–18.

Dougherty, Janet Wynne Dixon (ed.) 1985. *Directions in cognitive anthropology*. Urbana: University of Illinois Press.

Duncan, R. M. 1975. 'Color words in Medieval Spanish', in Beardsley, Brooks, Deyermond, *et al*. (eds.), pp. 53–71.

Durbin, Marshall. 1972. 'Basic terms – off-color?'. *Semiotica* 6: 257–78.

Durst, Uwe. 2004. 'The Natural Semantic Metalanguage approach to linguistic meaning'. *Theoretical linguistics* 29.3: 157–200.

Eastaugh, Nicholas, Valentine Walsh, Tracey Chaplin and Ruth Siddall. 2004. *The pigment compendium: a dictionary of historical pigments*. Oxford and Burlington, Mass.: Elsevier Butterworth-Heinemann. (For a list of errata, see the website of The Pigmentum Project at pigmentum.org.)

Edgeworth, Robert Joseph. 1992. *The colors of the Aeneid*. American University Studies, Series 17, Classical Languages and Literature 12. New York: Peter Lang.

Evans, H. Meurig and W. O. Thomas. 1958. *Y geiriadur mawr: the complete Welsh–English English–Welsh dictionary*, consulting ed. Stephen J. Williams. Llandysul: Gwasg Gomer; Llandybie: Christopher Davies.

Evans, Joan and Mary S. Serjeantson. 1933. *English mediaeval lapidaries*. Early English Text Society, Original Series 190. London, New York and Toronto: Oxford University Press.

Evans, Vyvyan and Melanie Green. 2006. *Cognitive linguistics: an introduction*. Edinburgh University Press.

Farfán, J. M. B. 1957. 'Onomástica de vehículos: el chofer en los nombres de sus vehículos'. *Folklore Americano* 5: 140–54; 285–6.

Farkas, Donka, Wesley M. Jacobsen and Karol W. Todrys (eds.) 1978. *Papers from the parasession on the lexicon, Chicago Linguistic Society, April 14–15, 1978.* Chicago Linguistic Society.

Forbes, Isabel. 1979. 'The terms *brun* and *marron* in modern standard French'. *Journal of linguistics* 15: 295–305.

2006. 'Age-related differences in the basic colour vocabulary of French', in Biggam and Kay (eds.), pp. 101–9.

Forster, Peter and Colin Renfrew (eds.) 2006. *Phylogenetic methods and the prehistory of languages.* Cambridge: McDonald Institute for Archaeological Research.

Fortson, Benjamin W. 2010. *Indo-European language and culture: an introduction.* 2nd edn. Malden, Mass., Oxford and Chichester: Wiley-Blackwell.

Fox-Davies, A. C. 1985. *A complete guide to heraldry*, revised and annotated by J. P. Brooke-Little. London: Bloomsbury Books.

Friedrich, Paul. 1970. *Proto-Indo-European trees: the arboreal system of a prehistoric people.* Chicago and London: University of Chicago Press.

Frisk, Gösta. 1949. *A Middle English translation of Macer Floridus* De viribus herbarum*: inaugural dissertation.* Uppsala: Almqvist and Wiksell.

Furbee, N. Louanna, Kelly Maynard, J. Jerome Smith, Robert A. Benfer, Sarah Quick and Larry Ross. 1997. 'The emergence of color cognition from color perception'. *Journal of linguistic anthropology* 6.2: 223–40.

Gaimar, Geffrei. 1960. *L'Estoire des Engleis*, ed. Alexander Bell. Anglo-Norman Texts 14–16. Oxford: Basil Blackwell.

Gardner-Chloros, Penelope. 2009. *Code-switching.* Cambridge University Press.

Gimbutas, Marija. 1973a. 'The beginning of the Bronze Age in Europe and the Indo-Europeans 3500-2500 BC'. *Journal of Indo-European studies* 1: 163–214.

1973b. 'Old Europe c.7000–3500 BC: the earliest European cultures before the infiltration of Indo-European peoples'. *Journal of Indo-European studies* 1: 1–20.

Gladstone, W. E. 1858. *Studies on Homer and the Homeric Age.* 3 vols. Oxford University Press.

1877. 'The colour-sense'. *The nineteenth century: a monthly review* 2: 366–88.

Glasgow, Kathleen. 1994. *Burarra–Gun-nartpa dictionary with English finder list.* Darwin: Summer Institute of Linguistics, Australian Aborigines and Islanders Branch.

Głaz, Adam. 2006. 'Beyond colour: modelling language in colour-like ways', in Biggam and Kay (eds.), pp. 73–87.

2009. 'Cognition, categorization and language: Cognitive Grammar meets vantage theory'. *Rice working papers in linguistics* 1: 242–59.

2010. 'Towards extended vantage theory'. *Language sciences* 32.2: 259–75.

Głaz, Adam and Keith Allan. 2010. 'Vantage theory: developments and extensions: introduction'. *Language sciences* 32.2: 151–7.

Goddard, Cliff. 2007. 'Semantic molecules', in Mushin and Laughren (eds.), pp. 1–14.

Gottlieb, Jens Erik Mogensen and Arne Zettersten (eds.) 2002. *Symposium on lexicography X: proceedings of the Tenth International Symposium on Lexicography, May 4–6, 2000 at the University of Copenhagen.* Lexicographica, Series Maior 109. Tübingen: Max Niemeyer.

Greene, Katherine S. and Malcolm D. Gynther. 1995. 'Blue versus periwinkle: color identification and gender'. *Perceptual and motor skills* 80: 27–32.

Greene, Richard Leighton (ed.) 1977. *The early English carols*. 2nd edn. Oxford: Clarendon Press.

Grieve, M. 1973. *A modern herbal: the medicinal, culinary, cosmetic and economic properties, cultivation and folklore of herbs, grasses, fungi, shrubs and trees with all their modern scientific uses*, revised edn. by C. F. Leyel. London: Jonathan Cape.

Grossmann, Maria. 1988. *Colori e lessico: studi sulla struttura semantica degli aggettivi di colore in catalano, castigliano, italiano, romeno, latino ed ungherese*. Tübinger Beiträge zur Linguistik 310. Tübingen: Gunter Narr.

Grzegorczykowa, Renata and Krystyna Waszakowa (eds.) 2000. *Studia z semantyki porównawczej: nazwy barw, nazwy wymiarów, predykaty mentalne*. Warsaw: Wydawnictwa Uniwersytetu Warszawskiego.

Gumperz, John J. and Stephen C. Levinson. 1991. 'Rethinking linguistic relativity'. *Current anthropology* 32.5: 613–23.

Gumperz, John J. and Stephen C. Levinson (eds.) 1996. *Rethinking linguistic relativity*. Studies in the Social and Cultural Foundations of Language 17. Cambridge University Press.

Haddon, A. C. (ed.) 1901. *Reports of the Cambridge Anthropological Expedition to Torres Straits, volume 2: Physiology and psychology*. Cambridge University Press.

Hage, Per and Kristen Hawkes. 1975. 'Binumarien color categories'. *Ethnology* 14.3: 287–300.

Hall, Alaric, Olga Timofeeva, Ágnes Kiricsi and Bethany Fox (eds.) 2010. *Interfaces between language and culture in Medieval England: a Festschrift for Matti Kilpiö*. The Northern World 48. Leiden and Boston: Brill.

Hardin, C. L. and Luisa Maffi (eds.) 1997. *Color categories in thought and language*. Cambridge University Press.

Harley, R. D. 1982. *Artists' pigments c.1600–1835: a study in English documentary sources*. 2nd edn. London: Butterworth Scientific.

Harrison, S. P. 2003. 'On the limits of the comparative method', in Joseph and Janda (eds.), pp. 213–43.

Haspelmath, Martin, Ekkehard König, Wulf Oesterreicher and Wolfgang Raible (eds.) 2001. *Language typology and language universals: an international handbook = Sprachtypologie und sprachliche Universalien: ein internationales Handbuch = La typologie des langues et les universaux linguistiques: manuel international*. 2 vols. Handbücher zur Sprach- und Kommunikationswissenschaft 20. Berlin and New York: de Gruyter.

Hattori, Shiroo. 1964. *Ainugo hoogen jiten* [Ainu dialect dictionary]. Tokyo: Iwanami.

Hays, David G., Enid Margolis, Raoul Narrol and Dale Revere Perkins. 1972. 'Color term salience'. *American anthropologist* 74.5: 1107–21.

Hegedüs, Irén. 1997. 'Principles for palaeolinguistic reconstruction', in Blench and Spriggs (eds.), pp. 65–73.

Heinrich, A. C. 1973. 'Systematics of Canadian Eskimo colour terminology'. Unpublished manuscript (see Kay 1975).

Henselmans, Arnold. 2002. 'The Munsell constraint', in Saunders and van Brakel (eds.), pp. 37–52.

Hiatt, L. R. (ed.) 1978. *Australian aboriginal concepts*. Canberra: Australian Institute of Aboriginal Studies.

Hickerson, Nancy P. 1971. [Review of Berlin and Kay's *Basic color terms*]. *International journal of American linguistics* 37.4: 257–70.

1975. 'Two studies of color: implications for cross-cultural comparability of semantic categories', in Kinkade, Hale and Werner (eds.), pp. 317–30.

1983. 'Gladstone's ethnolinguistics: the language of experience in the nineteenth century'. *Journal of anthropological research* 39.1: 26–41.

Hill, Peter M. 2008. 'The metaphorical use of colour terms in the Slavonic languages', in Wells (ed.), pp. 62–83.

Historical thesaurus of the Oxford English Dictionary with additional material from A thesaurus of Old English, by Christian Kay, Jane Roberts, Michael Samuels and Irené Wotherspoon. 2009. 2 vols. Oxford University Press.

Hough, Carole. 2006. 'Colours of the landscape: Old English colour terms in place-names', in Biggam and Kay (eds.), pp. 181–98.

[2010]. *Toponymicon and lexicon in north-west Europe: 'ever-changing connection'*. E. C. Quiggin Memorial Lecture 12. Cambridge: Department of Anglo-Saxon, Norse and Celtic, University of Cambridge.

Howard, Alexander L. 1947. *Trees in Britain and their timbers*. London: Country Life.

Irwin, Eleanor. 1974. *Colour terms in Greek poetry*. Toronto: Hakkert.

Isidore of Seville. 1911. *Isidori Hispalensis Episcopi Etymologiarum sive originum*, edited by W. M. Lindsay. 2 vols. Oxford University Press.

Jacobs, Wilhelmina and Vivian Jacobs. 1958. 'The color blue: its use as metaphor and symbol'. *American speech* 33: 29–46.

Jameson, Kimberly A. 2005. 'Why GRUE? An interpoint-distance model analysis of composite color categories'. *Cross-cultural research* 39.2: 159–204.

Jameson, Kimberly A. and Roy G. D'Andrade. 1997. 'It's not really red, green, yellow, blue: an inquiry into perceptual color space', in Hardin and Maffi (eds.), pp. 295–319.

Jameson, Kimberly A., Susan M. Highnote and Linda M. Wasserman. 2001. 'Richer color experience in observers with multiple photopigment opsin genes'. *Psychonomic bulletin and review* 8.2: 244–61.

Jespersen, Otto. 1924. *The philosophy of grammar*. London: Allen and Unwin, and New York: Henry Holt.

Jones, Andrew and Gavin MacGregor (eds.) 2002. *Colouring the past: the significance of colour in archaeological research*. Oxford and New York: Berg.

Jones, Rhys and Betty Meehan. 1978. 'Anbarra concept of colour', in Hiatt (ed.), pp. 20–39.

Joseph, Brian D. and Richard D. Janda (eds.) 2003. *The handbook of historical linguistics*. Oxford: Blackwell Publishing.

Jourdan, Christine and Kevin Tuite (eds.) 2006. *Language, culture, and society: key topics in linguistic anthropology*. Studies in the Social and Cultural Foundations of Language 23. Cambridge University Press.

Kay, Christian J. 2000. 'Historical semantics and historical lexicography: will the twain ever meet?', in Coleman and Kay (eds.), pp. 53–68.

Kay, Christian J. and Jeremy J. Smith. 2004. *Categorization in the history of English*. Amsterdam Studies in the Theory and History of Linguistic Science, Series IV:

Current Issues in Linguistic Theory 261. Amsterdam and Philadelphia: John Benjamins.

Kay, Christian J. and Louise M. Sylvester (eds.) 2001. *Lexis and texts in early English: studies presented to Jane Roberts.* Costerus New Series 133. Amsterdam and Atlanta: Rodopi.

Kay, Paul. 1975. 'Synchronic variability and diachronic change in basic color terms'. *Language in society* 4: 257–70.

1977. 'Language evolution and speech style', in Blount and Sanches (eds.), pp. 21–33.

1999. 'The emergence of basic color lexicons hypothesis: a comment on "The vocabulary of color with particular reference to Ancient Greek and Classical Latin" by John Lyons', in Borg (ed.), pp. 76–90.

2001. 'Color terms, linguistics of', in Smelser and Baltes (eds.), pp. 2248–52.

2004. 'NSM and the meaning of color words'. *Theoretical linguistics* 29.3: 237–45.

2005. 'Color categories are not arbitrary'. *Cross-cultural research* 39.1: 39–55.

2006. 'Methodological issues in cross-language color naming', in Jourdan and Tuite (eds.), pp. 115–34.

Kay, Paul and Brent Berlin. 1997. 'Science ≠ imperialism: there are nontrivial constraints on colour naming'. *Behavioral and brain sciences* 20.2: 196–201.

Kay, Paul, Brent Berlin, Luisa Maffi and William Merrifield. 1997. 'Color naming across languages', in Hardin and Maffi (eds.), pp. 21–56.

Kay, Paul, Brent Berlin, Luisa Maffi, William Merrifield and Richard Cook. 2009. *The World Color Survey.* CSLI Lecture Notes 159. Stanford, Calif.: CSLI Publications.

Kay, Paul, Brent Berlin and William Merrifield. 1991. 'Biocultural implications of systems of color naming'. *Journal of linguistic anthropology* 1: 12–25.

Kay, Paul and Willett Kempton. 1984. 'What is the Sapir–Whorf hypothesis?' *American anthropologist* 86.1: 65–79.

Kay, Paul and Luisa Maffi. 1999. 'Color appearance and the emergence and evolution of basic color lexicons'. *American anthropologist* 101.4: 743–60.

Kay, Paul and Chad K. McDaniel. 1975. 'Color categories as fuzzy sets'. Working Paper 44. Language Behavior Research Laboratory, University of California at Berkeley.

1978. 'The linguistic significance of the meanings of basic color terms'. *Language* 54.3: 610–46.

Kay, Paul and Terry Regier. 2003. 'Resolving the question of color naming universals'. *Proceedings of the National Academy of Sciences of the United States of America* 100.15: 9085–9.

2006. 'Language, thought and color: recent developments'. *Trends in cognitive sciences* 10.2: 51–4.

Kerttula, Seija. 2002. *English colour terms: etymology, chronology and relative basicness.* Mémoires de la Société Néophilologique de Helsinki 60. Helsinki: Société Néophilologique.

2007. 'Relative basicness of color terms: modeling and measurement', in MacLaury, Paramei and Dedrick (eds.), pp. 151–69.

Kikuchi, Atsuko and Frantisek Lichtenberk. 1983. 'Semantic extension in the colour lexicon'. *Studies in language* 7.1: 25–64.

Kinkade, M. Dale, Kenneth L. Hale and Oswald Werner (eds.) 1975. *Linguistics and anthropology: in honor of C. F. Voegelin.* Lisse: Peter de Ridder Press.

Koptjevskaja-Tamm, Maria and Inger Ahlgren. 2004. 'NSM: theoretical, methodological and applicational problems'. *Theoretical linguistics* 29.3: 247–61.

Kövecses, Zoltán. 2002. *Metaphor: a practical introduction.* Oxford University Press.

Kristol, Andres. 1980. 'Color systems in southern Italy: a case of regression'. *Language* 56.1: 137–45.

Kuehni, Rolf G. and Andreas Schwarz. 2008. *Color ordered: a survey of color order systems from Antiquity to the present.* New York: Oxford University Press.

Kuschel, Rolf and Torben Monberg. 1974. '"We don't talk much about colour here": a study of colour semantics on Bellona Island'. *Man* 9.2: 213–42.

Kytö, Merja. 1996. *Manual to the diachronic part of the Helsinki Corpus of English Texts: coding conventions and lists of source texts.* 3rd edn. Department of English, University of Helsinki.

Lakoff, George. 1987. *Women, fire and dangerous things: what categories reveal about the mind.* University of Chicago Press.

Lakoff, George and Mark Johnson. 1980. *Metaphors we live by.* University of Chicago Press. Reprinted in 2003 with a new afterword.

Lamb, Trevor and Janine Bourriau (eds.) 1995. *Colour: art and science.* Cambridge University Press.

Lapidge, Michael, John Blair, Simon Keynes and Donald Scragg (eds.) 1999. *The Blackwell encyclopaedia of Anglo-Saxon England.* Oxford: Blackwell.

Latham, R. E. 1965. *Revised Medieval Latin word-list from British and Irish sources.* Oxford University Press.

Lazar-Meyn, Heidi Ann. 1991. 'The colour systems of the modern Celtic languages: effects of language contact', in Ureland and Broderick (eds.), pp. 227–42.

1994. 'Colour terms in Táin bó Cúailnge', in Mallory and Stockman (eds.), pp. 201–5.

Leech, Geoffrey, Paul Rayson and Andrew Wilson. 2001. *Word frequencies in written and spoken English based on the British National Corpus.* Harlow: Pearson Education.

Lehmann, R. P. M. 1969. 'Color usage in Irish', in Atwood and Hill (eds.), pp. 73–9.

Lendinara, Patrizia. 1999. 'Glossaries', in Lapidge, Blair, Keynes and Scragg (eds.), pp. 207–9.

Lenneberg, Eric H. and John M. Roberts. 1956. *The language of experience: a study in methodology.* Indiana University Publications in Anthropology and Linguistics, Memoir 13 (Supplement to *International journal of American linguistics* 22.2). Baltimore: Waverly Press.

Lerner, L. D. 1951. 'Colour words in Anglo-Saxon'. *Modern Language Review* 46: 246–9.

Levinson, Stephen C. 2000. 'Yélî Dnye and the theory of Basic Color Terms'. *Journal of linguistic anthropology* 10.1: 3–55.

Lucy, John A. 1992. *Language diversity and thought: a reformulation of the linguistic relativity hypothesis.* Studies in the Social and Cultural Foundations of Language 12. Cambridge University Press.

Lyons, John. 1963. *Structural semantics: an analysis of part of the vocabulary of Plato.* Publications of the Philological Society 20. Oxford: Basil Blackwell.

1968. *Introduction to theoretical linguistics.* Cambridge University Press.

1977. *Semantics.* 2 vols. Cambridge University Press.

1995a. 'Colour in language', in Lamb and Bourriau (eds.), pp. 194–224.

1995b. *Linguistic semantics: an introduction*. Cambridge University Press.

1999. 'The vocabulary of color with particular reference to Ancient Greek and Classical Latin', in Borg (ed.), pp. 38–75.

Machen, V. 2002. 'Color naming by boys and girls'. *Perceptual and motor skills* 94: 348–50.

MacLaury, Robert E. 1982. 'Prehistoric Mayan color categories'. Unpublished manuscript, Language Behavior Research Laboratory, University of California, Berkeley.

1987. 'Color-category evolution and Shuswap yellow-with-green'. *American anthropologist* 89: 107–24.

1991. 'Social and cognitive motivations of change: measuring variability in colour semantics'. *Language* 67: 34–62.

1992a. 'From brightness to hue: an explanatory model of color-category evolution'. *Current anthropology* 33.2: 137–86.

1992b. 'Karuk color: the yellow-green-blue category of northern California'. Paper presented at the 91st Annual Meeting of the American Anthropological Association, San Francisco.

1997a. *Color and cognition in Mesoamerica: constructing categories as vantages*. Austin: University of Texas Press.

1997b. 'Ethnographic evidence of unique hues and elemental colors'. *Behavioral and brain sciences* 20.2: 202–3.

1999. 'Basic Color Terms: twenty-five years after', in Borg (ed.), pp. 1–37.

2001. 'Color terms', in Haspelmath, König, Oesterreicher and Raible (eds.), pp. 1227–51.

2002. 'Introducing vantage theory'. *Language sciences* 24.5–6: 493–536.

MacLaury, Robert E., Judit Almási and Zoltán Kövecses. 1997. 'Hungarian *piros* and *vörös*: color from points of view'. *Semiotica* 114.1–2: 67–81.

MacLaury, Robert E., Galina V. Paramei and Don Dedrick (eds.) 2007. *Anthropology of color: interdisciplinary multilevel modeling*. Amsterdam and Philadelphia: John Benjamins.

Maffi, Luisa. 1990. 'Somali color term evolution: grammatical and semantic evidence'. *Anthropological linguistics* 32.3–4: 316–34.

Maffi, Luisa and C. L. Hardin. 1997. 'Closing thoughts', in Hardin and Maffi (eds.), pp. 347–72.

Magnus, Hugo. 1877. *Die geschichtliche Entwickelung des Farbensinnes*. Leipzig: von Veit.

1880. *Untersuchungen über den Farbensinn der Naturvölker*. Jena: Gustav Fischer.

Malkoc, Gohkan. 2003. 'Color categories and the structure of color space'. PhD thesis, University of Nevada at Reno.

Mallory, J. P. and D. Q. Adams. 2006. *The Oxford introduction to Proto-Indo- European and the Proto-Indo-European world*. Oxford University Press.

Mallory, J. P. and Gerard Stockman (eds.) 1994. *Ulidia: proceedings of the First International Conference on the Ulster Cycle of Tales, Belfast and Emain Macha, 8–12 April 1994*. Belfast: December Publications.

Marsh, Robert. 1967. *Comparative sociology*. New York: Harcourt, Brace.

McMahon, April M. S. 1994. *Understanding language change*. Cambridge University Press.

McMahon, April M. S. and McMahon, Robert. 2006. 'Why linguists don't do dates: evidence from Indo-European and Australian languages', in Forster and Renfrew (eds.), pp. 153–60.

McNeill, N. B. 1972. 'Colour and colour terminology'. *Journal of linguistics* 8: 21–33.

Mead, William E. 1899. 'Color in Old English poetry'. *Publications of the Modern Language Association of America* 14.2 (new series 7.2): 169–206.

Mervis, Carolyn B. and Emilie M. Roth. 1981. 'The internal structure of basic and non-basic color categories'. *Language* 57.2: 384–405.

Middle English Dictionary 1956–2001. Edited by Hans Kurath, Sherman McAllister Kuhn *et al.* Ann Arbor: University of Michigan Press. (Internet: quod.lib.umich.edu/m/med/.)

Miles, Archie. 1999. *Silva: the tree in Britain*. London: Ebury Press.

Miller, David L. 1997. 'Over the rainbow: the classification of unique hues'. *Behavioral and brain sciences* 20.2: 204–5.

Mills, L. H. (trans.) 1887. *The Zend Avesta, part III*. Sacred Books of the East 31. Oxford: Clarendon Press.

Minkova, Donka and Robert Stockwell (eds.) 2002. *Studies in the history of the English language: a millennial perspective*. Topics in English Linguistics 39. Berlin and New York: Mouton de Gruyter.

Minnaert, Marcel. 1993. *Light and color in the outdoors*. New York, Berlin and Heidelberg: Springer.

Mithen, Steven. 1994. 'From domain specific to generalized intelligence: a cognitive interpretation of the Middle/Upper Palaeolithc transition', in Renfrew and Zubrow (eds.), pp. 29–39.

1996. *The prehistory of the mind: a search for the origins of art, religion and science*. London: Thames and Hudson.

2001. 'The Mesolithic Age', in Cunliffe (ed.), pp. 79–135.

Mollon, J. D., J. Pokorny and K. Knoblauch (eds.). 2003. *Normal and defective colour vision*. Oxford University Press.

Monier-Williams, Monier. 2008. *A Sanskrit–English dictionary etymologically and philologically arranged with special reference to cognate Indo-European languages*. New edn with collaboration of E. Leumann and C. Cappeller. Oxford: Clarendon Press. (Internet: www.sanskrit-lexicon.uni-koeln.de/monier/.)

Moore, Timothy E. (ed.) 1973. *Cognitive development and the acquisition of language*. New York, San Francisco and London: Academic Press.

Morgan, G. and G. G. Corbett. 1989. 'Russian colour term salience'. *Russian linguistics* 13.2: 125–41.

Moskovič, V. A. 1969. *Statistika i semantika: opyt statističeskogo analiza semantičeskogo polja*. Moscow: Nauka.

Moskovsky, Christo (ed.) 2004. *Proceedings of the 2003 Conference of the Australian Linguistic Society*. (Internet: www.als.asn.au.)

Moss, A., I. Davies, G. Corbett and G. Laws. 1990. 'Mapping Russian basic colour terms using behavioural measures'. *Lingua* 82: 313–32.

Munby, Julian (ed.) 1982. *Domesday Book: Hampshire*, general ed. John Morris. Domesday Book 4. Chichester: Phillimore.

Munsell, A. H. 1981. *A color notation: an illustrated system defining all colors and their relations by measured scales of hue, value and chroma*, ed. by A. E. O. Munsell. Baltimore: Munsell Color.

Mushin, Ilana and Mary Laughren (eds.) 2007. *Selected papers from the 2006 Annual Meeting of the Australian Linguistic Society, Brisbane, 7–9 July 2006*. (Internet: www.als.asn.au/proceedings.html.)

Narrol, Raoul. 1970. 'What have we learned from cross-cultural surveys?' *American anthropologist* 72.6: 1227–88.

Nielsen, Hans F. and Lene Schøsler (eds.). 1996. The origins and development of emigrant languages: proceedings from the Second Rasmus Rask Colloquium, Odense University, November 1994. Rask Supplement 6; *NOWELE* Supplement 17. Odense University Press.

Niemeier, Susanne. 1998. 'Colourless green ideas metonymise furiously'. *Rostocker Beiträge zur Sprachwissenschaft* 5: 119–46.

Nowaczyk, Ronald H. 1982. 'Sex-related differences in the color lexicon'. *Language and Speech* 25.3: 257–65.

Oja, Vilja. 2002. 'Some semantic problems in the translation of colour terms', in Gottlieb and Zettersten (eds.), pp. 253–60.

Oliphant, Robert T. (ed.) 1966. *The Harley Latin–Old English glossary edited from British Museum MS Harley 3376*. Janua Linguarum Series Practica 20. The Hague and Paris: Mouton.

Oxford English Dictionary [online]. 2nd edn with ongoing revision. Oxford University Press. (Internet: www.oed.com.)

Oxford Latin Dictionary. 1982. Edited by P. G. W. Glare. Oxford: Clarendon Press.

Packer, Dianne E. and Talib M. Ali. 1985. *The colours and markings of horses*. Ipswich: Farming Press.

Paramei, Galina V. 2005. 'Singing the Russian blues: an argument for culturally basic color terms'. *Cross-cultural research* 39.1: 10–38.

  2007. 'Russian "blues"', in MacLaury, Paramei and Dedrick (eds.), pp. 75–106.

Payne, Doris L. 2003. 'Maa color terms and their use as human descriptors'. *Anthropological linguistics* 45.2: 169–200.

Pitchford, N. J. and C. P. Biggam (eds.) 2006. *Progress in colour studies, volume II: Psychological aspects*. Amsterdam and Philadelphia: John Benjamins.

Plummer, Charles and John Earle (eds.) 1892–9. *Two of the Saxon chronicles parallel with supplementary extracts from the others*. 2 vols. Oxford: Clarendon Press.

Pokorny, Julius. 1959–69. *Indogermanisches etymologisches Wörterbuch*. 2 vols. Bern and Munich: Francke Verlag.

Pollnac, Richard B. 1975. 'Intra-cultural variability in the structure of the subjective color lexicon in Buganda'. *American ethnologist* 2.1: 89–109.

Popovic, Lyudmila. 2007. 'Prototypical and stereotypical color in Slavic languages: models based on folklore', in MacLaury, Paramei and Dedrick (eds.), pp. 405–20.

Prado-León, Lilia Roselia, Rosalío Ávila-Chaurand and Rosa Amelia Rosales-Cinco. 2006. 'Colour associations in the Mexican university population', in Pitchford and Biggam (eds.), pp. 189–202.

Preston, Christopher D., David A. Pearman and Allan R. Hall. 2004. 'Archaeophytes in Britain'. *Botanical journal of the Linnean Society* 145: 257–94.

Preston, Dennis R. 1994. 'Content-oriented discourse analysis and folk linguistics'. *Language sciences* 16.2: 285–331.

Pyne, Stephen J. 2001. *Fire: a brief history*. London: British Museum Press.

Rakhilina, Ekaterina V. and Galina V. Paramei. 2011. 'Colour terms: evolution via expansion of taxonomic constraints', in Biggam, Hough, Kay and Simmons (eds.), pp. 121–31.

Rätsep, Kaidi. 2011. 'Preliminary research on Turkish Basic Colour Terms with an emphasis on blue', in Biggam, Hough, Kay and Simmons (eds.), pp. 133–45.

Regier, Terry and Paul Kay. 2009. 'Language, thought and color: Whorf was half right'. *Trends in cognitive sciences* 13.10: 439–46.

Renfrew, Colin. 1987. *Archaeology and language: the puzzle of Indo-European origins.* London: Cape.

1998. 'Introduction: the Nostratic Hypothesis, linguistic macrofamilies and prehistoric studies', in Dolgopolsky, pp. vii–xxii.

2000. '10,000 or 5000 years ago? Questions of time-depth', in Renfrew, McMahon and Trask (eds.), vol. II, pp. 413–39.

Renfrew, Colin, April McMahon and Larry Trask (eds.) 2000. *Time depth in historical linguistics.* 2 vols. Cambridge: McDonald Institute for Archaeological Research.

Renfrew, Colin and Ezra B. W. Zubrow (eds.) 1994. *The ancient mind: elements of cognitive archaeology.* Cambridge University Press.

Rich, Elaine. 1977. 'Sex-related differences in colour vocabulary'. *Language and speech* 20.4: 404–9.

Rivers, W. H. R. 1901a. 'The colour vision of the Eskimo'. *Proceedings of the Cambridge Philosophical Society* 11: 143–9.

1901b. 'Vision', in Haddon (ed.), pp. 1–132.

Roberson, Debi, Ian Davies and Jules Davidoff. 2000. 'Color categories are not universal: replications and new evidence from a Stone-Age culture'. *Journal of experimental psychology: General* 129.3: 369–98.

Rosch, Eleanor H. 1973. 'On the internal structure of perceptual and semantic categories', in Moore (ed.), pp. 111–44.

1977. 'Human categorization', in Warren (ed.), vol. I, pp. 1–49.

1978. 'Principles of categorization', in Rosch and Lloyd (eds.), pp. 27–48.

Rosch, Eleanor H. and Barbara B. Lloyd (eds.) 1978. *Cognition and categorization.* Hillsdale, NJ: Lawrence Erlbaum Associates.

Rosch, Eleanor H. and Carolyn B. Mervis. 1975. 'Family resemblances: studies in the internal structure of categories'. *Cognitive psychology* 7.4: 573–605.

Rosch Heider, Eleanor. 1972a. 'Probabilities, sampling, and ethnographic method: the case of Dani colour names'. *Man* 7.3: 448–66.

1972b. 'Universals in color naming and memory'. *Journal of experimental psychology* 93.1: 10–20.

Rothwell, W. 1993. 'The legacy of Anglo-French: *faux amis* in French and English'. *Zeitschrift für romanische Philologie* 109.1-2: 16–46.

1994. 'The trilingual England of Geoffrey Chaucer'. *Studies in the age of Chaucer* 16: 45–67.

Ruhlen, Merritt. 1994. *On the origin of languages: studies in linguistic taxonomy.* Stanford University Press.

Saeed, John I. 2009. *Semantics.* 3rd edn. Introducing Linguistics 2. Oxford: Wiley-Blackwell.

Sapir, Edward. 1921. *Language: an introduction to the study of speech.* New York: Harcourt, Brace.

1929. 'The status of linguistics as a science'. *Language* 5.4: 207–14.

Saunders, Barbara. 1992. *The invention of basic colour terms*. Utrecht: Rijksuniversiteit te Utrecht–ISOR.

1993. 'On the concept of "basic" in Berlin and Kay's basic color terms'. *Antropologische Verkenningen* 12.1: 35–50.

1995. 'Disinterring *Basic Color Terms*: a study in the mystique of cognitivism'. *History of the human sciences* 8.4: 19–38.

1999. 'The ideology of a model of colour', in Aerts, Mathijs and Mosselmans (eds.), pp. 237–47.

Saunders, Barbara and J. van Brakel. 1988. 'Re-evaluating basic colour terms'. *Cultural dynamics* 1: 359–78.

1997. 'Are there nontrivial constraints on colour categorization'. *Behavioral and brain sciences* 20.2: 167–79.

1999. 'Colour word trouble'. *Behavioral and brain sciences* 22.4: 725–9.

Saunders, Barbara and J. van Brakel (eds.). 2002. *Theories, technologies, instrumentalities of color: anthropological and historiographic perspectives*. London, New York and Oxford: University Press of America.

Schalley, Andrea C. and Drew Khlentzos (eds.). 2007. *Mental states, volume II: Language and cognitive structure*. Studies in Language Companion Series 93. Amsterdam and Philadelphia: John Benjamins.

Schendl, Herbert. 2002. 'Mixed-language texts as data and evidence in English historical linguistics', in Minkova and Stockwell (eds.), pp. 51–78.

Schöntag, Roger and Barbara Schäfer-Priess. 2007. 'Color term research of Hugo Magnus', in MacLaury, Paramei and Dedrick (eds.), pp. 107–22.

Schumann, Walter. 1977. *Gemstones of the world*, translated by Evelyne Stern. New York: Sterling Publishing and London: N. A. G. Press.

Shields, Kenneth. 1979. 'Indo-European Basic Colour Terms'. *Canadian journal of linguistics* 24.2: 142–6.

Simpson, Jean and Arthur W. S. Tarrant. 1991. 'Sex- and age-related differences in colour vocabulary'. *Language and speech* 34.1: 57–62.

Smelser, Neil J. and Paul B. Baltes (eds.) 2001. *International encyclopedia of the social and behavioral sciences, volume IV*. Amsterdam: Elsevier.

Smith, J. Jerome, Louanna Furbee, Kelly Maynard, Sarah Quick and Larry Ross. 1995. 'Salience counts: a domain analysis of English color terms'. *Journal of linguistic anthropology* 5.2: 203–16.

Smith, Jeremy J. 1999. *Essentials of early English*. London and New York: Routledge.

Snow, David L. 1971. 'Samoan color terminology: a note on the universality and evolutionary ordering of color terms'. *Anthropological linguistics* 13.8: 385–90.

Stace, Clive. 1997. *New flora of the British Isles*. 2nd edn. Cambridge University Press.

Stanlaw, James. 2010. 'Language, contact, and vantages: fifteen hundred years of Japanese color terms'. *Language sciences* 32.2: 196–224.

Steinvall, Anders. 2002. *English colour terms in context*. Skrifter från moderna språk 3. Umeå Universitet (Sweden).

2006. 'Basic Colour Terms and type modification: meaning in relation to function, salience and correlating attributes', in Biggam and Kay (eds.), pp. 57–71.

Step, Edward. n.d. *Wayside and woodland trees: a pocket guide to the British sylva*. London and New York: Frederick Warne.

Summer, P. and J. D. Mollon. 2003. 'Did primate trichromacy evolve for frugivory or folivory?', in Mollon, Pokorny and Knoblauch (eds.), pp. 21–30.

Sutrop, Urmas. 2001. 'List task and a cognitive salience index'. *Field methods* 13.3: 263–76.

Swadesh, Morris. 1952. 'Lexico-statistical dating of prehistoric ethnic contacts: with special reference to North American Indians and Eskimos'. *Proceedings of the American Philosophical Society* 96.4: 452–63.

Swaringen, Sandra, Stephanie Layman and Alan Wilson. 1978. 'Sex differences in color naming'. *Perceptual and motor skills* 47: 440–2.

Swinburne, Algernon Charles. 1866. *Poems and ballads*. London: John Camden Hotten.

Taylor, John R. 2003. *Linguistic categorization*. 3rd edn. Oxford University Press.

Taylor, John R., Henrietta Mondry and Robert E. MacLaury. 1997. 'A cognitive ceiling of eleven Basic Color Terms', in MacLaury (1997a) (ed.), pp. 419–29.

Teubert, Wolfgang and Anna Čermáková. 2007. *Corpus linguistics: a short introduction*. London: Continuum.

Thomas, Lynn L., Anne T. Curtis and Ralph Bolton. 1978. 'Sex differences in elicited color lexicon size'. *Perceptual and motor skills* 47: 77–8.

Thomason, Sarah Grey and Terrence Kaufman. 1988. *Language contact, creolization, and genetic linguistics*. Berkeley, Los Angeles and Oxford: University of California Press.

Trask, Larry. 2000. 'Some issues in relative chronology', in Renfrew, McMahon and Trask (eds.), vol. I, pp. 45–58.

Traugott, Elizabeth Closs and Richard B. Dasher. 2002. *Regularity in semantic change*. Cambridge University Press.

Trotter, D. A. 1996. 'Language contact and lexicography: the case of Anglo-Norman', in Nielsen and Schøsler (eds.), pp. 21–39.

Turton, David. 1980. 'There's no such beast: cattle and colour naming among the Mursi'. *Man* 15.2: 320–38.

Uchikawa, Keiji and Robert M. Boynton. 1987. 'Categorical color perception of Japanese observers: comparison with that of Americans'. *Vision research* 27.10: 1825–33.

Ureland, P. Sture and George Broderick (eds.) 1991. *Language contact in the British Isles: proceedings of the Eighth International Symposium on Language Contact in Europe, Douglas, Isle of Man, 1988*. Tübingen: Max Niemeyer.

Uusküla, Mari. 2007. 'The Basic Colour Terms of Finnish'. *SKY Journal of linguistics* 20: 367–97.

van Brakel, J. 1993. 'The plasticity of categories: the case of colour'. *British journal for the philosophy of science* 44: 103–35.

    2004. 'The empirical stance and the colour war'. *Studia Culturologica: Divinatio* 20: 7–26.

Van Laar, Darren. 1997. 'Ekphrasis in colour categorisation: time for research or time for revolution?'. *Behavioral and brain sciences* 20.2: 210.

Walton Rogers, Penelope. 2007. *Cloth and clothing in early Anglo-Saxon England, AD 450-700*. Council for British Archaeology Research Report 145. York: Council for British Archaeology.

Warren, Neil (ed.) 1977–80. *Studies in cross-cultural psychology.* 2 vols. London and New York: Academic Press.

Waszakowa, Krystyna. 2000. 'Podstawowe nazwy barw i ich prototypowe odniesienia: metodologia opisu porównawczego' [Basic Colour Terms and their prototypical denotata: a methodology of comparative description], in Grzegorczykowa and Waszakowa (eds.), vol. I, pp. 17–28.

Weatherbys. 2008. *Identification of horses.* In conjunction with the Royal College of Veterinary Surgeons and the British Equine Veterinary Association. [Wellingborough]: Weatherbys.

Webb, D. A. 1985. 'What are the criteria for presuming native status? *Watsonia* 15: 231–6.

Wells, David N. (ed.) 2008. *Themes and variations in Slavic languages and cultures: Australian contributions to the XIV International Congress of Slavists, Ohrid, Macedonia, 2008.* Perth: Australia and New Zealand Slavists' Association.

Wenzel, Siegfried. 1994. *Macaronic sermons: bilingualism and preaching in late-medieval England.* Ann Arbor: University of Michigan Press.

Wescott, Roger W. 1970. 'Bini color terms'. *American anthropologist* 12: 349–60.

Whorf, Benjamin Lee. 1956. *Language, thought and reality: selected writings of Benjamin Lee Whorf,* ed. by John B. Carroll. Cambridge, Mass.: Technology Press of Massachusetts Institute of Technology, and New York and London: John Wiley.

Wierzbicka, Anna. 1996. *Semantics: primes and universals.* Oxford and New York: Oxford University Press.

2006. 'The semantics of colour: a new paradigm', in Biggam and Kay (eds.), pp. 1–24.

2007. 'Shape and colour in language and thought', in Schalley and Khlentzos (eds.), pp. 37–60.

2008. 'Why there are no "colour universals" in language and thought'. *Journal of the Royal Anthropological Institute* 14: 407–25.

Wilcox, Michael. 1991. *The Wilcox guide to the finest watercolour paints.* Cloverdale, Australia: Artways.

Willms, Johannes Eduard. 1902. 'Eine Untersuchung über den Gebrauch der Farbenbezeichnungen in der Poesie Altenglands'. Unpublished dissertation, Royal Academy of Münster.

Winters, Margaret E. 2002. 'Vantage theory and diachronic semantics'. *Language sciences* 24.5-6: 625–37.

Winward, Fiona. 2002. 'Colour terms in early Welsh literature'. Unpublished doctoral dissertation, University of Cambridge.

Witkowski, Stanley R. and Cecil H. Brown. 1977. 'An explanation of color nomenclature universals'. *American anthropologist* 79.1: 50–7.

1978. 'Lexical universals'. *Annual review of anthropology* 7: 427–51.

1982. 'Whorf and universals of color nomenclature'. *Journal of anthropological research* 38.4: 411–20.

Wolf, Kirsten. 2007. 'Snorri's use of color terms in *Gylfaginning*'. *Skandinavistik* 37.1: 1–10.

2010. 'Towards a diachronic analysis of Old Norse-Icelandic color terms: the cases of green and yellow'. *Orð og tunga* 12: 109–30.

Wooten, Bill and David L. Miller. 1997. 'The psychophysics of color', in Hardin and
    Maffi (eds.), pp. 59–88.
Yang, Yonglin. 1996. 'Sex- and level-related differences in the Chinese color lexicon'.
    Word 47: 207–20.
Yoon, Kyung-Joo. 2004. 'Korean *maum* vs. English *heart* and *mind*: contrastive seman-
    tics of cultural concepts', in Moskovsky (ed.) [not continuously paginated].
Zadeh, L. A. 1965. 'Fuzzy sets'. *Information and control* 8: 338–53.
    1996. *Fuzzy sets, fuzzy logic and fuzzy systems: selected papers by Lotfi A. Zadeh*,
    ed. by George J. Klir and Bo Yuan. Advances in Fuzzy Systems, Applications and
    Theory 6. Singapore and London: World Scientific.
Zipf, George Kingsley. 1949. *Human behavior and the principle of least effort: an
    introduction to human ecology*. Cambridge, Mass.: Addison-Wesley.

Subject index

achromatic colours, 4, 60, 84, 123
adopted words. *See* loan-words
age, influence on colour usage, 67, 68
Ainu language, 83
Allen, Grant, 13, 14
anglocentrism, 87, 91, 92, 93, 94
Avestan language, 185, 186, 187, 188, 191

Baines, John, 197
Basic Colour Terms, 20, 21, 22, 23, 24, 25, 26,
  27, 28, 29, 30, 31, 32, 33, 34, 36, 37, 38,
  39, 40, 41, 42, 43, 45, 46, 53, 56, 59, 60,
  65, 72, 102, 105, 147, 155, 156, 158, 159,
  191
  non-basic colour terms, 25, 27, 28, 30, 33,
  34, 36, 38, 40, 44, 46, 49, 50, 59, 60, 62
  relative basicness, 158, 159
basicness, 21, 85. *See also* categories, of
  colour, Basic Colour Categories
Berlin, Brent, 19, 22, 23, 24, 25, 26, 27, 28,
  29, 31, 32, 42, 70, 71, 72, 73, 78, 79, 80,
  84, 85, 86, 91
bilingualism (or multilingualism), 19, 64, 65,
  144
Bini language, 42
borrowed words. *See* loan-words
brightness, 4, 5, 74, 87, 95, 106, 122, 123, 124,
  125, 146
Burarra language, 95, 96, 97, 187

Casson, Ronald, 49, 50, 51
Catalan language, 164
categories, of colour, 20, 40, 58, 161, 170, 171,
  172, 180
  Basic Colour Categories, 20, 59, 60, 64, 65,
  66, 67, 68, 71, 73, 74, 76, 80, 82, 85, 88,
  91, 92, 103, 134, 174, 197
  category boundaries, 60, 64, 72, 78, 101,
  103, 108, 172
  category foci, 40, 60, 61, 64, 71, 72, 73, 74,
  75, 101, 102, 105, 108
  derived categories, 77, 79, 80

fuzziness, in categories, 77, 78, 81
macro-categories, 53, 61, 62, 63, 73, 74, 75,
  76, 77, 79, 80, 81, 82, 83, 95, 104, 105,
  106, 147, 160, 161, 172, 180
non-colour features, 53, 54, 55, 126
Chaucer, Geoffrey, 128, 129, 130, 131, 132,
  133, 136, 137
chromatic colour. *See* hue
classificatory use of colour terms. *See* type
  modification
code-switching (and code-mixing), 64, 143,
  144, 145
composite categories. *See* categories, of
  colour, macro-categories
conjunctivity (and disjunctivity), 55, 83, 84
Conklin, Harold, 52, 53, 54
consensus testing. *See* salience, psychological
consistency testing. *See* salience,
  psychological
contact-language influence, 55, 56, 57, 64, 65,
  69, 85, 144, 157
contexts, of colour terms, 7, 10, 11, 25, 26, 37,
  88, 89, 117, 118, 119, 120, 125, 129, 130,
  131, 139, 143, 153
contextual restriction, 25, 26, 45, 116, 126,
  155
controlled language. *See* metalanguage

Damara language, 195
Dani language, 74, 87
darkness. *See* tone
determinism, linguistic, 18, 19
disjunctivity. *See* conjunctivity
distributional potential. *See* morphology,
  derivational
dullness. *See* saturation
dye names. *See* paint and pigment names

Edgeworth, Robert, 193, 194
Egyptian, Ancient language, 197
elemental colours, 22, 77, 82, 85, 89
emergence hypothesis, 104, 105, 106, 180

Lightning Source UK Ltd.
Milton Keynes UK
UKOW05f0358280117
293022UK00002B/322/P